Contents

Contents

Introduction

"Every player, in his secret heart, wants to manage someday. Every fan, in the privacy of his mind, already does."

Who said that? I did, in a book I wrote a quarter of century ago called *A Thinking Man's Guide to Baseball*. It had one chapter devoted to "what a manager really does."

Now it's time to treat the subject more seriously, with a broader perspective. The position of major league baseball manager has unique appeal. He is the general of an army to which every fan has chosen to pledge loyalty. He makes the strategical and tactical decisions in battle, but also trains, selects, and assigns tasks to the troops, and looks after their health, housing, and morale. It is no coincidence that he is called "manager" rather than "head coach," which is the way his counterparts in other sports are designated. He is in charge personally, to a greater degree and with less delegation of responsibility to assistants than in most other sports, of every phase of the six-month campaign that constitutes a baseball season.

The term "armchair general," applied to those who take an interest in military and political affairs, acquires a different flavor when applied to baseball. Instead of suggesting a narrow, specialized, arcane interest that relatively few people share, baseball second-guessing (to give the process its correct name) is open to anyone and indulged in by millions. One can't anticipate, or even pretend to control, the physical actions that actually determine the outcome of games. But one can play the mental game along with the decision maker, in an armchair, a bleacher seat, in front of a television set, listening to the radio, or simply by letting the imagination roam after looking at a box score.

Well, who are these special and privileged people?

What sort of men are these major league managers, members of an exclusive club almost no one leaves voluntarily, whose position we would love to occupy even momentarily?

Introduction

What are they like? Where do they come from? How do they learn their craft? Why do some have one style and others another?

And, most of all, how come some are more successful than others, more respected, more important in the history of their field?

To explore such questions, we'll embark on a process I call "family tree analysis." More than five hundred men have actually managed a major league club, but they fall into three categories: (1) run-of-the-mill, (2) successful, (3) successful and influential. We will focus on the third group.

And this group, I believe, can trace its descent from three exceptional men who not only fashioned modern baseball's development in the first half of the twentieth century but whose direct influence is still visible and ubiquitous in every ballpark in the final decade of this century.

The three are John McGraw, Connie Mack, and Branch Rickey. They were distinct personalities, excelling in different ways, following different (and long) career paths, with their own methods and styles. But they produced so many disciples, who built on the successful practices they instituted, that an astounding number of later winners display their heritage in discernible ways, through what is now four generations.

I've come to this conclusion after forty-five years of direct contact with these dugout directors, absorbing (at first subconsciously) their endless references to their predecessors. I saw my first New York Giants game, as a child at the Polo Grounds, while McGraw was still managing (although he retired within weeks during that 1932 season). But Mack and Rickey were still active when I began writing about baseball professionally (for the *New York Herald Tribune* in 1948), and the first wave of managers I traveled with—Casey Stengel, Leo Durocher, Charlie Dressen—had worked for them directly. As the years went on, younger men, who had played for these three and their contemporaries, ascended to managerships. One couldn't help noticing how they did certain things the way the older managers had, with their own refinements and innovations, but still within the general pattern.

Ralph Houk said it best. He had been a third-string catcher, and later a coach, on Casey Stengel's Yankees. When Stengel was pushed aside as too old (in 1960, at the age of seventy), it was partly to make room for Houk as his designated successor, to

Introduction

prevent Houk from going elsewhere. And under Houk, the Yankees continued for three more years the dominance they had enjoyed under Stengel for twelve. But there were injured feelings, and Houk was as different from Stengel in personality as could be imagined. Stengel hadn't wanted to leave, wasn't sure he hadn't been undermined, and became more prominent than ever by taking over the newly formed New York Mets; Houk, a proud and assertive man, had every reason to establish his own authority, and many writers magnified the contrasts between them.

But when I asked him, one day, where he got certain ideas about how to manage and how to make certain moves, he said, "From Casey, of course; who else did I play for?"

Every manager, as a player, worked for some older manager. Each one got his ideas somewhere, and not out of books. None followed those ideas blindly (because circumstances change), but all adopted some basic philosophy as a starting point. Just as all later composers knew and absorbed what Beethoven did, and all later writers were steeped in the literature of prior giants, and all playwrights must be aware of Shakespeare, so all younger managers absorb the discoveries and methods of earlier creators.

Here's an example of how the family tree concept works, using only men who won pennants: McGraw, as a player, was part of a remarkable Baltimore Oriole team (in the 1890s) managed by Ned Hanlon. Frank Frisch (1934 Cardinals), Bill Terry (1933 Giants), and Stengel played for McGraw. Hank Bauer, Houk, Yogi Berra, Billy Martin, Al Lopez, and Whitey Herzog played for Stengel; Lopez also played for Frisch (in Pittsburgh). More circuitously, the McGraw influence can be found in such recent World Series winners as Chuck Tanner, Tony LaRussa, and Tom Kelly.

A much larger tree, the sequoia of my metaphor, grows out of Branch Rickey, who built the St. Louis Cardinal organization in the 1920s and 1930s and the amazing Brooklyn Dodger system in the 1940s. Managers of the 1980s who were directly Dodger trained included Sparky Anderson, Roger Craig, Don Zimmer, Dick Williams, Jim Frey, Tommy Lasorda, Bobby Cox, and Cito Gaston—all of whom finished first at least once.

However, the Rickey tree and McGraw tree intertwine. Frisch, a McGraw product (and favorite), began managing under Rickey at St. Louis. Durocher played for Frisch there, moved to Brooklyn before Rickey got there but stayed after he did, then took over a Giant team that produced its own cascade of managers (Alvin

Introduction

Dark, Whitey Lockman, Wes Westrum, Bill Rigney, Eddie Stanky, and Herman Franks just from the 1951 miracle team). Others, like Craig, were exposed to Stengel as well as the Dodger system. The cross-fertilization is considerable, and the amalgam of McGraw-Rickey hard to separate into constituent parts. Rigney alone, who modeled himself on Durocher in managing philosophy, had fourteen of his former players manage in the majors—and he started only in 1956.

These are the paths we'll try to follow, to see how strong personalities with powerful ideas handed down their principles to younger men strong enough, and smart enough, to put them to use.

In the process, we'll notice a significant shift in profiles. McGraw and Mack were above-average and very prominent players in their day, before managing. Rickey had no successful background as a player. In subsequent generations, and especially today, we see outstanding managers who were below-average players, some not reaching the majors at all. In the long run, Rickey's cerebral influence proved to be more valuable than the superior hands-on experience of the other two.

Anderson, a Dodger system product to the core, nevertheless considers McGraw the "greatest manager." He says, "Look at it this way: he won more than 2,800 games. Now suppose they give you a big-league club to manage at the age of 38 and leave you there until you're 66. If you won 100 games in every single one of those 28 seasons, you still wouldn't have caught up to McGraw."

In our book, we're not going to try to rank them—just understand them.

So let's be clear about what these descriptions do and do not do.

They deal with themes, not formulas. They intend to suggest, not prove. Exceptions are plentiful. The selection of managers is arbitrary, not all-inclusive, for the sake of illustration and to stimulate thought and curiosity about others in an open-ended fashion. And there is no attempt—and no point in trying—to sort out controversies that exist among serious historians about many events and motivations. Since influence and impact are two of the facets being considered in each case, the accepted mythical version of the past often has greater real-world effect than incontrovertible documented material turned up many years later by avid, but little publicized, research. Our enterprise is, above

Introduction

all, nonacademic. Our focus is how different managers have gone about being successful, and what the roots of that success are, from a baseball lover's point of view. Overriding all other theoretical considerations is the fact that individual personality counts. These men are heirs, not imitators, of identifiable traditions. If they have any single feature in common, it is that each has been true to his own nature and applied his inheritance in his own way, consistent with his own character. Those who try consciously to fit molds or simply please others don't get winning results over any length of time, and don't make the list we've compiled. And new ones are coming along all the time.

Finally, and above all, these character sketches are entirely my own, not posing as exhaustive or even objective biographies. Others (and they themselves) no doubt see these men differently. My impressions are drawn from an amalgam of extensive literature, hearsay, conflicting stories, and (in more recent times) personal contact. The factual material—dates, events, records, names, places—is certainly intended to be as accurate as I can make it; but the interpretations are one man's view, for what it's worth.

What may be most surprising is how deep the roots go and how far back in time; and how diverse the branches have become without losing their identifying characteristics. In my own mind, I've arrived at shorthand modifiers for each of the three originators, and it may help to keep them in mind from the start.

The key word for McGraw is *dictator.* He sought total control of everything all the time.

For Rickey, it's *organizer.*

For Mack, it's *talent scout.*

They, of course, had predecessors who influenced them. So let's see how they got that way, and how they shaped the future.

Part One

The Creators

1

The Antecedents

Birth of a Profession

Any society's idea of what's "normal" is always a generation behind the times, sometimes two. Men and women form their basic attitudes and habits of thought before they reach their twenties, but the decision makers who run things usually don't get the opportunity until their forties and fifties. But children and young people absorb their viewpoints from the adults around them—parents, teachers, clergy, employers, relatives, and neighbors—whose bedrock assumptions were acquired in their own childhoods. So the twenty-year-old who follows a fifty-year-old mentor is acquiring concepts and mores solidified twenty years before that moment, and filtered through a layer twenty years older than that.

Professional baseball in America developed its fundamental rules, organization, and place in society between the years of 1870 and 1900. That means the men (and it was an exclusively male enterprise at that time) who invented its practices and presided over their rapid evolution grew up between 1840 and 1870—influenced by adults whose own image of American norms was centered in the 1820s and 1830s.

It's important to keep such chronologies in mind if one is to understand how the unique position of a major league baseball manager developed. The process doesn't stop. A Jeff Torborg, managing in 1992 at the age of 51, finished college in the 1960s and his playing career in the early 1970s; his own life experience included the turbulent Vietnam era, but his baseball background was drawn from coaches and managers whose "normality" was the world of the 1940s and 1950s. So his personal generation gap with a twenty-five-year-old in the 1990s is not twenty-six years— the difference in their ages—but more like forty years in the difference between their unspoken assumptions.

The Creators

Now, a forty-year gap in perceptions today is much larger than it used to be. The world itself, and people's attitudes, changed more slowly in the past. The mind-set of 1850, operating in 1890, was certainly badly out of date, but not as far out of date as that of 1950 was in 1990. More to the point, at smaller intervals of say ten or twenty years, the changes were less dramatic. The ballplayer of 1939 could imagine the world of 1921 much more easily than a player of 1989 could visualize 1971—in earning power, boss-worker relationships, family life, physical surroundings, political issues, and educational background.

So to grasp how baseball's pioneer managers began defining their profession in the 1870s and 1880s, we have to start with a picture of American society in the 1840s, when systematic baseball rules were being written (and published) for the first time.

That America—the one de Tocqueville wrote about—was essentially English in its derivation. The United States had been formed, after all, by people who considered themselves Englishmen: betrayed by the Crown, but unswervingly English in cultural heritage. In actual fact, major waves of immigration from Ireland and German middle Europe took place in the 1840s and the 1850s, and westward-striking settlers were already reaching the Pacific Coast. But societal norms, firmly in the hands of a settled middle class in the Northeast (Boston, New York, Philadelphia, Baltimore) were modeled on English institutions.

For these respectable merchants and farmers, the dominant team game was cricket, and the natural method of association was to form clubs. However one traces the evolution of baseball's playing rules, through dozens of local varieties and refinements in preceding decades, the organizational model is unambiguous: the cricket club.

As the new game took hold (with New York's Knickerbocker Club leading the way in promulgating a coherent set of written rules in 1845), the word *cricket* was easily changed to *baseball*—but the word *club* has remained unchanged to this day, although it is totally inappropriate to what became a purely commercial business enterprise more than one hundred years ago. The correct designation for the New York Yankees or Los Angeles Dodgers should be a baseball "firm" or "company." But we still call them clubs.

Well, clubs have members, who vote on the admission of new

The Antecedents

members. But they also have clubhouses and other property, dinners and other social affairs, financial records and occasional excursions. These must be supervised on a continuing basis, so a club must have a manager to manage its organizational functions. He may be a volunteer or an employee, but if the club is of any appreciable size with an elaborate program of activities, a professional manager is soon needed.

And if the club's primary avowed activity is playing cricket, the manager should be someone who knows something about the game, able to teach and develop players as well as handle the noncricket chores of scheduling, housekeeping, and administration.

So there existed, in New York and Philadelphia particularly in the 1840s, a body of professional cricket coaches who took positions as club managers.

The most prominent of these turned out to be Harry Wright.

He was born in 1835, in Sheffield, England, where his father was a professional cricket player. The next year, his father moved the family to New York, where he continued his cricket-playing career. Harry (whose full name was William Henry Wright) grew up to be an outstanding player himself for the same club, the St. George Cricket Club based in Hoboken, New Jersey. It used the same grounds (called Elysian Fields) that the Knickerbocker Club used for its first baseball game (June 19, 1846) against an outside team under the rules written down by Alexander Cartwright. Was the eleven-year-old Harry a spectator? Possibly. But cricket was still the dominant game. In 1859, when an England–United States cricket match was played at Elysian Fields, a crowd of twenty-four thousand spectators turned out (requiring extra ferries to cross the Hudson River from Manhattan).

By then, Harry was of age, and attracted more and more to baseball as the faster (but as yet less skillful) game. That year, he joined the Knickerbocker Club. He listed his profession as jeweler; the clubs of those days were primarily social societies whose members came from similar classes. The Knicks were mostly merchants and clerks and some "professional" men, so he fit in well enough; but his prime credential was his playing ability, since clubs were already proselytizing good players and then finding them appropriate jobs (or making exceptions)—a system colleges adopted all too thoroughly when they went into the sports business within a few decades.

The Creators

Harry's instincts, however, apart from his training and athletic ability, were entrepreneurial. He was a businessman at heart. This blend—deep, sincere, and perceptive interest in the game and its techniques, and an eye for how to make a buck—soon became the driving force of the baseball world.

By 1863, he was staging "benefit games" with a 25-cent admission charge, and from one of them he cleared $29.65 for himself (not trivial in 1863 dollars). But by August 1865, with the war over and the economy uncertain, he returned to cricket, accepting a salary of $1,200 a year as cricket instructor at the Union Cricket Club of Cincinnati.

Interest in baseball was expanding explosively after the Civil War. Clubs no longer made any pretense of amateurism in scrambling for better players. In July of 1867, still in Cincinnati, Harry formed the Cincinnati Red Stockings Base Ball Team, of which he became captain and best player. By 1868, four of the team's players (including Harry) were openly professional, being paid just to play. And when Cincinnati businessmen put up some money for an all-professional team, Harry took charge of it. Thus the Red Stockings became the first truly professional baseball team in that every player was under contract for the full season.

That made Harry Wright the first baseball manager.

He was now thirty-four years old, and he knew his business. He played center field and maintained his salary of $1,200. But he had a younger brother, George, who was only twenty-two, and a better player even than Harry. He signed him up to play shortstop, and paid him more: $1,400. He recruited top players from all over the East. He paid the pitcher, Asa Brainard, $1,100, and his third baseman, Fred Waterman, $1,000. Five others got $800 apiece and a substitute $600.

Let's stop here for a moment and note the baseball mind at work.

Pitching had to be underhand (from a distance of forty-five feet) and the original idea that the pitcher's role was to put the ball in play rather than overpower hitters was still prevalent. (Balls and strikes as we know them weren't in use yet, and the batter had the right to ask for a high or low pitch; so if you didn't make pitches hittable, there would be no game.) But it was already known that a pitcher with stuff and control could make batters hit the ball weakly in a desired direction. Good fielding would then produce outs.

The Antecedents

Brainard was right-handed (and already knew how to keep batters off stride by changing speeds). Most batters were right-handed, and if they hit the ball solidly at all, they would tend to hit it to the left side of the infield.

So Wright put his best fielders at short and third—and paid them more than the others, on a level with the all-important pitcher. His own salary as an outfielder included his managerial duties.

Judge their abilities, put them in the right positions, and pay them accordingly. The managerial mind is taking shape.

Wright did not, of course, "invent" this use of position play. He got it from cricket, where fielders may be placed anywhere according to situation, and where the decision to place them is much more subtle and complex than in baseball. His genius lay in adaptation more than sheer innovation, and that has been the hallmark of good managing ever since. Football coaches "invent" new formations and tactics from time to time (and others quickly adopt the successful ones), but baseball managers adjust, tinker, revise, and make marginal (but significant) changes in what they already know will work.

The Cincinnati Red Stockings became the first legendary team. They went through the 1869 season undefeated, traveling coast to coast to play all comers (using the rail connection to California completed in 1868). In 1870, they ran their streak to 130 games without a defeat until the Atlantics in Brooklyn defeated them in extra innings before a crowd of nine thousand paying fifty cents for a ticket. No longer able to boast that they were undefeated, the Red Stockings became less of a gate attraction. No systematic promotional machinery existed. At the end of the season, the team disbanded, its financial backers disappointed.

But lessons had been learned. What was needed was a coherent way to determine an annual champion. The public had proved responsive to won-lost records. The best players expected guaranteed salaries. Investors needed structure. Over the winter, the first professional "league" was formed. The National Association of Base Ball Players, in existence since 1857, was the closest thing to a ruling body. It had hundreds of clubs as members. But it was dominated by amateurs in membership and philosophy. Now the leading players formed the National Association of *Professional* Base Ball Players, and that automatically meant a small number of clubs on whom public attention could be focused.

The Creators

They could schedule "official" games only with each other, keep track, publicize a pennant race, and produce an authentic champion.

The 1871 season began with ten such teams. One was in Boston, where its backers hired Wright as playing manager. He brought with him the name "Red Stockings"—and brother George. He also signed up two budding stars from the Chicago area, a pitcher named Al Spalding and an infielder named Ross Barnes.

But the first winning team turned out to be the Athletics of Philadelphia, whose leading player, Al Reach, had been one of the first open professionals back in Brooklyn in the 1860s. The schedule was thin—no team played more than 35 "championship games"—and Philadelphia wound up with a 22–7 record, Boston with 22–10, and Chicago (taking the name "White Stockings") with 20–9.

The next year, the schedule was almost twice as long, and the superior quality of the group Wright had gathered started to show. The Red Stockings won the next four championships, winning more games each year. Players jumped from team to team, often in midseason, whenever more money was offered or to play with "outside" teams, but Wright was able to keep his players together.

When the Red Stockings won 71 and lost only 8 in the 1875 season, the growing noncompetitiveness of such loose arrangements reached a dead end. A civic booster in Chicago named William A. Hulbert convinced Spalding and Barnes to "come home" and forestalled the disputes that would follow by advancing his own idea for a better way to organize. He conceived of a National League of Base Ball *Clubs*. Serious businessmen would be in complete control of the team's affairs, giving it continuity; the league would have centralized authority over scheduling and respect for one another's contracts; it would have unified policies about admission prices, discipline, and conditions of play.

That way, the "manager" of a club could concentrate on collecting and training playing talent, without the distractions of business management, raising capital, and paying bills; and sensible league rules could produce better-balanced competition, to convince the public that its games would be more competitive, honest, and "official." The players, now simply employees with no

The Antecedents

role in administrative decisions for which most had no talent and little interest, could concentrate on the special skill they did possess: playing ball. And in such an arrangement, there would be no ambiguity about responsibility and control, setting a pattern that has remained fundamental to this day: You do what the manager says, or you don't play.

Shakedown Cruise

The newly formed National League embarked on uncharted seas. The element of compulsion—to abide by league rules—had never before been seriously attempted. And the role of the individual club manager, in a league organization, lost the complete autonomy it had when each club was a law unto itself in a loosely formed association. The manager now had a responsibility to the league as a whole, and a league president to whom he was accountable for his behavior, so that he had lines of authority upward to contend with, as well as downward.

And the test came right away.

There was, at this point, a degree of separation between "manager"—fully in charge—and "captain," the player who was the team leader expected to train teammates and make tactical and strategic decisions regarding games. When the manager was a player—like Wright and Spalding (who was brought back to Chicago by Hulbert with the managership as an incentive)—he was, de facto, his own captain. But in some cases, the manager was really just that, a business manager with no on-field expertise, and he needed a player-captain who was really in charge of the ball playing.

In 1876, the first year of the National League (and therefore of "major league baseball" as we have come to think of it), these were the teams and their managers:

> **Chicago**—Albert Spalding, also the only pitcher
> **Boston**—Harry Wright, bench manager, available as outfield substitute
> **New York**—Bill Cammeyer, business manager only
> **Philadelphia**—Al Wright, business manager only, no relation to Harry and George

The Creators

St. Louis—Herman Dehlman, first baseman
Hartford—Bob Ferguson, third baseman
Louisville—Chuck Fullmer, shortstop
Cincinnati—Charlie Gould, first baseman

The fact that Cammeyer and Al Wright were not players proved to be of enormous significance. Harry Wright, we noted, was a rare combination of athlete and entrepreneur, as Spalding would prove to be. But Cammeyer was all entrepreneur. It was he who had the idea, way back in 1862 (during the war) to build a fence around a field so that one could charge admission, not just rely on passing the hat around. He had the diamond graded, built a clubhouse for player use, put some benches under a long wooden shed as the first "grandstand," and surrounded the six-acre enclosure with a seven-foot fence. (The playing area of a modern field is about two acres.) Inside the fence he also built a saloon, a storehouse for equipment, and offices. Admission was ten cents in the 1860s.

So when the National Association was formed in 1871, it was natural enough to have a New York team, but the best place to play was still over in Brooklyn—still a separate city at that time—at Cammeyer's Union Grounds. The New York Mutuals, inheritors of a name that referred to a club formed by firemen of the Mutual Hook and Ladder Company No. 1 back in the amateur pre-Civil War days, became a charter member. When Hulbert put forth his league arrangement, Cammeyer certainly grasped the possibilities better than most, got a franchise, and called the team the Mutuals, although it continued to play in Brooklyn.

The Philadelphia entry also adopted a hallowed name, the Athletics. More than one club had used it already. Back in the early 1860s, a Brooklynite named Al Reach, who was one of the first professionals, had made his fame with the Athletics.

Now, the key feature of the disciplined business organization Hulbert envisioned was inviolability of scheduling. The "championship" games were, after all, a minority of the total games being played by each club. Local and barnstorming rivals provided other moneymaking opportunities; but the league had to have top priority among its members. The credibility of the pennant race—the chief new marketing ploy—depended on every team completing its full schedule to the extent that weather would permit.

The Antecedents

In September of 1876, the Mutuals and the Athletics were supposed to make a western trip to complete their commitment.
Both, however, had losing records and no chance of being a factor
in the pennant race (which Spalding's Chicago team eventually
won with a 52–14 record). To go west would be expensive, and
they certainly wouldn't be an attraction out there. To stay home
and play nonleague games against local teams would bring in a
good deal of money. From a business point of view—short-term,
bottom-line, current-income thinking—it made little sense to
make the fruitless journey. The two pure business managers
made the decision that seemed natural: they stayed home.

But from the league—and long-term business interest—point
of view, establishing the integrity of the competition was more
important than any immediate profit or loss. So Hulbert, with the
firm backing of Spalding, Wright, and others who thought in
"baseball" terms, expelled the two largest cities in the new league
for violating the rules, and proceeded to operate a six-team
league in 1877.

This bold step put league authority on a sound basis and was
the key to all the success that followed. New York and Philadelphia weren't merely the biggest cities in the league, they were the
two biggest cities in America and the most important commercial
and publicity centers. Taking this step not only showed far-seeing
wisdom and a willingness to bear financial pain; it represented a
triumph of baseball-thinking by "baseball men" over purely commercial social-status thinking. It laid out the path baseball development would follow for decades, in which those with field-
managing experience would have greater influence than strictly-
business types. To this day, effective front offices pay great attention to their "baseball minds" in making business decisions,
regardless of who holds what title in the table of organization.
The game and the business are inseparable when the business
consists of presenting a marketable game—and this gave the field
manager a position of unique importance at the fulcrum of the
growing enterprise.

In 1877, Hulbert took the title of league president (which had
been bestowed the first year on a figurehead from the East,
Morgan P. Bulkeley of Hartford, an insurance magnate who later
became governor of Connecticut and a U.S. senator). That enabled Spalding to take on the presidency of the Chicago club.
Although he remained the team's manager, he no longer pitched

but switched to first base, and the team finished fifth. (As a pitcher, he had won 47 of those 52 victories in 1876.) And he had other things on his mind, as well. The entrepreneur portion of his brain had grasped another facet of the new industry faster than anyone else.

Only a handful of athletes had the special skills to be big leaguers, but millions of people were playing baseball. The big leaguers were not only producing gate receipts by their system-atized and marketable activity; they were stimulating interest in the game itself—among children, schools, clubs, town teams, and every level of society. And as they set the standard, so visibly, of what good baseball should be, the millions of followers would want the equipment necessary to emulate that level of play: bats, balls, and uniforms (no gloves yet) of manufactured and stan-dardized quality.

So Spalding and his brother Walter started a sporting goods company. Every ballgame, every newspaper story, was a free advertisement for their products. The era of home-wrapped balls and roughly whittled bats was still on; A. G. Spalding & Brothers would make it obsolete.

By 1878, Spalding couldn't devote most of his working hours to directing the ball club on the field. He gave up the managership and brought in Bob Ferguson, who had managed Hartford the first two years (as the Hartford club was dropping out). And in 1879, he made his most dominant player and field captain, Adrian (Cap) Anson, the manager as well, replacing Ferguson.

Anson had been a star hitter and infielder at Philadelphia in the association days. Spalding had persuaded him to join the new Chicago enterprise when the league was being founded; among other things, Spalding was an outstanding recruiter. Big, gruff, a terrific hitter who played third base, Anson was tremendously popular with the public. Ferguson, who was also a third baseman, had shifted to shortstop as manager in 1878 rather than displace Anson; and in 1879, Ferguson had moved on to a new team in Troy, New York, leaving Anson as the most important baseball figure in what was now the largest and most important city in the National League.

Meanwhile, also in 1879, another important development was taking shape as a result of the combined baseball-business orientation of the league leadership. One of the early problems the league was created to solve was the tendency of players to jump from team to team whenever a better offer came along (which was how Hulbert gathered his Chicago team). Full-season contracts were the first attempts to create stability at least for the current campaign. That was the policy Wright had adopted in Cincinnati back in 1869.

But the problem between seasons was severe. Some of the pioneers, like Wright, were much better than others at teaching and training the rapidly evolving techniques of play. When their best pupils were plucked away by better offers precisely because that training had made them so effective and so noticeable, they lost not only a financial asset—a player who could sell tickets—but the "intellectual product" of their teaching skill, now turned against them in competition on the field. The desire to retain good players was more than merely an economic interest: it was an idealized competitive interest too, in the minds of people who were conditioned to pursue victory for its own sake, beyond its monetary rewards.

So the system of putting a player "on reserve" came into use that year. This was, in effect, simply an option on that player's services for the next year. The basis upon which the league had been formed was that each club would honor each other club's contracts; it was easy enough to extend this to honoring the reserve list. The league members simply agreed not to make offers to a player on someone else's reserve list. That eliminated the competition for his services (within the league) and allowed a manager to plan on improving his team for next year with the knowledge that last year's best players would still be available.

At first, players were honored to be "put on reserve": it certified that they were among the best players, and guaranteed work for next year. Not all players were reserved: only five, then seven, of what was normally a fifteen-man squad. And those who were reserved, naturally, commanded the highest pay.

But it took only a couple of years for the business side of the baseball mind to realize what a weapon had been created. If you made all players reserved, there could be no competition at all for their services—and the better ones would have less bargaining position for salaries. The famous "reserve system," not to be cracked for almost one hundred years, was fully in place by the early 1880s.

As happens so often, however, success contains the seeds of its own destruction. The firm authority of the league, establishing uniformity of play, a valid pennant race, and high regard for "decency" within the ball grounds, made the National League the unchallenged top of the growing baseball pyramid. It was accepted that the league contained, and presented to the public, virtually all the "best" players in the country.

There were, of course, more good players than six teams could accommodate. In 1879, the league increased its membership back to eight teams, but more and more good players were coming along. While the reserve system locked players into their teams within the league, it did nothing to prevent them from playing outside it. Of course, there wasn't any place else to play at a comparable level of prestige and compensation.

But why shouldn't there be?

What success breeds, of course, is imitation. The league wasn't yet making any investors rich, but it was playing to an increasing audience with increasing attention. If those people could make money fielding ball clubs—other entrepreneurs argued—why can't we start another league and do the same?

Thus, in 1881, the American Association, a second major league, was born.

It started play in the 1882 season with six cities—Philadelphia; Cincinnati, St. Louis, and Louisville, whose National League teams had dropped out for one reason or another; and Baltimore and Pittsburgh, two of the most important metropolitan areas of the time.

And New York was still open. It had a professional team, all right, called the Metropolitans, who played their games on a polo field at the northeast end of Central Park. They played exhibition games (not counted in the standings) against National League teams and all sorts of other professional teams, 151 of them in 1881, and made good money doing so. Their manager, Jim Mutrie, explained that they couldn't join the new association because that would disrupt their relationship with National League teams.

Nevertheless, the AA made a success of its 1882 season. Meanwhile, Hulbert had died (at the age of forty-nine) in the spring of 1882. The opportunity to reverse his expulsion decision was at hand, and the need to enforce it was no longer relevant. For the

The Antecedents

1883 season, the National League placed a team in New York (today's San Francisco Giants) and Philadelphia (today's Phillies), replacing the small towns of Troy and Worcester, Massachusetts. It kept Chicago, Boston, Providence, Buffalo, Detroit, and Cleveland.

And the AA responded by expanding to eight teams, bringing in Columbus, Ohio, and New York.

New York?

Sure, the Metropolitans.

The new National League franchise, you see, had been awarded to John B. Day—who also owned the Metropolitans. The Polo Grounds was large enough to accommodate two playing fields (with two sets of stands) separated by a canvas fence. With a foot in each camp, Day had a good thing going—but he was able to do it only because the league and the association had come to an agreement to observe each other's contracts and reserve lists, and to coexist instead of conflict.

But this only created another opportunity. In St. Louis, a wealthy real estate operator named Henry V. Lucas became the chief backer of another new league, called the Union Association. This group pointedly rejected the reserve, although it said it would honor in-season contracts, and plenty of established players, now locked into reserve systems and salary limits by the agreement between the National and the AA, were willing to work for more money elsewhere.

So in 1884, there were three major leagues in operation, with a total of thirty-three teams: eight in the National, thirteen in the AA, and twelve in the Union Association.

This was too much, and the union lasted only one season. In 1885, the AA was back down to eight, the same as the National.

What does all this have to do with managing?

Well, the explosive expansion created a need for instant managers. Player-manager was still the preferred mode, but there weren't enough good ones to go around. Only fifteen of the thirty-three teams in 1884 had them; in 1883, in contrast, ten of the sixteen did. So a large number of former players, not-quite-so-proficient players, and nonplayers were given the chance—or the exposure—for managerial ability. What this did was highlight the difference between the better ones and the ordinary or incompetent ones, and clarify what would be expected of managers when the shakedown came.

The Creators

It would also highlight which managerial methods worked and which didn't.

Management versus Labor

The player-managers soon found themselves in a peculiar situation.

A firm two-league setup, with eight teams in each and a great surplus of players with major league experience, put club owners in a favorable position in 1885. They now had a reserve system, a monopoly product (the only "big league" baseball available), representation in almost all the biggest markets, and the ability to impose salary ceilings. They also had a great new promotional gimmick, a postseason series between the champions of the two cooperating leagues, something they promptly named "the series for the baseball championship of the world," or, in shorter form, "the World Series." Its structure varied from year to year, and it was not a commercial success right off the bat, but the idea of it was irresistible. Fans who didn't buy tickets, especially in nasty weather in the Northeast in October, still followed the result avidly. And players and managers had an added incentive in going after a pennant, since playing in the World Series meant a bit of prize money (very little) and a lot of national prestige.

Natural processes were at work. By the middle of the 1880s, players in their twenties had been reading box scores since childhood and absorbing the mystique of big league glory. They considered themselves, rightly, celebrities and the actual producers of the show: it was their skill people paid to see. Club owners, enjoying prosperity and local celebrity, just as naturally considered it "their" game. Didn't they put up the capital, take the risks, organize the proceedings, and sign the checks?

Throughout America, at this time, the conflict between the working man and the capitalist boss was taking shape in the emergence of labor unions, labor legislation, and labor-management strife. Professional baseball—the only team spectator sport at which an athlete could make a living then—was not, and could not be, exempt.

In 1884, in the first real attempt at a World Series, the AA New York Mets lost 3 straight to the NL Providence Grays.

The Antecedents

In 1885, NL Chicago and AA St. Louis played 7 games, each winning 3, with 1 tie.

In 1886, they played 6, with St. Louis winning 4.

In 1887, St. Louis and the NL Detroit Wolverines played 15 games, 10 of them in other cities—New York, Brooklyn, Philadelphia, Baltimore, Washington, Chicago, Pittsburgh, Boston. Detroit won 10 of the games. Attendance dwindled into the hundreds for the last two games in late October, but the exposure was terrific.

And by now, the owners had specific plans to hold salaries down and the players had had their consciousness raised. Just how the labor war erupted, and what it led to, we'll come to in a moment. But consider the position of the player-manager.

As manager, he was in charge, the direct representative of the owner: the foreman. As a player, he suffered all the limitations, contract inequities, and grievances, real or imagined, his teammates did. How can one be a boss and a teammate at the same time when those forces oppose each other? (What was so bad about the contract? As a judge pointed out, it bound the player for many years and the club for only ten days.)

The popularity and stability of the game in the mid-1880s had produced some charismatic managers who commanded a great deal of fan loyalty. The St. Louis Brown Stockings, a true dynasty in the AA, were led by their star first baseman, Charles Comiskey. The revived New York franchise in the National League had a glamorous young man named John Montgomery Ward—known as Monte—who had been to college, turned himself into an infielder when a sore arm ended his pitching career, and managed the team briefly in the closing days of the 1884 season. Cap Anson was a fixture in Chicago. John Morrill in Boston was a regular and popular infielder. Fans identified with them primarily as players and "team captains."

Up to now, the assumption that players and management of any particular club were in the same boat, with the same interest in success, had seldom been questioned. But if club owners were putting league regulations (like salary limitation, blacklist, and mutual observance of disciplinary punishments) above their own team's interests, and players were trying to act collectively to alter what they saw as onerous rules, what was the right side for the player-manager to choose?

The Creators

We'll see how different men made different choices, and how this shaped the nature of managing from then on.

The Brotherhood

Late in the 1885 season, National League players started to meet secretly to form the Brotherhood of Professional Ball Players. The name had a two-edged connotation. The players pointedly avoided forming a labor union, which would bargain collectively with employers—but many an early union, at that time, did use the word *brotherhood* in its title, referring to the brotherhood of working men. What the players had in mind, primarily, was a group that could help former and present players needing financial help, but that could also present complaints and requests to management with one voice. Since no player had any bargaining power with his own club, only a committee operating across club lines could have any hope of getting a hearing.

The key chapter was in New York. Some of the biggest stars— Tim Keefe, the pitcher; Buck Ewing, the catcher; Roger Connor, the slugger—signed a document stating their objectives. The organization would try to protect its members' collective interests, uphold the highest standards of professional and personal behavior, and encourage "the interests of baseball." They elected as their president Monte Ward, who had finished the 1884 season as their manager, appointed by John B. Day.

As owner of both New York clubs, Day had contributed to their raised consciousness. The National League charged fifty cents admission, did not permit the sale of beer on the grounds, and did not permit Sunday games. The American Association charged twenty-five cents, did sell beer, and did play on Sunday (where local law permitted it). Day's AA Mets had been good enough, in 1884, to win a pennant, while his National League team had finished fifth. If you owned a bunch of good ball players and had the choice of displaying them for twenty-five-cent tickets or for fifty-cent tickets, how would you handle it? That's how Day handled it. He shifted some of his best Met players (Keefe was one) to the National League team. And he also shifted Jim Mutrie, who had proved his capabilities as a manager with Mets, to the league team.

The Antecedents

"My men are giants," Mutrie declared, and the name stuck. The New York Giants they became, playing on the better of the two fields at the Polo Grounds.

The players throughout both leagues had two principal complaints. They didn't like being shifted from team to team, at management's whim, with no say in the matter. And they were flatly opposed to any formula for salary scales, called "classification." When the club owners instituted such rules, but didn't try to enforce them too strictly, the situation was irritating but bearable. But when they intended to make the classification formula stick, players stopped thinking about brotherhood and started thinking about bargaining.

The brotherhood had announced its existence late in 1886. During 1887, now ninety strong, the brotherhood sought recognition as a bargaining agent. Ward issued a public manifesto, calling the player's status under a baseball contract "serfdom" and demanding reforms. A committee of Ward, Ned Hanlon (remember that name), and Dennis Brouthers appeared at a league meeting and won some contract adjustments, but not actual abolition of the salary classification system being evaded by under-the-table payments.

In 1888, the beefed-up Giants won the National League pennant and defeated Comiskey's St. Louis Browns in the World Series, 6 games to 4. Immediately afterwards, Spalding took two all-star teams on a tour to Australia, which turned into a globe-circling tour by way of Egypt, France, and England to New York. Games were played alongside the Pyramids, the Eiffel Tower under construction, and in front of British royalty. It was a super promotion for baseball, for America, and for the sporting goods business.

But during the tour, which included Ward and Anson, the club owners back home announced that the classification system (that is, salary cuts) would be imposed for the 1889 season. When the ship docked at New York, only a few days before the season was to open in April, Keefe and other players were on the pier waiting for Ward. They wanted to strike.

After talking things over, however, they got a better idea. They would play out the 1889 season, as contracted, but would spend the year lining up backers to form a league of their own, in which the players would be shareholders. It was a bold plan with one major factor in its favor: since 1884, there had grown again a supply of playing talent and eager investors. It also ignored, however, one major factor against it: the National Association of 1871–75 had demonstrated that getting players involved in the operation of teams could create more problems than it solved.

A factor was emerging that would be evident seventy-five years later, when the players formed their present union. Top athletes are aggressive, competitive, determined, and strong-willed individuals, sought out for those qualities because they help make them winners. When they become embroiled in an off-field conflict, they may or may not follow the wisest course, but they will certainly put up an all-out fight.

So the Players' League, as they envisioned it, would not be merely an alternative to the National League. It would be a head-on challenge with survival at stake. The new league, which would enlist most of the established players and recognizable stars, would place its teams in National League cities, build its own ballparks, and play on the same dates. This would be war to the finish.

The American Association was a not-quite-innocent bystander in all this. It had smaller financial resources, fewer star players (outside of St. Louis), a less militant attitude toward player contracts, and smaller cities. (In 1889, it contained Brooklyn, St. Louis, Philadelphia, and Baltimore, but also Cincinnati, Columbus, Louisville, and Kansas City.) Some of its players would join the brotherhood, but essentially this was a National League versus players war.

The plan worked. In 1889, the Giants won their pennant, and Brooklyn won its. New York and Brooklyn were still separate cities, but the Brooklyn Bridge had been opened in 1883 and connections were tightening. It was a tumultuous World Series, getting more press coverage than ever before, won by the Giants, 6 games to 3. But the off-field baseball news was already clashing with accounts of ball games. Investors had been lined up. There would be another league—called the Brotherhood League, or the Players' League, in 1890. It would have teams in New York, Chicago, Boston, Philadelphia, Pittsburgh, Cleveland, Indianapolis, and Washington, all National League cities. In Chicago, it would use the same ballpark. In New York and Pittsburgh, it would have new fields adjacent to the National League's.

But the National League had been doing some maneuvering too. The brotherhood had consciously avoided going after association players, hoping to keep that league neutral. But the Brooklyn team (1889 AA champion) was taken intact into the National League, and so was Cincinnati, while Indianapolis and Baltimore were dropped. Thereupon the Players' League also took Brooklyn, forgot Indianapolis, and made Buffalo its eighth team (instead of Washington). This left a wounded—fatally, as it turned out—American Association with teams in St. Louis (its stronghold), Philadelphia, Columbus, Rochester, Syracuse, Louisville, and Toledo, and an entry sharing Baltimore and Brooklyn— hardly a major league image even in 1890.

All told, about 100 of the National League's 130 or so players wound up in the Players' League, essentially all the regulars. A notable exception was Anson, who remained loyal to Spalding in Chicago. But Comiskey abandoned St. Louis and joined the brotherhood, as player-manager of the Chicago entry. And a twenty-seven-year-old catcher named Cornelius McGillicuddy, with a few years of experience in Washington, switched to Buffalo.

Ward managed Brooklyn, Buck Ewing New York, Ned Hanlon Pittsburgh, King Kelly Boston, and Jack Rowe Buffalo, all playing regularly.

It is not surprising that the result was disaster all around. The idea of players forming their own league may or may not have had merit, but a head-to-head war for customers was sheer suicide. Some cities had three leagues playing the same day. In an age when ancillary income—from radio and television—didn't exist and when concession income (always important) was limited to the physical presence of fans inside the enclosure, there simply weren't enough ticket buyers to go around. And one of the basic features that had made major league baseball so appealing in the first place—the sense of order in competition and the focus on games, not on financial squabbles and name-calling and business maneuvers—was negated by the three-league confusion and constant speculation about which player intended to go where.

All three leagues were reduced to the edge of bankruptcy. The National, with more experienced ownership and larger reserve resources (including Spalding's growing bankroll from his sporting goods empire) survived. The Players' League, with its over-enthusiastic or naive or sharpie backers, folded completely. And the American Association, after limping through one more season in 1891, expired forever, leaving only its name to be picked up by a minor league at the turn of century.

The Creators

This searing experience, which set the course of the baseball business for three generations, also had a permanent effect on the concepts and practice of field management. It made clear how sharp the line had to be between manager and players, and that democracy was not applicable to the game on the field. And it also showed that the line between field manager and policy maker must be equally distinct. The manager could still recruit, negotiate salary, and make player movement decisions for his own club, and would continue to do so for many years. But he could not be involved (as Spalding and Wright had been) in league regulation matters that were the province of club owners—the people whose money was invested—and league presidents. The manager could not afford to be the tool or point man of ownership's purposes concerning player rights, any more than he could be the buddy of his players, sharing a "brotherhood" relationship. Such distinctions existed from the start, but were fuzzy; they were better defined after the Brotherhood War in the minds of the men who lived through it. And the men who fashioned twentieth-century baseball were taught and led by those who had lived through it.

But there were three more stages to go through before modern times arrived.

The Monopoly

Starting in 1892, the National was the only major league in existence. It had twelve teams. The density of outstanding players was greater than ever before. The authority of management was unchallengeable. The pay scale had come down. But it wasn't so easy to get the fans back, and having a twelve-team standing, in which half the teams were identified as seventh or lower, didn't help. In a 132-game schedule (12 against each opponent), noncontenders (defined as teams in fourth place or lower) were your "attraction" 81 percent of the time.

Even before trying such a setup, the club owners could see its flaws. They tried breaking the season into halves, with the first-half winner playing the second-half winner for the championship (the way many minor leagues do today, but without a playoff involving other teams). The 1890 World Series, between NL Brooklyn and AA Louisville (which ended 3–3 with a tie game) had been a complete flop, because it didn't include the Players' League. In 1891, the dying AA didn't even agree to take part, and since all the stars were back in the National League, it was probably just as well. So the 1892 split-season winners were matched in what was called "the World Series." Boston defeated Cleveland, five games to none, with one tie, and attendance wasn't bad, about five thousand a game.

However, attendance during the second-half race had fallen off, and the danger signal was there. Why wouldn't the first-half winner be expected to win again? And by the time the first-half winner showed that it would not repeat, much of the second-half season had been played. Either way, interest lagged.

Besides, by 1893, the owners had their monopoly under control. They limited rosters to fifteen men, cut salary levels in half, and lived up to a $30,000 team salary limit. They could afford to have an eleventh-place team come to visit when the fans, as well as the players, had nowhere else to turn. So from 1893 on, the league played in a single twelve-team standing.

To create a postseason series, they had the top two teams meet in a Temple Cup Series, named after a cup put up by Pittsburgh's William C. Temple. This was done for four years, 1894 through 1897, but it didn't have quite the same panache as "World Series."

The twelve-team league also accepted cross-ownership of clubs. The shakedown of 1892 had been accomplished by a complicated series of agreements (and disagreements) to settle ownership rights among Players' League, American Association, and old National League investors. Franchises were moved and exchanged, players were assigned to various teams, ballparks were exchanged. (The Giants, at the new Polo Grounds location in upper Manhattan, moved into the better ballpark the Players' League had built immediately adjacent to their new one of 1889, and that's the one that became the Polo Grounds twentieth-century New Yorkers knew.)

Here, then, is the National League alignment of 1893, with an asterisk next to the names essential to our managerial theme:

Team	President	Manager
Boston	Arthur Soden	*Frank Selee
Pittsburgh	Al Buckenberger	Al Buckenberger
Cleveland	Frank Robison	Patsy Tebeau
Philadelphia	*Al Reach	*Harry Wright

The Creators

Team	President	Manager
New York	C. C. Van Cott	*Monte Ward
Brooklyn	Charles Byrne	Dave Foutz
Cincinnati	*John T. Brush	*Charles Comiskey
Baltimore	*Ned Hanlon	*Ned Hanlon
Chicago	James A. Hart	Cap Anson
St. Louis	Chris Von de Ahe	Bill Watkins
Louisville	Fred Drexler	*Billy Barnie
Washington	George Wagner	Jim O'Rourke

It must be noted that "president" does not necessarily mean "owner." Who actually owned how much stock is often a tangled tale, but a club's president is the one who represents that interest in league meetings. The special circumstances of Philadelphia, New York, and Baltimore need amplification.

The actual owner of the Phillies was John Rogers, and he was the one who attended league meetings and took an active role in the events of the 1880s and 1890s. Al Reach, however, was a person of great importance. After his playing career as one of the first full professionals, he went into the sporting goods business in Philadelphia and then consolidated his company with Spalding's. His great asset was a partner, Ben Shibe, who had invented machinery for making baseballs of great uniformity and reliability. The Spalding-label baseball was the official ball used by the National League (thanks to Spalding)—but it came off the same Reach-Shibe machines that supplied the American Association (and later the American League). So Philadelphia's voice in league councils carried weight out of proportion to its fortunes on the field, which were uniformly poor.

In New York, during the Brotherhood War, several other club owners had advanced money to John B. Day, who finally pulled out in 1892—leaving, in effect, some rival owners (like Soden in Boston and Spalding in Chicago) actually part owners of the Giants. The president of the Giants in 1893 and 1894 was essentially a league delegate to the league. And Baltimore's majority owner was Harry Von der Horst, who hired Hanlon as manager and took a secondary role after Hanlon became part owner. As for Spalding, he had turned over directorship of Chicago to Hart in 1892.

By 1898, interlocking ownership had spread. Von der Horst and Hanlon had acquired an interest in Brooklyn, and Hanlon moved

The Antecedents

there with his best Baltimore players. (We'll learn a lot more about this in the chapter about John McGraw, because this is what gave McGraw his big chance.) The Robison brothers in Cleveland acquired St. Louis and shifted some of their best players there. (Remember the Mets and Giants in 1885?) And the Giants had passed into the hands of Andrew Freedman, a highly controversial and influential New York political figure who not only behaved on the baseball scene like an early-day George Steinbrenner, but took the lead in a plan (nearly adopted) to make the league a single business entity owning shares in every club and moving players around at will to "arrange" close races.

Meanwhile, on the field, Boston won three straight pennants (1891–93) and Baltimore the next three (1894–96). Then Boston won in 1897 and 1898. This didn't do much to stimulate excitement in the ten other cities. And in 1899, Hanlon, transplanted to Brooklyn, won there.

In short, the time was ripe for another challenge. The monopoly which promised—and delivered—"total control" also delivered stagnation and corruption. Once again, there were cities eager to house teams, good players (and managers) available, and the example (thanks to the monopoly) of how profitable a ball club could be.

The American League

Byron Bancroft (Ban) Johnson was a sportswriter in Cincinnati in 1893. He got friendly with Comiskey, who had become the team's manager after the Brotherhood War. A minor league called the Western, founded in 1879, was in the process of folding in 1893. Comiskey, on a scouting trip to that area, persuaded the troubled owners to make Johnson their league president. Johnson took charge of a league, for 1894, that consisted of Sioux City, Toledo, Indianapolis, Detroit, Kansas City, Milwaukee, Minneapolis, and Grand Rapids. The owner of the Indianapolis team was the same John T. Brush whose major league franchise there had been extinguished by the Brotherhood War, and who had been allowed to buy Cincinnati instead. It was Brush who brought Comiskey to Cincinnati.

Within a year, Brush fired Comiskey, who then bought the Sioux City team and moved it to St. Paul. Cornelius McGillicudy, known as Connie Mack, had gone from the Players' League to Pittsburgh, and had become the manager late in the 1894 season. Now Johnson persuaded him to buy (with silent backers, of course) the Western League's Milwaukee franchise, which was moved in due course to Philadelphia, even as Mack continued to manage Pittsburgh through 1896.

By 1899, the National League's problems had come to a head, and for the 1900 season it cut back to eight teams, dropping Cleveland, Washington, Louisville, and Baltimore.

At that point, Johnson changed his league's name to "American." He moved St. Paul to Chicago, as a direct challenge to the National League. He took in Cleveland, in place of Grand Rapids. But he didn't claim major league status—yet.

For 1901, however, he did. His league now contained Chicago, Detroit, Cleveland, and Milwaukee as a western unit, and Baltimore, Philadelphia, Boston, and Washington in the East. And it went after National League stars in the time-honored way, offering more money—something easy enough to do since the old league was clinging to its $2,400 ceiling on individual salaries.

The raids succeeded. A new war was fought. Recriminations flew. Players got more money. New stars got opportunities to develop alongside the established ones, so many of whom jumped to the new league. In Chicago, Philadelphia, and Boston, fans had a choice. Publicity flourished.

In 1902, Milwaukee moved to St. Louis, so that the two leagues were in direct competition in four cities.

Only one piece was missing: New York. Attempts to put a New York team there were being stymied by political influence (tied to Freedman) which prevented finding a suitable spot for a ballpark. But far more important was the issue of competing for players, which the National League had worked so long to avoid. To end such a situation, it had entered into an agreement with the American Association in 1883. Both had fought off the short-lived challenge of the Union Association in 1884. The civil war with the players in 1890 had been followed by more strife with the dying American Association before it folded after 1891. Now, only a decade later, they were facing again the one thing these dedicated free-enterprise capitalist entrepreneurs loathed above all else: competition.

There was only one thing to do.

Make a deal.

The Antecedents

In the fall of 1902, agreement was reached. The American League could put a team in New York (moving its Baltimore franchise). It would not go into Pittsburgh. Lists of which players could stay with which clubs were negotiated and accepted, and from then on both leagues would observe each other's contracts (and reserve rights). There would be a three-man commission (the two league presidents and a third "neutral") to handle interleague disputes. The minor leagues, who had formed a National Association of their own, joined the agreement with certain protections for their own contracts.

Thus was Organized Baseball born, and that's the system we've had ever since.

Synthesis

The year 1903 is the real beginning of our story, and not only because that's when the major leagues took their present form.

The game itself, in playing rules, had been evolving and changing year by year. In the nineteenth century, the changes were so drastic and so frequent that the "generalship" function we associate with managing had limited applicability. To "play the percentages," rules and styles have to be stable enough to determine what favorable percentages might be. When the number of balls for a walk, and even the number of strikes for an out, kept shifting; when the pitching distance kept getting longer; when what constituted a legal delivery was radically different in one era than in another; when the home team could choose whether to bat first or last (and usually chose first); when the nature of home plate and the pitcher's box was not yet in its present form; when gloves were just being developed; when the catcher didn't yet crouch right up under the hitter, but stood back; in those circumstances, the strategic decisions made by a manager were important enough, but not systematized.

His more important task, from Harry Wright in the 1860s well into the 1890s, was to train, teach, condition, and control his players. The teaching of mechanics—throwing, batting, catching the ball—was a significant element in dealing with young players who came to teams with little or no previous professional instruction. Conducting practice, to master those techniques, was a serious matter. Getting players to stay in shape, combatting drunkenness and other rowdy behavior, instilling habits of thought that we now consider "instinctive"—these were of greater concern, taking up more time than deciding when to change pitchers, when to bunt, what pitch to call, and setting up a pitching rotation.

The manager, at least until 1891, also retained administrative functions concerning travel arrangements and finances. He didn't just give orders or input concerning decisions about a preferred procedure (as today's managers do), but he had to actually carry out the tasks.

In 1903, however, the shape of the game on the field had settled into its modern form, and the sixty-foot-six-inch pitching distance, so fundamental to everything else, had been in use for ten years. The time was ripe for a shift in managerial thinking to a higher priority for tactics and strategy in a fixed context more suitable for analysis.

A few dates illustrate this evolutionary process.

1884 Overhand pitching is allowed.

1887 A batter may no longer call for a "high" or a "low" pitch but must swing at any delivery in the newly established "strike zone" or take a called strike.

1888 Three strikes is out. (It was four the year before.)

1889 Four balls is a walk. (It was as high as nine.)

1893 The pitching distance is changed from 50 feet (the front end of the pitching box in which the pitcher must remain upon completing his delivery) to sixty feet six inches (where his rear foot must maintain contact with the pitcher's plate).

1894 A bunt deliberately hit foul counts as a strike up to two strikes.

1901 Any foul counts as a strike up to two strikes (National League only).

1902 A foul bunt on the third strike is out.

1903 The American League adopts the foul-strike rule.

Only at this point do we have the game we are familiar with (something to remember when you look at statistics in record books). The pitching pattern, and therefore what the hitter can expect, is set. The catcher is in position to throw out a base stealer. Gloves make fielding a surer proposition. The home team always bats last.

The game will keep changing in physical terms. The liveliness of the ball will vary, fences will be at different distances, a new

The Antecedents

ball will be put in play frequently, trick pitches will be outlawed, artificial turf and lights will create their own playing conditions, athletes will be bigger and faster.

But conceptually, there has been only one significant change since 1903: the American League's adoption of the designated hitter in 1973. And even that has less effect on strategy than people think.

So 1903 is a proper dividing line. Two of our three "originators," who are the subject of the rest of this section, played and managed before 1903—but their impact on others, and their own full development, rests on what happened after that. The third, Branch Rickey, was twenty-two years old at that time and playing minor league baseball to support a college education.

The point to remember is that baseball's development was not a series of individual "inventions" by isolated geniuses. Wright and Spalding in their generation, Selee and Hanlon and Comiskey later, all knew and tried techniques that their successors would build upon. But they were like early builders who found, refined, and polished various kinds of stones, determined their strength and utility, learned where to find and how to shape them. Full-fledged architects, who could use this knowledge, came later, and in baseball they came at the start of this century.

2

John McGraw

A Troubled Youth

John McGraw had a terrible childhood. His father, an Irish immigrant, eked out a living as a railroad track inspector and occasional farmhand in the town of Truxton, New York, in the years right after the Civil War. Truxton was in a rather lovely portion of New York State, east of the Finger Lakes region, about twenty miles south of Syracuse, sixty miles west of a village named Cooperstown, which had not the slightest inkling that someday it would be designated as a baseball shrine. The father, also named John, was a widower with a daughter when he married Ellen Comerfort, whose family was well situated in the little community for many years and not thrilled by her choice. Living in a small house on the outskirts of town, this couple had eight children, four girls and four boys. John, Jr., was the third, born April 7, 1873. It is fair to describe the family as dirt poor.

In the winter of 1884–85, just before John turned twelve, his mother and four of the children died of what was called "black diphtheria". The survivors moved into a house in downtown Truxton, nearer the in-laws, but John wound up bearing the brunt of a shattered and embittered father who took out his frustrations on the oldest surviving boy, often by beating and berating him for his time-wasting interest in playing ball.

The young boy was already fascinated by baseball. He kept a homemade ball with him at all times, and managed to get annually published rule-and-record books, which he studied avidly and kept lovingly all his life. He played as much as possible, and this created additional friction with his father, who was not only insensitive to his needs but insistent that the boy concentrate on productive labor on the railroad or the farms. After one particularly violent incident, John moved out and was taken in by the widow who ran the hotel across the street, getting a bit of mothering and better living conditions in exchange for looking after the stables. He did work briefly for the railroad, as a candy butcher—walking through a car, selling refreshments and magazines.

At sixteen, he was already on his own, and known locally as a good pitcher. He was small, about 5 feet 5 inches tall and weighing about 110 pounds, but he could throw hard and his active mind was focused completely on baseball (whose rules were changing every year, and whose techniques were still being individually rediscovered more often than taught). In 1889, major league baseball promotion was at its height, well reported in all newspapers, and every community had a town team with some tradition behind it playing neighboring towns. McGraw became a regular on the Truxton team, and opponents noticed his ability.

He was offered $2 a game to pitch for the team in Homer, a slightly larger town five miles away. He did well enough to demand a raise to $5, and then $5 plus transportation back and forth. (Up to then, he walked the five miles there and back.)

The owner of another hotel in Truxton also ran a professional baseball team in Olean, way off in the southwestern corner of the state, just north of the Pennsylvania line, about 150 miles away. He offered McGraw $40 a month plus room and board to join that team. McGraw accepted instantly, and after a terrible row with his father (he was still underage), off he went.

He was a flop. They didn't want him to pitch, but to play third base. He could catch the ball all right, but most of his throws to first were wild. He made nine errors in six games, all losses, and wound up on the bench. But by hours of extra practice every morning, he learned to throw straight. The next spring, after starting at Olean, he drifted eastward to Hornellsville and Canisteo, ending up at Wellsville, where the manager was someone he already knew, Al Lawson.

Here he was in the Western New York League, and he always referred to this as the "real start" of his baseball career. He was seventeen.

You don't have to be a trained psychologist to suspect that such a childhood would produce an unhappy man who, if he also had special talents, would be both driven and complex. Here's how Frank Graham, an outstanding sports columnist and biographer, who covered McGraw in New York and knew him well, described him:

The Creators

"He was, distinctly, a robust temperament. He was generous and loyal to his friends, implacable toward his foes. He was vain about some things, extremely modest about others. He irritated persons in the mass and charmed them as individuals. His charities were numerous, and he genuinely resented any attempt to publicize them. He forgave many injuries done him—but forgot none of them. He enjoyed many fine friendships and had many quarrels."

All those tendencies were already in him when, at seventeen, he got his first exposure to the larger world.

In Wellsville, he had enjoyed his first taste of "being someone," an identifiable professional ballplayer acknowledged as such with admiration by the people around him. That winter (1890–91), Lawson organized a team to play in Florida, representing Ocala. He took McGraw along. They went through New York City and Jacksonville—the largest places McGraw had ever seen—to central and very rural Florida. While there, they got an offer to visit Cuba (still under Spanish rule) and played 17 games in Havana against other American teams wintering there. When they got back to Tampa (the point of embarkation), Lawson told the press that McGraw was his best player.

The team resumed barnstorming in Florida. This was 1891, with the baseball world in shambles after the Brotherhood War, as we have seen. The Cleveland team, restocked with regulars, came down for practice games. Lee Viau was a veteran pitcher of high reputation, and one day in Gainesville McGraw got three doubles and a single off him. Of course, Viau was just throwing easily, trying to loosen his arm, not bearing down against nobodies. But that didn't show in the box scores, which went out over the telegraph wires showing four hits.

Within days, McGraw had offers from Rockford, Fort Wayne, and Davenport. He didn't jump at the first one, but accepted $125 a month from Cedar Rapids. The rights to a player—any player—was a disputable issue throughout baseball in the aftermath of the Brotherhood War. The clubs he spurned carried their claims to higher authority and even threatened legal action, but nothing came of it. He played for Cedar Rapids, in the Illinois-Iowa League, and the manager (Bill Gleason, who had been the shortstop on the triumphant St. Louis Browns of the 1880s) was impressed.

On Gleason's recommendation, after only 31 games, McGraw was hired by Bill Barnie, who ran the Baltimore club in the

John McGraw

American Association. He finished the season there without making much of an impression, hitting only .245.

Then, suddenly, everything changed. A rising tide lifts all boats, as they say. The association folded. The National League, expanding to twelve teams, took in Baltimore. Von der Horst, the club's owner and a major beer wholesaler, brought in the bright young Ned Hanlon as manager after the season had started, impressed by the initiative and originality Hanlon had displayed by his role in the player revolt and in managing Pittsburgh's National League teams in 1889 and 1891 and the brotherhood team there in 1890.

Hanlon became the formative influence on McGraw (and others) over the next decade, a Socrates to McGraw's Plato. But at the beginning of 1892, McGraw was just a borderline substitute on an undistinguished team that Hanlon intended to rip apart.

McGraw had just turned nineteen.

The Young Old Orioles

Hanlon had strong ideas, a wealth of experience, and an air of authority. Baseball had been plagued, from the 1850s on, by lack of discipline. Players, including many of the best, were known for dissolute or disreputable life-styles. Gamblers infested the spectator communities, and offers to fix games were often made and not too seldom accepted. Rowdiness in the stands, paralleling the abuse on the field of umpires and opponents, constantly troubled the owners who wanted so much to create a "respectable" environment in which even ladies would feel welcome. (Ladies Day was invented in hopes of softening crowd behavior in their presence.) In fact, a cornerstone of establishing the National League had been the desire to create a climate of decency and discipline (for excellent commercial reasons, not simply out of idealism). But the problems had persisted, and the players and owners were not setting a good example. The owners were constantly arguing among themselves about this advantage or that, and had just gone through an all-out conflict with the players en masse, while players individually hopped from team to team not always with full justification. It was a chaotic time.

Hanlon had lived through it all. He had reached the majors, as an outfielder with Cleveland, in 1880, before the American

Association existed. He spent the next eight years as a journey-man player with Detroit, on teams that went nowhere under Frank Bancroft and Jack Chapman, but did win a pennant in 1887, under Billy Watkins. He had played against teams managed by Anson, Harry Wright, Bob Ferguson, Johnny Morrill, Jim Mutrie and, in the World Series, Comiskey. He had seen the disorder of 1884. He matched wits with the best players of his day in the Players' League (and had finished sixth), and in 1891 with Ward and Selee as well—and had been fired in midseason because his teammates (who finished last) rebelled at his attempts to impose discipline on the drinkers. But the manager, Al Buckenberger, was ready to have him as team captain in 1892 when a broken leg put Hanlon out of commission. At that point, the Baltimore offer came, and Hanlon took it.

Through all this, he had observed, absorbed, analyzed, learned, and exchanged views with the best baseball minds of his time. With the authority granted him in Baltimore, he was ready to put his own ideas into practice. He was thirty-four years old.

His ideas were:

1. Tactics to gain a small edge—bunting, a hit-and-run play, cutoff throws—could be developed further than they had, and could make a big difference to winning and losing if refined "scientifically."

2. Personal discipline and physical conditioning were essential to season-long effectiveness.

3. The manager's authority had to be accepted as absolute, not only in game play decisions but in practice and off-field self-care, to make better tactics work.

4. Aggressiveness was a primary asset.

5. Speed—of foot and brain—helped you win.

6. Deciding where and when a man should play was as impor-tant as recognizing his generalized abilities.

7. It's us against them.

That list became McGraw's Bible, which he fleshed out in greater detail as time went on. But not right away.

Hanlon began by seeking trades to get the kind of players he wanted. (And players were available in the contraction of jobs that followed the player war and AA demise). He couldn't do much for 1892, already under way, and he didn't think the boyish McGraw was ready for the majors. He wanted him to go down to the minors at Mobile. When McGraw refused, and argued his case,

John McGraw

Hanlon was more impressed by his determination and fiery spirit than by physical ability, and kept him on as a utility infielder. McGraw played about half the time, didn't hit much, and the Orioles finished last in the first half and tenth in the second. However, McGraw made a lasting friendship with the team's catcher, a larger man eight years older than he, named Wilbert Robinson.

In 1893, Hanlon made McGraw his regular shortstop and acquired a sensational young outfielder named Joe Kelley. And by 1894, he had the team he wanted in place. He added Willie Keeler and Steve Brodie as young outfielders, and Hughie Jennings as a young shortstop, shifting McGraw to third (where, by now, he had his throws to first down pat). Henry Reitz (called "Heinie") had been installed as a rookie second baseman in 1893. He liked Robinson as his catcher. And for first base, he acquired a thirty-six-year-old slugger of reknown, Dan Brouthers.

This is the team that won the 1894 pennant, and six of its eight regulars are now in the Hall of Fame. Only Reitz and Brodie didn't make it.

This team became famous for its offense, based on place hitting and aggressive base running, as well as its character (which we'll get back to in a moment). But its attack must be seen in perspective, especially the fact that all eight regulars hit well over .300 and that the team's batting average was .343. The mound had just been moved back, and pitchers did not yet know how to adjust, so the whole league hit .309. This put a premium on Hanlon's methods. If home runs were not a factor (with distant fences and a dead ball in play much of the time), and pitchers were easier to hit, the bunt-steal-take-an-extra-base offense was the best way to get runs in bunches.

By the same token, defensive play was at a premium, especially if the best pitchers were less dominant than they had been at the shorter distance. The 1894 Orioles did not have a dominant pitcher, but several who could contribute in turn. In this, too, Hanlon was ahead of his time.

Then something happened in the Temple Cup playoff that made a deep and permanent impression on McGraw.

The Orioles had finished first, three games ahead of Monte Ward's New York Giants, with the three-time champion Boston Beaneaters (as they were now called) falling to third. The split season hadn't worked in 1892, and there had been no postseason excitement (and extra money) at all in 1893. In putting up his cup, Temple stipulated that the winners get 65 percent of the net after expenses and the losers 35 percent, to be divided among the players.

This made little sense to the Orioles, who felt they had earned their championship. They threatened not to play unless the arrangement was a 50–50 split; the second-place team could gain glory and a trophy by winning a short series, but it shouldn't be able to get more money. McGraw, still twenty-one, was a ring-leader in what threatened to be another player strike. When Temple wouldn't agree to this arrangement, it took all of Hanlon's persuasive powers, hours before the first game, to get his players to take the field—whereupon they promptly made private deals with their opponents, player to player, to split the prize money however the games came out.

But it was the way the games came out that focused McGraw's thinking. Upon winning the pennant, the Orioles had been wined, dined, and idolized on their return to Baltimore, and had become, almost overnight, neither physically nor mentally prepared to play seriously. The Giants whipped them in four straight, 4–1, 9–6, 4–1, and 16–3.

Although ready to refuse to play altogether over a money issue, McGraw was outraged at his teammates' willingness to play half-heartedly once they took the field. He blamed Hanlon for failing to maintain the discipline that he had advocated all season. Already a team leader by force of personality, despite his youth, he began to talk more openly about being "the real brains" behind the new style the Orioles were displaying.

This experience solidified, in McGraw's mind, three principles that he would apply throughout his career.

1. The manager's absolute authority must be exerted at all times in all places, especially with respect to off-field behavior and conditioning.

2. Since a player could challenge that authority, as he was challenging Hanlon's and getting away with it, he would never allow such insubordination if he were ever a manager, and he became all but paranoid in his ability to recognize its stirrings.

3. The postseason was important.

During the next four years, the legend of the Old Orioles took shape. They won the pennant again in 1895, but lost the Temple Cup series again (to Cleveland) in 5 games. They won in 1896 and

John McGraw

this time polished off Cleveland in 4 games, and in 1897, after finishing 2 games behind Boston in the pennant race, defeated the Beaneaters in the Temple Cup series in 5 games.

Their reputation for "inside baseball" grew in the retelling after the fact. At the time, they were more recognized for playing dirty. With only one umpire working a game, it was easy to get away with holding or tripping a base runner. Systematic abuse, by incredible profanity and threat of fisticuffs (often enough actualized), was part of the winning technique, directed at opponents as well as umpires. Fans in other cities hated them and they needed police protection often enough. But they turned this hatred to their advantage in three ways: it disrupted the concentration of enemy players, it helped keep the Orioles steamed up within their siege-mentality motivation, and it did intimidate umpires for subsequent decisions no matter how many times they lost a particular argument. McGraw, at least, was convinced that this aggression-intimidation pattern worked, and remained dedicated to it all his life. The Orioles also perfected and popularized the hit-and-run style, but their main characteristic was rowdiness-with-a-purpose.

In this period, McGraw developed four important personal relationships.

One was with Robinson, the team captain as well as catcher, whose more placid personality fit well with McGraw's passion for leadership. Robinson was married with children, and when, in February of 1897, McGraw married, the two families lived in close contact. Almost immediately, the two players became partners in purchasing and operating the Diamond Café, which became Baltimore's prime social milieu for the sporting crowd. Then they bought adjacent homes.

Another was with Hughie Jennings. Hanlon had brought him to Baltimore to take McGraw's place at shortstop, despite his light hitting. McGraw not only didn't mind being displaced to third base, but found a soul mate in this slightly older (by two years), fun-loving, extremely intelligent young redhead from the eastern Pennsylvania mining country. They became inseparable, and with Robinson and Joe Kelley the nucleus of the "always talking baseball" group that refined the style Hanlon had set in motion. McGraw then taught Jennings how to be a better hitter.

The third was, of course, his young bride, Minnie Doyle.

The fourth had an earlier beginning. Back in 1890, when he had played briefly in Olean, he had become friendly with a priest named Joe Dolan, who was on the faculty of Allegany College, a small Catholic school run by Franciscan monks in Olean. Dolan was a baseball fan and preached to the seventeen-year-old McGraw the value of education. After the 1892 season, with no guaranteed prospects of success in Baltimore, McGraw had little reason to hang around a strange city with no income, and no desire to go back to Truxton. (Players got paid only during the season.) So he got in touch with Dolan and asked him to negotiate a deal: if the college would let him take classes and provide room and board, he would coach the college baseball team until it was time to go back to the National League.

The school, which soon became St. Bonaventure, accepted the deal, and that's where McGraw spent the winters of 1892–93, 1893–94, 1894–95, and 1895–96. He didn't get enough credits for a degree, but he certainly "improved himself" to the point where he could move comfortably among, and communicate easily with, the well-educated and prominent people with whom he would rub elbows for so much of his later life.

And after the 1893 season, he persuaded Jennings to come with him, as a fellow student and assistant coach. Father Dolan, by the time he attended McGraw's wedding in 1897, had become vice-president of St. Bonaventure.

But fate was not finished with providing tragedy and hardship for young Johnny. He suffered various injuries and illnesses in these years, including malaria. Within weeks of his wedding, the news came that Father Dolan had suddenly died, still a young man. And in August of 1899, Minnie died of a ruptured appendix.

By now he was the manager of the Orioles (after a sequence of events we'll describe presently), but he was devastated emotionally. He left the club, which was on the road, and went into seclusion for a couple of weeks. He escaped a nervous breakdown, but not by much. He was still only twenty-six years old. It was fourteen years since half his original family had been wiped out by disease. The loss of so young a wife, childless, in such circumstances, tested his resiliency to the utmost degree. He did return to work in September, but he was shaken and uncertain.

He had already frayed old friendships and loyalties with his sharp tongue and unending belligerence. What his fate might have been if baseball, at that point, had been in a "normal" mode, no one can say. But because the business was again going through extraordinary ferment, opportunities arose that helped

John McGraw

his innate ambition and drive recover from the double blow of widowhood and physical deterioration of his playing ability.

Baseball was entering a revolutionary period that would produce its modern form, and McGraw was right in the middle of the maelstrom.

The Move to New York

As the twelve-team league was starting to unravel, Hanlon and Von der Horst bought a half interest in the Brooklyn club, and transferred half interest in the Orioles to Fred Abell and Charley Ebbets, who owned Brooklyn. This was in February of 1899, and it made a lot of sense.

In 1898, Boston had again beaten out the Orioles in the pennant race, but what really mattered was that Baltimore attendance had fallen to half of what it had been during the middle 1890s (below 150,000 for the season). Brooklyn had just become one of the five boroughs of Greater New York, and its population was exploding as bridges across the East River, subway connections, and a network of trolley cars opened (or promised to open) new residential areas. Its "market potential"—a phrase not then in general use, but a reality well grasped by all businessmen—was incomparably greater than Baltimore's. Brooklyn's tenth-place team in 1898 had drawn 300,000.

So Hanlon went to Brooklyn as manager, taking Keeler, Kelley, Jennings, and some others with him.

He would have taken McGraw and Robinson, too. But they wanted to stay in Baltimore because their Diamond Café was a thriving business, and they now had family roots there. (Robinson had four children, and Minnie McGraw's father was a respected citizen.) So they offered McGraw the managership, and Robinson stayed as his assistant manager and best player.

The Brooklyn caper worked the way it was supposed to. The (recently named) Trolley Dodgers won the pennant, beating out Boston. The Baltimore residue, under McGraw's leadership, did better than others expected, with the team winning 86 games and finishing fourth. In September, John T. Brush offered McGraw the managership of Cincinnati for 1900, improving the grieving McGraw's morale; but the Baltimore business was too lucrative to leave. At the same time, rumors were circulating that the league would cut back to eight teams in 1900, with Baltimore being eliminated. This, in turn, stirred talk of reviving the American Association, dead since 1891. Ban Johnson's grand plan for upgrading his Western League was not yet generally known.

The situation in New York had become deplorable. When andrew Freedman took control of the team in 1895, it had been a contender for six of the previous ten seasons, including a second-place finish in 1894 (with a Temple Cup victory to boot). Freedman not only dumped Monte Ward but used eight different managers during his first five seasons, finishing ninth, seventh, third (the only time one manager, Bill Joyce, stayed all season), seventh, and tenth. If the National League was going to be challenged again, it could not afford a weak franchise in New York. Beefing up Brooklyn helped, but that wasn't a real answer.

Freedman favored the one-company-eight-subsidiaries reorganization plan. He also had an ace in the hole concerning any possible rival. With his Tammany Hall and other political and real estate connections, he could have the city plan to run a street through any property on which someone seemed ready to build a ballpark; and as owner of the Polo Grounds, he certainly wouldn't let anyone use that. But keeping out competition was one thing; putting the laughingstock Giant operation on its feet was something else.

McGraw and Robinson knew Baltimore was doomed. They got backers for a Baltimore entry into the proposed American Association, but that dream evaporated before the 1900 season began. When the National did cut to eight teams, all the Baltimore contracts were moved to Brooklyn (as were Cleveland's to St. Louis, with Washington and Louisville players divided up in various ways). Hanlon then promptly sold McGraw, Robinson, and Billy Keister, the shortstop, to St. Louis.

McGraw and Robinson refused to go. They had nothing against the St. Louis management, they said, but they couldn't afford it: their investment in their Baltimore business was too great. If they could play for an East Coast team, they'd be close enough to look after it, but St. Louis was far away.

They approached Freedman. He said he wasn't interested. (One owner, even Freedman, wasn't about to encourage free choice by players who were another owner's "property.") He advised them to go to St. Louis.

They did, but with a sweetener: the reserve clause would be stricken from their contracts. After 1900 they would be free to go anywhere. They reported to the Browns three weeks into the 1900 season and played out the year, finishing in a tie for fifth.

By now, however, McGraw was aware of Johnson's plans for 1901, and included in them. The new "major" league, recruiting National League players, would put a team in Baltimore. He had no contractual obligation to anyone, even under the reserve theory, and was free to take that franchise.

Brush offered him Cincinnati, a National League survivor, again. McGraw refused again. He had other things in the works, as head of the Baltimore club in the American League for 1901, and was scouring the country with Johnson, Mack, Comiskey, and Clark Griffith, recruiting National League players for what would soon be called "the Junior Circuit."

They succeeded, eventually, in getting more than 100 former National League players to join the American, at a time when the entire population of an eight-team league was about 180.

So in 1901, McGraw, at twenty-eight, was manager and part owner of a charter member of the American League, managing strictly from the bench. His team finished fifth, barely over .500, but did arouse a lot of local enthusiasm. The Diamond Café hummed.

And during this year, he was courting Blanche Sindall, nineteen-year-old daughter of a prosperous building contractor. Her brother had befriended many of the Baltimore players and invited them to the Sindall home. These visits were the beginning of a healing process that McGraw sorely needed.

He and Blanche were married in January 1902.

What happened next is clear enough in its effect, but there are various versions of what really went on. Different historians give different accounts.

The facts are:

McGraw became manager of the New York Giants midway through 1902, bringing some good Baltimore players with him, but not Robinson.

Opposition to an American League entry in New York and a playing site for it evaporated.

The Baltimore franchise was sold to New Yorkers whose Tammany connections were as good as Freedman's.

Brush, who owned Cincinnati and supported Freedman's plans to form a single-entity league, wound up buying full control of the Giants after selling his Cincinnati team, and Freedman left the baseball scene.

The Creators

The two leagues entered into a peace agreement that started in 1903 and remains in place today.

The public perception, at the time and for a long time afterward, was that McGraw and Johnson quickly developed irreconcilable differences; that McGraw's rowdyism on the field and frequent suspensions, including one in July of 1902, made McGraw switch sides; that Johnson considered McGraw a "traitor"; and that Brush's move from Cincinnati was coincidental, as was the discovery that an American League park could be built at 168th Street and Broadway, barely a mile northwest of the Polo Grounds.

But was it, as Blanche McGraw later wrote, all based on private agreements known to all parties? Was the illusion of hostility a way to keep public interest stirred up? Was McGraw in New York the National League's fee for letting an American League team in? Or had McGraw, whose daily differences with Johnson were real enough, forestalled a move by Johnson to move into New York without him, leaving him holding the bag with a defunct Baltimore franchise? Or were there cross-purposes and unintended consequences that produced a better resolution of the war than anyone had consciously planned? And what exactly was the role of Spalding, who took an active part in derailing the Freedman-Brush plan within the National League, and whose sporting goods cartel now included Wright and Ditson (started by George Wright back in the 1870s in Boston) as well as Reach? Did he pull invisible strings in accordance with his consistent belief that (1) the more major league activity, the more ordinary customers for equipment and publications and (2) the illusion of rivalry (like Spalding versus Reach) was a better marketing device than acknowledged monopoly?

It doesn't matter here. What does is that McGraw had reached a position of total authority, under Brush, in the publicity center of America, New York City. His ideas about managing could now get full play, without restraint and with adequate resources, in a limelight that would maximize the impact of his example.

The Mathewson Years

All this personal history of one man is necessary because, in his case, it became such an integral part of the managing style he passed on to so many others. We won't need it in comparable

John McGraw

detail on the others—these are essays, not biographies—but McGraw was exceptional in both his approach to the job and the breadth of his influence.

He was monomaniacal about winning. It was all that counted. If breaking rules supplied an advantage, fine, break them. (It doesn't always work that way; breaking rules in ways you can't get away with is counterproductive.) But to break rules advantageously, you have to know them inside out.

What didn't matter was decency. Abuse—verbal and occasionally physical (again, if you could get away with it)—was a legitimate weapon if it aided the chance of victory. People could be cajoled, encouraged, instructed, and guided into doing better—but many could also be frightened or whipped into trying harder. Insult in the foulest terms, sarcasm, carping criticism, and humiliation were not to be avoided whenever they might pay a dividend. "The main idea," he said again and again, "is to win."

Later generations might associate this frame of mind with a Vince Lombardi ("Winning isn't the main thing, it's the only thing") and Leo Durocher ("Nice guys finish last"), but McGraw was totally committed to it in 1902. And probably in 1892.

This attitude has corollaries.

To get away with abuse, you have to be absolute boss.

To become absolute boss, you have to win a test of wills, and the techniques of intimidation can help you win that test.

To win the confrontation, you must seize the intiative so that the combat is instigated on your terms, on your turf.

Once your absolute authority has been established, you can afford to be kind, even gentle, understanding, and supportive—at times and circumstances of your choice. But you have to keep your dictatorial powers on display often enough, dramatically enough, to keep the general atmosphere of fear alive. If you don't use it, you may lose it.

Finally, to act this way effectively, you must maintain unshakeable faith in your own judgment. In every circumstance, you must be right and your way must be seen to be right. To question is to doubt; to doubt is to undermine obedience; but since your way is the only right way—because you've thought it out and come to that decision—any disobedience means doing it less than right.

Belief in his own infallibility manifested itself on three levels, which came to characterize his methods for the rest of his life. First there was the matter of judging talent, a player's capabilities. On this score he was uniformly excellent. Second, there was a conviction that he could "straighten out" players who had proved troublesome to other managers, especially those with drinking problems. In this respect, he had some notable successes, at least temporarily. The third was a tendency to play hunches and make unorthodox moves in tactical situations during games, rather than stick to "precentages." Here, too, his instincts were marvelous; but this was one reason why he needed his orders to be followed blindly, and eventually this technique began to backfire.

Nevertheless, such abnormal self-confidence was essential to his approach. And while it can become excessive, as it did eventually in McGraw, it must be a substantial part of any manager's equipment. The troops must be convinced that the general knows what he's doing.

McGraw arrived in New York on July 17, 1902, amid great fanfare, ready to put all his ideas into practice. The Giants were in last place. Freedman still owned the club, and McGraw was his fourteenth manager in eight seasons—but McGraw had a four-year contract promising him "absolute control." The first step was to carry out a previous plan to wreck Baltimore by buying up (through an intermediary) its stock and transferring some players thus acquired to the Giant roster. Was this intended to cripple the American League by having one of its teams fold in midseason? Or was it part of some private understanding to clear the way for a move to New York without losing the "warfare" momentum that was creating so much publicity? In any case, Johnson denounced McGraw and pieced together enough players for Baltimore to finish its season (with Robinson as manager). McGraw denounced "Czar" Johnson and scoffed at the American League's future. It was run by a Chicago-Boston-Philadelphia "clique" (with which he had been recruiting National League players less than two years before), and in Philadelphia, McGraw said, the league had a "white elephant" on its hands in Connie Mack's team. The papers lapped it up.

Then he turned to the serious business of telling Freedman where to get off. He gave nine of the twenty-three players on the roster their release. Freedman protested that they had cost $14,000; McGraw declared they'd cost him more if they stayed, and listed the ones he intended to acquire. Freedman protested again; McGraw told him he'd run the club his way and Freedman would like it—picking the fight he wanted to pick to assert himself. Freedman gave in. (Did he give in knowing he'd soon be leaving? Probably.)

John McGraw

The Giants had a young player named Christy Mathewson, tall, handsome, the prototype of the All-American boy. He had been a college star at Bucknell in football, baseball, and basketball, class president, and an outstanding student. He also pitched semipro ball. When offered a professional contract, he took it because his family could use the money ($90 a month). Strong and hard-throwing, he developed a "reverse curve," a right-handed delivery that broke into instead of away from a right-handed batter. It became known as his "fadeaway"; now we call it a "screwball," used mostly by left-handers. At Norfolk in 1900, he won 20 of his 22 starts by July, rejected an offer from Philadelphia, and accepted one from the Giants. In 1901 for the Giants, he won 20 games (of the team's 52), including a no-hitter. In 1902, on an even weaker team, he wasn't doing quite as well, and just before McGraw arrived they had him playing first base for a few games.

McGraw seized upon that rather silly experiment to castigate Freedman's previous managers (Harry Fogel and Heinie Smith), and boasted publicly right then (and for years afterward) that he had to "convert" Mathewson back to pitching because of the ignorance of the management that preceded him. Actually, there was no question that Mathewson was a pitcher, but McGraw was making his point about who was in charge.

The Giants finished the 1902 season with a 48–88 record, 53½ games out of first place (the deepest finish in the club's history, to this day). But McGraw had gotten rid of the players he didn't want and had brought in some players he did (Joe McGinnity and Roger Bresnahan, for instance).

By the time the 1903 season opened, Brush had bought out Freedman and the peace treaty between the two leagues was in effect. With Brush, who had sought him for Cincinnati, McGraw had nothing to prove and nothing to demand. A tightwad in other respects, who had fought for years to keep player salaries down, Brush turned out to be always willing to spend when McGraw wanted money to acquire a player by purchase or trade. In Brush, McGraw had exactly the kind of owner he needed: a check signer who didn't interfere with baseball decisions, and a strong force in league councils, able and willing to stick up for his club's rights in the endless disputes that McGraw helped provoke.

For spring training in 1903, McGraw took the team to Savannah, Georgia. The newlywed Mathewsons and the McGraws, married only a little more than a year, became close friends and shared an apartment. Matty, only seven years younger than his manager, appreciated immediately the baseball wisdom McGraw exuded, and shared the older man's competitive fire without losing his own gentlemanly instincts. McGraw, cognizant of (and even a little awed by) Matty's talent, warmed to the presence of so intelligent a disciple (much as he had responded to Jennings). And since the two wives took to each other so well, the relationship was cemented for years to come.

And in Savannah, McGraw learned a lesson in managing that confirmed his paranoia. The hotel was a long walk from the ballpark. Some players asked if they could rent bicycles to go back and forth. Thinking this would be a fine conditioning device, McGraw gladly gave permission. The players then started to have races, with frequent spills, narrowly escaping serious injuries. Within a week, he had to stop the bike riding. The lesson: You have to watch these dumb ballplayers every second, or they'll do something foolish.

That 1903 team had plenty of talent, and McGraw started teaching it the Oriole techniques. The rules had been stabilized, so his own skill of fouling off pitches endlessly to wear out an opposing pitcher was no longer useful. But the hit-and-run play was a fundamental weapon. The Baltimore chop—hitting down at the ball to get a high first bounce off the ground in front of home plate (hardened by the home groundskeeper)—was a good way to beat out infield hits. Stealing bases as often as possible not only put men in scoring position but disturbed pitchers and forced moving infielders to leave holes or commit errors. And when it came to making choices about which pitch should be thrown to which hitter when, McGraw would make the final decision and call it from the bench.

And he adopted a routine instituted by Hanlon at Baltimore. When at home, every morning at ten o'clock everybody had to show up for two hours of practice. Then they could go home for lunch and a rest, and return to the park at two o'clock (since games usually started around four o'clock). The extra practice time honed skills to a degree most other teams didn't attain, and it put at least some pressure on the night-life crowd by eliminating the possibility of sleeping late the next morning.

That season, the Giants won 84 games and finished second, 6½ games behind Pittsburgh, 12½ ahead of fifth-place Brooklyn, still under Hanlon. McGraw's opinion about which of them was the real baseball brain was confirmed in his own mind, and he didn't hesitate to say so. (The Brooklyn team, incidentally, was now being called the "Superbas," because there was a famous vaudeville act named Hanlon's Superbas." The name persisted, in occasional tabloid headlines, into the 1940s.)

The 1903 Giants, even as nonchampions, broke many attendance records, and Brush started adding to the seating capacity of the Polo Grounds. The American League team, managed by Clark Griffith, had finished in the middle of the pack and was no rival for public affection. McGraw, in one year, was emerging as New York's dominant sports figure.

Since the two leagues were no longer at war, the idea of reviving a World Series seemed natural. Boston, the American League champion, challenged Pittsburgh to a best-of-nine series. Pittsburgh accepted, confident it could display the superiority of the older league (and not without reason, since it had a truly outstanding team managed by Fred Clarke and starring Honus Wagner). But after taking a 3–1 lead, the Pirates lost 4 straight, 2 to Cy Young and 2 to Bill Dinneen, and American League prestige made a quantum jump. Sixty-three years later, a comparable shift in perception occurred when the New York Jets of the American Football League defeated Baltimore, the National Football League champion, in Super Bowl III.

For the Giants, Mathewson and McGinnity had posted thirty and thirty-one victories in 1903. They could pitch half the games in a four-day rotation, so McGraw needed two more starters. He now put his evaluative talents to work.

He traded for Bill Dahlen, a shortstop branded "lazy" at Brooklyn. He had found a young third base prospect named Art Devlin. His third pitcher of 1903, Dummy Taylor, had done well enough, and now he found George (Hooks) Wiltse, a young left-hander. Dahlen and Devlin completed a superior infield anchored by Dan McGann at first and Billy Gilbert at second, both brought over from Baltimore. He played Bresnahan, who would be a Hall of Famer as a catcher, in the outfield, and let two others share the catching: Jack Warner, batting left-handed, and Frank Bowerman, batting right-handed—a platooning device he would use persistently and that became copied much sooner than contemporary fans (and players) believe.

In a schedule expanded to 154 games (partly to take advantage of the increased attendance the two-league system was stimulating), the 1904 Giants won 106 games and the pennant by a

13-game margin over the Chicago Cubs. Matty won 33 games, McGinnity 35, Taylor 21. The team led the league in hitting (.262) and stolen bases (283 under the new definitions, which we still use). It also made the fewest errors and the most double plays.

Everything McGraw wanted as a manager had worked perfectly.

But the other New York team had also caused a flurry of excitement, losing the pennant only on the last day on a wild pitch. McGraw was the toast of New York, but the American League was not to be sneered at. Boston, having won the pennant again by such a narrow margin, issued a challenge to the National League champion, as it had the year before. Another World Series was an intriguing prospect.

It wasn't that simple, however.

Brush had been opposed to the peace treaty with the American League from the start, having cast the lone vote against it (as owner of Cincinnati) after being bypassed in most of the negotiations. McGraw, of course, had his animus against Johnson (real or exaggerated for effect). At the end of the 1903 season, when the opposite-league members in Chicago and St. Louis had played a postseason exhibition series, the Giants haughtily rejected such a suggestion in New York.

As early as July of 1904, the two league presidents, Johnson and Harry Pulliam, were talking about formalizing a World Series. (The 1903 arrangement had been made strictly by the two clubs involved, with no preexisting rules about format, choosing umpires, or dividing the receipts. It turned out that Pittsburgh's losing share was bigger than Boston's winning share, and there was a big fuss about that anamoly.) But Brush, publicly and truculently, said his team wouldn't take part, and since his team was leading the league, the two presidents did not pursue the matter.

Now, with the season over and the prospect of big money to be made in a Boston–New York confrontation, players as well as fans were clamoring for staging such an event.

But Brush was adamant and McGraw went along, although in later years he claimed he had wanted to go ahead. Brush had made enough money in a highly prosperous Giant season, and didn't want to give any indirect boost to the American League's New York entry. McGraw didn't want to risk the adulation he had just won by losing a short series (in which "anything could happen," he knew) as Pittsburgh had the year before.

John McGraw

So there was no World Series in 1904, but its very absence created the pressures that led to its formal establishment for 1905. The criticism of the Giants was so severe that Brush actually took the lead in putting forth a plan for the future. It would be a best-of-seven series. The receipts from the first four games only (after certain expenses) would constitute the pool of prize money for the players, so that they would have no incentive to prolong the series to increase their shares. The prize money would be divided so that the winning team got 75 percent and the losing team 25 percent, with each team deciding internally about how to break up its pool into individual shares. If the series went beyond a fourth game, the clubs would keep the receipts except for a certain share assigned to the two league offices.

These became known as the Brush Rules, although officially they were adopted and administered by the three-man commission set up in the peace treaty between the leagues.

The 1905 Giants were even stronger. Late in the 1904 season, McGraw had made a deal for Mike Donlin, a Cincinnati outfielder who had battled Honus Wagner down to the wire for the batting title in 1903. He had a reputation as drinker and roisterer, and fought with the new (after Brush's departure) Cincinnati management. McGraw was sure he could handle a man like that—who could play like that. With Donlin in centerfield, Bresnahan could go back to catching. In later years, McGraw would say that this team was his best; even in 1905, he was saying it was better than the Orioles of the 1890s.

With such talent at his disposal, McGraw intensified his aggressiveness. He insulted everybody in sight and antagonized crowds wherever he went. He never let up on umpires, and was often thrown out of games and suspended by the league. He got into fistfights, and triggered others. Many who knew him best insisted it was all calculated: "Everything he did was intended to boost the gate," one recalled. And this was clearly part of his conscious motivation. But his behavior also contained an element of loss of self-control. There may have been method in his madness, but it did spill over, at times, into authentic madness.

Two aspects of this side of his character became visible to all around this time. He loved to gamble—on horses, on billiards, at gaming tables—and flaunted this activity in public. And his appetite for good food turned him into a rotund figure as soon as he stopped actually playing. His silhouette, short with a protuberant belly, fit the common image of the name that was being attached to him semisarcastically but increasingly taken at face value: Little Napoleon.

At the same time, his sharp mind took pursuit of victory beyond traditional boundaries. Sure, a scrappy team on the field would win ball games and pull in the customers. But players leading better lives would perform better too. In those days, pay scales were low and in a home city many players lived in fourth-rate hotels and ate cheap food. On the road, a club was responsible for travel and accommodation expenses, but most clubs took the cheapest facilities available.

McGraw set out to upgrade the living conditions of his players. He paid good salaries, by the standards of the day, but more than that he improved club-directed responsibilities. He made sure that travel was first-class, in Pullman cars. He booked the team into first-class hotels. He provided better transportation from hotel to ballpark, at a time when visiting teams still had to dress at their hotel because not every park had a visitors' dressing room. He improved the clubhouse facilities—showers, lockers, trainer's table—in his own ballpark. He helped, out of his own pocket, players who developed a legitimate need (in his eyes) for assistance. He wanted high morale and a sense of self-respect, as well as obedience. (That his foul mouth and endless criticism undermined self-respect was a self-defeating element that he would pay for later.) He wanted players focused on playing ball, not on discomfort.

So he was also aware of psychology—inconsistently, but sometimes brilliantly. When the 1905 Giants won another pennant (105 victories, 9 games ahead of Pittsburgh, leading the league in hitting and stolen bases), he prepared a masterstroke for the World Series, which this time would pit him against the Philadelphia team he had called a white elephant three years before.

He ordered special new uniforms: all black, with white trim, with "Giants" spelled out in large white letters across the front. The impact was everything he expected. He had not forgotten how a great Baltimore team, in 1894, had not taken postseason play seriously enough. If a gimmick could help, he had thought of a good one.

But it was only incidental, of course, to the main impact the Giants had to offer: the right arm of Christy Mathewson.

John McGraw

It's fair to call the 1905 World Series the first real "modern" one, launching a tradition unbroken since. And there hasn't been another like it.

Mathewson was at his peak. He had been 31–8 during the regular season, with 8 shutouts and an earned-run average subsequently computed as 1.27. (No such statistic was kept in those days.) In 339 innings, he had struck out 207 batters and walked only 64. Of the 37 games he started, he completed 33. Used in relief 6 times, he won 3, saved 2, lost 1.

Until now, America had not had such a transcendent sports hero, projecting manly virtues and moral rectitude while displaying competitive fire and consummate skill, in so bright a spotlight.

He won the opener, 3–0, in Philadelphia. McGinnity lost the second game by the same score, in New York. Then Matty won again at Philadelphia, 9–0, on two day's rest (since there had been no game on Sunday). Back at the Polo Grounds, McGinnity won 1–0. The next day, also in New York, Matty won 2–0.

He had pitched three World Series shutouts in six days.

The status of Mathewson the Model Warrior and McGraw the Genius General was universally accepted as unprecedented and unmatchable.

And it was Mathewson's presence at McGraw's side that set the tone of the next decade, the most significant portion of McGraw's career.

McGraw didn't win another pennant for six years, or another World Series for sixteen. But during the period 1906–17 his fame and influence continued to grow. His teams, almost always in contention, became involved in a series of dramatic incidents that became baseball legend. All we can do here is summarize the sequence of events and pick out some revealing items about his managerial methods.

In 1906, Mathewson came down with diphtheria (and one can imagine what feelings that stirred in McGraw), but was able to pitch by May and did wind up with 22 victories. But Donlin broke his leg, McGann broke his arm, and Bresnahan was beaned. Even so, the Giants won 96 games—and finished 20 games behind the Cubs, who won 116.

In 1907, the Cubs won 107, and the Giants fell to fourth.

In 1908, the Cubs won again, but this time by only 1 game after a disputed tie, which became the most storied single game in baseball history until Bobby Thomson's 1951 homer supplanted it. We'll get back to it in a moment.

In 1909, Pittsburgh outsprinted the Cubs, 110 victories to 104, with the Giants a distant third.

In 1910, the Cubs were back on top, winning 104 and leaving the second-place Giants 13 games behind.

In 1911, finally, the Giants won another pennant, beating out an aging Chicago team with a group entirely different (except for Mathewson) than the 1905 squad. But they lost the World Series to Mack's Athletics in 6 games.

In 1912, they finished first again, well ahead of the Cubs and the Pirates, but were beaten in the World Series by the Boston Red Sox in the tenth inning of the seventh and deciding game.

In 1913, they made it three pennants in a row, but were polished off again by the Athletics, in five games.

In 1914, they seemed well on their way to a fourth straight when they and the rest of the league ran into a baseball miracle. The Boston Braves, in last place in mid-July, 11 games below .500, were at the exact midpoint of the 154-game schedule. Then they won 61 of the remaining 77 and went on to sweep the Athletics in the World Series in four straight. The Giants finished second.

In 1915, Mathewson finally gave out, able to win only eight games. Amid this and other complications, the Giants fell to last place.

In 1916, they bounced back to fourth place, only seven games behind the pennant-winning Dodgers.

And in 1917, they were National League champions again, losing the World Series in six games to the Chicago White Sox, a truly powerful team that would tarnish itself forever two years later by becoming the Black Sox who fixed the 1919 World Series.

From this period, we have to focus on five topics:

1. McGraw's skill in finding and nurturing young players who could develop into stars.

2. The nature of the Cubs and Pirates who were able to beat the Giants.

3. The melodramatic incidents of 1908 and 1912, and their aftermath.

4. His role in the Federal League War, which rocked baseball in 1914 and 1915, when a third major league set up shop.

5. His roster of protégés.

Let's take them in reverse order.

John McGraw

In 1911, McGraw resumed his interrupted relationship with Wilbert Robinson, now heavier than ever and usually addressed as Uncle Robby. After 1902, Robinson had remained in Baltimore, running the Diamond Café. McGraw had sold his interest in it to Robinson as part of the money-raising scheme to buy out the Baltimore franchise. Robinson was active from time to time in minor league baseball, in Baltimore and elsewhere, and occasionally went to spring training with the Giants to help out. In 1911, McGraw had a promising pitcher named Rube Marquard who needed special tutoring, and Robinson joined his staff as a full-time coach, working first base during games.

The old intimacy, however, could not be revived. McGraw was now king of the hill, dictator, more arbitrary and arrogant than ever, drinking more than before and turning nasty when drunk. No one dared contradict or criticize him, and few even dared to try. But to Robinson, he was his old buddy, the unpolished kid who had shown up in Baltimore when Robinson was an established big leaguer, subsequently his confidant and willingly followed leader. Robby wasn't afraid to say what he thought, or see anything wrong in giving his honest opinion.

In the 1913 World Series, McGraw took defeat even harder than usual, and blamed Robinson for a mix-up in signs. At the customary season-end party, they had a row, and McGraw fired him on the spot.

Whereupon Robby went out and signed on as manager of the Brooklyn Dodgers. The breach between the two old Orioles had been entirely public, and fit perfectly the mystique of hatred that was supposed to exist between Brooklyn and New York. Whatever his private feelings after he cooled down (if he did), McGraw played the "hated rival" routine to the end and once again fanned the flames of fan involvement in an "us versus them" context.

The imprint of Robinson was so strong that the Brooklyn team, back to Dodgers from Superbas, began to be called the Robins, depicted as such in cartoons, and referred to in newspaper headlines as "the Flock." When they won National League pennants in 1916 and 1920, the personal vendetta in the neighborhood rivalry solidified what became baseball's most intense (and profitable) promotion.

As manager, however, Robinson was clearly a McGraw disciple—totally different in personality, laid back instead of insistent on dictatorial control, but entirely attuned in strategic concepts to the McGraw-Oriole way of playing baseball.

One story from a later time illustrates the difference. In the late 1920s, Babe Herman was one of Robinson's best hitters but a less than graceful right fielder. One day he chased a curving line drive which ended up foul in the right field corner while Herman sacrificed his body by crashing into the box fronts. He thought he'd given it a helluva try.

When he got back to the dugout, Robinson said, "Why were you playing so far off the line?"

"Why don't you go and [etcetera, etcetera]," yelled Herman, losing his temper.

Without another word, Robinson yanked Herman out of the game, and wouldn't put him in the lineup for the next three days.

Now they came to a late-game situation where a hit would win it, and there was Herman sitting on the bench. One of the other players said to Robinson, "Why don't you send Babe up to pinch hit?"

Robinson said, "I'm not talking to him. Get somebody else to ask him to do it."

Somebody did. Herman got a hit and the Dodgers won. The next day he was back in the starting lineup.

At any rate, Robinson was one offshoot of the McGraw school.

And also, among the men who played for McGraw in 1903–17, were:

Bresnahan (Cardinals, 1909–12, Cubs 1915)
Art Fletcher (Phillies, 1923–26)
Hans Lobert (Phillies, 1938, 1942)
Mathewson (Cincinnati, 1916–18)
Buck Herzog (Cincinnati, 1913–16)
Bill Dahlen (Brooklyn, 1910–13)
Fred Tenney (Red Sox, 1905–7, 1911, before and after he played for McGraw)
Frank Bowerman (Braves, 1909)
There would be many, many others.

The Federal League story involved McGraw directly, and the whole course of baseball history might have been different if he had made other choices.

The ten years of baseball peace that followed the 1903 agreement had the usual result. Outsiders wanted in. With the major league scene bigger and more successful than ever, wealthy men and business firms wanted to share the glamor as well as the revenue that baseball insiders enjoyed. One way was to buy an existing team, and McGraw was involved in a key incident of that type too. But with more buyers than sellers, it seemed simpler to start another league from scratch, offer more money to the established players, and engage in good old-fashioned capitalistic competition head on.

The backers of the Federal League aimed for a 1914 start-up and were already proselytizing during the 1913 season. They did operate in 1914 and 1915, then gave up. Some of them bought into the two existing leagues. Some of them dropped out altogether. But some set in motion the antitrust suits that shaped the future.

McGraw's place in what was happening was complicated. Right after the 1912 World Series, with its last-gasp defeat, he started a fifteen-week vaudeville tour (the 1912 equivalent of a series of talk show appearances for today's celebrities). In Chicago, he met Comiskey and they laid out plans for a world tour of their baseball teams after the 1913 season. Then, in November, Brush died.

Ownership of the Giants passed on to his heirs. The one who took charge was Harry Hempstead, a son-in-law who had been taking care of the original clothing business back in Indianapolis. With no knowledge of baseball or even any special interest in it, he could not have the kind of relationship his father-in-law had enjoyed with McGraw. So he brought in an acknowledged baseball expert to act as secretary of the club, John B. Foster, editor of the annual Spalding Guides and an authority on playing rules with a long background as a sportswriter. Foster would have primary personal loyalty to Hempstead.

McGraw, at this point, considered it "his" club and any questions to be "interference." He was a central figure in New York's social and show business communities, as well as an object of public adulation. He had countless friends in the theater-hotel-restaurant-nightclub-partygoing circles to which some wealthy "society people" were also attracted.

Through these circles, he knew Col. Jake Ruppert, heir to a brewery fortune, and Cap Huston, a retired army engineer who had made his fortune in Cuba (where McGraw met him in 1911). They were baseball fans, Polo Grounds regulars, and often guests of Brush. They sounded McGraw out about buying the Giants.

McGraw told them that the family had no intention of selling, but that if they wanted a team they could probably buy the Yankees. The Giant-Yankee relationship had become warm (no pun intended) after a fire destroyed most of the Polo Grounds

The Creators

early in the 1911 season. The Giants were invited to play at Hilltop Park as guests of the Yankees until an improved, enlarged, and modernized Polo Grounds was built (in time for the 1911 World Series, in fact).

The two colonels, as they were usually referred to, then paid $450,000 for the franchise that Tammany-designated purchasers had acquired just ten years before for $19,000. In 1913, they moved the Yankees into the Polo Grounds as tenants.

If not for that, Ruppert and Huston (or one of them) would probably have bought into the Federal League.

The Feds were putting teams into Chicago, St. Louis, Pittsburgh, and Brooklyn, taking the majors head on, and into such high-minor locales as Buffalo, Baltimore, Indianapolis, and Kansas City. What they needed was a superstar personality for instant credibility, and the greatest superstar in existence was McGraw, bigger than any player could be. They were ready to give him a five-year contract worth $250,000 (in 1913!) to manage Brooklyn or Chicago or anywhere he wanted, with an eye to eventually putting a team in New York.

Since McGraw got, and took, so much credit for reviving the National League merely by coming to New York in 1902, few could deny the possibility that he could help establish the Feds (who would then seek amalgamation with organized baseball instead of remaining as outlaws).

When McGraw returned from the world tour of 1913–14, the offer was there and the scramble for players was on.

McGraw rejected the offer, and denounced the players who moved.

This time, unlike 1890 and 1901, the majority of the players stayed put. They used their increased bargaining power to get more money and long-term contracts from the existing teams, but for the most part they stayed. What kind of stampede McGraw might have started will never be known.

His instinct, however, served him well. The Federal League's future was dimmed by the outbreak of World War I that August, creating uncertainty for everyone and particularly for financiers. And the organized baseball two-leagues-plus-minors structure was now strong enough, and wealthy enough, to fight off challengers. It outmaneuvered the antitrust actions the new league brought against it, kept promoting its own product, offered reasonable surrender terms after 1915, and outlasted the threat.

John McGraw

(One dissolution arrangement was not settled satisfactorily. The Baltimore Feds had been promised a chance to buy into the St. Louis Browns but were not allowed to do so. They brought a new antitrust suit against baseball. This became the landmark "Federal Baseball" case in which the Supreme Court, in 1922, ruled that baseball was not subject to federal antitrust laws because staging games was not "commerce" in the sense that Congress had intended under the interstate commerce clause of the Constitution. Upheld in 1952 and 1972, this antitrust exception has been prized by baseball ever since, and has enabled it to withstand all subsequent external challenges, which succeeded in football, basketball, and hockey.)

In the process, however, McGraw had demonstrated the full force of a manager as superstar, raising that position to a higher level of prestige than ever before in the public imagination.

On the other hand, the season-end incidents of 1908 and 1912 showed the manager as thoughtful human, and had a profound effect on later managerial outlooks.

The 1908 case was the Merkle Play, about which entire books have been written. On September 23, the Cubs and the Giants were playing their final scheduled game against each other, at the Polo Grounds, in a close pennant race also involving Pittsburgh. Fred Merkle, a rookie first baseman, singled with two out in the ninth inning of a 1–1 game, sending a teammate from first to third. When Al Bridwell lined a single to center, the winning run came in from third, the crowd started to pour out of the stands, and Merkle did what almost all players did in those days—he didn't bother to touch second base and sprinted for the clubhouse in center field to avoid being engulfed by the crowd.

Technically, of course, if Merkle didn't touch second and the Cubs got the ball there, he would be forced out, and on such a force play for the third out, the run doesn't count.

In a wild scene (which doesn't have to be described here), the Cubs claimed they did get the ball to second. The two umpires made no on-the-spot decision, but ruled that night that the run didn't count and that the game had ended in a tie.

For his "boner," Merkle was castigated as few athletes have ever been in any connection. He was called "criminally stupid." After much protest and turmoil, the ruling stood, and this meant that the tie would have to be replayed if needed to decide the pennant race.

The Creators

The season ended on October 7 with the Giants and Cubs tied at 98–55 and the Pirates finished at 98–56. The tie had to be played off at the Polo Grounds on October 8, in the most bally-hooed ball game ever played until that time. And the Cubs won it, 4–2, as Mordecai (Three Finger) Brown outpitched Mathewson.

Now the venom heaped on young Merkle, a nineteen-year-old introvert from a small town in Wisconsin, increased beyond reason. He was never allowed to forget what happened, branded forever for a "dumb" play, the target of every fan who wanted to show off his knowledge of baseball. It poisoned his life to the point that Bridwell, sympathetically describing Merkle's fate many years later, said "I wish I'd never got that hit. I wish I'd struck out instead."

But what about McGraw, the dictator, the infuriated warrior, the curse-spewing taskmaster so intolerant of mistakes?

He never blamed Merkle for a moment. He not only didn't blame him, he defended him at every turn—face to face, with the writers and with the public. What had happened wasn't Merkle's fault, he insisted; the kid had only done what he'd seen veteran players do every day. What robbed the Giants of a pennant—and they were robbed, McGraw declared, make no mistake about that—was incompetent umpiring. They had no right to call an out in all that confusion, when it wasn't clear the Cubs had actually retrieved the ball in play and got it to second. But if they had, the umpires were obligated to clear the field and continue the game into a tenth inning, 1–1. How could you blame Merkle for that?

By being supportive, he enabled Merkle to function, wounded emotionally but not crippled. He made him his first baseman for the next seven years and used him in three World Series. In 1916, Merkle wound up with the pennant-winning Dodgers (under Robinson) and eventually completed a productive sixteen-year major league career.

The managing lesson was: Be fair. Know whom to blame for what. And when one of your players is treated unfairly, defend him.

A similar issue came up again in 1912. The second game of the World Series had ended in an eleven-inning tie, so the deciding game, in Boston on October 16, was actually the eighth played although only the seventh to count. It was 1–1 after nine innings, with Mathewson pitching against Smoky Joe Wood, who had come in as a relief pitcher in the eighth. The Giants scored in the top of the tenth and it was up to Matty to nail down the 2–1 victory.

Matty got the first batter to hit a routine fly to center field.

Fred Snodgrass muffed it for a two-base error.

Harry Hooper followed with a long drive to right center, where Snodgrass made a great running catch, preventing an extra base hit. But the runner moved to third after the catch.

Matty then issued a walk to Steve Yerkes, which brought up Tris Speaker.

Speaker hit a high foul along the first-base line.

Merkle, the first baseman, seemed to freeze. Chief Meyers, the catcher, drifted out after it, lunged, and couldn't reach it. Speaker had another chance.

He singled, tying the score. And Larry Gardner's single gave Boston a 3–2 victory.

The papers concentrated on Snodgrass. "A $30,000 muff," they screamed, referring to the difference between winning and losing club shares. McGraw had bawled him out, they said; he would be traded, they said; it was the Merkle treatment all over again.

But McGraw didn't go along. It was Merkle's fault this time, he explained. Speaker's foul was his ball to catch. Even Matty could have come over to get it when he saw Merkle wasn't going to get it. The catcher never had a chance. As for Snodgrass, his hit-robbing catch on Hooper certainly made up for the routine error. Snodgrass was one of the best players in the league and not only wouldn't be traded but next year would get the best contract he ever had. His play was not what cost the game. It was Merkle, who should have moved, and Matty, who should have yelled at him when he didn't move.

The lesson: Be fair. Put the blame where it belongs.

However, as a result of all this, instead of a possible four straight World Championships, the Giants had none.

Who were these Cubs and Pirates who kept beating them out in the 1906–10 interval?

They had dynasties of their own under managers who probably deserve chapters of their own.

Frank Selee was a nonplayer. He came to managing from the administrative side, back in the 1880s, when playing managers were the rule. A mild-mannered New Englander, he excelled at judging and recruiting talent, then letting it play—a forerunner, in a way, of Connie Mack. He used the standard tactics of his day but didn't emphasize signals from the bench, expecting his players to know what to do. He expressed his philosophy this way: "If I make things pleasant for the players, they reciprocate."

In the monopoly league, he managed Boston to pennants in 1891, 1892, 1893, 1897, and 1898, holding his own and better with the flashy Orioles. In 1902, he moved to Chicago and started to put together one of the greatest teams ever. By 1905, he had most of it in place, chasing McGraw's dominant team: Frank Chance at first, Johnny Evers at second, Joe Tinker at short, Johnny Kling catching, Ed Reulbach pitching, and so on. But midway through that season he contracted tuberculosis and turned the managership over to Chance, a suitable protégé. Selee lived long enough to see some of the fruits of his effort, dying in Denver in 1909; but there's no reason to believe that the team would have been any less successful if he had remained in charge.

The Cubs, in winning National League pennants in 1906, 1907, 1908, and 1910, and trailing the Pirates in 1909, won 530 games in five seasons. Their rivalry with the Giants was the foundation of burgeoning baseball interest in that era, the epitome of sports glamor.

Pittsburgh's Pirates had acquired that name in 1891, in the aftermath of the Brotherhood War, by signing a player whose rights were in dispute. (They pirated him, critics said.) In the twelve-team league, they finished higher than sixth only once (in 1893). But in the contraction to eight teams in 1900, they were bought by Barney Dreyfuss, who had been operating the Louisville team now being eliminated. He brought with him Honus Wagner, Fred Clarke, Rube Waddell, Deacon Phillippe, and a few others, and the Pirates were instant contenders. They ran second to Hanlon's Brooklyn in 1900, then reeled off three straight pennants, lost out to the Giants and Cubs in the next five races, and won again in 1909, the year they moved into baseball's second steel-and-concrete stadium (Forbes Field). They remained a contender through 1913, when all those great players were gone.

Dreyfuss had made Clarke their manager in 1900, as he had been in Louisville the three preceding years with losing teams. He was an outstanding hitter and outfielder, and only twenty-four years old when first promoted to manager in 1897. His approach was always orthodox and low-key: he saw and understood what the Orioles were doing, and applied it; he knew talent and where to put it; he had leadership qualities but little flamboyance. But he was also strict about discipline and conditioning.

John McGraw

And he had an interesting background. Growing up on a farm in Iowa, he got a job as a delivery boy for a Des Moines newspaper whose circulation manager formed a "Newsboy's League" in which Clarke played. That circulation manager was Ed Barrow, who would eventually change Babe Ruth from pitcher to full-time outfielder in Boston and take charge of the Yankee dynasty from 1920 into the 1940s. Baseball has always been a small world.

At nineteen, Clarke saw an ad in *The Sporting News* for ballplayers. Using a railroad ticket a friend had bought before deciding not to try, he went to Hastings, in the Nebraska State League, for a tryout and made the team in 1892. Two leagues that he played in during 1893 folded in midseason, so in September he took part in the land race into Oklahoma Territory but failed to stake a claim. (He was, in effect, a late Sooner.) So he went back to baseball, and in 1894 found himself stranded in Memphis with the Savannah team, which had just gone broke. Dreyfuss, in Louisville, offered to pay off the team's debts in return for Clarke's contract, proving the value of good scouting. Clarke, successfully insisting on getting a $100 bonus before taking the field, then played regularly until 1911 and wound up with a .315 lifetime average.

Despite their success, Selee and Clarke differed from McGraw in important respects. The first lacked the technical expertise, especially about giving signs and making instantaneous tactical decisions, that only a first-rate player could develop in those days. The latter, by remaining a player, could not give as much attention to other matters as a nonplayer could.

To put it another way, McGraw made clear the limitations of a player-manager, who could handle his teammates but not rebuild or repopulate a club when the best players aged; and he showed how field experience was fundamental in devising the right procedures for everything else. Selee could recognize talent but had to let it perform, in essence, on its own. Clarke could lead, compete, and play the game, but not scout for new talent. Chance, taking over the Cubs, was in Clarke's situation. The managership as we have come to know it—neither a super captaincy nor a chief executive officer—was fashioned by McGraw and Mack.

And it is the scouting function, long since departmentalized in the more elaborate organizations baseball has now, that remains a major facet of managerial responsibility. McGraw, Mack, and their contemporaries did much scouting personally, almost haphazardly, through trusted friends. Today's managers don't do that, but have equally influential input to final evaluations after studying farm system performances and reports.

McGraw's method was particularly effective with very young players who caught his fancy in some way. He wouldn't send them to the minors, but would keep them alongside him on the bench, teaching them and letting them mature.

There were several striking examples.

In spring training in 1907, he liked a cheerful and naive twenty-year-old kid from Illinois, who could play second base and spray line drives. He kept him and played him in only about half the games that year. But Larry Doyle became a mainstay of his three straight pennant winners a few years later.

In spring training in 1908, in an exhibition game against the minor league Dallas team, the Dallas shortstop began yelling insults at the famous Giant players even before the game began, almost provoked a fight, and told off McGraw directly, calling him "yellow-bellied" and a "bum." He was so belligerent, and so tough in the game itself, that McGraw decided he liked his spunk. He made arrangements right then to buy him after the season. When he brought Art Fletcher to the Polo Grounds in 1909, he used him as a part-timer for two years before making him his regular shortstop for the next nine years. And Fletcher's postplaying career as a coach was also distinguished, especially as Joe McCarthy's right-hand man with the Yankees.

In 1908, a pitcher named Richard Marquard won 28 games for Indianapolis in the American Association, then a top minor league. He was called "Rube" because his hard throwing reminded people of the celebrated Rube Waddell. McGraw persuaded Brush to pay $11,000, an unheard-of sum, for his contract. But Marquard wasn't ready to pitch in the majors, lacking control and finesse. In 1909 he was 5–13 with the Giants, in 1910 only 4–4.

McGraw believed in his ability and, instead of giving up, brought in Robinson to coach him as a special project. Uncle Robby knew his stuff. In the next three pennant-winning seasons, Rube won 24, 26, and 23 games, picking up where Joe McGinnity had left off as Mathewson's partner.

McGraw's protective attitude toward Merkle has already been mentioned. In grooming him to take Fred Tenney's place, McGraw used him in only 38 games in 1908 (when he was nineteen) and 78 in 1909. Then he was the regular first baseman for six years until he was traded to Brooklyn late in the 1916 season.

John McGraw

In the spring of 1912, McGraw had a young outfielder who had come up from Utica in time to play a few games the previous September. The natural thing would have been to farm him out for another year in a higher minor league. But (according to Frank Graham) McGraw told George Burns:

"You may not play much this year, but I want you with me. Sit next to me on the bench and I'll tell you all I can about the way they play ball up here. And I'll stick you in there now and then. I don't want you to get impatient. Understand?"

Burns got into only 29 games that year. But starting in 1913, he was the Giants' left fielder for nine years and played on three pennant winners.

McGraw's most famous prodigy project, of course, was Mel Ott. Mel was sent north as a sixteen-year-old catcher from Louisiana with a letter from one of McGraw's many friends. One look at Ott in batting practice convinced McGraw that he was such a natural that no minor league manager must ever get a chance to tamper with his unorthodox swing. He kept him with the Giants in 1926, converted him to an outfielder, and didn't let him play regularly for two years. After that, Ott hit 511 home runs, which was the National League career record until Willie Mays broke it in 1966.

By that time, however, McGraw was well into the last phase of his career, which began with unprecedented success and gradually deteriorated into illness, querulousness, and ineffectiveness. He aged, but he never mellowed. Yet his influence on others was even greater in this era than before.

Little Napoleon

World War I had cut short the 1918 baseball season, which ended abruptly on Labor Day because of the government's "work or fight" order. The Giants were 10½ games behind the Cubs and unlikely to catch them in any case, but McGraw had a more important matter on his mind.

The Brush heirs were ready to sell. Even when the war ended in November, they wanted a more secure investment for their money than baseball seemed (to them) to be. McGraw had experienced increasing friction with Foster, who stood between him and Hempstead, with whom McGraw had little rapport anyhow. If he could line up backers, McGraw could realize his desire to own a piece of the club himself, as he had so briefly in Baltimore, and nail down his position as complete boss.

The Creators

McGraw tried to put together groups among his Broadway friends (including George M. Cohan), but when negotiations dragged on he found a principal buyer unknown to the sports and newspaper community. Charles Stoneham was a stockbroker of dubious reputation with lots of money at his disposal. He put up $1,000,000 to buy 58 percent of the club's stock, far more than anyone had ever paid for a ball club before. And he took a note from McGraw for most of the $50,000 McGraw needed but did not have to buy his minority shares.

This was January 1919. McGraw was now vice-president and part owner of the team he was managing—but, as time proved more and more, he was no longer its number one decision maker as he had been with Brush's blessing and through Hempstead's passivity. Stoneham was a baseball fan, a loyal admirer of McGraw, and a willing spender—but he had his own ideas too, and whenever his own purposes did not coincide with McGraw's, Stoneham's prevailed.

At first, things looked better than ever. With a completely rebuilt team, McGraw won four straight pennants in 1921 through 1924, displaying brilliantly the most important of all managerial characteristics: adaptability. In 1920, the Yankees had acquired Babe Ruth, whose home runs were so fascinating that baseball changed itself almost overnight to take advantage of their appeal. A livelier ball was introduced. Trick pitches, like the spitball, were forbidden. A fresh baseball was to be used at all times. As home-run possibilities multiplied, the basic weapons of offense—hit-and-run singles and stolen bases—became less important, and the proper way to pitch changed too.

McGraw showed that he was able to adjust to these changes even when he spoke disparagingly of them. He selected players for more appropriate skills, like Ott's long-ball capability. He altered his tactics in accordance with the new percentages. One would have to be stupid, he pointed out, to risk an out by trying to steal a base if there was a better chance that the next batter would drive in the run with a homer or an extra-base hit. He had never liked the sacrifice bunt, except by a pitcher (for which he had been roundly second-guessed in the dead-ball days), preferring to hit-and-run. "If the player can't execute the hit-and-run, why have him?" he'd say. Now that viewpoint was more valid than ever, but power was becoming as necessary a trait as bat control. He sneered at Ruth, but got the message.

These conditions also required a new approach to pitching.

John McGraw

The day of dependence on a couple of 30-game winners was gone. McGraw developed larger staffs, with more variety, needing more rest, and used relief pitchers more frequently. The home-run threat in so many enemy bats made choice of pitches even more important, so McGraw called them from the bench with greater frequency—and authoritarianism—than ever. A famous incident illustrates how he operated. In 1921 and 1922, his Giants defeated the Yankees in the World Series (played entirely in the Polo Grounds with the teams alternating in batting last). The first time, his pitchers held Ruth to four singles and a homer in 8 games; the second, to two singles in 5. But in 1923, when the teams met again, the Yankees had moved into their own new stadium, right across the Harlem River, and Ruth hit 3 home runs, a triple, a double and two singles, and had been walked eight times. This had helped the Yankees take a 3–2 games lead, but the Giants took a 4–1 lead into the eighth inning of the sixth game with their best pitcher, Art Nehf, on the mound. But with one out, Nehf suddenly gave up two singles and two walks, and had to be replaced by Rosy Ryan, who promptly walked in another run. Now the lead was down to 4–3, with the bases loaded and Ruth up.

Ryan got two strikes on him, and McGraw called time.

He sent a coach out of the dugout with instructions for the catcher, Frank Snyder, to relay to Ryan.

His order was: Throw it in the dirt; Ruth will swing at anything you throw now; aim at his spikes.

Ryan, doubtful but obedient, did.

Ruth swung and missed.

That's the way McGraw managed.

But he didn't always win. The next batter, Bob Meusel, hit a grounder up the middle, past Ryan, over second base, into center-field, and when Bill Cunningham's throw went past third, all three runners scored and the Yankees had a five-run inning and a 6–4 decision that ended the series.

And he lost in an even more frustrating manner in 1924, when the World Series reached a seventh game in Washington. This time the Giants had a 3–1 lead in the eighth when the Senators filled the bases with one out. A short fly provided the second out without letting a run score, and Bucky Harris—the twenty-seven-year-old boy wonder player-manager of the Senators—hit what looked like an inning-ending grounder to the third baseman, McGraw's latest protégé, an eighteen-year-old rookie named Freddie Lindstrom.

But the ball hit something, the proverbial pebble, and bounced high over Lindstrom's head for a two-run single, tying the score.

Now Walter Johnson, no less, came in to pitch for Washington, and the game went to the twelfth inning (the longest seventh game of any World Series). The Giants got six men on base against him in four innings, but couldn't score. In the bottom of the twelfth, with one out, Muddy Ruel hit a high foul pop-up. Hank Gowdy, the catcher, went after it but tripped over his discarded mask, and Ruel got another chance.

Remember 1912? You can be sure McGraw did.

Ruel ripped a double past third.

Johnson, batting for himself, grounded to short—where Travis Jackson fumbled the ball. Ruel, of course, had stayed at second.

A ground ball double play could still get the Giants out of the inning, and Jack Bentley got Earl McNeely to hit one, at Lindstrom.

And this one, too, bounced high over his head (hitting the same pebble? people wondered). Ruel raced home with the series-ending run. Johnson, thirty-six years old and winner of 376 major league games, had his first World Series victory.

Bentley, in the clubhouse, got off a classic line.

"Cheer up, boys" he said. "It just looks as though the Good Lord couldn't stand seeing Walter Johnson get beat again."

But McGraw never reached the World Series again.

From that point on, his ill-temper and cruel tongue became increasingly destructive. His merciless criticism and second-guessing turned more and more players against him. Where he was once able to inspire as well as intimidate, he was now more often simply infuriating—and unfair.

It's a process we'll see again and again. A manager, in his earlier years, not that far removed in age from his players, achieves a positive rapport on the basis of respect even with men who don't particularly like him. Then, as he gets older, and the generation gap widens, and his frustrations mount, he "communicates" less and becomes perceived as a nag, less respected, less obeyed, more frequently rebelled against. McGraw, in 1923, had passed into his fifties. His world view had been formed in the 1890s, and it was increasingly difficult for him to relate to the feelings of the young people of the 1920s.

At the same time, his health was deteriorating. He had to miss trips and turn direction of the team over to a coach or veteran

John McGraw

player. The Giants finished second in 1925, then fifth, then third, second, third, third, second. Frisch, McGraw's pet coming out of Fordham in 1919 and in his mind a possible successor, walked out on him in disgust in 1926, forcing a trade that brought Rogers Hornsby to New York. McGraw let Hornsby function as manager when he was ill in 1927, and Hornsby insulted Stoneham, and Stoneham traded him away. No question now whose club it was.

McGraw still had his successes. He was still able to persuade Bill Terry, who had quit minor league baseball because he could make more money in business, to come back, convert from pitcher to first baseman, and become a .400 hitter and his successor when McGraw finally gave up managing in 1932. He nurtured Ott, and accepted Carl Hubbell when other clubs had discarded him because the "screwball" he threw would certainly wreck his arm. (McGraw knew it hadn't hurt Mathewson.)

But his time ran out. He was no longer king of New York; Ruth was that, and of all baseball. He was in debt, not only because of his gambling but because of ill-advised land deals in Florida. A couple of months into the 1932 season, with the team in sixth place, he saw the futility of going on. He called in Terry and asked him if he wanted to take over.

Only if he would be complete boss, said Terry, without McGraw looking over his shoulder or passing along suggestions. That's the way it would be, McGraw assured him.

On June 3, 1932, Lou Gehrig hit four home runs in Philadelphia's Shibe Park, but that wasn't the lead sports story that day. At the Polo Grounds, where a double-header was being rained out, the announcement was made that John McGraw was retiring. It was six weeks short of the thirtieth anniversary of his arrival in New York, which had changed baseball history in so many ways.

He had one more great ceremonial moment. In July of 1933, they held an all-star game in Chicago, the first one, between American and National League teams. The managers had to be Mack and McGraw; how else could "all-star" be justified?

McGraw's team lost, 4–2, as Ruth hit a two-run homer.

That fall, led by Terry, Ott, and Hubbell, the Giants won the World Series. McGraw already knew he had cancer.

On February 25, 1934, in a hospital in New Rochelle not far from his Pelham home, at age sixty, McGraw died.

His influence never has.

3

Connie Mack

LEARNING THE ROPES

Connie Mack was the complete opposite of John McGraw. That's the way the public saw it, and the public was right.

He exuded calm and dignity. He didn't shout or curse. He didn't drink or carouse. He managed from the bench in street clothes, which meant he couldn't enter the field of play (to coach or argue with an umpire) during a game. He wore a high starched collar for two generations after it was no longer standard garb.

In less visible activities, he was also different. He didn't bawl out players for their mistakes or criticize them in front of others but always waited to say in private (and usually in gentle terms) what he wanted to point out. He didn't preach aggressiveness as a virtue in itself (although he certainly understood its proper value). And he didn't second-guess.

What did he do, then, to be so successful and influential?

1. He was a superb judge of talent.

2. He was ahead of his time in analyzing the way to pitch to particular hitters and to place fielders.

3. He helped players develop by using patience, instruction, and a fatherly manner, rather than by "pushing" them.

4. He was, in his own quiet way, as daring and original in decision making as many more flamboyant "thinkers."

5. And he carried unchanging, long-lasting equanimity to the ultimate degree, win or lose, decade after decade.

McGraw commanded respect. Mack engendered affection.

Players understood McGraw's brilliance, welcomed the success his leadership gave them, admired the way he got results, feared and obeyed him.

Players loved Mack and had just as much faith in his judgment.

When a Giant player did something wrong, he knew he risked

Connie Mack

McGraw's wrath. When a Philadelphia player did something wrong, he felt guilty about letting Mr. Mack down.

And he was "Mr. Mack" to them as a matter of being respectful to an older mentor, like a Mr. Chips schoolmaster, not as an expression of subservience.

Mack was ten years older than McGraw. He was born on December 22, 1862, while the Civil War was on. His father, Michael McGillicuddy, was an Irish immigrant who settled in East Brookfield, Massachusetts (about halfway between Springfield and Worcester) and worked in the cotton mill there. He served in the Union Army and afterwards died while Cornelius was still a teenager. Connie's mother, Mary, had to rear him and his six siblings without the father's presence during the war and after his death. In Lawrence Ritter's book, *The Glory of Their Times,* there's a wonderful picture of her at the opening of the 1911 World Series, surrounded by Connie, his second wife, and two sons from his first marriage.

East Brookfield, in 1862, had a population of three hundred. (Even today, it has only about two thousand people.) But it did have a town baseball team. Connie had begun to work in the cotton mill, for thirty-five cents a day, at the age of nine while his father was still there too. Later, at sixteen, he left school to work in the local shoe factory to help support the family. The way he reminisced about those days reveals much about his nature. They worked twelve hours a day, six days a week, in the mill, but it wasn't so bad, he said. Most of the kids in his part of town had to go to work early, and they did get a whole hour for lunch, spending most of the time playing ball.

He grew exceptionally tall and exceptionally thin, so naturally he was called "Slats." He became the catcher of the town team (when catchers still stayed well back from home plate, had no protective equipment, and handled the mandated underhand deliveries on a bounce). The town team won the Central Massachusetts championship.

In 1883, when he was twenty, Cap Anson's Chicago team came through East Brookfield for an exhibition game, and Connie decided to give professional baseball a try. His mother disapproved, warning him he'd never get anywhere drinking and fighting. He didn't think he'd have to do that, but just play ball, which he loved. "There's room for gentlemen in every profession," he'd say

The Creators

later, "and my profession is baseball." So when a team in Meriden, Connecticut, needed a catcher in 1884, and a friend recommended him, Connie insisted on a good salary—$90 a month—got it, and went.

Obviously, "Cornelius McGillicuddy" could not fit in a newspaper box score, so he became Connie Mack.

He proved so popular in Meriden that the fans gave him a gold watch at the end of the season. But that didn't prevent him from accepting $125 a month to go to Hartford the next year. In 1886, he and four other players were sold to Washington, of the National League, for $3,500, and he was a big leaguer.

Overhand pitching was now allowed, and Mack became one of the first catchers to learn how to handle it and develop its potential by moving up just behind the batter. For three years, he was an established player, though not a star. He married and started a family. Then came the Brotherhood War, in which he was a willing participant with the other players. He invested all his money in the Buffalo club (which had been planned for Washington originally) for which he played—and lost every cent. In 1891, he returned to the National League as Pittsburgh's catcher under Ned Hanlon, who was dismissed late in the season after a player revolt in which Mack was not involved.

Late in 1894, Mack was made manager as well as catcher. The team finished above .500, in the middle of the pack, the next two years, but then he was fired and finished as a player. He was not quite thirty-four, a widower whose three children stayed with their grandmother while he pursued his profession.

Ban Johnson, with whom he had become friendly, offered him a chance to manage the Milwaukee team in the Western League, still in its minor league phase. Mack took that post and held it for four years, 1897 through 1900. When Johnson decided to go major, he gave Mack the Philadelphia franchise, in which Mack kept a 25 percent interest and financed the rest through Ben Shibe and the Reach Sporting Goods Company (already a part of the Spalding cartel). Shibe, inventor of ball-winding machines, would give him whole-hearted support through all that followed.

So the Philadelphia Athletics of the American League played their first game under the managership of Connie Mack, and the next 7,877 (plus 43 World Series games) under his direction for fifty years.

Now his two finely honed talents, recruitment and pitching analysis, came into play.

His first job for Johnson was to raid the National League for talent. This involved persuasion, which was simple enough (offer more money) and evaluation (make sure the money is well spent). His first and most obvious target was the best hitter of the National League Phillies, Napoleon Lajoie, and he got him. In a league that had not yet adopted the foul-strike rule (as the National had that year), Lajoie hit .422. But the A's got off to a bad start and finished fourth; that's why McGraw, moving to New York the next year, sneered at them as a "white elephant"—even though his own Baltimore team had finished fifth, $4\frac{1}{2}$ games behind Mack's.

Then the courts ruled that the Philadelphia National League players who had switched leagues could not play for the American League in the state of Pennsylvania. So Lajoie was transferred to Cleveland and skipped that team's visits to Philadelphia in 1902. After that, the leagues made their peace treaty and everyone could play anywhere, but Lajoie remained with Cleveland.

But Mack's better source of players was a population he exploited more than others did: the colleges. He got a pitcher named Eddie Plank out of Gettysburg College. Later he would get Eddie Collins out of Columbia, Chief Bender out of Carlisle, Mickey Cochrane from Boston University, and many others.

THE WHITE ELEPHANTS

When McGraw uttered his insulting put-down, "In Philadelphia, the American League has a white elephant on its hands," he was using a cliché then universally understood, now pretty much forgotten. In Siam, the Victorian world had been told, albino elephants were so revered that they could not be sold or used for work or for any other useful purpose—but had to be fed and tended, at great expense, because technically they belonged to the king. The term, then, came to mean a grandiose but useless entity expensive to maintain and therefore, when referring to an investment, an unwise purchase with which one is stuck.

Mack's response tells a lot about his whimsical mind as well as his tough-under-the-soft-glove character. He adopted the white elephant as his team's emblem, simultaneously expressing defiance and good humor.

The White Elephants proceeded to win the American League pennant in 1902. Since there was no peace agreement, there was no attempt to play the National League champion Pirates.

Lajoie was gone, and so were two former Phillies' pitchers who had won 39 games between them in 1901. But Mack had found an even more important figure, the left-handed Rube Waddell, the ultimate fast-ball pitcher of his age.

Usually described as "crazy" and "just a big kid" by roommates and other acquaintances, always in affectionate terms, Waddell marched to his own drummer. He would show up only when he wanted to, he drank too much too often, he set records for unreliability. When Clarke, managing Louisville in 1897, offered him $500 to join the team after seeing him pitch in some semipro games, Waddell woke him up at 2:00 A.M. to announce his arrival. Later that year, when Clarke fined him $50 for getting drunk, Waddell jumped the club. In 1898 and 1899, he bounced back and forth between semipro ball and Johnson's Western League, where several of his victories were against Mack's Milwaukee team.

Mack remembered.

Late in 1899, Waddell rejoined Louisville and Clarke, won 7 games, and went along in the transfer to Pittsburgh for 1900. But he and Clarke were perpetually at war. He'd skip games to go fishing. By mid-July, he had a 9–11 record and a long list of fines, so he jumped the club again and holed up in a small town called Punxsutawney in Pennsylvania—a town subsequently famous for the presence of Punxsutawney Phil, the ground hog who emerges and does or does not see his shadow on February 2 in front of the television cameras.

Mack, still in Milwaukee, decided to track Waddell down. Pittsburgh didn't object when Mack asked Dreyfuss for permission, since the Western League was still not challenging the National, and Mack went to Punxsutawney. He paid off Waddell's debts, dried him out, brought him back to Milwaukee, and then pretty much left him alone.

Waddell was already famous, a big drawing card. He won 10 games in the next two months, including a double-header in which he won the first game in seventeen innings and the second 1–0.

That got Pittsburgh's attention, and it asked to have him back.

Connie Mack

Mack, acknowledging that he had made no formal agreement, let him go. But as soon as 1901 started, Waddell resumed his conflict with Clarke, and was traded to Chicago.

Then Waddell was such a big hit with the fans in Los Angeles during a postseason exhibition tour that he stayed out there and began the 1902 season in the Pacific Coast League. He had already won 12 games when Mack sent two Pinkerton detectives to bring him back to Philadelphia. Even with a late start, but happy to be working for Mack, Waddell won 24 games (losing only 7) and led the league with 210 strikeouts—50 more than Cy Young, as runner-up, accumulated in over 100 more innings. He got as high as 349 in 1904 and set strikeout records unapproached until the days of Bob Feller.

Waddell and Plank were the backbone of Mack's first pennant winner. In 1903 and 1904, the Boston Pilgrims were simply a better club, but in 1905 the A's won again with Chief Bender added to the rotation. This produced the first McGraw-Mack World Series, the one in which every game was a shutout. Mathewson pitched his 3 and Joe McGinnity 1 for the Giants, and Bender 1 for the A's. But Waddell didn't pitch at all because he had injured his shoulder in September.

These A's were a relatively weak hitting team at this point, and Mack needed to do more talent scouting. They finished fourth in 1906 when the White Sox, themselves called "the hitless wonders," startled everyone by beating the mighty Cubs in the World Series. Then, for the next three years, the A's were eclipsed by the Detroit Tigers, whose manager was McGraw's old friend Hughie Jennings and whose outfield included baseball's newest star, Ty Cobb.

By 1910, however, Mack had his whole team in place. The infield of Stuffy McInnis at first, Collins at second, Jack Barry at short, and Frank Baker at third became known as "the $100,000 infield," indicating unimaginable value in those days. (Now the minimum salary for any major league rookie is more than $100,000; values change.) Waddell had moved on, having worn out himself and even Mack's patience by 1908, and died of tuberculosis at the age of thirty-seven in 1914. But the new staff was even stronger; Bender, Plank, and Jack Coombs, and later Joe Bush and Herb Pennock.

These A's won four pennants in five years in 1910–14, running third in 1912 to a pair of remarkable Boston and Washington teams. They excelled in every way: hitting, fielding, running, pitching. In the 1910 World Series, they polished off the Chance-led Cubs; in 1911 and 1913, they beat McGraw's Giants. But in 1914, they were swept by the Miracle Braves, and there was more to that than your garden-variety upset. The team had become a white elephant in fact.

THE FIRST DEMOLITION

Fans and writers blamed the 1914 defeat on "overconfidence," which seemed plausible. That does happen, after all, to dynasties. But Mack, with considerable bitterness, blamed it on something else. The Federal League, from 1913 on, had been making overtures to all prominent players, pushing up the general salary scale and leaving the highest-paid players wondering if they were getting paid enough and asking for multiyear contracts. Mack, as operating owner, had to deal with finances, not just victories. With no real external resources, as the Federal League millionaires had and as the new purchasers of the Yankees had, he had to watch pennies. And his heritage was, after all, both Irish and New Englander.)

His players, he claimed, stopped concentrating on baseball and started concentrating on maximizing contracts. At the same time, his gate receipts shrank. Perpetual victory dulled fan appetite as it became taken for granted. The A's had opened the 1909 season in sumptuous Shibe Park, the first steel-and-concrete stadium (beating Pittsburgh's Forbes Field to completion by a couple of months), and had averaged 600,000 in attendance for the first three years. The next two years, attendance fell to 540,000, and in 1914 to below 350,000.

Mack was always realistic. World War I had begun in Europe, making all economic forecasts shaky. The Federal League was ready to go again in 1915. There was no way he could pay competitive salaries in that climate, and no way to get the money to make that possible. So he decided to sell off what assets he could.

He sold Collins to the White Sox for $50,000. He sold Barry to the Red Sox. Plank and Bender were going to the Federal League, so he simply released them along with Coombs (whose arm was gone and who wound up in Brooklyn). Home Run Baker—a title he had acquired by hitting home runs off McGinnity and Mathewson in consecutive games in the 1911 World Series—retired.

The A's finished eighth and last in each of the next seven seasons.

It wasn't until 1925 that he started to put together another great team.

THE SECOND DYNASTY

Let's pause here and evaluate Mack as a manager at the age of 62 as the 1925 season was about to begin.

He had become a familiar figure, in his dark suit, standing on the dugout steps, pointing with the scorecard he always had in his hand, telling defensive players where to move. This had become a cartoon figure, a caricature, but the scorecard was also his primary weapon. He had always made detailed notes on where particular hitters hit the ball off particular pitchers (and pitches), and positioned his fielders accordingly. Today, every team has reams of diagrams and computer printouts analyzing exactly this, and an "eye in the sky" coach with a walkie-talkie high in the stands constantly checking with the bench. All good managers, including McGraw, had a rough idea of such information in their heads, and paid attention to it. But Mack was ahead of his time in the degree of attention and depth of analysis he gave this factor. McGraw, trusting his instinct and experience, would call pitches; Mack would drum into his pitchers and catchers the patterns he wanted in pregame meetings, then let them play their game—and concentrated on making sure the fielders were where they were supposed to be when the pitcher made the right pitch.

Of course, if your players aren't good enough, it doesn't matter. The ball won't be pitched, or hit, where it's supposed to be (or caught, if it is). And for a decade, after discarding all that talent, Mack had bad ball clubs. He could survive as manager only because he was also the owner: He wasn't going to fire himself; but because this traditional and easy illusory remedy didn't come into play, his club also retained the special talent he represented.

After 1920, the baseball economy boomed, and once again a rising tide lifted all boats. Mack's basic problem had been lack of operating capital. Now, thanks to Babe Ruth and new ballparks (from which visiting teams got more for their share), and amid the general prosperity of the country, while the baseball rich got richer, the not-so-poor got enough.

And he was more avuncular, and fatherly, than ever. He had remarried in 1910, and had six more children. His older boys worked with him as coaches and scouts. A man in his sixties might as well be Methuselah as far as most ballplayers in their twenties are concerned, but Mack's personality turned the grand-old-man image into an advantage. The aging but younger McGraw, in these years, was getting nastier and deteriorating physically. Mack had an iron constitution (which he had never subjected to dissolute habits) and that warm combination of sharp mind and gentle manner that made young players comfortable.

The Yankees, with Babe Ruth and a host of other former Boston players, had won three straight pennants in 1921–23. The Washington Senators had won the next two, barely beating out the Yankees in 1924 and beating them easily in 1925 as the Yankees collapsed to seventh place. But then, with Ruth restored to health, Lou Gehrig and Tony Lazzeri added, and more pitching than ever, the Yankees won the next three.

In 1925, the year of the Yankee collapse, the A's finished second. Mack had finally acquired some quality players: Cochrane to catch, Max Bishop at second, and a slugging outfielder named Aloysius Harry Szymanski who, making the same kind of concession to journalism that Cornelius McGillicuddy had, changed it to Al Simmons. The pitching staff acquired Lefty Grove and Rube Walberg. Another fine outfielder was Bing Miller. These acquisitions were the result of his improved finances. He paid more than $50,000 for Simmons, and $100,000 (in ten installments) for Grove, whom McGraw had rejected as too expensive. To get Cochrane, he invested $200,000 to buy the Portland club in the Pacific Coast League that held his rights.

But the Yankees were at the peak of their effectiveness. They let the A's and Cleveland fight it out for second place in 1926, then finished 19 games ahead of the second-place A's in 1927, and were out of sight again by the middle of 1928. However, the A's had kept building. Their younger contingent included Jimmy Foxx and Jimmy Dykes, who started as utility men but eventually wound up at first and third, and an outfielder named Mule Haas. Joe Boley was their shortstop. Grove, his blazing speed nullified by wildness the first two years, had acquired control, and George Earnshaw, who could throw almost as hard as Grove and was right-handed, arrived as a twenty-eight-year-old rookie.

The A's also had three forty-year-old players ending their careers: Ty Cobb, Tris Speaker, and Eddie Collins (about whom more in a moment).

They won 25 games in July, and suddenly the Yankee lead was down to $3\frac{1}{2}$ games. On September 8, they were actually half a game ahead, but the Yankees fought them off hand to hand and finally won by $2\frac{1}{2}$ games.

In 1929, the A's took up where they left off, had a 10-game lead by June, and won by 18 as the Yankees started to wear out.

The A's won the World Series, and the next pennant race and World Series, and the 1931 pennant by a huge margin, although this time they lost the seventh game of the World Series to the Cardinals. That year they peaked at 107 victories, and there wasn't much wrong with winning 94 games in 1932 (as Foxx hit 58 homers), except that this time it was the Yankees who won 107.

These were, clearly, Mack's best teams and are listed among the greatest teams ever any time such a list is made. For our purposes, we want to zero in on three items from this period: the Cobb-Speaker-Collins presence, the celebrated and unorthodox pitching choices in the 1929 World Series, and the let-them-play philosophy.

In the 1920s, memory of the Black Sox scandal was fresh. Judge Landis had been made sole commissioner and given extraordinary powers partly to help the image of self-policing. Actually, the more important reason had to do with squabbles over player rights that the three-man commission had been unable to resolve, but as far as the public was concerned, Landis was the czar who "cleaned up" baseball.

After the 1926 season, a story surfaced accusing Cobb and Speaker of being involved in a fixed game back in 1919. Cobb was managing Detroit and Speaker was managing Cleveland, both still playing. Suddenly, both were released without explanation. Then Landis cleared them, and Ban Johnson, who had vowed publicly that they'd never play in his league again, resigned as American League president. (Again, the Landis-Johnson feud wasn't really about this case, but it served as a focal point.) Even when Cobb and Speaker were cleared, however, in the face of some damning evidence, it was felt they should not resume managing.

The overriding consideration was baseball's image of integrity. Cobb seemed more at fault than Speaker, and was the stronger personality anyhow. His resurrection seemed most important. So he went to Philadelphia, to play for Mr. Mack; if Mr. Mack would accept him, the whole world could believe he was a worthy fellow, because if he weren't, Mr. Mack wouldn't have him around.

Speaker, meanwhile, signed with Washington, whose owner, Clark Griffith, also had a high standing in the baseball community. And Cobb's experience in Philadelphia was so good (he hit .357 in 1927 at the age of forty, playing right field full time), that Speaker came over in 1928. Meanwhile, Collins had been an untarnished member of the Black Sox, and manager of the White Sox in 1925 and 1926. After two fifth-place finishes, he was released—and he returned to the man who had sold him to the White Sox twelve years before.

In othe words, Mack's aura of propriety and righteousness was so strong that it could be used to sweeten unsavory developments.

The start of the 1929 World Series produced a legendary anecdote. During the season, Earnshaw was 24–8, Grove 20–6 and, Walberg 18–11, each appearing in more than 40 games and relieving occasionally. Ed Rommel won 12 and two other pitchers 11. Then there was Howard Ehmke, thirty-five years old, with a 7–2 record in only 11 games. He had started in the Federal League, back in 1915, and had knocked around Detroit and Boston for ten years before being traded to the A's in June of 1926. For them, he was a second-line pitcher for the next two years.

Who would open the series, Grove or Earnshaw? When the A's saw Ehmke warming up, they were as disbelieving as the writers. "Him?" they asked.

But Mack had been plotting. He had high regard for Ehmke's pitching intelligence. He sent him out to follow the Chicago Cubs around during the last couple of weeks of the season, to make notes and see for himself.

"And he knew what he was doing," said Joe McCarthy, manager of the Cubs, in retrospect. "Our club was loaded with powerful right-handed hitters, and Ehmke had a way of pitching to right-handers that was tough on us."

Tough indeed. Ehmke struck out 13, a World Series record at that time, and won 3–1. The next day Earnshaw started—and Grove finished, taking over in the fifth. After a day off for travel, Earnshaw started again, pitched nine innings—and lost 3–1. But Grove didn't start the fourth game either, and the A's were losing 8–0 when they scored 10 runs in the seventh inning. Then Grove came in and nailed it down. Ehmke started the fifth game, gave way to Walberg when he fell behind 2–0 in the fourth inning—and watched the A's score three in the bottom of the ninth to end the series with a 3–2 victory.

So Grove never started at all.

Murray Kempton, star liberal columnist and as sharp-eyed a critic of baseball (which he loved) as of politicians, wrote a column in 1969 poking fun at President Nixon's citation of the Ehmke incident as something brilliant. Kempton was ridiculing Nixon's general acumen and his pretension to baseball expertise, and wrote as follows:

> Let us begin with the Ehmke case, although I must confess I dream of the day when hardly a man is now alive who can remember that one. It is baseball's classic example of a command decision; and, like most text-book examples of such, it could as well have been made by an idiot. Three of the eight players Mr. Mack fielded besides the pitcher that day are now in the Hall of Fame. He had Grove and Earnshaw in reserve. He won that series in five games; if Ehmke had been knocked out in the first inning, the Athletics would have won that series in six. I have always assumed that Mr. Mack acted from whim and out of boredom in hopes of making something all too assured seem doubtful.

Style and skepticism is what made Kempton so great a columnist, and as his admirer and one-time teammate on the *New York Post,* I would be the last to take too seriously the wicked wit he applied to so many situations. But in this case, his conclusion is wrong, and relevant to our discussion. Mack's choice of Ehmke was not an attempt to stir up interest or relieve boredom. It was a clear instance of his total belief in his knowledge of how hitters should be pitched to, and confidence in a man whose understanding and control (Ehmke) were of a higher order than that of the flame-throwers he held out. The significance of the incident lies in the 13 strikeouts by a nonpower pitcher, testimony to proper placement and changes of speed against big hitters. The setting made this game startling and historic. But day by day, inning by inning, Mack counted on choosing the right pitch, the right man to throw it, and the right situation to use him in.

That's what the scorecard in his hand represented. Moving the fielders was part of the pitch-selection process. When McGraw needed a strikeout of Ruth in the World Series, he sent word to the catcher to tell the pitcher what to throw. Mack's less visible method was illustrated by a story Dykes told about Cobb playing right field. Mack's scorecard started moving him over, and Cobb seemed doubtful, but went along. Mack kept moving him more and more, and Cobb, more and more reluctant, moved. Then the batter hit the ball to exactly where Cobb had wound up, and he caught it without needing to take even one step. When he got back to the bench, Cobb (who had been a manager himself, against Mack) said: "I've heard a lot about your scorecard, and from now on I'm going to believe it."

Still, he who lives by astute manipulation of talent dies by the absence of talent. In 1932, Mack found himself right back where he had been in 1914.

THE SECOND DEMOLITION

The first time, it had been the challenge of an outlaw league, the start of a war, and falling attendance. This time it was the Depression. And once again, too many victories had made the customers too blasé about excellence. In 1928–30, attendance had averaged 750,000, peaking at 840,000 in 1929, the first pennant-winning year. In 1931, for a third straight pennant, it was down to 630,000, and in 1932, for a strong second place with Foxx chasing Ruth's home run record, 400,000.

Attendance was down everywhere, of course, from its Jazz Age peaks, because the customers were out of money. But so were banks and backers, except for the exceptionally rich. The only way Mack could see to keep the A's in business was to sell off the best players to clubs that could afford to pay for them. Salaries, this time, were not an issue; there was no rival league, the reserve clause was in full flower, and everyone was keeping salaries down. But the only source of cash to pay the bills of operation was the main asset the franchise had: the contracts it owned.

In Boston, the Red Sox had been at the bottom of the league for more than a decade, ever since they had sold Ruth to the Yankees. They had a new owner who did have money, Tom Yawkey. In Detroit and Chicago, the clubs were in pretty good shape financially, yet not recently successful on the field.

So Mack opened the store.

After the 1932 season, he netted $100,000 in a deal that sent Simmons, Dykes, and Mule Haas to Chicago.

After the 1933 season, in which the A's finished third (and drew 300,000), he got $100,000 from Detroit for Cochrane, and $125,000 from Boston for Grove, Walberg, and Bishop.

In 1934, the team dropped to fifth, and Yawkey gave him $300,000 for Foxx, Doc Cramer, Eric McNair, and Johnny Marcum.

Connie Mack

The A's then finished last or next to last in eleven of the next twelve years, achieving a tie for fifth only in the totally war-distorted season of 1944.

THE GRAND OLD MAN

Just before Christmas in 1934, Mack turned seventy-two. It was certainly time to retire. McGraw had not only retired two years before but had died earlier that year. Clark Griffith, the only one left from the group who had formed the American League, was almost seven years younger, but had given up managing as far back as 1920. Like Mack, he was a principal owner of his club, but confined his activities to the front office. Comiskey and Johnson had died in 1931. Having dismantled his championship squad, aware of how long it might take to rebuild, Mack could certainly have retired gracefully and with honor.

Instead, he stayed in the dugout for another sixteen years. It wasn't a question of stubbornness or ego; it was simply his family business. Tom Shibe, Ben's son, had died in 1936, and Mack had taken on the club presidency. In 1940, he acquired majority control from other Shibe heirs. His own salary, as manager and president, was his only source of income; his sons Earle, Roy, and Connie, Jr. held various positions as team executives and coaches. And he loved what he was doing. Many more fine young players came under his wing: Sam Chapman, Nellie Fox, Ferris Fain, a dozen good pitchers, but never enough at one time to reach the first division. Finally, in 1948, the A's did come in fourth while the Yankees, Red Sox, and Indians battled for the pennant to the final day, with the Indians beating the Red Sox in a one-game playoff the day after that.

But not even Mr. Mack could go on forever. At the end of the 1950 season, approaching his eighty-eighth birthday, he stepped down. His handpicked successor was Jimmy Dykes, who had managed the White Sox for twelve years after Mack sent him there. Mack's sons took over the business side.

The franchise was beyond repair. In 1938, the Phillies had moved in as tenants, abandoning their lopsided Baker Bowl a few blocks away, and when they were bought by a member of the DuPont family after World War II, they had the resources to become a pennant winner by 1950. In 1953, Shibe Park's name became Connie Mack Stadium, but the Phillies were now Philadelphia's team. After the 1954 season, the Mack family decided to sell out, and the team was moved to Kansas City for 1955. Mack, who had created it out of nothing, lived to see that, but died the following winter, at the age of ninety-three.

There were great ironies in his Grand Old Man phase. During the 1930s, hastened by the Depression, independent minor league operators began disappearing and the success of major league teams began to depend on building farm systems. Mack's eye for talent should have made him excel at this, but the farm system required investment—buying or supporting minor league teams—and he had no capital. If the farm system idea had come along earlier, he could have taken part.

By the same token, if it had been a later time, with jet airplanes on the drawing board, national television, and pressure for expansion, he might have moved the team himself and prospered, perhaps in California; but that was a process that would start only in the 1950s. From the mid-1930s on, he was in a developmental blind alley.

There was a third possibility, but here too the timing wasn't right. Mack could have turned to the Negro leagues, so prominent in Philadelphia and the rest of the eastern seaboard, for new and exciting talent. However, although he was a fine man, he was in no sense a revolutionist, and that social breakthrough was not possible before World War II set in motion forces for equality. Even Branch Rickey, who did finally break the color line for the 1946 season, admitted he would have liked to do it a decade earlier, but couldn't even bring it up in a society that still took segregation for granted and in a baseball world presided over by Judge Landis, whose bigotry was plain and well known.

Two anecdotes from the last segment of Mack's career appeal to me as illustrations of the flavor of his regime. The first is told by Joe DiMaggio at dinners. A colorful pitcher named Louis (Bobo) Newsom had just rejoined the A's in emergency circumstances, and had to pitch against the Yankees the same day. Mack asked him if he knew how to pitch to each hitter, and Bobo (who was thirty-nine years old and late in a career in which he would change teams eighteen times) said "Sure." In the first inning, DiMaggio hit an upper-deck homer off him.

"What pitch did you throw him?" Mack asked.

"My fast ball."

"Louis, don't ever throw DiMaggio another fast ball. Throw him nothing but curves. You understand? Curves."

In the third inning, Bobo served up a luscious curve, and DiMaggio hit it over the roof.

As DiMaggio circled the bases, Newsom ran off the mound toward the A's dugout and, cupping his hands, shouted:

"Mr. Mack! Mr. Mack! He hit yours farther than he hit mine!"

The other involves Fain, a fiery first baseman who would win the American League batting title in 1951, but broke in under Mack in the late 1940s. He became famous, very quickly, for his aggressive play on bunts. He would come all the way down the line to field the ball and throw out a runner at second or third.

In one game, he made his play, and threw the ball into left field. Two runs scored.

A few innings later, the same thing happened. In both cases, he had passed up a sure out at first.

"Why did you throw to third?" Mack asked him, after the second disaster.

Fain, mad at himself as well as at everyone else, snapped back, "What am I supposed to do with the ball, shove it down my throat?" Only he didn't say "throat" after "shove," and said "up" instead of "down."

"Well, young man," said eighty-five-year-old Mack, "it would have done less harm there."

Humanistic, therefore, is the key word concerning Mack. He had a feel for people, an innate empathy. McGraw had a sadistic streak that emerged even when he was being playful; his practical jokes involved humiliating someone, provoking rage. Mack was concerned about the feelings of others. The difference permeated their managerial styles. McGraw knew the answer in any situation, told you what to do about it, and demanded that you do it that way. Mack knew the answer but wanted you to learn it too, and do it on your own. McGraw's way was more applicable to offense; Mack concentrated more on defense, which is fundamentally pitching. McGraw pushed men to play with injuries, if they could at all; Mack didn't. And Mack was more conscientious about giving pitchers proper rest than most of the managers of his time. McGraw played his hot hand to the point of overusing arms; Mack showed more self-control.

Their professional inheritors, we'll see, reflected those differences to a remarkable degree.

4

Branch Rickey

Ohio

To the world at large, the name of Branch Rickey is more familiar than those of McGraw and Mack and always will be. It's associated with his role in breaking baseball's color line by bringing in Jackie Robinson in 1946, perhaps the most visible single desegregation action ever taken, and its importance transcends baseball and goes to the heart of fundamental social issues. Even among baseball buffs, McGraw and Mack are remembered essentially for what happened on the field in ball games, while Rickey is a figure on a different level. His role in opening organized baseball to blacks is only the second great change he wrought, because long before that he was identified as the architect of farm systems.

Now, the Robinson story, as important as it is, has been described in detail in many fine books, available in all libraries. It does not need retelling here. Our subject is the narrower one of managing major league baseball teams, and to Rickey's role in that evolution, his sociological achievement is not relevant. His farm system concept is. Glossing over the racial issue would be impossible in a biography or a history of baseball, but this is neither. We must assume that the reader is generally familiar with the main events, significance, and ramifications of major league baseball's racial integration, and Rickey's central position in it.

Rickey is also different from McGraw and Mack in four other ways.

1. He belonged, almost, to the next generation. When he was born, in 1881, Mack was almost nineteen and McGraw eight; but more to the point, he had no real contact with the baseball business until after it had settled into its modern form in 1903.

Branch Rickey

2. He was a fully trained and experienced teacher-coach before he was a major league manager. The other two ascended to authority through the ranks as outstanding players. Rickey was never more than a marginal player and coached extensively at the college level before he ever got charge of a professional team.

3. He was a well-educated man in orthodox academic terms, through formal schooling, before he turned to baseball as a profession, with degrees in literature, liberal arts, and law.

4. And he came from much deeper traditional American cultural roots, in religion and intellect, than the descendants of recent immigrants.

All four of these differences had a profound effect on the way his baseball concepts took form.

Wesley Branch Rickey was born on December 20, 1881, in a small farming community in the southern part of Ohio, called Little California. It soon changed its name to Stockdale, and was located in Pike County, about forty miles north of the Ohio River, eighty miles due east of Cincinnati, sixty miles due south of Columbus. But the family farm was in Duck Run, six miles from Lucasville, the largest town in the immediate area: population 350 then, 3,300 now.

On his mother's side, Rickey's ancestors came from Scotland to Massachusetts as early as 1646. One of them was a principal founder of the Methodist Church in America, another served in President Millard Fillmore's cabinet. His father's family came from Vermont and Connecticut. By the time his father, Jacob Franklin Rickey, and mother, Emily Brown, married in 1873, both families had been living in that Ohio district for a generation at least. The Rickeys were Baptists, but both parents were fervently religious and wound up as Wesleyan Methodists, attracted by that group's adherence to John Wesley's declaration, "Think and let think."

Their first son was named Orla. Branch was the second. Orla became a schoolteacher and a terrific baseball fan (of the Cincinnati team in the 1890s), and a pretty good local pitcher. Branch followed him in all his interests, and became his catcher. In 1892, when Branch was ten, the family moved into Lucasville to take advantage of better schooling. At that time, a national depression was making life especially tough for farmers, and the Rickeys just barely got by. But they wanted their sons to be educated.

The Creators

When Branch was seventeen, he got a job teaching elementary school in a one-room schoolhouse in nearby Turkey Creek, where he had to handle particularly unruly students nearly his own age. But his goal was to go to college at Ohio Wesleyan University, in Delaware, Ohio, near Columbus. His athletic ability at Lucasville had been well recognized, and some of the other Lucasville boys had come to Ohio Wesleyan. The athletic director got Rickey to go out for football, and he was soon the starting halfback, scoring a touchdown in a notable victory over Ohio State. In the spring— this was 1902—he and his friends made up the backbone of a good baseball team, with Branch as the catcher very volubly taking charge of all the play in front of him.

Through all this, he was taking part-time jobs and carrying the heaviest possible academic load. When the Portsmouth semipro team offered him $25 a game during the summer, he accepted and traveled with it all over the South.

Back at college that fall, the school president confronted him with newspaper stories about his playing for pay, which the just-organized Ohio Conference had decided, retroactively, would mean ineligibility. The manager of the Portsmouth team had sent the president a handwritten letter flatly denying that he had paid Rickey anything.

It wasn't true, Rickey said. He had been paid.

The president said, "I understand," and that was that.

With his eligibility gone, he could now also play semipro football, for $50 a game. He also helped coach. But he broke an ankle and that source of income ended. Then, in the spring (1903), the baseball coach suddenly quit and the college president offered Rickey the job while he was still an undergraduate. Honesty had proved the best policy.

One of his players, Charles Thomas, was black. Thomas had no trouble inside the college community, but his twenty-one-year-old rookie coach found he had to deal with opponents refusing to play, hotels refusing to give accommodations, and so forth. This experience in sticking up for his player, usually successfully, was the beginning of an awareness that would prove so vital later.

Now Rickey's father mortgaged the farm to pay for his remaining college years, to ease the work burden the young Rickey had imposed upon himself. That summer, he played minor league baseball, and in the fall more semipro football—and wound up on crutches again. In the spring, Ohio Wesleyan made him football coach as well as baseball coach. In June, he got his B. Litt. degree, having completed a 5-year program in 3⅓ years.

Rickey, determined to pay back his parents, needed money badly, so when he heard that Dallas would pay $175 a month for a catcher, he went. In September, he was called up to the Cincinnati Reds. He arrived on a Tuesday. After Saturday's game, he intended to go home to Lucasville to spend Sunday and go to church, since he would not dream of playing baseball on Sunday.

The manager—Joe Kelley, of the Old Orioles—fired him on the spot, and sent him over to the owner's office to get his release.

The club president was Garry Herrmann, installed the previous year when Brush had sold the Reds and bought the Giants. He was also the third man on the three-man commission Organized Baseball had set up in the 1903 peace treaty. (The two league presidents were the other two.) Hermann was impressed with the young man's sincerity and loyalty to his convictions, and wound up giving him expenses as well as one month's salary when Kelley refused to take him back on the team.

His contract went back to Dallas and was sold to the White Sox, but Rickey didn't care. Playing baseball was just a way to earn extra money. He had been in love with, and informally engaged to, a Lucasville girl his own age since they were sixteen. Her father was the wealthiest merchant in town, and getting married meant carving out a respectable career. He headed back to Ohio Wesleyan to get his B.A., but found that his friends there had recommended him for a job at Allegheny College in Meadville, Pennsylvania. (not to be confused with the Allegany College that became St. Bonaventure and McGraw's academic home). At Allegheny, for two years, he coached basketball and football and taught freshman English, Shakespeare, German, and Greek drama.

But never on Sunday.

In 1905, the White Sox passed his contract along to the St. Louis Browns. To make the team, he'd have to go to spring training. Would Jane Moulton marry him if he became a professional ballplayer?

No, she wrote, she wouldn't.

He told the Browns he'd play only between June 15 and September 15, to keep his school jobs, and not on Sunday. The owner, Bob Hedges, was agreeable. But as soon as he joined the team in Philadelphia, he had to turn around and go home because both his parents were seriously ill. They recovered, and he went back to the Browns in August, and to Allegheny College in September. Now he was determined to study law.

In 1906, the Browns offered him $450 a month, and Jane relented. They scheduled the wedding for June 1. And he had his best year as a player, hitting .284. The manager, Jim McAleer, tried to renege on his September 15 leaving date (the season ran into October) by threatening to withhold some of his pay. Rickey got the school to accept the delay, but told Hedges in no uncertain terms that he'd never play for McAleer again.

His 1906–07 Allegheny football and baseball teams won conference titles. By Christmas, he had his Bachelor of Arts degree in hand. Hedges, taking him at his word, traded his contract to the New York Highlanders—whose manager was Clark Griffith.

That winter, in the gym, Rickey had injured his throwing arm, nullifying his outstanding asset as a catcher, his ability to throw. He notified Griffith of his condition, and said he thought he'd be useless. Griffith suggested he go to Hot Spring, Arkansas, for two weeks of hot mineral baths and massages. It didn't seem to help, but he went to New York anyhow, reporting June 28. The regular catcher, it turned out, was hurt.

"Try it," said Griff.

On the first few steal attempts, he tried to throw but didn't get anybody. By the end of the day he wasn't even throwing. The record of 13 stolen bases in one game against one catcher is still in the book. He stuck around for 52 games, hitting .182, and knew his playing career was over.

Back at Allegheny, he coached, taught, studied law, made speeches in favor of Prohibition, and worked to elect Taft president, keeping up his customary breakneck pace. He turned twenty-seven. And he got sick.

It was tuberculosis. In those days, that was often considered a death sentence. But there was a famous sanitarium at Saranac Lake, in New York, which offered hope. (Christy Mathewson would die there in 1925, of complications from being gassed in World War I.)

He recovered, and went home to Lucasville. He had $200 to his name. If Jane stayed with her parents, he could just barely afford to be a student enrolled at the University of Michigan Law School. In his second year there (1911–12), the school's baseball coaching job opened up. He got it.

Branch Rickey

He also got his law degree. For one who had recently recovered from tuberculosis, climate was a consideration in planning a career. He and two other young lawyers decided to set up a firm in Boise, Idaho. He continued to coach at Michigan, but in the summer he would go to Boise.

Suddenly, Bob Hedges showed up in Ann Arbor.

The owner of the Browns had liked Rickey, even when his manager hadn't, and admired his capabilities. He was thinking of buying a minor league team in Kansas City, and wanted Rickey to run it. That didn't pan out, but Rickey agreed to do some scouting on the West Coast when he went to Boise. In August, Hedges had another proposition. Would Rickey join him as his second-in-command of the Browns? To become, in effect, a general manager as we now know the position, but which didn't exist then? Make trades, sign players, scout, evaluate the minor league draft, build a team? For $9,000?

At Michigan he was making $1,200. The Boise firm was breaking up because (1) the partners were on opposite sides in the 1912 presidential campaign and (2) they had no clients.

The Rickeys moved to St. Louis.

St. Louis

In June 1913, when Rickey moved into the Browns' office in Sportsman's Park, the Federal League threat was just getting started. But it wasn't much of a threat to the Browns. The Feds were after stars, and the Browns didn't have any. They had finished seventh, eighth, eighth, and seventh the last four years, and were well on their way to finishing last again. McAleer, the manager Rickey had his dispute with, had departed after 1909. In 1911, Bobby Wallace was a great shortstop but thirty-seven years old, and also the manager. Halfway through 1912, the reins were given to George Stovall, a first baseman nicknamed "Firebrand" during his eight years as a regular in Cleveland, who had come over in a trade, and Wallace went back to just playing. As the 1913 season was winding down, Hedges fired the firebrand, and made Jimmy Austin, an outstanding third baseman, temporary manager with the announced intention of putting Rickey in the dugout in 1914. (Stovall did go to the Feds, as manager of Kansas City.) But 8 games later, with 11 games to go, Hedges insisted that Rickey become manager then and there.

The Creators

Rickey kept that job only two years, but that was enough to reveal why his methods were so different from the others of his time, and a direct outgrowth of his unusual background.

For one thing, he was a teacher first, a "boss" second. He had learned how to deal with unruly pupils, how to devise drills, how to deal with feelings, and how to organize a curriculum.

More important, he had coached football. Even in those days, under what we consider primitive rules, football was a game that required far more analytic preparation than any other. It was a "rehearsed" sport, in which set plays were diagrammed and the proportion of practice time to actual combat was 10 to 1 or more. The kind of planning that football required as a matter of course was simply not applied to baseball because it didn't seem necessary; but Rickey did apply it.

Finally, he was a man of words, backed by evangelical fervor for what he believed in, an indefatigable explainer. Few of his contemporaries in the baseball world were that.

For spring training in 1914, he took his team to St. Petersburg, Florida, the first team to train in that city. He set up three batting cages, three handball courts, a sliding pit, and a sprinting track. The handball would improve conditioning and sharpen hand-to-eye coordination. In the sliding pits, the correct way to hook-slide to either side of a base would be practiced. Since speed was fundamental to success (in his view), and few players had ever received any systematic instruction in how to run efficiently, the track would give them a place to learn.

He continued routines he had refined at Michigan: the best way to make rundown plays, the best way to take a lead off base, timing runners to first with a stopwatch, hitting fungoes to outfielders just out of reach to judge how much ground they could really cover, and endless bunting practice.

Every morning, at 9:00 A.M., the workday would start with a blackboard lecture—like football. (McGraw, remember, used morning workouts for batting and fielding practice.) These were lecture sessions, which most players found boring. But they were part of a pattern that Rickey was sure would have long-range benefits and that represented the core of what would become "the Rickey system": Master the fundamentals.

There's a right way to catch the ball (two hands). There's a right place to throw the ball (to the cutoff man). There's a right way to stand in against close pitches; and to force players who pulled back to break the habit, Rickey devised a rope and pulley gadget that would trip the batter if he stepped back.

Rickey already knew, though he had not yet told the world, his formula for the five basic baseball skills: run, throw, catch, hit, and hit with power.

All this couldn't help the Browns very much, although they did rise to fifth place in 1914.

And in 1915 George Sisler showed up.

Rickey was not exactly surprised.

Back in 1911, at the age of seventeen, Sisler was already known as an outstandinig prospect in his native area around Manchester, Ohio. He signed a contract with the Akron club of the Central League, but never reported or accepted any money because he changed his mind and decided to enroll at the University of Michigan. Akron sold the contract to Columbus, which sold it to Pittsburgh, and Pittsburgh put him on its suspended list.

At Michigan, his coach was Rickey, who could see the potential in one of the greatest hitters of all time as soon as he laid eyes on it.

And Rickey had just finished studying law, too.

He gave Sisler good advice. The existence of the contract, even though not fulfilled, was a threat to his college eligibility. And Sisler had signed it while underage, without parental consent. He urged both Sisler and his father to write to the National Commission to certify that he didn't belong to any club.

The head of the commission was Garry Herrmann.

Here was a knotty problem. A club's property rights were involved, since the Pirates had paid Columbus to acquire the contract. Sisler was asking for free agency, the one thing baseball owners had been dreading and resisting for forty years. Yet, legally, there was no way to deny the claim of the two Sislers that an innocent teenage boy had been "duped" into signing a contract that had no legal force.

Baseball's hierarchy reacted in its most typical fashion: It did nothing, to see if the problem would go away.

It didn't. It got worse. By 1914, Sisler, as a junior, was universally recognized as the best college player in the country, a prize for any club that got him.

Now, the commission's National League president had every need to uphold Pittsburgh's claim, since Dreyfuss, the club owner, was one of his employers. The American League president had every reason to hold out the possibility that one of his league's teams could get him. Herrmann, a National Leaguer but an intimate of Ban Johnson's, was the "neutral" vote, and offered a compromise: Sisler could be a free agent but Pittsburgh should get the first chance to sign him.

By this time, Rickey was with the Browns and the Sislers knew exactly what they wanted: for George to play for Rickey, with whom he'd had such a good relationship at Michigan.

Sisler's attorney, a Detroit judge, injected the words "antitrust suit" and "triple damages" into the discussion.

Baseball was already facing antitrust suits from the Federal League.

The commission decided Sisler was a free agent, no strings attached.

Upon graduation in 1915, Sisler sorted out bids from the Federal League and from Pittsburgh—and chose St. Louis.

Dreyfuss screamed that he had been betrayed within his own industry. He hated Rickey from then on, and looked for every opportunity to unseat Herrmann. It was this case that set in motion the events that led to the single commissioner system and Landis in 1920. In other player control cases, it had become impossible for the three-man body to settle ownership disputes across league lines.

So Sisler became a Brownie, playing first base and the outfield for the remaining half of the 1915 season. Starting in 1917, he hit .353, .341, .352, .407, .371, and .420, averaging 39 stolen bases a year and fielding impeccably, before sinus trouble affected his vision and brought him down into the .320 neighborhood for the rest of his Hall of Fame career.

But Rickey wasn't there to get the benefit.

As manager, he had a Sunday problem. He stuck to his resolve never to go to a ballpark on the Sabbath. His "Sunday manager" was Austin at first, then Burt Shotton, one of his outfielders. Hedges accepted that.

At the end of 1915, however, Rickey suddenly had an owner problem. Hedges sold the team to Phil Ball, an outspoken millionaire who had backed the St. Louis Feds and had helped engineer the peace settlement. Ball had no use for Rickey, told him to stick to the office, and hired Fielder Jones, who had managed his Federal League team (and before that, the Hitless Wonder White Sox of 1904–08) as the new manager of the Browns. If Rickey wanted to go elsewhere, it would be all right with Ball.

Branch Rickey

Well, there were a lot of people in St. Louis who liked Rickey. Hedges had left him with the protection of a contract through 1916. At the end of that season, the other St. Louis team, in the National League, finished last and actually went backrupt. There was a public sale of stock to pay off debts, and the investors asked the sportswriting community for advice in hiring a president. The recommendation was unanimous: Get Rickey.

Now Ball balked. Go anywhere, said Ball, but not across the street. He reneged on his verbal release. And Ban Johnson, Ball's friend and up to now a friend of Rickey's, didn't like the idea of any talented person going from his league to the National.

Rickey went, but both sides sued each other (and eventually settled).

In 1918, at the age of thirty-six, father of four children and a lifelong pacifist, Rickey yielded to patriotic fervor and joined the war voluntarily. Given the rank of major, he went overseas with a gas regiment in the Chemical Warfare Service, the same unit that contained Capt. Ty Cobb, Capt. Christy Mathewson, and Lt. George Sisler. They were home four months later, three unscathed, Mathewson with fatally scarred lungs.

So 1919 began with him back in total charge of the St. Louis (National League) team, which he renamed Cardinals. But not for long.

The 1919 Cardinals were so poor that they couldn't go to Florida for spring training, but had to work out at Washington University in St. Louis. Rickey took over the field managership, to save $10,000, and brought in Austin and Shotton as his Sunday managers. His office staff consisted of a young stenographer named Bill DeWitt. The team finished seventh, drawing only 167,000 in old Robison Field.

The investors had to do something. To borrow $18,000, they gave Sam Breadon 72 percent of the stock, leaving Rickey with the rest. Breadon was another hard-bitten self-made millionaire (as a car dealer) who had little use for Rickey's piety and blatant intellectualism. He demoted Rickey to vice-president and made him continue as field manager (both for one salary), but he did give him the opportunity to take and keep the baseball limelight. Breadon was strict, not to say tight, about spending money; but he left baseball matters to Rickey and let him speak as much as he liked, with full authority, about baseball affairs.

Breadon also sold off the land where Robison Field stood and moved the team into Sportsman's Park as a tenant of Ball and the Browns'.

And now it was 1920, with the vistas of prosperity that Mack had recognized equally evident to Rickey—who had his own ideas.

When Hedges had asked Rickey about running a minor league team in Kansas City, back in 1912, Hedges had expressed a vague plan. "Syndicate baseball," with common ownership of more than one club, had become a dirty word in the 1890s, and was obviously unsuitable within a league. But what if you also owned a minor league club with which you could, by "gentleman's agreement," exchange players for developmental purposes or in case of injury? Nothing came of it then, but Rickey had been thinking about it while in the army in France.

What if you owned several minor league clubs, at different levels, and skimmed off the best players for the major league club as the need arose?

As it was, teams got good prospects from the minors by buying their contracts. A team like the Cardinals would always be outbid by teams like the Giants, Yankees, and Cubs (as Mack was finding out). But the new Cardinal owner was, unlike Mack, a millionaire too. He had money if he could be persuaded to spend it. Rickey had to prove that he had a plan that would get results on the field and make a profit too. Breadon wouldn't "spend," but he might "invest."

This way, through the first half of the 1920s, Rickey started building a farm system. There were many intermediate steps, but the end result was this: Hundreds of players could be examined in tryouts and assigned to minor league teams at various levels, with the minor league team committed by contract to give the Cardinals first crack. (The 1921 National agreement with the minors permitted this.) You didn't have to guess which of the hundreds of hopefuls would turn out to be major leaguers; they would identify themselves in the process of progressing through the system. The ones you wanted, you'd keep; the other good ones, you'd sell off at a profit (the way the independent minor league owners did); and whenever you had a replacement ready for a respected veteran, you could sell or trade the veteran for more profit.

That was the idea. Breadon liked it.

For the system to work well, there were certain prerequisites. The universality of the reserve, now that no rival leagues were operating, enabled you to control players in the minors. But it would do you no good to control them unless you made consistently correct evaluations of every player, not only in your own system but elsewhere (to make decisions about exchanges). This is where Rickey's refined analytic methods, his tireless energy, and his ability to form a large-scale organization came into play. You needed the right kind (and number) of scouts, reliable reporting systems, consistent terminology, internal communication, and even a jigsaw puzzle of travel arrangements. Instinct (McGraw) or detail (Mack) weren't enough; you needed the kind of intellect Rickey had to organize and administer on such a scale. And he had a network of college, church, and political contacts to draw upon.

He continued to manage into the 1925 season, without notable success, although he did climb to third in 1921 and 1922. But he was accumulating some high-caliber talent: Jim Bottomley, Jesse Haines, Chick Hafey—and Rogers Hornsby, whom he had described as "a remarkable hitter, indeed" as far back as 1918, when Hornsby was twenty-one years old in his second full season.

Less than a third of the way through the 1925 season, there was an abrupt change. Rickey had asked Breadon to be relieved of managing several times, and had been told no; now, when he felt things were about to start clicking, Breadon decided to have him step down and have Hornsby manage. Or, to put it more accurately, step "up" and concentrate only on the front office and farm system affairs.

Rickey didn't like it, and Hornsby (who respected Rickey) didn't either, but what Breadon wanted, Breadon got. Angered, Rickey sold his stock to Hornsby, and that was to make trouble later.

Under Hornsby, in 1926, the Cardinals beat the Yankees in the seventh game of the World Series, in one of baseball's oft-told tales—and Hornsby promptly told off Breadon about pursuing dollars instead of players and scheduling too many exhibitions. The Giants had long wanted Hornsby; Rickey had long wanted Frank Frisch. Now Frisch had just walked out on McGraw. Breadon and Stoneham made the deal over the phone—but then it was held up until the question of Hornsby's stock was settled.

From then on, Rickey concentrated on farm system affairs. Judge Landis became his main foe: Landis hated the idea and turned farmhands loose whenever there was any hint of "covering them up" by stockpiling them in the minors when they might have played for some other major league club (a legitimate enough complaint most of the time). But the structural advantage of a farm system was too great to be ignored, and when the Depression hit, it also became the savior of independent minor league operators.

The Cardinals continued to thrive under different managers. They won in 1928 under Bill McKechnie, in 1930 and 1931 under Gabby Street, in 1934 under Frisch, and in 1942–44 under Billy Southworth.

By that time, however, Rickey had moved on.

Mahatma in Brooklyn

For ten years after 1920, Uncle Robby's Brooklyn team did well enough in drawing customers and interesting its fans, but couldn't win another pennant. By the early 1930s, it was in desperate straits and taken over by the banks. To revive the franchise, the owners brought in a flamboyant figure named Leland Stanford MacPhail. In 1935, MacPhail had introduced night baseball to the majors while putting a deteriorated Cincinnati franchise on its feet. In 1938, moving to Brooklyn, MacPhail installed lights on Ebbets Field, broke an agreement that had existed among the three New York teams to avoid radio broadcasting, turned Red Barber loose on the metropolitan public, and hired Leo Durocher as a charismatic and controversial manager. By 1941, the Dodgers were pennant winners again, loaded with older ball players collected by trades, and the darlings of an underdog-loving nation far beyond Brooklyn.

And MacPhail was a Rickey protégé. Back in 1932, he had acquired an option on a failing minor league team in Columbus, and sold it to Rickey with the proviso that he could run it. Rickey, impressed with MacPhail's drive and energy, made the deal and started to teach MacPhail about baseball; MacPhail needed no help in matters of promotion. Columbus got a new ballpark, night baseball, and lots of fine Cardinal players as a high link in the farm system chain. But Rickey also thought MacPhail was spending too much money and had a double purpose in recommending him for the Cincinnati job: It would be good for Cincinnati and good for the St. Louis balance sheet.

In 1942, both men were at the end of the line. In St. Louis, Rickey's conflicts with Breadon had become irreconcilable, and the warfare with Landis over farm systems had escalated. Rickey's current contract was up and he was determined to leave. MacPhail, famous for some spectacular adventures in World War I, was determined to go back into service (in his fifties) once Pearl Harbor brought the United States into World War II in December of 1941. The 1942 pennant race, one of the best on record, ended with the Cardinals making up a 10-game August deficit and beating out the Dodgers, 106 victories to 104. The Cardinals, consisting almost entirely of their own farm products, had beaten Brooklyn's collection of older all-stars, and now proceeded to win the World Series from a Yankee team that had its own elaborate farm system.

MacPhail left. Rickey quit. And the Brooklyn owners hired Rickey as MacPhail's replacement.

In the next seven years, as unfettered boss of the Dodger operation, Rickey put the finishing touches to his farm system conception. Landis died, removing that obstacle. The war ended. The economy entered a postwar boom. There was a backlog of playing talent available, at all levels, as servicemen returned to civilian life.

In this context, Rickey also went ahead with his integration project, but what concerns us here is how he took the "organization" system to its logical conclusion and set the parameters almost all managers would have to follow in the future.

The original idea had been to own minor league clubs as repositories for players on the way up, to fill need at the top. But if you controlled the minor league club financially, why not also control its baseball operations?

There was, Rickey had long believed and demonstrated, a certain way to teach and perfect baseball fundamentals. If you got all your minor league managers and coaches on the same wavelength, teaching the same techniques the same way, throughout the system from Class D through Class AAA, you would wind up with an inventory of players thoroughly prepared to play baseball your way by the time they reached the majors. The baseball curriculum, Rickey was convinced, would help any player reach his personal potential; the most talented would benefit most and supply the parent club with a higher quality of uniformly trained regulars to use or trade or sell.

Thus evolved the Dodger System, capital *S*, which permeates baseball to this day. Its virtue is not secret formulas or trick devices, but consistent and uniform application of time-tested basics, constantly revised.

Those basics included:

1. Speed is the greatest asset. It must be found, not taught, although proper training can refine the natural gift.

2. Pitching is the greatest need. It can be taught, but only if natural arm strength is there in the first place. So sign strong arms.

3. Game tactics—position play, response to the count on a hitter, substitutions, base running decisions—become second nature by repetition, so build in awareness of them through correct repetition from the lowest classification on up.

4. "Hitting alone will not win ballgames," Rickey had declared as early as 1913, when he was setting up his first training camp. But you needed sufficient hitting, of course, and it was important to seek the right balance of two different kinds: hitting for average and hitting for power. A Hall of Famer could do both, but clubs could not be composed simply of Hall of Famers. What mattered was identifying which ability a man had best, and making sure he worked on it on the way up.

5. Make sure reports are thorough and judgments valid.

What did all this mean to field managers in the majors?

1. It downplayed the teaching function, which had been a major part of the McGraw-Mack duties.

2. It forced the manager to pay much more attention to what was lower in the system and to be familiar with a player's capabilities by the time he arrived in the majors.

3. It meant, as time went on, that "bright" ideas would filter through to the opposition faster than ever, so that success depended on carrying out the right principles consistently more than on inspired instinct.

"Luck," preached Rickey, "is the residue of design."

4. Well-organized record keeping became necessary. Rickey hired a statistician, Allan Roth, to chart pitches and compile detailed records beyond what managers had been keeping in their heads or in the form of rudimentary notes in a little black book. Objective measurements by stopwatch of every action had to be taken into consideration, along with "impressions."

5. Attention to pitching decisions—rotation of starters, when to use relievers, special matchups—became a larger part of the manager's preoccupations than devising batting orders or looking for players.

The New York papers christened Rickey "The Mahatma," in

reference to Ghandi, who had been described as "a combination of your father and Tammany Hall." They harped on his reputation for penny-pinching (honed beyond his own frugal inclinations by years of Breadon's carping) and called him El Cheapo. His farm system made him a "plantation owner" or "chain gang operator"—ironic similies that evaporated once the Robinson saga began. His Sunday rule was attacked as pretentious hypocrisy (which it wasn't).

But the results were unmistakeable, and everybody started to imitate his "system."

He put it in place, when the war ended, by acquiring Vero Beach, Florida. Early in 1947 he heard that a Naval Air Station there was to be closed. He bought it, despite the objections of one of the club's owners (a fellow named Walter O'Malley) that it was too much money to waste on a frivolous idea. The barracks could house up to five hundred people. There were buildings for administration, recreation, and meals. Any number of baseball fields could be laid out, for use simultaneously, and a central one could be built (with stands) for exhibition games.

Everyone in the system could train together, learn the same things together, be observed easily by all concerned, from the lowest rookie league to the parent club. And aside from spring training, the facility could to used all year round for other developmental projects.

Vero Beach became, and still is, the model for every baseball complex. And it gave the major league manager a dimension he had never had before: daily contact and exchange of views with all the minor league managers who would be sending players to him, and early acquaintance with young players.

The Dodger dynasty was a monument to Rickey's vision. The foundation of the team's success for the last forty years and more rests on what he built. But not even Rickey could escape what McGraw always confronted, and what Mack escaped only by becoming an owner himself: conflict with the ownership. Rickey owned 25 percent. So did O'Malley. The other 50 percent was in the hands of passive heirs of previous owners. In a power struggle between Rickey and O'Malley, O'Malley had the home-court advantage as a native New Yorker. By the end of the 1950 season, O'Malley was victorious and Rickey stepped out by selling his share.

Rickey's teams had reached the World Series in 1947 and 1949, and missed by the narrowest of margins in 1946 and 1950. The farm system was in place. O'Malley would reap its benefits, and through his own astuteness, maintain and extend it. But Rickey was gone.

The Grand Old Man

By the time he left Brooklyn, at the age of sixty-eight, all Rickey's innovations were complete. More than any individual, he had revolutionized (and modernized) the talent procurement, team development side of baseball. The Cardinal and Dodger systems, now virtually self-sustaining, were copied as much as possible, wherever possible. What followed was noteworthy in its own right, but added nothing to the influence he had already wielded. If he had completely retired at that point, nothing that has been said so far would have to be changed.

But he had too much energy for that. The Pittsburgh Pirates had passed into the hands of John Galbreath, an Ohioan of Rickey's generation who had made a huge fortune in a world-spanning construction business and was prominent as an owner of race horses—and incidentally, a fraternity brother of Rickey's. The Pirates had fallen to last place, dissipated a strong tradition, and had nothing to offer the public but Ralph Kiner's home runs. Galbreath brought Rickey to Pittsburgh and put him in charge. A new farm system could be built from the ground up.

The five years he spent there seemed to be a failure, as the Pirates finished the last four years in a row with an ineptitude that provided the material for Joe Garagiola's budding career as a raconteur. Yet, a viable system was being built and eventually paid off in a World Series triumph in 1960, five years after Rickey had resigned. Many of the scouts and executives he had brought along from Brooklyn stayed on. The process took longer than expected because external conditions had changed. The continuing peacetime military draft took two years out of every young player's development, and sidetracked some for good during the Korean War. The growth of other sports, especially pro football, had injected a bonus necessity into signing prized youngsters, and that changed economics. Other systems, in existence because of Rickey, provided stiff competition. The timetables he had come to rely on at St. Louis and Brooklyn were stretched out, but they did eventually produce the intended result.

Branch Rickey

Two acts remained, both with downbeat endings. In 1958, the cyclical pressure for outside challenge had come around again. Five teams had moved, including the Giants and Dodgers to the West Coast, and many enlarged American cities wanted a piece of the major league pie. With Organized Baseball resisting expansion, plans surfaced for a third major league, the Continental, and Rickey was called out of retirement to head it. The majors then accepted (under antitrust threat) expansion as the lesser of evils, took in four teams in 1961 and 1962, and killed the Continental League idea. At least indirectly, however, Rickey helped bring about the New York Mets.

Finally, in 1962, Rickey started one last go-around with the Cardinals. The Cardinals had not won a pennant since 1946, and had been purchased in 1953 by the Busch Brewery, whose owner, Gussie Busch, was having them run by a tandem of Dick Meyer (from the beer business) and Bing Devine (up the baseball ladder after starting as an office boy in Rickey's original regime). They got along well and did, in fact, run the team well. Busch, impatient, decided Rickey should be some sort of senior advisor, and the predictable friction resulted. The 1963 Cardinals made a run at the Los Angeles Dodgers, led by Sandy Koufax and Don Drysdale, but didn't quite make it, and in August of 1964 were running fifth.

Devine and Meyer believed Rickey was trying to take too much control. Busch believed (a congenital failing of his, in my opinion) that everybody in the world was wrong but himself. So Busch fired Devine, to Rickey's surprise. He also approached Leo Durocher, coaching with the Dodgers, to become manager of the Cardinals in place of the colorless Johnny Keane—without telling Rickey or Meyer, and also without preventing the rumors from getting out.

Then the Cardinals surprised the whole Western world by getting hot and winning the pennant when the Phillies blew a 6½-game lead with 12 to play. They also won the World Series in 7 games from the mighty Yankees.

Whereupon Keane quit and moved to the Yankees, who fired Yogi Berra. It all made lots of headlines and left a lot of bad taste in a lot of mouths.

So Busch completed the process by firing Rickey.

Rickey died a little over a year later, within two weeks of what would have been his eighty-fourth birthday.

Part Two

The Developers

5

Miller Huggins

The Cincinnati Kid

Miller Huggins is the first of three transitional figures in managerial evolution. Like Joe McCarthy and Bill McKechnie, he formed his ideas as much from observation of contemporaries and opponents as from direct instruction under the masters. These men absorbed and passed on the respective frameworks of the originators without being actual disciples. Casey Stengel, the fourth member of this group, went beyond that in becoming a conscious, specific, and dedicated pupil of McGraw. Collectively, however, these four were the ones who spread the various gospels.

Huggins was a city boy, in itself a significant difference from the rural upbringing of the McGraw-Mack-Rickey group. He was, however, of Rickey's generation and, in fact, almost two years older. He was born in 1880 in Cincinnati, where his father, who had been born in England, was a grocer. A Methodist, the elder Huggins was as much opposed to Sunday baseball as Rickey was, so the son played semipro ball under an assumed name (since so much of it was played on Sundays) to avoid embarrassing the father.

Miller was tiny, five feet four inches tall, under 130 pounds in weight, but tough and athletic. He was also very bright. His father wanted him to study law, so he did, at the University of Cincinnati. One of his teachers, William Howard Taft, would become president of the United States. Huggins did get his law degree, but never did go into practice because he found he could make his living from baseball right from the start.

At nineteen, he played in the Inter-State League as an infielder who experimented earlier than most with switch-hitting. Either way, he was only a fair hitter, but an outstanding fielder. The next year, 1900, he played for a semipro team in the Catskill Mountain resort area for a hotel run by the Fleischmann brothers, Max and Julius, who would eventually buy the Cincinnati Club. In 1901, he was back in the minors and spent three years playing for St. Paul at the highest minor league level, through the time when the American and National leagues and the minors got together and the playing rules stabilized.

In 1904, he was purchased by the Reds and installed as the regular second baseman by the manager, Joe Kelley—the same Joe Kelley who had been such a big star on Ned Hanlon's Orioles in the 1890s, and who had gone with Hanlon to Brooklyn in 1899. Kelley went back to Baltimore, where McGraw was running the American League team, in 1902, and when McGraw went to the Giants in midseason, Kelley went to Cincinnati and became the player-manager.

Huggins played for Kelley for two seasons. In 1906, Kelley became only a player again as Hanlon came over to manage, and Huggins was the regular second baseman under Hanlon for the next two years. In 1908, the Cincinnati manager was John Ganzel, the first baseman, who had played a couple of years for McGraw in New York before that. In 1909, Griffith arrived but before the season was half over, traded Huggins to St. Louis, where the manager, Roger Bresnahan, had made a special effort to acquire him.

In 1913, Huggins succeeded Bresnahan as manager.

So the Oriole lineage of Huggins was impeccable: Hanlon and Kelley, and Bresnahan, who had just spent eight years as McGraw's catcher in Baltimore and New York. All the technical details of winning baseball represented by the McGraw school, offensively and defensively, were internalized by Huggins.

As a personality, however, he was entirely different. His toughness was essentially mental, not physical. He wasn't noisy or belligerent in baseball, nor rowdy or flamboyant in private life. He distilled the intellectual portion of Oriole baseball into a more orderly and self-controlled approach. In fact, one of the reasons the owner of the St. Louis team, Mrs. Helene Britton, put Hug in charge was that he was "gentlemanly" while Bresnahan had been much rougher in speech and manner.

The Cardinals (who were already being called that because of the color of the trim on their uniforms, before Rickey formalized the redbird emblem), had little talent. When Huggins lifted them to third place in 1914, it was their highest finish since 1876. But they dropped back to sixth in 1915 and last in 1916. At that point, Mrs. Britton decided to sell the team, and offered Huggins a chance to buy all or part of it. While he was trying to raise the money from the Fleischmanns, she went ahead and sold it to someone else—and the new owners of the bankrupt franchise brought in Rickey to run it.

Huggins had no problem with Rickey, but he felt betrayed by the circumstances of the sale. He was still under contract to manage in 1917, and did, having turned second base over to a young hitter named Rogers Hornsby, who had arrived in 1916 as a rookie third baseman. But he had no desire to stay, and the new owners wanted Rickey to manage in the dugout as well. Huggins was thirty-seven, finished as a ballplayer, qualified as a lawyer, as well trained for managing as anyone could be, and available.

A Controversial Choice

The two colonels, Ruppert and Huston, had acquired the New York Yankees at McGraw's urging in 1915. They made Wild Bill Donovan, famous as a pitcher for Detroit, their manager, and finished fifth, fourth, and sixth. They were sure they wanted someone else for 1918, but they had distinctly different ideas about who and what type the new manager should be.

In April 1917, the United States had entered World War I, and Huston had gone back into service, so Ruppert was, in effect, in sole command. At the 1917 World Series, Ruppert met Huggins and was impressed, especially since Hug was being highly recommended by Ban Johnson, the American League czar-president who had always stayed close to his Cincinnati roots and knew Huggins well. Huston, in France, had made clear his preference: He wanted to hire Wilbert Robinson away from the Dodgers. Ruppert went ahead and hired Huggins, causing a breach between himself and Huston that was never healed, and led to Huston finally selling his share to Ruppert after the 1922 season.

In the war-shortened season of 1918, Huggins's first Yankee team placed fourth and got little notice from anyone. In 1919, with the war over, Ruppert and Huston started spending their money to acquire some quality players. They wound up with Wally Pipp at first, the unretired Home Run Baker (of Philadelphia fame) at third, Roger Peckinpaugh at short, Duffy Lewis (of Boston Red Sox fame) and Ping Bodie in the outfield, and Muddy Ruel as a catcher. In Bob Shawkey, Ernie Shore, and a few others, they had a pretty good pitching staff. And in midsummer, they provoked a tremendous intraleague fight that would lead to the commissionership of Judge Landis.

Carl Mays was an outstanding pitcher who walked out on the Red Sox, dissatisfied with salary. He was suspended. While he stayed away, the Yankees offered to buy him, and the Red Sox, owned by Harry Frazee, were quite willing to sell him. But Ban Johnson insisted that this would constitute rewarding a disobedient player, and that Mays must return to Boston to uphold the sanctity of player contracts. The Yankees went to court, got injunctions, signed Mays, and with his help finished third behind the White (soon to be Black) Sox and Cleveland. Johnson, insisting Mays should have been ineligible, held up the third-place money. Ruppert and Huston, deciding that the arrogant Johnson must be forced out, actually took part in a scheme to break away and join the National League. It was this row, after the 1919 season but before public acknowledgment of the World Series fix, that turned a majority against Johnson's authority and brought about the single commissioner.

The other remarkable aspect of the 1919 season was Babe Ruth. He had come to Boston in 1914 as a left-handed pitcher, and had become the best in the league by 1918. But he was also such a good hitter that during the 1918 season the Red Sox manager started letting him play the outfield between starts. He pitched only 20 games, half his usual number, and played 75 in the outfield and at first base—and hit 11 home runs, playing part time in a war-shortened season. No American Leaguer had hit more than 12, playing full time in a full schedule, since 1903.

That was evidence enough for Boston's manager. Let others pitch, and let Ruth concentrate on being in the lineup every day as a hitter. In 1919, Ruth hit 29 home runs, shattering all previous records.

The manager was Ed Barrow, the same Ed Barrow whose newsboy league had turned Fred Clarke on to baseball back in Iowa. He had moved to Pittsburgh, hoping to sell a soapsuds invention

Miller Huggins

he and his brother had come up with but wound up broke, so he went to work as a hotel clerk. In 1894, he hooked up with Harry Stevens, the concessionaire at the Pittsburgh ballpark. (Stevens, as a teen-ager in the 1880s, had run across John McGraw, who helped him get into baseball; baseball is a *very* small world.) The next year, they helped organize a minor league, the Interstate, and invested $100 each in the Wheeling, Virginia, franchise, of which Barrow became the manager. His team finished first, but the league folded, so he moved it into the Iron and Oil League (in which McGraw had made his start a few years before).

Then Barrow, on his own, bought the Paterson, New Jersey, franchise, in the Atlantic League and signed a good-looking hitter named Honus Wagner for $25 more than the league's limit of $100 a month. That year he had his team play a night game, under makeshift lights, in Wilmington, Delaware, and at the end of the season was elected president of the league. In 1897, he sold Wagner to Louisville for $2,100, and during his three years as league president tried letting a woman pitch and hired heavyweight champions as umpires (John L. Sullivan, Jim Jeffries, and Jim Corbett). He retained side business interests in the theater and as a fight promoter.

For all that, the Atlantic League folded after 1899, so he bought a 25 percent interest in Toronto of the Eastern League and went back to managing. The next year, 1901, he lost fourteen of his players to the new American League, but won the pennant anyhow. In 1903, he followed them and became manager of the Detroit Tigers; but when the Tigers were sold in 1904 to Frank Navin, he and the new owner didn't get along, and he went back to the minors to manage in Indianapolis. There he decided not to pay $500 for the contract of one Ty Cobb; well, nobody's perfect.

Then he went into the hotel business for three years, resumed managing in Montreal, became president of the Eastern League, and renamed it the International (with it is today). In 1917, as league president, he was making $7,500 when the league's club owners decided to cut it to $2,500, so he quit. Harry Frazee, who had recently acquired the Red Sox, promptly hired him as manager, and the 1918 Red Sox just as promptly won the pennant and the World Series.

Clarke as a young boy, Wagner, Ruth—Barrow had a pretty good eye for talent, along with entrepreneurial nerve and a strong will.

The Developers

Frazee had even stronger entrepreneurial instincts, but they were focused on producing Broadway shows. He was always out of money. He knew Ruppert, who was a socialite stage-door Johnny in a New York just about to enter the Jazz Age.

Huggins, managing the Yankees in 1918 and 1919, had seen (along with everyone else) what Ruth was capable of. He urged his colonels and the Yankee business manager, Harry Sparrow, to try to buy him.

Ruppert made the deal. He gave Frazee a $300,000 personal loan and $125,000 outright for Ruth's contract.

Ruth then hit 54 home runs for the 1920 Yankees, who finished third during the confusing final week when the Black Sox scandal erupted and Cleveland won the pennant. And in the Polo Grounds, the Yankees outdrew McGraw's Giants (just purchased by Stoneham) by 1,300,000 to 900,000. Never before had a baseball team sold 1,000,000 tickets in a season.

Stoneham and McGraw let Ruppert and Huston know they wouldn't be welcome at the Polo Grounds when the lease ran out.

Meanwhile, early in the 1920 season, Sparrow had died, and the Yankees needed a business manager. How about Barrow? Frazee, as usual, was willing. Barrow, aware that the Red Sox could go only downhill, was more than willing. So he was installed as what we now call a general manager, in charge not only of all the business aspects of the operation (for which he was well qualified) but for player personnel decisions like trades and minor league purchases (for which he was also qualified). Most important of all, he became a complete buffer between the ownership and the field manager—an arrangement Huggins welcomed. Barrow was total boss of the Yankees, the way Mack was of his team, without field managing duties; and Huggins, not burdened with the power-craving ego drive that McGraw and Rickey had, was satisfied to be boss in the dugout. This was the first such tandem that really worked: a specialist general manager and a nonplaying bench manager who operated on the same wavelength.

So now, in 1921, Huggins had Ruth, a flock of other outstanding players (to which Barrow had added some other Boston products, including the battery of Waite Hoyt and Wally Schang), and a perfect relationship with the front office. The owners, for their part, concentrated on finding a new home and decided to build their own stadium in a lumberyard directly across the Harlem River from the Polo Grounds.

Miller Huggins

That triad—Ruth, Huggins, Barrow—was the foundation of the most successful sports operation America has ever known.

In 1921, Ruth hit 59 home runs. He hit .378, batted in 171 runs, got 144 walks. His 457 total bases meant a slugging average of .846. He even stole 17 bases and threw out 17 base runners. No one had ever imagined, let alone seen, that anyone could have a season like that. No one has had one since, either.

The Yankees won their first pennant, but lost the World Series to the Giants.

In 1922 they won the pennant again, and again lost the series to the Giants.

Huston, never fully reconciled to Huggins even after two pennants, demanded he be fired for (1) "not controlling" Ruth and (2) losing to McGraw.

Ruppert, scoffing at (1), was worried by (2) because huge Yankee Stadium was nearing completion. How many of its seats would be filled if the "Number One" label stayed at the Polo Grounds?

They argued bitterly, noisily, all through November.

Barrow, hearing them, threatened to quit. If they wanted him to run their club, they should shut up and let him. If not, get somebody else.

Huston gave in. He promised to sell his half to Ruppert, and a few months later got $1,500,000 for it—more than six times what he had paid seven years before, more than 150 times what it had been worth only nineteen years before when it was transferred from Baltimore.

That gave Barrow a degree of authority a nonowner had rarely achieved. He and Huggins worked hand-in-glove in every respect. They were delighted. They promptly got two more prize pitchers from Boston (George Pipgras and Herb Pennock), won the 1923 pennant *and* the World Series, beating McGraw in their own Yankee Stadium. They drew 1,000,000 customers while the Giants, with the Polo Grounds all to themselves, drew 800,000.

Huggins, with total support upstairs, was in total command in the dugout. Steeped in the old ways of playing baseball, by his own experience as well as his Oriole training—run, steal, hit-and-run, hit 'em where they ain't—he adapted more quickly than anyone to the new reality implied by Ruth, the lively ball, and cleaned-up pitching. Don't decrease the chances of a big inning by running into unnecessary outs. Don't get upset by Babe's strikeouts, which were also reaching unprecedented totals, since they were the price of the homers. And since hitters would inevitably try to imitate Ruth's success, choose some who had long-ball capability, not merely long-ball desire.

As for pitching, the main thing was consistency rather than brilliance. You needed someone everyday who could keep you in the game until the hitters broke loose; you didn't have to rely on someone who could win 1–0 or 2–1. That meant a large number of good arms in a well-rested rotation, and patience with a starter in early-inning trouble.

However, neither hitting nor pitching would save you in the long run unless you also had first-rate fielding, getting all the outs your pitchers earned and giving your side a chance to come to bat not too far behind. So you chose good defensive players too.

Discipline, then, didn't mean a signal on every pitch, lots of orders to be followed blindly, or extra practice sessions. It meant be on time, stay in shape, play where and when you're asked, and accept instruction gracefully.

And that left one, and only one, problem to be confronted: Ruth himself.

He was, perhaps more than any athlete has ever been, larger than life. He was crude in manner and language, a glutton, a drinker, a tireless carouser, gregarious, fun-loving, "childlike" (if you include "unruly" and "Peck's Bad Boy" in your image of a child), self-centered (although not selfish), and a god in the eyes of the public. He was also kind, good-natured, smarter than his lack of education would lead you to think, a true lover of children and his profession, and (now) well-heeled.

He was, in short, a law unto himself. He had respect for Barrow, from the Boston days. He had no respect whatever for Huggins. How could he? The man was tiny and old (forty-four in 1924), spoke softly, used long words, couldn't punch anyone out. All the great success the Yankees were having was his, Ruth's, doing; what had Huggins ever done before he had Ruth? Managers had a place, he conceded, but that was because the other players needed one, not him.

Huggins didn't push him. Ruth didn't want to play "sun fields"— where the fielder has to look up into the sun—so he played left field or right, according to the ballpark. Huggins was glad to cater to such a preference, since eyesight was so basic an asset to hitting.

Miller Huggins

But during 1924, friction started to show. The Yankees had no easy time that season. There was a certain degree of over-confidence after three straight pennants, there were some key injuries, there was some fall-off in pitching efficiency. But more than anything, there was a team able to stay with them. The Washington Senators were hot from the start and the Detroit Tigers, in the best season they would ever have in the six years of Ty Cobb's managership, made it a three-team race through August. Then, in a furious stretch run, the Senators beat out the Yankees by 2 games.

Ruth had had another spectacular year (a .378 average, 46 homers), so the fault must have been Hug's, right? (Logic was not one of the Babe's strong points.) And in the middle of the Jazz Age, wasn't a man making more than $40,000 a year entitled to enjoy life even if his teammates didn't manage to finish first?

The Yankees went into 1925 at a high simmer.

For spring training, they went to St. Petersburg for the first time, joining Rickey's Cardinals. This sleepy retirement area offered less scope for Ruth and others for nonbaseball activities than New Orleans did, but it didn't slow them down entirely. On the way north, when the exhibition tour with the Dodgers reached Asheville, North Carolina, Ruth was suddenly hospitalized with the most famous stomachache of the 1920s. Amid all sorts of rumors about the direct cause or exact nature of his illness, the fact remained that he was quite sick and unable to start the season.

When he was able to play, about two weeks into the regular schedule, he was still weak and ineffective. But the whole team was coming apart. A difficulty we'll see again and again had arisen: The very players who had produced so many victories were aging and slowing down, yet too established to be discarded too precipitously. The 1925 Yankees were a ball club with weaknesses—and they weren't used to handling such a situation.

So instead of merely being inadequate, they turned out to be really bad. By the end of May, they were 10 games below .500; by the end of July, 15 under and solidly imbedded in seventh place. Ruth was hitting less than .250 with only 15 home runs.

He paid less and less attention to baseball and more and more to fun at night. Huggins would complain loudly in front of the others without citing Ruth by name; Ruth would tell him off, just as loudly, about what a lousy manager he was, second-guessing every decision, humiliating him with even more insults than in the past. The blow-off came in St. Louis in late August. Ruth, sleeping late after a late night, got to the clubhouse late and started to undress. Huggins told him not to bother.

"You're fined five thousand dollars and suspended indefinitely," Huggins told him.

Ruth couldn't believe it. Screaming that Huggins would never get away with it, he headed for New York within a couple hours to see Ruppert personally. His train journey was covered at every stop by press and radio with maximum hysteria. Five thousand dollars! Most players didn't make that much in a year. And suspended? The greatest drawing card in the world forbidden to appear in uniform?

He got off the train at Grand Central Station, greeted by a mob of reporters and cameras. They all went to his hotel. There he told them, in ringing terms, that he'd never play for the Yankees again as long as the manager was Huggins, who was trying to use him as an alibi for his own failings.

Then he went to the Ruppert Brewery, at Ninety-third Street and Third Avenue, for his private meeting with Barrow and the Colonel.

Huggins, of course, had talked to Barrow first, by telephone, before taking his action. Barrow had promised support as long as Huggins didn't back down. Huggins assured him he wouldn't.

So in the meeting, Barrow and Ruppert backed their manager 100 percent. A half-hour later, a contrite Ruth and a grim Ruppert faced the press. The fine stood. The suspension stood. Ruth would stay with the Yankees and report to Huggins when the team returned from the road trip. He would apologize and promise to behave.

The inmates would not run the asylum. Not in Yankee pinstripes, they wouldn't.

When the team did come home, Ruth did apologize. Huggins reinstated him and he played better the final month, raising his average to .290 and hitting 10 more homers, although the team never got out of seventh place. The fine was enforced. Never again did he give Huggins any trouble.

This crucial incident was no mere victory for Huggins, or even for the Yankees, although it was a turning point in the club's glorious history. It was a triumph for the office of field manager, serving the interest of all future managers everywhere.

Miller Huggins

No star can be any bigger than Ruth was; no star ever has been; but if the whole enterprise is to function, no star can be bigger than the manager. Huggins had the guts to establish the fact. He couldn't have done it alone, but he understood the implications thoroughly enough to have Barrow back him up, and that was the point. The manager doesn't have to be the smartest or the strongest man in the world, but he does have to *be* the manager. McGraw, bigger than any player, could always intimidate. Huggins proved a manager mustn't be intimidated.

The Mighty Mite

No one suspected, at the time of the Ruth suspension fuss, that Huggins had only four years to live. Yet, in those four years, Huggins nailed down the managerial principles he represented by unprecedented success, because in sports, victory certifies proper procedure and impels everyone to copy it.

During 1925, he had rebuilt the Yankees around Ruth. Lou Gehrig, Tony Lazzeri, Bob Meusel, Joe Dugan, and Benny Bengough were worked into the lineup. They won a tough pennant race in 1926, but lost a World Series to the Cardinals in the seventh game. Then, acquiring the name "Murderers Row," they won 110 games in 1927 as Ruth raised his home run record to 60, and swept Pittsburgh in 4 games in the World Series. And they won again in 1928, holding off the rising Philadelphia A's, and swept the Cardinals in 4 straight in the series.

Now Huggins had six pennants in eight years, and no one had ever done that, not even McGraw. He had two straight World Series sweeps, and no one had done that. Results like that meant that the "Mite Manager" was the official genius of the baseball world. McGraw was in decline after 1924; Mack had been in eclipse since 1914; and in New York, the articulate and "gentlemanly" Huggins was at the center of the nation's image-forming publicity mechanism. Ruth had become a well-behaved, solid citizen. The whole team radiated irresistible efficiency rather than flash, the glamor of excellence rather than colorful personalities.

Therefore, his way must be the way. What way was it?

1. In ball game terms, all the basic Hanlon-McGraw techniques adjusted for the lively ball.

The Developers

2. In handling men, calm and kind consideration for players' needs combined with hardheaded evaluations, along the lines of Mack.

3. A new, intimate relationship of perfect communication with a professional general manager who hired the scouts who procured the talent.

4. Unassailable authority exercised as necessary but not flaunted.

5. Pitching and defense, pitching and defense, pitching and defense, no matter how many sluggers also showed up.

In 1929, the Yankees seemed headed for a fourth straight pennant, but the A's had become too strong. By mid-August, the Yankees were 25 games over .500, a better-than-normal pennant pace, but the A's were 45 over. Meanwhile, from August on, Hug had been losing weight, getting sicker and sicker, suffering from a type of blood poisoning. Art Fletcher, once McGraw's favorite and much less fiery after his own managing experience, had become the third base coach in 1927, and he took over the team in September of 1929. On September 25 Huggins died at the age of forty-nine.

Most of Huggins's players had loved playing for him. Many had prospered following his sound investment advice in the years that "everyone" had gone into the stock market. Even Ruth was moved to tears. A monument to his memory was placed in Yankee Stadium's spacious center field, too far from home plate (490 feet then) to interfere with play. The practice field in St. Petersburg was named Huggins Field. They called Yankee Stadium "The House That Ruth Built." But the Yankee legend, which was to last into the 1960s, was the legend that Huggins built.

Miller Huggins
(National Baseball Library)

Joe McCarthy
(National Baseball Library)

Bill McKechnie
(National Baseball Library)

Casey Stengel (right) with Mickey Mantle
(New York Yankees)

Leo Durocher
(National Baseball Library)

Al Lopez
(National Baseball Library)

Frank Frisch
(National Baseball Library)

Cap Anson
(National Baseball Library)

Charles Comiskey
(National Baseball Library)

Harry Wright
(National Baseball Library)

John McGraw
(National Baseball Library)

Connie Mack
(National Baseball Library)

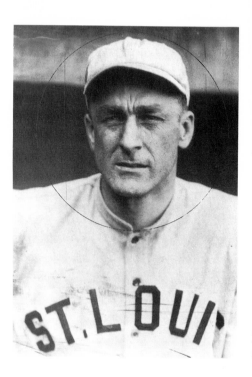

Branch Rickey
(National Baseball Library)

Earl Weaver
(Baltimore Orioles)

Sparky Anderson
(Cincinnati Reds)

Tommy Lasorda
(Los Angeles Dodgers, A. Bernstein)

Whitey Herzog
(St. Louis Cardinals)

Tony La Russa
(Oakland Athletics)

Roger Craig
(San Francisco Giants)

Walt Alston
(National Baseball Library)

Clark Griffith
(National Baseball Library)

Paul Richards
(National Baseball Library)

Ralph Houk
(Detroit Tigers)

Alvin Dark
(San Francisco Giants)

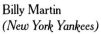

Dick Williams (right) with Reggie Jackson
(Oakland Tribune)

Billy Martin
(New York Yankees)

6

Joe McCarthy

Chicago

What Huggins started, Joe McCarthy took to even greater heights, but he was a distinctly different man with a different kind of history. Still, there were similarities also, and they involved more continuity than simply the Yankee uniform.

McCarthy never did reach the major leagues as a player, the first one of the principals in this book to become a great manager anyhow, but not the last. He was born in 1887 in Philadelphia and grew up there, playing sandlot and high school ball. He went to Niagara University in Buffalo but, after two years, committed himself to a baseball career. He was fairly short and stocky, five feet eight inches, 170 pounds, played infield and outfield, and hit fairly well without power, making his living with his glove. Turning pro in 1907, he needed only two years to reach Triple-A level, at Toledo, but he never got any higher. Settling in as a second baseman, he found himself down a notch at Wilkes-Barre in 1912, and the next year managed that team at the age of twenty-five. Then he moved back up to Triple-A at Buffalo in the International League in 1914 and 1915. Ed Barrow, still president of the league at that time, recommended him to the Yankees, but McCarthy decided to sign with Brooklyn of the Federal League—which never opened for the 1916 season. So he went to Louisville of the American Association, and that's where he made his reputation.

He became known as one of the best fielders and smartest players in the league. In the middle of the 1919 season, he was made the manager, won a pennant in 1921, and another in 1925. He was widely regarded as the best manager in the minor leagues, comfortably settled and relatively well paid in Louisville.

The Chicago Cubs, at this time, had fallen on evil days. Their status as perennial, or at least frequent, contenders had been taken for granted for nearly half a century, from 1876, when the league started, through 1919, when they finished third after winning the abbreviated 1918 pennant race. But as the lively-ball 1920s began, they fell to fifth, seventh, fifth, fourth, fifth, and (in 1925) eighth. William Wrigley, the chewing gum magnate, had purchased the club in 1918, and this was not what he had in mind. In 1919, he installed William Veeck (Senior) as club president, and they had tried five different managers without getting anywhere.

John B. Foster, the editor of the Spalding Guides, with whom McGraw had had such conflict the previous decade, suggested McCarthy. Wrigley offered him the job and McCarthy took it, aware that he was risking the security he had built up in Louisville.

Taking over a last-place team, and aware of what big league ballplayers think of someone who was never one of them, McCarthy knew that the first thing he had to do was establish his authority. The biggest name on the Cubs was Grover Cleveland Alexander, generally accepted as the best pitcher in the National League since Mathewson, but now in his late thirties and a notorious drinker (which he had not been in his earlier years). McCarthy had understood fully what the Ruth-Huggins conflict of the previous year meant in terms of managing. So he pointedly got rid of Alex by putting him on waivers. The Cardinals claimed him, got 9 victories out of him that helped them win the 1926 pennant, and won the World Series with him as the hero in the seventh game. (He relieved with the bases full and a one-run lead in the seventh inning, struck out Lazzeri, and closed out the 4–3 victory.) The Cubs finished a respectable fourth, but no one on McCarthy's team doubted who was in charge.

McCarthy also understood that this was the age of power, and that Wrigley Field—the ballpark built by the Federal League that the Cubs occupied as their home in 1916—was often a hitter's heaven when the wind blew out. He started to collect hitters: squat Hack Wilson, sent back to the minors by McGraw in 1925, Riggs Stephenson, Kiki Cuyler. He already had Charlie Grimm at first base and Gabby Hartnett catching. As he worked to put together a pitching staff, he finished fourth in 1926 and 1927, and third in 1928.

After the 1928 season, he told Veeck and Wrigley that if they got Rogers Hornsby they could win the pennant. They listened, and sent $200,000 plus five players to Boston to deliver. McCarthy also delivered. With Hornsby hitting .380, the Cubs won the 1929 pennant by 10½ games, running away from the Pirates in the last two months. In the World Series, they were the victims of three historic feats by Mack's A's—Ehmke's 13 strikeouts in the opener, a 10-run inning in the fourth game, and a 3-run bottom of the ninth in the fifth game—and were trounced. But the first Cub pennant since 1918 was not to be sneered at.

Then McCarthy discovered a baseball truth of his time: He who lives by the Hornsby, dies by the Hornsby. Usually described as the best right-handed batter who ever lived, Hornsby was also an exceptionally plain-spoken, uncompromising, pull-no-punches type of man with ultimate confidence in his own opinions, not as smart as he thought he was, and guaranteed to not get along with anyone he worked for or (as a manager) anyone who worked for him. In St. Louis, he had replaced Rickey as manager during the 1925 season and won the World Series in 1926. Unwelcome even after that, he was traded to the Giants and acted as manager when McGraw was sick, alienating the owner, Horace Stoneham, enough to get himself traded to Boston. There, early in the 1928 season, he supplanted Jack Slattery as manager after only 31 games and led the team to a 50–103 record even though he hit .387 himself and had George Sisler hitting .340 as his first baseman.

In 1930, McCarthy became convinced that Hornsby was after his job and trying to undermine him. The National League baseball, that year, was juiced up beyond reason—the whole league hit .303 and the last-place Phillies .315—so whatever degree of advantage Cub power provided was a relatively smaller factor. In an eventful four-team race involving the Cardinals, Giants, and Dodgers, the Cubs wound up second to St. Louis by 2 games. But 4 games before the schedule ended, when they were out of it, McCarthy quit in disgust and Hornsby took over. (In 1931, Hornsby brought the Cubs in third, 17 games behind the Cardinals, and in 1932, after he was replaced in midseason by Grimm, the Cubs came on and won the pennant.)

Within days, McCarthy had a new job, and a better one.

At the 1930 World Series, he met with Ruppert and Barrow. After the death of Huggins, they had turned to Bob Shawkey, their veteran pitcher, as manager for 1930. The team ran a distant third (8 games behind Washington, 16 behind the A's) and they wanted someone else, someone closer to Huggins in character. McCarthy had shown many of the managerial traits they were looking for:

The Developers

sound tactics, stable atmosphere, ability to handle stars (except Hornsby) and to operate a homer-powered machine, an infielder's outlook, a low-key ego. And, as perhaps the most important factor, he could have the same close working relationship with Barrow, since they knew each other from International League days and enjoyed mutual respect.

Of course, Ruth wanted the job and had said so openly. Some of his teammates and much of the press and public felt the same way. McCarthy would have an even bigger prima donna problem on his hands than Hornsby. But he and Barrow were confident he could handle it, and Ruppert, having acquired a wisdom so many owners resist, was confident that any decision Barrow made would be right.

McCarthy became the eleventh manager of the Yankees. He would hold that job longer than anyone else, before or since.

New York

Ruppert's idea of "a good ball game" was one in which the Yankees scored 11 runs in the first inning, then pulled away. He told McCarthy, not really in jest, that he had one year of grace as a newcomer to the American League, but he'd better finish first after that. McCarthy took him at his word. The 1931 A's were uncatchable at 107–45 and the Yankees finished second, $13\frac{1}{2}$ games out. But that showed McCarthy what you had to do to win, so in 1932 *his* team won 107 (and lost 47) and finished 13 ahead of Philadelphia. Evidently, Joe was a fast learner. He then had the satisfaction of winning the World Series in 4 straight against the Cubs, who had fired Hornsby in midseason, having replaced him at second base too with a young fellow named Billy Herman.

This was the Babe's last truly Ruthian season. At thirty-eight, he hit .341 with 41 homers, and hit his famous "called shot" homer in the World Series at Wrigley Field. As his production dropped off sharply in the next two years, his desire to manage became stronger and more openly stated.

But McCarthy, as the Babe and the other Yankees found out right from the start, was a much stricter boss than Huggins had been. He didn't have petty rules and he didn't try to micromanage a ball game à la McGraw, but he was perpetually at war with any hint of complacency or frivolous behavior. In spring training the first year, he made it clear he wanted victories and all-out effort even in exhibition games. When they got to the stadium, he not only ruled out card-playing in the clubhouse but had the equipment man smash the card table with an ax in front of the players to make his point.

"This is a clubhouse, not a clubroom," he told them. "In here I want you to have your minds on baseball and nothing else."

He put in a dress code: ties and jackets when on the road, the idea being to build self-respect and a self-image of pride in being "classy" and "special." (In the 1930s, it was still considered "improper" for respectable men to walk around without ties, jackets, and hats.) He was not chatty with his players, although he didn't embarrass them with criticism in front of others, and in everything he did hammered away at the central theme: Think baseball.

All this left Ruth with little room for maneuver or complaint. McCarthy showed him all the respect and consideration he was due as baseball's living legend, with full acknowledgment of his elder statesman status—but McCarthy ran the club in such a businesslike and fair manner, there was little to second-guess.

What's more, the old cronies who might have rallied around Ruth were quickly being replaced. Ruth had always been a loner, as far as his teammates were concerned, in afterhour activities, but he had certainly been a role model for other fun lovers. The new players coming into the McCarthy regime were not going to follow that example if McCarthy could prevent it.

On that 1932 team, his top pitchers were Lefty Gomez, a skinny left-hander from California with a Hall of Fame fast ball and a Hall of Fame wit, who was 21–9 as a rookie the year before and 27–7 now; Red Ruffing, the last great steal from Boston, engineered by Barrow on Shawkey's advice, who was transformed from a 9–22 Red Sox pitcher in 1929 to an 18–7 Yankee in 1932; Pipgras, and an aging Pennock. McCarthy had a young Italian second base combination in the experienced Lazzeri and the newcomer Frank Crosetti at short, with Lazzeri already something of a cult hero to New York's Italian community as "Poosh-'em up Tony." He had a new outfielder, Ben Chapman, who would lead the league in stolen bases. Earle Combs, the centerfielder who was a holdover from Murderer's Row, had played for McCarthy at Louisville. The dynamic young catcher who could hit and throw, Bill Dickey, had

The Developers

arrived only in 1929. And Lou Gehrig, now the second-ranking veteran to Ruth, was as nonpolitical a person as one could imagine, totally different from Ruth in quiet life-style and work ethic, and no particular buddy of the Babe's anyhow.

The Babe was isolated and McCarthy knew how to keep him that way. But when Ruth slowed down in 1933 and 1934, the Yankees weren't the team they had been with him at full power. They ran second to Washington in 1933 and to Detroit (where Mickey Cochrane had become player-manager) in 1934. At the end of that season, Babe made one more pitch, directly to Ruppert, to replace McCarthy. Instead, he was offered a chance to manage the minor league club they had acquired at Newark, at the top of the farm system under construction. He turned that down and made a deal for himself with the Boston Braves, as player, assistant manager, and vice-president. The Yankees let him go, and McCarthy was finally beyond challenge.

In 1935, the Yankees finished second again, behind the Tigers. In Boston, Ruth played only about a month, and after an amazing 3-homer game in Pittsburgh, retired.

Marse Joe

In five years, McCarthy had developed two close relationships, one with Barrow, one with Art Fletcher, who had stayed on as his third base coach. They had managed against each other in 1926, when Fletch had finished last with the Phils, and the one-time brash tormentor and later pet of McGraw had no further taste for being a manager. He was the perfect second-in-command for McCarthy. Barrow, meanwhile, had been working on the farm system idea Rickey had profitted from in St. Louis. When the Cardinals won pennants in 1930 and 1931, the rest of the baseball world—always ready to mimic a winner—started to pay attention to the much-maligned and Landis-opposed format. That winter, a friend sold Ruppert the Newark franchise and Barrow, with his unerring eye for talent, hired George Weiss, a longtime minor league operator he didn't particularly like as a person, to run it. Weiss began propagandizing his bosses to get more clubs and start a full-fledged chain, and they finally agreed. McCarthy, hitherto consulted on trades and purchases from the high minors, was now being consulted on farm club promotion decisions too, increasing his already excellent communication with Barrow.

Joe McCarthy

However, in five years, McCarthy had won only one pennant. After three straight years as runner-up, he was being called "second-place Joe." He had brought in some younger players, and the farm system was about ready to produce a bumper crop, but the missing piece wasn't there yet.

It arrived in 1936, named Joe DiMaggio. Barrow's scouts had recommended purchasing him from San Francisco for a big price ($25,000 and players) even when a leg injury put his career in doubt. Barrow paid it for future delivery and in 1936 a healthy DiMaggio rode across the country in a car with Crosetti and Lazzeri, not telling them until Utah (when they first asked him) that he couldn't take his turn at the wheel because he had never learned to drive.

With DiMaggio added, the Yankees won four straight World Series in 1936–39, finishing first by margins of 19½, 13, 9½, and 17 games. That matched McGraw's string of four pennants, but the four world championships were unprecedented: 4–2 and 4–1 over the Giants, 4–0 over the Cubs and Reds.

In 1940, in the aftermath of the emotional shock of losing Gehrig to illness the previous year, the Yankees floundered for four months, made a terrific pennant run, but wound up third behind Detroit and Cleveland by a narrow margin. Then they reeled off three more pennants, beating the Dodgers in the 1941 World Series, getting upset by the Cardinals in 1942, and beating them in 1943 when most of baseball's stars were away at war.

Seven pennants in eight years! McCarthy was no longer second-place Joe. He was now Marse Joe, intended as a good-natured term in an era still insensitive to ethnic and racial slurs, as in "Master Joe" of the plantation spoken with a slave's accent. It was a double reference. The plantation simile came from his function at the top of the farm system, now spewing forth stars in incredible profusion: Joe Gordon, Charlie Keller, Spud Chandler, Phil Rizzuto, and a dozen others in an apparently endless stream. At the same time, his strict, firm command of all baseball activities fit the overseer image. He didn't crack the whip, but every player knew he had it in his hand.

It's the Marse Joe persona that concerns us here.

McGraw had played favorites, developing pets and hates; Mack seemed to like everyone he kept (and quickly got rid of those he didn't). Rickey dealt in huge numbers and wasn't in the dugout anyhow. But McCarthy, always keeping a certain distance from his players, had no pets. He gave special attention to young players, to hasten their improvement; he gave full measure of respect to the older ones; but he offered no special privileges and didn't have a doghouse (as players called the condition of being in trouble with the boss). He wanted everyone concentrating only on baseball, and he led that by example. Personal feelings were minimized.

As a tactician and teacher, he was an expert on infield play and defense in general, incorporating Fletcher's McGraw-ingrained basics but following the big-inning philosophy set down by Huggins. McCarthy expected men to play hurt and abhorred alibis, but he was not unreasonable or sadistic about it. He believed in choosing a lineup and letting it play (and why not, with the talent he had available?). He rarely platooned. Jimmy Dykes called him a "push-button manager" half in jest, and McCarthy was offended by that idea. But he did have tremendous resources at his fingertips—and knew exactly how to use them.

McCarthy had his own ways of using psychology. Here's an example Crosetti told me about fifty years after the event.

In the 1930s, the pregame infield drill was conducted with such verve and all-out effort that fans used to watch it as a show in itself. It was in line with McCarthy's bear-down-in-training theory, and part of the mental preparation for a ball game beyond the routine need to loosen up.

One day he said to Cro:

"I want you to do me a favor. Lou [Gehrig] has been dragging a bit lately. I don't want to talk to him about it, but I'd like to see something pep him up. When you do infield, throw real hard to him, and talk it up. With your help, we can wake him up."

Crosetti did as he was told, chattering and firing the ball hard, especially at close range. At first, Gehrig looked at him as if he'd gone crazy. Then Lou started to fire back, and to get mad. Finally, after a couple of days, he yelled at Crosetti, "What's got into you?" He also got a bunch of hits in those games (which was nothing unusual), and Cro made peace with him, and things went back to normal.

The plan had worked, and Crosetti was proud of himself and of the confidence McCarthy had put in him.

Many years later, Crosetti and McCarthy met at an Oldtimers Game, and reminisced about the incident.

McCarthy laughed. "Now I can tell you," he said. "There wasn't anything wrong with Gehrig. You were the one who needed pepping up, and that was my way of doing it."

Another example isn't as benign, but it does show McCarthy's obsession with never enough victories and "class" as a motivational tool.

In 1939, the day before Gehrig played his last game (on April 30), DiMaggio tore up his ankle in the muddy Yankee Stadium outfield and was out of action for more than a month. He didn't play again until June 7, then started to hit better than ever.

On September 1, the Yankees had a 13½-game lead and Joe was hitting well over .400. He peaked at .410 on September 3, after a double-header in Boston, with 25 games to play.

He caught a bad cold, and it led to a sinus condition that interfered somewhat with his vision. He started to slump, and within a week his average was down to .401—still leading the league by a comfortable margin.

He suggested that he might sit out a few games until he felt better. The pennant was safe, after all.

"I think you should keep playing, Joe," McCarthy said. "If you sit down and win the batting title, they'll call you a cheese champ."

DiMaggio continued to play. In the last 25 games, he hit .266, and finished (as batting champion and Most Valuable Player) at .381.

"But if I'd taken a few days off, I might have hit .400 two years before Williams did," he would say, half a century later.

At the time, though, he made no complaint and no excuses. He didn't like McCarthy's decision, but had no intention of disputing it or even putting up a serious argument about it.

But the "cheese champ" argument was nonsense, and McCarthy knew it. Nobody would have questioned DiMaggio sitting out a few games with a legitimate illness, then coming back strong. What McCarthy really wanted was DiMaggio playing every day and contributing to victories—even with a 16-game lead. The Yankees clinched on September 16, but DiMaggio kept on playing right through to the end even after that. The Yankees finished 106–45, including a 19–7 September.

Marse Joe wanted results.

And he wasn't afraid to experiment. He was one of the first to pick up fully on the relief-specialist technique, and used Johnny Murphy that way in the 1936–39 period. Murphy earned the name "Fireman" in the press (for coming in and putting out the fire) and "Grandma" in the clubhouse (because of his fussy manner). But McCarthy also was flexible about pitching rotation, preferring to give adequate rest. When Ruffing got older, McCarthy used him as

The Developers

a "Sunday pitcher," with six days off between starts. In winning those 107 games in 1939, he used eight different starting pitchers, none making more than Ruffing's 28 starts and the others no fewer than 11. The two years before that, without quite such even distribution, had had used twelve starters in each.

He shifted Joe Gordon, the most acrobatic second baseman of his or any other day, to first base, and although he was a right-handed power hitter in Yankee Stadium, used him to lead off for a while. He used Ruffing as his preferred right-handed pinch hitter.

Nevertheless, he didn't preside over a club with a solemn atmosphere. The Yankees became perceived as arrogant, annoyingly confident, with superior airs, and inhuman in their mechanical efficiency, radiating wealth and power, welcoming the cry of "Break up the Yankees" they heard everywhere. But among themselves they enjoyed a cheerful tone when it wasn't actually ball playing time. Gomez alone would be enough to lighten any environment, as thousands of afterdinner listeners found out when his playing career ended. But Tommy Henrich, who signed for a bonus after Landis freed a bunch of Cleveland farmhands in 1937 in one of his raids on the farm system, was also a jovial sort. So was Red Rolfe, the third baseman from Dartmouth, and Joe Gordon, and others. They played bridge on the trains instead of poker (because McCarthy had put a limit on stakes), they sang, they went to the theater in New York and movies everywhere, they ate in the good restaurants, and needled each other into bearing down before McCarthy would have to call them on it—which was the way he wanted it.

Gomez found ways to tease him, just enough. McCarthy didn't want smoking in the clubhouse. One day in Fenway Park, that death trap for left-handers, Gomez was waiting around as the starting pitcher and sneaked out of the visitors' dressing room for a smoke. He was sitting in the phone booth across from the clubhouse door, puffing away, when McCarthy came out. (Someone had squealed.)

"What do you think you're doing?" Marse Joe demanded.

"I'm pitching today, right, Skipper?" Gomez said.

"Yes, and why aren't you in the clubhouse?"

"I'm in here," said Gomez, indicating the phone booth, "trying to acclimate myself to the ballpark."

"Bah, get inside," ordered McCarthy—but he couldn't help laughing.

Gomez was in no more awe of Mack, for that matter. He had been chosen to start the first All-Star Game in 1933, and Mack went into his usual routine of going over the opposition's hitters in a pregame meeting. How to pitch to each hitter, after all, was Mack's main stock in trade.

"Frisch, fast-ball hitter; Traynor, fast-ball hitter," started Mack, going down the starting lineup, warning them what to avoid. "Medwick, fast-ball hitter; Cuyler, fast-ball hitter; Berger, fast-ball hitter; Terry, fast-ba—

"Mr. Mack," Gomez broke in, "Maybe you'd better get another starter. A fast ball is all I've got." P. S.: Gomez was the winning pitcher.

Solemnity was never a problem when Gomez was around. During the war he worked in a war plant. How was it?

"It was strange," he said. "I work all day and there's no Murphy to relieve me."

And this aspect of team spirit was an important ingredient in Yankee success, for a well-concealed reason.

Through all this, McCarthy had a personal problem hidden from the public but not from his players. He was a heavy drinker, a solitary drinker. He kept the habit under control and it didn't interfere with his work for a long time, but during the war it started to catch up with him. The Yankees of 1944 and 1945 were nondescript, and it was hard for him to handle the situation.

Meanwhile, changes were piling up. Ruppert had died in January of 1939, with Barrow assuming the club presidency. Weiss was more autonomous as farm director. The heirs (Ruppert had never married) were ready to sell, but the war set back such plans. Landis died in 1944. Early that year both Barrow, now seventy-six, and McCarthy, now fifty-seven, had serious illnesses.

And in February 1945, the club was sold, for $3,000,000 to a three-man partnership: Dan Topping, usually described as a "millionaire sportsman" and heir to a tin plate fortune, well known in cafe society and still in service in the Marines; Del Webb, a self-made millionaire contractor from Arizona; and—just released from his army duties—Leland Stanford MacPhail, erstwhile baseball operator in Columbus, Cincinnati, and Brooklyn and a headline maker of unparalleled skill.

MacPhail would run the club (as he would any club he had), and Barrow retired. Weiss stayed. Lights would be installed on the Yankee Stadium roof. A brand-new concept called the Sta-

The Developers

dium Club—a restaurant and bar for season-ticket patrons—would be introduced.

For the 1946 season, all the stars were back from the war. But none of the conditions McCarthy had enjoyed for fifteen years existed. Old, not well, hiding his drinking less, he could hardly be "Marse Joe" to men coming back from World War II. His rapport with the front office was shattered. On May 21, 1946, he resigned and Bill Dickey, still active as a catcher, took over.

Boston

All through 1947, McCarthy stayed home in Buffalo. He turned sixty, he was fixed financially, and his health improved. Meanwhile, some changes were taking place in Boston. Joe Cronin, managing the Red Sox since 1935 (and spending most of that time chasing McCarthy's Yankees without catching them), had finally won a pennant in 1946. Now, after the 1947 season, he was moving up to the front office as general manager. The Red Sox had exactly the kind of power club that had been McCarthy's trademark but had a traditional—not to say notorious—reputation as a "country club" under Cronin's genial and teammate-oriented regime. It seemed a good fit, and Cronin offered him the job.

McCarthy accepted. His departure from the Yankees had been tinged with ill feeling, and their World Series victory of 1947 (under Bucky Harris) didn't make McCarthy feel any better. What better way to restore his own status than to beat them with the Boston team he had always beaten? (McCarthy's ego was low-key and never flaunted, but he did have one.)

He almost did it. His 1948 Red Sox beat back the Yankees in a September drive, eliminating them on the next-to-last day, but finished in a tie with Cleveland—and the Indians won the 1-game playoff by having their playing manager, Lou Boudreau, hit 2 homers and 2 singles. How could a bench manager outthink that?

And in 1949, McCarthy brought the Red Sox to Yankee Stadium for the final 2 games of the season with a 1-game lead—and lost both in such dramatic circumstances that best-selling books were still recreating that pennant race forty years later.

In June of 1950, with the Red Sox in second place, McCarthy resigned and retired to Buffalo. (Actually, his home was in nearby Tonawanda.) He was elected to the Hall of Fame in 1957 and in

Joe McCarthy

1976, to mark his eighty-ninth birthday, a plaque honoring him was placed on the centerfield wall of the just rebuilt and reopened Yankee Stadium, alongside monuments to Huggins, Ruppert, Ruth, Gehrig, and Barrow.

In our family tree diagram, we place McCarthy on the Mack branch, for one excellent reason. "Connie Mack was my idol," he told Donald Honig in 1977. Beyond that, his basic method—identify the good ones, let them play, don't embarrass them, and be kind to pitchers—was derived from Mack, even though he never actually worked for him. And the McGraw principles of hit-and-run, steal, antagonize, and challenge were never a part of his *modus operandi.*

He died in 1978, at the age of ninety.

7

Bill McKechnie

A CONSERVATIVE'S LIBERAL EDUCATION

If Miller Huggins came across as a "gentleman" and Branch Rickey as "devout," Bill McKechnie combined the two. They called him "Deacon," and everybody knew he didn't drink, cuss, or raise his voice, although he did play on Sundays. But the adjective *nice,* which Leo Durocher would contend consigned a person to finishing last, didn't prevent Deacon Bill from winning pennants with three different clubs and being voted Manager of the Year in a season when his team finished in the second division. A string of titles with one organization, like the Yankees is one thing. Three with three different sets of people is a harder achievement.

McKechnie also finished last, but only once in twenty-five years of major league managing.

And his baseball life was intertwined with virtually every significant figure in major league history between 1910 and 1950.

He was born in 1887 in Wilkinsburg, Pennsylvania, where he became a member of the church choir as a boy and remained active in it for twenty-five years. His parents had come from Scotland and took their religion seriously. He was a Methodist.

At eighteen, instead of going to college, he signed a pro baseball contract with Washington—Washington, Pennsylvania, that is, in the Pennsylvania-Ohio-Maryland League. He was an infielder who couldn't hit much but was a good glove man. Within two years, he got a brief look (three games) at Pittsburgh, where Clarke and Wagner were in their heyday, but spent the next two years back in the minors. In 1910, he came back to the Pirates to stay, as a utility infielder. He was a switch-hitter, of ordinary size (five feet 10 inches, 180 pounds) and a good fielder, In 1912, however, he was shipped back to the minors to St. Paul. At the end of the season he was drafted by the Boston Braves, who let him start 1913 there, called him up after 32 games, had him play 1 game for them in the majors, and let him go on waivers to the New York Yankees, for whom he played 44 games before the season ended.

It's not surprising that in 1914, he figured he had better opportunities in the new Federal League, and he was right. As the third baseman of the Indianapolis team, he hit .305 for the pennant winner. The next year, Indianapolis was replaced by Newark, and both McKechnie and his Indianapolis manager, Bill Phillips, went there. In June, still only twenty-seven years old, McKechnie replaced Phillips as manager for the rest of the year. Then there was no more Federal League.

McGraw signed McKechnie and his best Newark player, Edd Roush, for the Giants in 1915. In July, he sent both of them with Mathewson to Cincinnati for Buck Herzog, so that Matty could manage. The three stayed at Cincinnati through 1917, then Mathewson went to war and McKechnie was sold to Pittsburgh. He played 126 games at third base in the war-shortened season, his only experience as a major league regular (not counting the Federal League), and in 1919 was out of baseball altogether.

Let's review his baseball education to this point.

At Pittsburgh he had been exposed to Clarke and Wagner. Phillips, his Federal League manager, had been a pitcher for Cincinnati under Joe Kelley, then fresh from his Oriole experience. Even half a year under McGraw, at the peak of his powers in 1916, meant a lot, and in Mathewson he was serving with and under one of the top pitching minds of the time, McGraw-oriented. A cerebral sort himself, McKechnie was absorbing high-quality pitching lore from Mathewson and Phillips, and thinking about how to apply it. He was also being well schooled in the percentage play the Oriole tradition had universalized. Not being a big talker, he was a fine listener.

In 1920, McKechnie returned to the Pirates as a utility infielder. Their manager now was George Gibson, a prominent catcher for Clarke's teams (1905–16) and McGraw (1917–18). In 1921, at the age of thirty-five, McKechnie wound up his playing career back in the minors at Minneapolis, and rejoined the Pirates in 1922 as one of Gibson's coaches.

PITTSBURGH

In July, with the team in sixth place at 32–33, Gibson was fired and McKechnie named in his place. He went 53–36 the rest of the way and finished a strong third behind the Giants. On his team were some impressive players: Charlie Grimm at first base, Rabbit Maranville at shortstop, a young Pie Traynor at third base, Max Carey in center field, Wilbur Cooper pitching.

The next year, he added Kiki Cuyler to the outfield and moved Maranville to second to make room for shortstop Glenn Wright. The Pirates finished third again, and again in 1924 as the Giants ran their pennant string to four straight.

And in 1925, the Pirates won everything, their first pennant since 1909 and the World Series in 7 games from the Senators. McKechnie had traded Grimm, Maranville, and Cooper, his free spirits, to the Cubs for Granny Grantham, a second baseman he switched to first, and Vic Aldridge, a pitcher.

But 1926 brought trouble. While Huggins was wrestling with his Ruthian problem in New York, McKechnie had a rebellion of his own to deal with. Dreyfuss had brought back Clarke, still one of his stockholders, as a coach in 1925. For 1926 he appointed Clarke vice-president and assistant manager. A better design for disruption could hardly be imagined. Administratively, Clarke outranked McKechnie, and was stuck with his perception of Bill as one of his inferior young players. In the dugout, McKechnie was supposed to be boss, but there was Clarke, also in uniform, loudly second-guessing and criticizing players, who were getting very mixed signals. Carey, the team captain, called a meeting to resolve the situation and the squad voted 18–6 for Clarke. When the news reached Dreyfuss, vacationing in Europe, he resolved to clean house. Carey was suspended and waived to Brooklyn; other players were released; Clarke sold his stock and went back to his ranch in Kansas; and McKechnie, whom Dreyfuss had supported strongly, wouldn't be around any longer either. Leaving what had been an impossible situation, he joined Rickey as a coach with the Cardinals, who had won the 1926 World Series under Hornsby and had then turned to Bob O'Farrell as manager after trading Hornsby to the Giants.

ST. LOUIS

Rickey, needless to say, had high regard for McKechnie's religion and demeanor, but also recognized how expert he had become in handling pitchers. O'Farrell was a catcher for nine years with the

Bill McKechnie

Cubs before coming to St. Louis, and had been the one to end the 1926 World Series (after Alexander's famous seventh-inning strikeout of Lazzeri) by throwing out Babe Ruth trying to steal second with the score 3–2 and two out in the last of the ninth at Yankee Stadium. (Ruth, who had walked, revealed the basic mindset of baseball in the early stages of even the lively-ball era: "I wasn't going to do any ——ing good on first," he explained.) So O'Farrell knew something about pitchers too.

In 1927, the strong Pittsburgh team McKechnie had built, managed by Donie Bush, beat out the Cardinals by $1\frac{1}{2}$ games for the privilege of being swept by the Murderers Row Yankees. Breadon, the owner, was disenchanted with O'Farrell, who was criticized for leaving starters in too long, and wanted him replaced. Rickey preferred McKechnie anyhow. So they gave O'Farrell a $5,000 raise to return to catching only, made McKechnie the manager, and unloaded O'Farrell and his big contract to the Giants in May.

Under McKechnie, the Cardinals won the 1928 pennant and took their turn at being wiped out by the Yankees.

McKechnie's way with pitchers was getting results. He handled the aging and unreliable Alexander well enough to get 16 victories out of him. He helped Bill Sherdel (21 victories) and Flint Rhem improve, and had another 20-game winner in Jesse Haines.

Breadon, overriding Rickey again, reacted to the World Series sweep the same way he did the year before. He demoted McKechnie to managing the top farm club at Rochester, and brought up Billy Southworth, who had managed that team in 1928 after his fine career as an outfielder had ended with the 1927 Cardinals. It was a mistake, and as the Cardinals sank below .500 in July of 1929, Breadon acknowledged it and let Rickey bring McKechnie back, with Southworth returning to Rochester.

The Cardinals finished fourth, and McKechnie did not take the humiliation in stride. When offered a three-year contract by the Boston Braves, he got Breadon's permission to take it. He'd rather be in charge of a bad club (which Boston certainly was) than a yo-yo in the hands of an owner of a good club.

BOSTON

The Braves were, indeed, bad. They had just finished last after three straight years in seventh. In 1928, they had switched to

The Developers

Hornsby in midseason without improvement. In 1929, they were managed part of the time by their owner, Judge Emil Fuchs, and Maranville. Fuchs was searching desperately for stability, let alone improvement, and McKechnie would be a healing force.

He was, and stayed for eight years, making the club somewhat more respectable but never a winner. It got as high as fourth in 1933 and 1934 but slipped back to eighth in 1935, the year that started out with the complexities of Ruth's arrival and retirement. After finishing sixth and fifth the next two years, McKechnie was ready to listen to a better offer.

It came from Cincinnati. MacPhail had left to go to Brooklyn, and the new general manager was Warren Giles, who had been in charge of the Rochester club when McKechnie was sent there in 1929. He was a Rickey disciple. Right after World War I, he had entered minor league baseball as an executive in Moline, Illinois, and was running a successful team in St. Joseph's, Missouri, when Rickey—building the St. Louis farm system—hired him to take charge of the top of the chain at Syracuse (the franchise that was moved to Rochester in 1928).

By the public, the self-effacing McKechnie was considered nothing special, but within the baseball community he was highly regarded and fully appreciated. Giles had taken over a franchise MacPhail had put on its feet financially (with night baseball and other innovations) but not yet competitively. It had tried a lot of managers, including Donie Bush, Bob O'Farrell, Burt Shotton, and Charley Dressen (whom Giles had fired as a player in Moline back in 1919), while finishing last four years in a row in 1931–34. Dressen got it up to sixth and fifth under MacPhail, but in 1937 it was back to last. Giles fired Dressen again. Yet, there were some good players being accumulated. They needed a teacher and a guide, especially one who knew pitchers.

McKechnie was clearly the man Giles needed.

CINCINNATI

It took McKechnie one year to lift the Reds to fourth place, winning 82 games instead of 56 (the 1937 total), and one more to win the pennant, seizing a lead in May and finishing comfortably ahead of the Cardinals, Dodgers, and Cubs. In the World Series, McKechnie was swept again by a superstar Yankee team, but in

Bill McKechnie

1940, after finishing far ahead of MacPhail's refurbished Dodgers, he won a 7-game World Series against Detroit.

The next year, both the Dodgers and the Cardinals passed McKechnie, and in the war years the Reds clung to the first division. But when everyone's stars started coming back in 1945 and 1946, the Reds sank to seventh and sixth and McKechnie's managerial career was over. He was fifty-nine.

What kind of career had it been?

He was the purest of pure "book" managers, playing the percentages in every circumstance. This was considered stodgy by some, but those who felt that way didn't understand what McKechnie had learned: The "percentages" will work for you only if you *do* stick to them consistently; otherwise, you're just trying to outguess random fluctuations. If you follow them only sometimes, you don't give them the chance to produce the benefits they are supposed to contain. McGraw might operate on brilliant intuition. Huggins and McCarthy might rely on power. McKechnie's best chance was to follow the book.

And he arrived at that view by a process that Huggins, Rickey, and McCarthy had traversed. As a player, he had only limited talent and had to survive by thinking rather than by physical ability. As an infielder (like Huggins and McCarthy; Rickey was a catcher), he lived in the middle of the action with lots of opportunity to note what had to be figured out at close range. This, in turn, made him knowledgable about the relation between pitching and position play, and a fine instructor of infielders.

We'll see the same background forging winners out of Sparky Anderson, Earl Weaver, Billy Martin, and others.

Most of all, however, McKechnie became an expert handler of pitching staffs and developer of individual pitchers to their full potential.

His Cardinal pennant winner of 1928 had a strong orthodox four-man rotation. But his 1925 Pirates had used five: a 19-game winner (Lee Meadows), three 17-game winners, and a 15-game winner, all making between 26 and 31 starts.

At Boston, despite the team's weakness, he turned Lou Fette and Jim Turner, overage rookies (past thirty) in 1937 into simultaneous 20-game winners on a team that won only 39 other games—a fact Giles noted.

At Cincinnati, he inherited a truly great pitcher in Paul Derringer, and a rookie fireballer named Johnny Vander Meer who promptly pitched consecutive ho-hitters. And just before the trading deadline in 1938, he and Giles got Bucky Walters from Philadelphia for $50,000 and two regulars, even though Walters had been converted to pitching less than four years before after four seasons as an infielder. He had records of 9–9, 11–21, 14–15, and 4–8 up to the time of the trade. Just turning thirty, Walters became Derringer's partner in one of the great tandems of the lively-ball era. In the two pennant winning years he was 27–11 and 22–10, while Derringer was 25–7 and 20–12.

"I learned more from McKechnie about pitching than anyone else," Al Lopez said later, "about always trying to keep a regular rotation." Lopez caught for him in Boston for only two seasons, 1936 and 1937, but the impression was that strong.

TUTOR

In 1947, the Cleveland Indians had been acquired by Bill Veeck, Jr., son of the Chicago Cub president through 1933. He was back from the Marines with a shattered leg and eager to let his exceptional promotional talents flower. The team's manager, since 1942, had been Lou Boudreau, an outstanding shortstop who had asked for the job at the age of twenty-four and been given it by the previous owner, Alva Bradley. Lou was ambitious, intelligent, a leadership type, a terrific hitter, and good position-play short-stop—but he had little real baseball background. His greatest athletic success, in fact, had been as a basketball player at Illinois, before his bat won him star status in the American League. Boudreau was extremely popular in Cleveland, and too valuable a player to be tampered with, but Veeck knew he needed help and, as a baseball insider, knew all about McKechnie.

He hired McKechnie as a coach–tutor–assistant manager, particularly in the realm of handling the pitching staff. So far, Boudreau had finished fourth, third, fifth, fifth, and sixth. Bob Feller had come back from the army in 1946, won 26 games, struck out 348 (apparently breaking Rube Waddell's record which had been listed as 343 instead of 349), and pitched a no-hitter at Yankee Stadium; but the only other pitcher able to win even 11 games was Allie Reynolds.

In 1947, the Indians were fourth, but they had a promising pitcher named Bob Lemon who, like Walters, was a converted

Bill McKechnie

infielder. In 1948, Lemon won 20, Feller 19, and a rookie left-hander named Gene Bearden 20, including the playoff game at Boston (thanks to Boudreau's bat). The Indians won the World Series in 6 games, from the Boston Braves, and Veeck's promotions had sold 2.6 million tickets. In 1949, the Indians were a close third behind that sensational Yankee–Red Sox final weekend showdown but added another strong right-hander, Mike Garcia, as well as the veteran Early Wynn (from Washington).

Then McKechnie retired for good, as Veeck sold the club and Hank Greenberg became its president. After the 1950 season, Greenberg discarded Boudreau and brought up Lopez, who had been managing the Indianapolis farm club. Since the Indians then won 570 games in the six years Lopez stayed, never finishing lower than second, boasting one of the strongest and deepest pitching staffs ever assembled, it's fair to say that the McKechnie influence lingered and paid off.

In 1952 and 1953, when Boudreau became manager of the Boston Red Sox, McKechnie came out of retirement to join him as a coach. McKechnie died in 1965, at the age of seventy-eight.

8

Casey Stengel

The Player

Charles Dillon Stengel grew up in a happy, close-knit, affectionate, reasonably well-to-do family in Kansas City, Missouri, at the turn of the century. Why this quintessentially American middle-class upbringing produced a rambunctious professional ballplayer and subsequently one of the sages of the modern world is something for psychologists to figure out.

He was born on July 30, 1890, the third child of an insurance salesman of German ancestry married to a bright woman whose family was Irish. Their oldest child was a daughter, the second a boy about two years older than Charley. The brothers were close friends and companions from the start, with Charley's somewhat larger build minimizing the difference in age. Both became good ballplayers by their early teens. Grant was much in demand on pickup and semipro teams, with Charley included at first because Grant insisted but soon accepted for his own proficiency. They led a cheerful, busy, mischievous existence, which Robert Creamer, one of the best of Stengel's countless biographers, compares to the world described by Mark Twain. It certainly seems true that only someone like Twain could have invented the Stengel character if the man himself had not existed.

School was of no concern to the Stengel boys, although they attended it obediently enough. Charley was left-handed, and in accordance with the mores of the time, was forced to write right-handed. He learned to do it, but it certainly didn't increase his taste for laborious schoolwork. In high school he blossomed as a three-sport athlete winning local reknown, acquiring the nickname "Dutch" routinely applied to kids of German extraction. He didn't enter high school until he was fifteen, and when he left at nineteen he didn't have enough credits to graduate. He pitched Central High to the state high school championship in 1909, even though he was playing a good deal of semipro ball by that time, and in January of 1910 he signed a contract to play with the Kansas City Blues of the American Association at the top level of the minor leagues.

Within weeks, it was obvious he was not good enough as a pitcher, but he could hit and run and did have a strong arm, so they made him an outfielder and sent him down to Class C, at Kankakee, Illinois. That league folded in midseason and they moved him down to Class D at Shelbyville, Kentucky. After a few weeks, that team was sold and transferred to Maysville, Kentucky, and as the season ended he was brought back to Kansas City and got into a couple of games.

He had impressed nobody, but had taught himself to play the outfield and to slide.

During the winter, he tried dental school, but all the instruments were designed for right-handers, he complained later. For 1911, the Blues sent him to Aurora, near Chicago, in Class C. There his dedicated practice and natural ability started to show. He hit .352 and led the league in stolen bases. A Brooklyn Dodger scout came out to see him, liked what he saw, and told the Dodgers to draft him. For 1912, they optioned him out to Montgomery, Alabama, the next level down from Triple-A.

There he became the protégé of an old shortstop, Kid Elberfeld, then thirty-seven years old. Elberfeld had played thirteen seasons with five major league teams, most of the time with the Yankees, whom he managed for part of 1908. He took it upon himself to teach the twenty-one-year-old Stengel major league tricks, like the best way to execute the hit-and-run, and an attitude Stengel internalized for life: "If you're going to be a big leaguer, act like a big leaguer."

What Stengel was actually acting like much of the time, however, was an overage juvenile delinquent. He loved practical jokes, including mean ones, as well as verbal jokes. He was aggressive and boisterous and got into fights, in ball games and after hours. He was serious about playing baseball to win, but never solemn about it (or anything else). He was the prototype of what older players then called "a fresh busher," and a later generation called "flaky."

The Developers

He hit .290 and in September was called up to Brooklyn. It was the last season the Dodgers were playing in Washington Park, the third version of a ballpark first used in 1884 on the site of George Washington's headquarters during the Battle of Long Island. Harry Ebbets, the owner of the Dodgers, was building a magnificent new baseball palace way out in Flatbush, to be named after himself, and slowly acquiring enough good players to climb out of the second-division residence the Dodgers had fallen into ever since 1903, even before Hanlon left. His manager the last three years had been Bill Dahlen, the shortstop McGraw had considered his key acquisition when he had first come to the Giants. It was Dahlen who became Stengel's first big league manager, and he had a rich background: eight years on Cap Anson's Chicago Cubs, five under Hanlon in Brooklyn, then four with McGraw including the first two pennants in 1904 and 1905.

Dahlen put Stengel in center field, batting second, the day after he arrived, and Stengel broke in with a bang. The visiting team was Pittsburgh, carrying a 12-game winning streak, and its pitcher was Claude Hendrix, with whom Stengel had played semipro ball a few years before back in Kansas City. Stengel got 4 singles and a walk, stole 2 bases and drove in 2 runs, each breaking a tie, as the Dodgers won, 7–3. He played the remaining three weeks of the season and wound up with a .316 average.

The Dodgers started 1913 by opening Ebbets Field, and Stengel was their center fielder. By May 1, he was hitting .352, but by the end of June he was down in the .290s, and on July 4 he injured his ankle and was out of action for nearly a month. When he came back, he didn't play well and the whole team, after a promising start, was settling into sixth place.

Dahlen had noticed, in going over last September's events, that Stengel's .316 broke down to .351 with 11 runs batted in against right-handers, and only .250 (5 singles) and 2 runs batted in against left-handers. In mid-August, he started using a right-handed rookie instead of Stengel when a left-hander pitched.

Eventually, Stengel as manager became known as the master of platooning. He came by the idea honestly: he was being platooned in his first full season in the majors.

He was also acquiring his familiar name. His teammates started calling him "K.C." because he talked so much about Kansas City. At the same time, vaudeville was featuring DeWitt Hopper's recitation of "Casey at the Bat." Fans and players started saying, "Here comes Casey to the bat again", and one of baseball's most celebrated names quickly became permanent.

In 1914, Wilbert Robinson came over to manage the Dodgers, having had his falling out with McGraw at the end of the 1913 World Series. At his very first press conference, a few days after being hired, Uncle Robby gave an optimistic rundown of the Dodger lineup but noted it had too many left-handed hitters. He hoped he could get some right-handed outfielders, he said, to alternate with Stengel. Throughout his career, Casey would not be platooned always, but he would be repeatedly.

In 1913, he had hit .272. In 1914, Uncle Robby moved him to right field and he hit .316 as the Dodgers inched up to fifth place. The fans loved him for his panache and occasional clowning. The writers loved him for his uninhibited talk.

In 1915, though, he reported sick and underweight, and by midseason was hitting about .150. He revived, hit .300 the rest of the way (for a final .237), and by endless practice became a master of caroms off the odd, tilted right-field wall in Ebbets Field. The Dodgers moved up to third.

In 1916 they won the pennant. Stengel and his more famous teammates—Zack Wheat, Jake Daubert, Rube Marquard—were the toasts of Brooklyn, as was, of course, Uncle Robby. Stengel hit .279 and was frequently platooned.

And in 1917, the United States entered the war about the time the baseball season began. Casey, however, was already at war with Ebbets over salary. In 1915, with the Federal League available as an alternative, he had obtained a big ($6,000) two-year contract. Now, with the Feds gone, Ebbets and all the other club owners were systematically cutting salaries, and Stengel was offered a $1,400 cut. Casey held out, he wrote letters, he spoke freely to the press and anyone else who would listen; but in the end, of course, he had to give in, even with the public on his side. The other Dodgers, also disgruntled, had a bad year and finished seventh. Stengel knew his days with Ebbets were numbered.

That winter he was traded to Pittsburgh, where he promptly got into a salary squabble with Dreyfuss. In June, on the first visit by the Pirates to New York and Brooklyn, Stengel suddenly enlisted in the navy, and got a cushy job in the Brooklyn Navy Yard, running the baseball team and working in the commissary. By

The Developers

November the war was over, and he was soon a civilian again, going back to the Pirates.

In August of 1919, the Pirates traded him to the Phillies, but he refused to report unless he got more money. He didn't, so he went back to Kansas City and organized a barnstorming tour that went all the way to California. For 1920, however, he did sign, played the full season, and hit .292 for a last-place team. But he was unhappy in Philadelphia, and ecstatic when, at the end of June 1921, he was traded to McGraw's Giants.

He had already admired McGraw as an opponent; he worshipped him as an employee. That year and in 1922, the Giants won the World Series with Stengel playing only part time but hitting .368 in 1922 when McGraw platooned him (but in an unorthodox manner, as we shall see). In 1923 he played even less, but hit .339 and 2 home runs in the World Series, which the Giants lost this time to the Yankees.

In New York, he was one of the most popular players, out of proportion to his playing performance, because of his talent for clowning and publicity. McGraw also liked him for his pugnacious nature and quick, all-embracing baseball mind, and would invite him out to his home in Pelham to talk baseball by the hour.

That didn't prevent McGraw, however, from shipping him off to Boston right after the World Series, as part of a major trade that brought Billy Southworth to the Giants and also sent Dave Bancroft and Bill Cunningham (Stengel's right-handed platoon partner) to the Braves. Bancroft, the shortstop, would be Boston's manager, and he made Stengel a regular again, at the age of thirty-four. Casey hit .280 for another last-place club (while the Giants won again, a bitter pill). But it was a good year for him in other ways. Edna Lawson, whom he had met in 1923 and to whom he proposed within two weeks, agreed to marry him, and the wedding took place in August, during a trip to St. Louis. After the season, their honeymoon consisted of the gala European tour by two baseball teams organized by McGraw and Comiskey, at McGraw's invitation. They hit London, Paris, and Rome, met King George V of England, and enjoyed two luxurious ocean crossings.

In 1925, however, it was increasingly clear that Stengel was washed up as a player. But since his name still had marquee value, he suited the needs of Judge Fuchs, Boston's owner, when Fuchs bought the minor league team in nearby Worcester.

Casey Stengel

He installed Casey as its president, field manager, and regular outfielder.

The Minor Leaguer

Casey played 100 games and hit .320 in Worcester in 1925, and was supposed to move with the club when Fuchs transferred the franchise to Providence for 1926. But the Giants, who had a working arrangement with Toledo, needed a manager there, and McGraw wanted Stengel. So Casey, as president, released himself as a player, fired himself as manager, and felt free to take the Toledo job. Judge Fuchs appealed to Judge Landis to return Stengel as Boston's property, and the commissioner was prepared to do that until Fuchs relented and said, "Okay, let him go."

Stengel managed Toledo for the next six years, continuing to play part time (for himself) through 1929.

Home was now Glendale, California, where Edna's family had real estate interests. Every year they'd spend the off-season there. In 1927, his roster loaded with former major leaguers, he won the pennant for the first time in Toledo's history, setting off a three-day civic celebration. However, minor league rosters change rapidly, and two years later the Mud Hens were last. The Stengels invested some of their money in the team, and it did get back to third place in 1930. But by now the Depression was in full swing, and when Toledo finished last again in 1931, the team went bankrupt.

Casey was out of work, and out his $40,000 investment.

A livelihood was not in question, since the California real estate activities were doing all right, but at forty-one, the only thing Casey knew how to do, or really cared about doing, was baseball. He went to the winter meetings looking for a job, any sort of job, and an odd sequence of events that had been building for years in Brooklyn provided him with one.

When Ebbets died, in 1925, control of the Dodgers had passed to two factions, each with 50 percent ownership. To avoid giving the presidency to either side, they made Robinson president. But as time went on, one side liked him, the other didn't. By 1929, the squabbling was so bad that the league had to step in to force a compromise in which Robinson would be no longer president but manager for two more years. Now, after the 1931 season, Uncle

The Developers

Robby was going into retirement at sixty-eight, and the new manager was Max Carey.

Stengel had played with Carey in Pittsburgh, long before Carey had been shipped off to the Dodgers because of the rebellion against McKechnie in 1926. Max approached Casey about being one of his coaches, and the Dodger ownership, remembering Casey's popularity in Brooklyn and eager to have any positive development to counteract the departure of good Ol' Uncle Robby, agreed.

So in 1932, Casey was back in the majors right where he had started, the community of Brooklyn with which his character had such a remarkable rapport.

The Dodger

The Dodger team of 1932 did rather well, finishing third and ahead of the fourth-place Giants for the first time since 1920. But Carey, as manager, was doomed to anonymity. At the Polo Grounds, McGraw had turned the Giants over to Bill Terry, a blockbuster story if ever there was one. At Yankee Stadium, the Yankees, in Joe McCarthy's second year, were tearing the league apart and dethroning the Philadelphia A's. And at Ebbets Field, where the zaniness of the Robins had been so firmly impressed on the public consciousness for a decade, the voice that the town's brightest baseball writers gravitated to was the familiar one of Stengel's, more garrulous than ever, not the rather grim and straight utterances of Carey.

The Dodger team of 1933 didn't do so well. It fell to sixth while the Giants, under Terry, won the World Series. Attendance, which had peaked at 1,000,000 in 1930, was down to 600,000. The Depression was pinching harder and harder, and the two-faction ownership remained paralyzed. In an attempt to get some direction, they brought in a professional general manager, Bob Quinn, who saw the need for attracting attention was well as trying to win more games.

Shortly after Quinn took over, Terry made an offhand remark that became baseball legend. While summing up prospects for 1934, he was asked about Brooklyn. "Haven't heard a peep from there," said Terry. "Is Brooklyn still in the league?"

Quinn seized upon this comment to whip up Brooklyn's always available antagonism for New York, blasted Terry for issuing such an insult, and expected Carey to jump into the war of words. Carey, home in Florida, had no taste for that sort of thing. Quinn got angry at him, and they had words that led to Quinn firing Carey even though the manager had a year left on his contract.

Then Quinn offered the job to Stengel, who certainly could provide the colorful regime he was looking for. After checking with Carey—since loyalty was at the top of the list of Casey's self-imposed morality—he accepted the job with Carey's blessing, and got a two-year contract himself.

Two days later, McGraw died.

As a mouthpiece, Casey was everything Quinn could hope for. He pounced on the Terry remark and wouldn't let up. Terry became Brooklyn's most hated enemy. But that didn't alter the fact that the Giants had a good team and the Dodgers didn't. As the 1934 season reached its final weekend, the Giants were fighting the Cardinals for the pennant and the Dodgers were locked solidly into sixth place.

All through September, which the Giants entered with a big lead, the Cards kept winning and the Giants kept breaking even. With two days to go, the teams were tied for first place—and the Giants had to play the Dodgers at the Polo Grounds while the Cards played Cincinnati.

On Saturday, Stengel unleashed his fire-balling right-hander, Van Lingle Mungo, who stifled the Giant hitters and won 5–1. A Cardinal victory that day clinched at least a tie for St. Louis. On Sunday, although the Giants got off to a 4–0 lead, the Dodgers came back and won again, 8–5. The Cardinals won too, and finished 2 games ahead.

Yes, chortled all of Brooklyn toasting Stengel, we're still in the league.

But still sixth, and in 1935 fifth, and in 1936 seventh. After the 1934 ending, Quinn had given Stengel a three-year contract, but in 1936 he himself had moved to Boston to try to straighten out the Fuchs-Ruth-McKechnie debacle there. The bank, which held all sorts of notes from the Dodger owners, was taking a greater role in demanding Dodger improvement, while pinching pennies harder than ever. Stengel was being perceived more and more as a clown, a role he played to the hilt, which was fine with fans and writers but not with bookkeeper mentalities. And, as a manager, Stengel was trying to apply McGraw principles (about tactics, practice, and mechanics) to insufficient talent.

The Developers

After the 1936 season, management decided to replace him with Burleigh Grimes and paid off Stengel's final year. "I'm getting paid more not to manage than he is to do it," Stengel observed, not concealing his sense of embarrassment at being in such a situation. He spent 1937 out of baseball, learning something about the oil business (in which one of his 1936 players from Texas had persuaded him to invest), missing the New York spotlight, and most of all missing baseball itself.

And once again, unrelated events worked in his favor. Quinn, in Boston, was working for new owners, with Fuchs out of the picture. McKechnie had just left for a better situation in Cincinnati. Quinn had liked Stengel in Brooklyn. He brought him now to Boston. He also changed the name of the team to the Boston Bees and let Stengel buy a small piece of the club.

The Bee

In Boston, Casey did his managing while coaching at third base, as he had much of the time in Brooklyn and as McGraw had in his early years. He concentrated, as he did in Brooklyn, in trying to help the too-few young players with talent improve themselves. He was reunited with Lopez, who had been his catcher in Brooklyn and whom he respected so much. (Lopez had also invested in the oil venture, so in that sense they were partners.)

As for the team on the field, it wasn't much good, but no worse than the Dodgers had been. And the city itself was highly appealing to the Stengels, who appreciated its cultural ambiance, its uniqueness, and the slight edge of hysteria on which so many of its citizens seemed to live. What it didn't have was a receptive press corps. In New York, the writers had been Casey's best friends and loved his crazy humor; in Boston, a more narrowly competitive newspaper community took itself more seriously and judged acceptability only in terms of winning and losing—and not without reason, one must say, since in the nineteen baseball seasons from 1919 through 1937, their two baseball teams had finished seventh or eighth twenty-one times and never as high as third.

So what had been funny in Brooklyn brought sneers and increasing antagonism in Boston. Casey's 1938 team did just about what McKechnie's 1937 team had done, finishing fifth at 77–75 instead of 79–73 (but still 7 games better than the Dodgers under

Casey Stengel

Grimes). Then the Bees settled into seventh place for four years in a row. In addition, the ballpark itself, Braves Field, was deteriorating; attendance was averaging less than 300,000 a year; and there was a war on.

Stengel's tenure came to an end in 1943. There were new owners, headed by a construction magnate named Lou Perini, who didn't relate to Casey's double talk. Just before the season started, Stengel was hit by a car and had to spend weeks in the hospital, acquiring the permanent limp that would characterize his gnomelike movement from then on. After a sixth-place finish, Quinn told him the new owners wanted him gone. "Let them buy me out," Stengel said, referring to his stock, and went quietly.

He was fifty-three, financially secure enough, with a nice place to live in Glendale. Always aware of what was going on in the world at large, he knew that the twentieth century, in 1944, was passing through a fulcrum point, with the war still undecided. His profession had been baseball for thirty-four years, and the shape of postwar baseball wasn't at all clear. Maybe it was time to adjust to another way of life.

The Outcast

Sitting in Glendale, Stengel could not turn off his restless mind. His ideas about managing a ball club, taken entirely and consciously from McGraw, had been refined by experience, even though that experience had no "you could look it up" success to point to. He knew exactly how he wanted to run a club and what he thought would work. The only trouble was that he had no place to apply his painstakingly accumulated skill. The jokes and double talk served their purpose: one of the things he had noted about McGraw was the old man's cultivation of the press. McGraw had always made friends with beat writers and columnists and used publicity for his purposes. He fought and argued with those who disagreed, but he always made up quickly. McGraw considered propaganda one of his important weapons, in controlling players and in conflicts with ownership, and was constantly giving parties and dinners for the journalists who could rely on him to make news. Younger writers, especially, tended to idolize him (since he was famous when they arrived) until some incident flared up to hurt somebody's feelings. What Stengel saw, however, better than his contemporaries, was that dealing with the press was a basic feature of a manager's job, a responsibility to his club from a promotional standpoint, and capable of helping or hurting his players and results on the field.

He also appreciated McGraw's mental flexibility in changing from dead-ball baseball to lively-ball baseball. Stengel himself, after all, had made the majors as a singles hitter and base stealer, before the lively ball arrived. But he understood that you had to play differently when power became available; problem was, he never had enough of it on the clubs he managed.

Stengel identified with McGraw's unrelentingly competitive spirit, readiness to fight, and verbal aggressiveness, because he was that way himself. Yet he was, essentially, a softer person, loving argument more for its own sake than as a way to exert dominance. He fought for the fun of it, not with anger, as McGraw did. So in Stengel, the desire for control took the form of wanting to teach and impart special knowledge rather than to issue orders like a commanding general.

Finally, he understood the value of McGraw's intuitive responses and willingness to gamble. You had to know the book, of course, inside out, to always be aware of what percentage was in your favor. But you also had to feel—feel, not "know"—when to go against the book and not worry about the consequences. The percentages would see to it that you won as much as you should if you followed them; but to win more than you should, you had to be able to go beyond them.

There was, for example, the central question of platooning.

In the standard way of looking at it, one was simply taking advantage of baseball's built-in advantage of opposite hitting: Lefties did better against righties and vice versa. This was playing the percentages. Of course, your best players could hit either way and were in the lineup every day regardless. But if no one player was clearly superior at his position, you could get more out of that slot in the batting order by alternating the righties and lefties.

Stengel saw it as a much more complex instrument. He factored in the reality that players have hot streaks and cold streaks; that injuries can allow you to play with decreased effectiveness, not only keep you out altogether; that all humans, including ballplayers, are subject to fatigue over a six-month season of games every day, mentally as well as physically; that concentration and motivation wax and wane.

What made the outstanding regulars outstanding was not that they were free of these natural cycles but that a great player at 75 or even 60 percent of his potential was still giving you more than a lesser talent at 100 percent. That's why you played him every day regardless (as, we've seen, McCarthy did with DiMaggio).

But usually you didn't have eight everyday players of such quality. That meant that at least a couple of your positions would have to be shared. Whatever choice you made about some player being only somewhat better than another, you weren't going to get 150 good games out of either one. But you could, if you handled it right, get 75 better games out of each and avoid the 75 weaker performances that would be included in one man's full season.

Platooning, then, was first and foremost a division of labor, an attempt to have each man pour his best effort into carrying a smaller burden.

"Now, if I know I'm gonna have to use both of them," he would explain later, "I might as well use each of them the best way."

So the lefty plays against righties, and the righty against lefties, not because he "can't" hit the other way, but because if he's going to be out there only part of the time, it might as well be the part that's most in his favor.

More important, however, is that each one gets to play enough to stay sharp. So if there's a change of pitchers in the middle of the game, and you shift to the other platoon member, it's not primarily a "tactical" decision in that game (which may be one-sided at that point). It's a disciplined way of seeing that each of the two gets his turns at bat sufficiently often.

Then, when one or the other is hurt or in a long slump, you can play the other one against all kinds of pitching and still have a position being more productive than if the healthy one had been rotting on the bench for weeks at a time. That's how McGraw had used him.

The lefty-righty bit, therefore, was only one factor, not the whole rationale, for the platoon system.

This kind of thinking was fully worked out in Stengel's mind at this stage of his life. So was his philosophy of pitching. McGraw, with his gambler's guts and killer instinct, played hot hands. It's possible to overuse a pitcher, especially a reliever, by calling on him too often, or by letting him work with an apparently mild injury. He can still get the job done, but he may wind up with a damaged arm and shortened career. McGraw didn't worry about the consequences too much. An especially valuable arm, like Mathewson's, had to be preserved at any cost, because it meant victories down the road for a long time. But below that level, a hot pitcher could be used until he ceased being hot, and if he had a bad reaction afterwards, you could always find another pitcher of comparable capability.

Stengel subscribed to that philosophy wholeheartedly. On the other hand, unlike McGraw, he had more sympathy (from his own experience) for the player's desire to earn more money and keep making a living. So he added an element of loyalty McGraw seldom showed. If he got another chance to manage, Casey thought, he'd see to it that faithful service was properly rewarded with dollars, in the form of being kept on the payroll for a while beyond the point of full usefulness, or by working extra hard to help a man improve his "weaknesses" so that he could earn more money by becoming a better player.

But when it came to starting pitchers, Stengel would give less weight to the regularity of assignments (in terms of days off) than to favorable matchups: he wanted his best pitchers facing his toughest opponents, however the schedule broke, and certain pitchers facing certain teams (the Mack-Ehmke principle carried to greater lengths).

In all these matters intuitive and split-second decisions would make you go against the book sometimes. One of the worst effects of book managing, he felt, was that it protected you against the second-guessers on your own bench and in your front office, as well as in the stands. If you made the book move and it didn't work, who could blame you? It was simply a failure of execution. But if you did something unorthodox that did work, you'd be called lucky; and if it didn't, you'd be blamed. Since being blamed led to being fired, there was constant pressure to make "safe" decisions. You'd win often enough in the normal course of things operating that way; but if you wanted to win a lot or (to be honest) every time, you'd have to risk brilliance backfiring and the consequences of carping criticism.

So to do your best as a manager meant never worrying about keeping your job. McGraw had that going for him by the power of his position; Mack had it as part owner; Rickey didn't have it, and wound up in the front office. Huggins and McCarthy had it through their relationship to Barrow.

And Stengel, if he ever got another chance, knew he'd have it because he had enough outside income at his age not to need the job for financial reasons. He needed the job, desperately, to be himself.

In 1944, therefore, the full-fledged persona of Casey Stengel, manager, was complete and in place. And sitting in Glendale.

And again, outside forces were at work.

Bill Veeck, Jr., and Charley Grimm had invested in the Milwaukee club of the American Association, with Grimm as its manager. Jolly Cholly had managed the Cubs in the 1932 and 1935 World Series, and through the first half of the 1938 pennant-winning year, so his credentials were real. Now the Cubs wanted him back again when they started 1–9 under Jimmie Wilson in April of 1944.

Grimm had a problem. Veeck was off in the Pacific, in the Marines. To simply abandon Milwaukee, which had won the pennant in 1943 and was in love with Grimm's Teutonic *gemütlichkeit* and cheerful zaniness (Cholly was a pretty good clown himself, and as gregarious as Stengel), would threaten their investment. To go back to the Cubs, he needed someone special to take over Milwaukee.

He called Casey.

Do a friend a favor and get back into action? Sure. Who was doing the favor for whom?

On May 7, Casey took over the Brewers. He brought them home first again. Grimm, the next season, got the Cubs into the World Series.

But Veeck, when he heard about the change, was furious. He knew Stengel only by reputation—as a clown—and had no use for him. Word of his attitude surfaced. Years later, Veeck and Stengel turned into a mutual admiration society, but at the time Stengel was stung by the young man's opinion. He resigned at the end of the season without waiting for any friction to become a public issue.

What had become evident to everyone in Stengel's Milwaukee performance was his ability to develop young players. In the fall of 1944, the Yankees were in the process of being sold to Mac-Phail, and Weiss would no longer be under Barrow's thumb (but very much under MacPhail's). Weiss had been running the New Haven club when Stengel was at Worcester. Their paths had crossed various times, and they had respect for each other. Weiss asked Casey if he'd take over the Triple-A Yankee farm club in Kansas City—still bearing the name Blues and descendants of the team that had signed Stengel to his first contract.

So Stengel spent 1945 back in Kansas City, managing a team that finished seventh (since the Yankee system, depleted by the war, did not yet have its players back), and not having much fun seeing Milwaukee win again. Not one of his Kansas City players ever became a recognizable Yankee. Besides, MacPhail had taken over in New York, and Weiss found out that Larry's thumb was even bigger and heavier than Barrow's. There was no reason for Stengel to stick around.

However, the Oakland Oaks of the Pacific Coast League had been purchased by Brick Laws, and he was looking for a manager. Would Casey be interested? This top minor league, coming out of the war, was a haven for ex-major leaguers as well as prospects, in an exploding population region, working itself up to ask for semi–major league status (which it never got). Oakland was only 400 miles north of Glendale, and the Coast League schedule called for week-long visits to a town, two of which were Los Angeles and Hollywood. It sounded like a good deal, and Casey took it. After all, he was still a young chicken of fifty-five.

With a 188-game schedule and a roster full of veterans, Stengel started to put into practice all his ideas about lineup juggling, unorthodox moves, and motivation now so clear in his mind. He had, now, that key ingredient: He didn't need the job. He had himself a ball in Oakland, and was beloved by the community (and West Coast writers), and as funny as ever, and successful. The Oaks finished second, fourth, and first, selling more than 500,000 tickets each year—more than his teams had ever done in Brooklyn and Boston. It wasn't the majors, but it was pretty good fun for a spry, affluent fifty-eight-year-old with a limp.

And, for the umpteenth time, the outside world was moving in strange ways. MacPhail had hired Bucky Harris to manage the Yankees in 1947, and they ran away with the pennant and beat the Dodgers in a 7-game World Series. Immediately afterward, in an emotional scene, MacPhail announced his retirement. That left Weiss as the only high-ranking baseball man in the organization whom Topping and Webb could turn to—and Harris wasn't Weiss's man. (Weiss never had any use for anyone who wasn't indebted to him, at least in Weiss's eyes.) In 1948, the Yankees failed to repeat, missing by 2 games in that three-way finish with Boston and Cleveland, after many disputes between Weiss and Harris about bringing up farm products for help during the season. That was all the excuse Weiss needed to unload Bucky.

Weiss wanted Casey. Topping was against it. Webb, who had met Stengel casually in Oakland, was won over. Yankee scouts who had been covering the Pacific Coast League endorsed him heartily as the best manager out there.

In New York, of course, Stengel was as firmly identified as a clown as the Statue of Liberty was as a statue. The Daffy Dodger managing the lordly Yankees? That would be a joke in itself. His old friends in the Big Town were delighted to see him and Edna again, but no one thought it made much sense. Publicity? Yes, the best. Victories? Never.

But it was no joke.

The Yankee

In twelve seasons with the Yankees, Stengel won ten pennants, starting with five straight World Series championships. When that streak was broken in 1954, his team won more games than it ever had before (103), but Cleveland won an American League record 111. Then he won four more pennants in succession, although he lost the World Series in 7 games to the Dodgers in 1955 and to the Milwaukee Braves in 1957—then beat each of them in a return match the following year. His only poor team, barely over .500, was in 1959, when it finished behind the White Sox and Indians. Then the Yankees won the pennant in 1960—the league's last season as an eight-team circuit—and lost the World Series to Pittsburgh in 7 games.

No manager had ever done anything like that. None ever will again, because the conditions that made it possible are long since gone.

The most important feature of this achievement, from a managerial point of view, was the ability to keep winning without letting complacency sap the drive of long-term regulars and to handle personnel turnover without loss of efficiency. Of the thirty-seven players who got into a game for the 1949 Yankees, only one—Yogi Berra—was still playing for them in 1960.

It's a major league truism that it's harder to repeat than to win the first time. To repeat time after time becomes exponentially more difficult, and the true measure of Stengel's accomplishment lies in that.

The 1949 season has been chronicled in detail in David Halberstam's *Season of '49* and many other books. The library is full of volumes that tell the story of Stengel's dozen years through the eyes of one or another of the participants and countless observers. Our concern is with the particular managerial problems, solutions, and characteristics made evident in this twelve-year period.

1. Gaining control. The team Stengel started with had many men accustomed to winning under McCarthy, whose decisions they respected and rules they followed. In their maturity, they had enjoyed Bucky Harris's more easygoing manner. Stengel's clown reputation offended their Yankee pride, but more than that, they had no reason to feel confident that he knew what he was doing. And when he displayed methods they weren't used to—lots of platooning, hunches that violated orthodox logic, incomprehensible chatter, a taste for kooky publicity—their doubts increased. He could win them over in only one way: What he did had to work. He had to be proven right by results and victories. By the end of the third year, Casey had convinced them. They still didn't understand what he was doing, and shook their heads at "crazy" moves that seemed to turn out right by sheer luck. But you couldn't argue with success.

Older players, however, automatically phased themselves out as time went on. The newer ones had no reason to disbelieve. The problem with them was to teach them to be "big leaguers," shore up their weak points, and keep improving their strong points. The best form of discipline for them was the oldest one, made easier to carry out in a platoon system: Do it my way or sit.

2. Maintaining continuity. Each year the farm system would produce high-quality new talent, and for specific needs, Weiss was good at making in-season trades. But even outstanding talent, arriving from Triple-A, needed more instruction and refinement. Rickey's system was getting impressive results from specialized coaching, departmentalization in training camp, and expert instructors traveling through the minor leagues. The Yankees had a lot of that too under Weiss. But why couldn't you apply the same idea to the parent club? Couldn't the coaching staff be made larger, given more clearly defined responsibilities, used to greater advantage? Traditionally, a manager had one close confidant (perhaps the third base coach), as a drinking buddy; someone to take care of the bullpen; and a general-purpose assistant. Stengel wanted more.

He brought in Jim Turner, who had pitched for him in Boston after having McKechnie's tutelage, as his pitching coach—and put him in charge, as if pitching were a subdepartment of the ball club. The pitchers were "his" to look after—not just their mechanics and their training and their rotation, but their problems and desires as a group. Turner was their delegate to the central brain trust, protecting their "interests," as well as their foreman. Then, having given Turner this responsibility, Stengel deferred to his judgment most of the time.

Berra was obviously a potential hitting star, but he had been played in the outfield a lot because he had deficiencies as a catcher. Stengel brought back Bill Dickey as a special coach who could, as Yogi put it, "learn me his experiences."

Crosetti, who had worshipped McCarthy and stayed on as a player-coach under Harris, now took over as full-time third base coach in games, and concentrated on sharpening the skills of infielders in practice.

Dickey, of course, could help all the hitters, although Casey subscribed to McGraw's precept that it's better not to tamper with natural styles. (When a kid infielder named Gil McDougald showed up in 1950 and won a job although he had played only in the Class AA Texas League the year before, he had one of the craziest stances anyone had ever seen; but he had hit .336 that way at Beaumont, where Rogers Hornsby, his manager, had sense enough to leave him alone. Stengel also let him do it his own way while McDougald hit .306 as a rookie in 131 games. When, in 1951, his average slipped to .263, it was time enough to get him to make adjustments.)

And Stengel felt he could teach the outfielders what they had to know.

None of this was new in itself. Casey just applied it more thoroughly.

3. Versatility. Injuries and slumps were forever upsetting the smooth course of any ball club. Stengel's first Yankee season was marked by an abnormal run of them, meticulously counted by the publicity man, Red Patterson, and included the loss of DiMaggio for the whole first half of the season. The best protection was to have good players able to shift around and play different positions when needed, rather than to always be looking for suitable emergency replacements. But in this, as with platooning, why wait for emergencies? Sure, every player preferred to be settled in one position, feeling secure, learning all the fine points, "getting in a groove," playing every day. But if you could move people

around in the field, you could also use different batting orders every day to get the best matchups against particular pitchers. Then, when injuries did occur, you'd have people ready and in game playing form to put where needed.

So, in those first five championship years, people like Mc-Dougald, Billy Martin, and Jerry Coleman wound up playing at all three infield positions (excluding first), and outfielders were expected to play any of the three fields when asked. In 1952, for instance (one of the years I kept track of this), Stengel used more than one hundred different batting orders, with McDougald batting in each of the eight slots at least once, Hank Bauer in the top seven, Irv Noren in seven of the eight (not cleanup), Gene Woodling in six of the top seven (not cleanup), Berra in every slot from second through seventh, and even Don Bollweg, a part-time first baseman, in every slot but leadoff.

He used pinch hitters at odd times, and sometimes let pitchers hit, and it worked. He brought in lefties to face righties (like Bob Kuzava in the 1951 and 1952 World Series) and it worked. He made established 20-game winners, Allie Reynolds and Johnny Sain, into terrific relief pitchers, but saw it wouldn't work with Vic Raschi. He bunted when others would hit-and-run, and vice versa, but that was "intuition." Moving players around and making them flexible, mentally comfortable with multiassignments as well as physically proficient, was planning ahead and maintaining the efficiency of the whole.

4. Morale and discipline. Given his own history, he certainly didn't expect his players to be celibate nondrinkers who curled up with a good book in the hotel room. But he wanted the high life to stay reasonably within bounds and could ignore it until and unless it interfered with performance. He had other concerns in this department.

"On every club," he would say, "you'll have eight or ten men who hate you. Make sure you room those kind together so they don't contaminate all the others."

And "The hotel bar is mine. Let the players go somewhere else where I won't see them."

Like McGraw, but to a lesser degree, Casey wasn't concerned about hurting a player's feelings by a sarcastic or sharp criticism in the dugout, in front of others. But he stuck to a pattern. When the club was losing, he wouldn't criticize much. When it was winning, he became almost intolerably edgy and nasty, trying to forestall a letdown. ("They know when they're losin' and feel bad enough," he'd say. "But they'd better not fall asleep on me when they think everything is going la-de-dah.") In the same way, he was hardest on the best talents (like Mickey Mantle), driven by what he saw as unrealized potential even beyond Mantle's imposing accomplishments, yet quite tolerant toward those with lesser ability (whom he would replace as soon as possible, but not demean while they were around).

5. The double talk. He was always a nonstop talker, and his mind often raced ahead of his syntax, but in the Yankee spotlight, so much brighter than any he'd had before, he cultivated the stream-of-consciousness style and brought it to new heights. I can't reproduce it on paper—and I certainly tried often enough in writing about him through fifteen years of traveling with his clubs—and even word-for-word transcriptions from tape can't catch the quality of his monologues because the unexpected stresses and accents, the facial expressions, the hand movements, and the body language were too integral parts of it. But it was, most of the time, an act—an act he enjoyed so much and got so proficient at that he would begin to do it in relatively private surroundings and, I suppose, out of habit. If you listened carefully enough, long enough, you always got back to the thread of the thought and the basic point being made (well, almost always). It was, simultaneously, a defense mechanism (against outsiders), an attention getter (if you stopped listening you *really* got lost), a sort of secret communication (for insiders present), and a guarantee against interruption.

Players marveled at it, usually from a distance. Writers tried to capture gems of obfuscation. Strangers were fascinated. But when he had a specific message to transmit, especially to a player, there was nothing confusing or ambiguous about it, and as often as not, the clarity didn't leave the listener's ego unbruised.

Familiarity, they say, breeds contempt. In Stengel's case, it certainly bred fatigue at least. His players had heard his act too often. In his twelfth year as a Yankee, Casey passed his seventieth birthday. For all his success, he was never as popular with Topping as with Webb. Now, as Topping was taking more and more control of club operations with Weiss also in his late sixties, time was running out. As 1960 played itself out, Topping had determined that both Stengel and Weiss were "too old" and should be retired. And it was true that Stengel's outspoken and often unkind motivational methods were getting less effective with a younger generation, simultaneously more sensitive to insult and more secure about its rights.

The 1960 World Series was lost partly because Stengel made a bad decision about his pitching rotation, holding Whitey Ford out of the first game, so he was able to pitch only twice instead of three times. (He pitched two shutouts.) The details of Stengel's departure belong to the Ralph Houk story, later on. But Casey was always a realist, and proud, and wouldn't swallow the word *retirement*.

"I've been discharged," he said, "because there's no question I have to leave."

His career was over—again—but now his place in the Hall of Fame was assured.

The Met

The saga of the early Mets, which Stengel created, is even better documented than his Yankee history. This coda added only one item to his method of managing and needs only the briefest summary here.

The attempt to start a third major league, The Continental, was driven by New York's desire to find a replacement for the Giants and the Dodgers, who had fled to California in 1958. It seemed possible in 1959, but was sidetracked when the majors offered to expand. The American League took in Los Angeles (the Angels) and Washington (to replace the original Senators, still owned by the Griffith family, who became the Minnesota Twins) for 1961. The National would add its two teams, New York and Houston, in 1962.

The guiding force behind the New York effort was Bill Shea, a lawyer with strong political connections, brains, and energy. The new franchise, to be called the Mets, belonged to Mrs. Charles Shipman Payson, a Whitney and a sincere New York Giant fan. Rickey, between Pittsburgh and his last St. Louis connection, was advising her, along with Shea. They hired Weiss as club president (a sham title to get around his contractual obligation to the Yankees not to take another "general manager" job), and Weiss got Stengel. The rationale was sound. An expansion club would be hopelessly uncompetitive at first, so it needed attention and identity. Who could give it that better than Stengel in New York?

Casey Stengel

For their part, both Weiss and Stengel nurtured the hope of somehow embarrassing the Yankees for discarding them.

The Yankees, of course, reeled off three more pennants under Houk and a fifth straight under Berra in 1964. The Mets, forced to play their first two seasons in the Polo Grounds because Shea Stadium wasn't completed until 1964, lost 120 games the first year and 111 the second. Then they moved into Shea Stadium and lost only 109. In July of 1965, leaving a party at Toots Shor's, Stengel fell and broke his hip. It was impossible to manage anymore, and in August, out of the hospital and leaning on a cane, he made his formal farewells. Wes Westrum took the reins and finished a 112-loss campaign.

The expansion Mets, becoming cult figures by losing in an amazing variety of ways, had no chance no matter who managed them. Casey, in his seventies, certainly lacked some energy and alertness, but what was remarkable was how much of both he retained. He tried to teach, knowing he was going to lose games anyhow; some players responded, some did not. But he really put more effort into promoting the team than into managing it. (Among the coaches he had in the first three years were Hornsby, Cookie Lavagetto, Solly Hemus, Westrum, and Don Heffner, all of whom managed in the majors before or after, and pitchers like Red Ruffing, Mel Harder, and Ernie White.) And he really did sell tickets, more than the Yankees were selling, while spreading baseball's gospel.

Both in promoting and teaching he was "giving something back to baseball," an obligation he felt with the deepest sincerity. His remarks became more sarcastic, funnier, and more pointed about his team's deficiencies. The players hated this, but a new generation of writers ate it up and the public loved it. He wouldn't deny what anyone could see: His team was a "fraud." He had expected the expansion assignment to be tough, but never imagined the team would lose as much as it did, for so long a time.

And the last item of his managing technique? The very insults and wisecracks that his players resented were a method of protecting them in a way they never understood. The day of locker rooms crammed with microphones, cameras, and tape recorders after every game had arrived. By going into his harangue in his office, for half an hour, he was keeping a mob of reporters away from the lockers of players who had just messed up another day. No matter how much they resented reading the critical remarks he made at their expense, they would have read and heard worse

The Developers

if they had to face an onslaught of immediate and embarrassing questions on their own. Casey's jibes were, at least, selective and limited in number. If the whole squad had been exposed to the journalistic wolfpack after every daily disaster, their feelings would have been hurt much worse than they were.

In his own way, Casey felt he was acknowledging tender egos and contributing to the future of those young players who might have a future, offering a bit of protection until they grew harder shells.

It was a technique later managers would formalize, without comparable wit and liveliness, by funneling reporters through their offices for the first wave of postgame questions.

And it was a technique derived from one of McGraw's viewpoints developed in a simpler time but profound enough even then: Since a manager has to deal with the press, whose activity can affect his club's performance in various ways, a manager should understand how the press (not yet the "media" then) does its work, just as you want to know how the groundskeeper does his.

Knowing when to bunt is not enough.

Part Three

The Descendants

9

Leo Durocher

Gas House Gangster

There are many similarities between Leo Durocher and John McGraw, but there are important differences too. In a thick book called *Who's Who in Professional Baseball,* published in 1973 by Gene Karst and Martin J. Jones, Jr., the Durocher entry starts this way:

"Synonymous with controversy, noise, argument, shouting, rhubarbs, litigation, Durocher has been supreme egotist, brash loudmouth, natural ham, narcissistic monologist, hunch player, strategist. Has been strutting clothes horse, manicured, pedicured, perfumed; ruthless, sarcastic, bitter, amiable, flirtatious, charming, dapper."

That's pretty good for starters, and it is an accurate reflection of how Leo was perceived throughout his turbulent career.

Strictly as a manager, however, in a narrower framework than his total publicity-attracting persona, Leo can be described more simply. In everything he did, he looked for an edge.

His sharp, quick mind grasped instantly where his edge lay. He didn't always grasp it correctly, but he never doubted at that moment that he was right. The phrase "He's got the guts of a burglar" was applied to him again and again, because he had unfailing nerve to act upon his hunches and little regard for the consequences to anyone else. And in all his personal as well as professional relationships, he subscribed to the precept that the best defense was an aggressive offense. Act first. Beat the other guy to the punch. Get them before they get you. "Nice guys finish last."

All these traits are reminiscent of McGraw but, of course, not peculiar to the two men. Many of the most successful competitors have them. They believe intimidation of others helps them win.

The Descendants

They harass umpires to tilt future calls in their favor, as a matter of policy. They resort to fists without hesitation, as long as they're young, and more subtle forms of attack later. They have unshakeable conviction that they can outsmart, as well as intimidate, any opponent. And they see other people—players, business associates, superior officers, and anyone who happens to be around—as tools to be used in pursuit of their own goals.

They wouldn't get away with it, and wouldn't be the leaders that they were, if they didn't combine that drive with considerable charm, accurate reading of the psychology of others, and a sense of when to pull back (and most of all, with whom to pull back). Durocher, like McGraw, had the knack of being attractive to other celebrities and the world's movers and shakers, precisely because his reputation for rowdiness, which aroused their curiosity in the first place, was not directed at them when they found him so warm and interesting a companion in social situations.

Just as McGraw became a darling of the Broadway crowd once he got to New York, Durocher, almost half a century later, was lionized in the later equivalent milieu, Hollywood. Both loved to gamble and enjoyed hobnobbing with gamblers. Both loved the limelight for its own sake.

McGraw and Durocher were fundamentally different, however, in significant ways. McGraw's driving impulse was for dominance: He wanted dictatorial control of everything and everyone he dealt with. Leo didn't care about control, he just wanted the result favorable to Leo. McGraw wanted it done his way; Leo didn't care how you did it, as long as it got done. McGraw had social aspirations and yearned to be a club owner, i.e., a successful capitalist. Leo didn't have either ambition, the first having become fairly irrelevant in the culture of his time, and the second so unquestionably out of reach that he just didn't bother about it.

They also had a different effect on the men they influenced. McGraw generated tremendous loyalty and affection among many, especially in the first half of his career, and was venerated by his disciples (among the writers as well as baseball people). He was also hated passionately by many others, of course. Leo also wound up being hated by a lot of people, but never venerated. His disciples admired his ability, imitated his methods, appreciated his help, learned lessons from him, and understood

Leo Durocher

what made him exceptional; but no one ever spoke of him in awesome terms, or seemed to "love" him. They could be deeply grateful, like Willie Mays, and feel perpetually indebted to his guidance and teaching, like Alvin Dark and Bill Rigney; but few felt any sense of personal loss when he moved on to another venue, or would talk of him affectionately until he and they were into their sixties and seventies.

Nor did Leo give any indication that he sought, wanted, or missed that sort of emotion from them. He wanted to be respected and feared, acknowledged for his "brilliance," treated as he wished, aided toward his purposes (which might well coincide with yours in certain circumstances), but if you didn't like him—well, that was *your* problem, not his.

Finally, McGraw was an inventor, a tinkerer, and a worker for perfection in technique. Leo didn't invent anything and left mechanical work to others. He mastered, completely and with insight, the McGraw principles of play and tactics, and applied them with hunch and instinct, both grounded in solid baseball reasoning. But he was applying—or reversing for his own reasons—what had become standard knowledge, not adding to it.

And that's the part where we see Leo as the first hybrid of McGraw and Rickey.

In his approach to playing the game, he was pure McGraw, filtered through Frisch and his own observations.

In preparation and talent procurement, he was content to be the recipient of the Rickey system in which he worked, accepting the product of its methods as well as its personnel.

All his managerial descendants would contain both strains.

Durocher was born in 1905, in West Springfield, Massachusetts, and grew up poor. He was small (five feet nine inches), fairly quick and strong for a ballplayer, but never much of a hitter. His brain, however, made him an outstanding fielder by enabling him to excel at proper positioning and fast release as a shortstop.

In 1925, when he was turning twenty, Durocher played a full season at Hartford, hitting .220. (That year, Weiss was running the New Haven team and Stengel was at Worcester, in the same Eastern League.) The Yankees liked his fielding well enough to buy his contract, and sent him to Atlanta in 1926 and St. Paul, at the Triple-A level, in 1927. His aggressive approach to fielding is shown by the fact that he led the league in putouts, assists, and errors. He also hit .253, and the Yankees promoted him to the big club for 1928.

He was not a hit. The nonstop talking of this brash rookie promptly earned him the name of Lippy Leo, supposedly pinned on him by Will Wedge of the New York *Sun*. The proud and self-assured members of Murderers Row—Ruth, Gehrig, Lazzeri, Meusel—were annoyed, not intimidated, by a loudmouth busher. What's more, he was filling in for two of the most popular members of the team, Lazzeri at second, Mark Koenig at short. A shoulder injury kept Lazzeri out for almost a third of the season, so Leo played mostly second, getting into 102 games. He hit .270, which was less than any of the eight regulars and the other utility infielder, Gene Robertson. In the World Series sweep, he got into every game as a late-inning replacement.

In 1929, he started to win the shortstop job from Koenig, who was slowing down. But many of the older Yankees openly despised him, and an ugly story circulated about him stealing something out of Babe Ruth's locker. That's the year Huggins died, the A's dethroned the Yankees, and Barrow bought a hotshot shortstop named Lyn Lary from the Pacific Coast for big bucks. At the end of the season, the Yankees waived Leo and Cincinnati claimed him.

He was the shortstop for a seventh-place Cincinnati team in 1930 and started a long association with Charley Dressen, no longer the regular third baseman. In 1932, the Reds under manager Dan Howley finished last. In 1933, they did it again. But Leo had escaped less than a month into that season: On May 7, he was part of a three-for-three trade that brought Paul Derringer from St. Louis to Cincinnati.

Rickey, as always, knew the abilities of every player everywhere. The Cardinals had won pennants in 1930 and 1931 with Charley Gelbert, an outstanding shortstop. But after the 1932 season, a hunting accident ruined Gelbert's career (nearly destroying one of his legs) and Rickey needed an immediate replacement. He got Durocher to play between Frisch at second and Pepper Martin at third, and never mind the hitting; the rest of the team would take care of that.

In midseason, Frisch replaced Gabby Street as manager, and the Cardinals came in fifth but only 9½ games behind Bill Terry's champion Giants. They had pitching, led by Dizzy Dean, power, led by Joe Medwick, and balance.

Leo Durocher

They also had a collection of uninhibited nuts, led by Dean and Martin, and not much reined in by Frisch. Here Leo's personality fit perfectly. What became known as the Gas House Gang stormed to a World Series triumph in 1934, and Leo was an integral part of it. Frisch's managerial tactics were pure McGraw, and Durocher absorbed them into what he had already learned. They lost close pennant races in 1935 and 1936, as Rickey's farm system kept turning up new stars (like Johnny Mize and Terry Moore), and in 1937 slipped to fourth (partly because Dean got hurt in the All-Star Game). More changes were on the way.

MacPhail had just taken over Brooklyn and needed a colorful player—among other things—to revive the franchise. The manager he had inherited, Burleigh Grimes, had left the Cardinals before Durocher got there, but liked his play as an opponent. MacPhail, of course, had Rickey's ear. The Dodgers sent four players to St. Louis for Leo, but what Rickey knew was that he had a young shortstop down in Rochester who wasn't quite ready but would be far better than Durocher in every way, a tall skinny guy named Marty Marion.

So Durocher came to Brooklyn in 1938, and it was a marriage made in heaven, or maybe someplace else.

Brooklyn's Hero

MacPhail's whole approach to rebuilding the Dodgers was to promote, get attention, stir up Brooklyn's latent patriotism. (The word *Brooklyn* itself was a guaranteed laugh for the new radio comedians like Bob Hope, Fred Allen, and Jack Benny.) Brooklynites saw themselves as tough, street smart, irreverent toward humans (but not toward religion in what was called "the city of churches"), pushy, outspoken, and proud representatives of the Century of the Common Man, then getting full appreciation in Franklin Roosevelt's second administration. The Yankees and the Giants had enjoyed—were still enjoying—an endless flow of glamorous figures and victories. Brooklynites were sick of it. Above all, they would respond to self-assertion—and Leo the Lip was self-assertion squared.

Grimes knew his baseball—he was the last of the pitchers licensed to keep using a spitball after 1920, because it was already his stock in trade before the rules were changed—and had wide experience, a gruff manner, and authority. But he was a public relations zero, and Leo, in one undistinguished season, eclipsed him as a presence. (Leo hit .219 for a seventh-place club, but that was still better than his .203 the previous year in St. Louis.) He had the honor (?) of making the last out of Johnny Vander Meer's second consecutive no-hitter in the first night game ever played at Ebbets Field—a soft fly to center fielder Harry Craft. Leo didn't always win, but he was always in the center of the action.

So MacPhail made Leo manager of the 1939 Dodgers.

He knew what he was doing. He was loading his roster with veterans and a few truly outstanding rookies. They needed a leader who could keep them fired up, make the moves during ball games, get them an extra edge. They didn't need teaching or a housemother. Leo got them home third in 1939 and second in 1940, with all his adventures and rhubarbs faithfully described to millions of new radio listeners by Red Barber's dazzling style. By 1941, Leo had nearly an all-star team: Dolph Camilli, the home run hitter, at first, Billy Herman at second, Cookie Lavagetto at third, Dixie Walker and Joe Medwick in the outfield, Mickey Owen catching, Whitlow Wyatt and Kirby Higbe starting, Hugh Casey relieving. And the youngsters were Pee Wee Reese, broken in at shortstop by Leo himself (he could teach *that!*) after MacPhail bought him from the Red Sox farm club in Louisville, and a whiz named Pete Reiser, stolen out of Rickey's own farm system in 1937 for a $100 bonus when Judge Landis went on one of his free-the-farmhands sprees.

The Dodgers gave Brooklyn its first pennant since 1920, and Leo epitomized the community's cocky triumph—even if they did lose the World Series to the Yankees—a shocking defeat that occurred after Casey threw a third strike past Tommy Henrich and also Mickey Owen with two out in the ninth inning of the fourth game, setting up a 7–4 loss in what would have been a 4–3 victory.

In 1942, with Arky Vaughan added at third base and Augie Galan to the outfield, they won 104 games but finished second to the streaking Cardinals. With a 10-game lead in August, MacPhail called a team meeting to tell them they could still lose and got precious little satisfaction from being proved right.

But MacPhail went off to war, and the new boss of the Dodgers was Rickey.

He certainly appreciated Leo; in fact, he was one of the few people Leo would listen to with respect. Leo would agree to try to control himself (try, not necessarily succeed). He still got into fist fights, one with a fan, one with an umpire. Brooklyn churches threatened to boycott the team for one of his offenses against morality (having to do with a divorce). Rickey always smoothed things over, but he also had in mind a more important fact. Leo could not control the older group of independent-minded players of his own generation, and didn't try; but when Rickey's plan to stock the team with young players from his own new farm system matured, Leo's charisma, reputation, and knowledge would make them receptive to his control.

After the war, that's exactly how it turned out.

The 1946 Dodgers still had Walker, Lavagetto, Higbe, and Galan—but they also had Reese and Reiser back from service, Eddie Stanky taking Billy Herman's job at second, and a rifle-armed outfielder named Carl Furillo. On the way were Gil Hodges, Duke Snider, and Ralph Branca (already on the team, and just about to blossom into a 20-game winner). Jackie Robinson was being groomed in Montreal, and Roy Campanella would be brought in once the color line was broken. For such a group, Leo was not only the riverboat gambler he'd always been, but an authority figure too.

They did finish first, but lost the playoff to the Cardinals (to Rickey's chagrin, since the Cardinals consisted almost exclusively of his products). But with Robinson added, Leo would do even better in 1947.

Only he couldn't. He had learned to control his fists, but not his mouth.

He had institutionalized his philosophy by saying something like "Nice guys finish last," referring to Mel Ott's Giant team. Now he spouted off, to the press, about the presence of "known gamblers" in MacPhail's Yankee box at an exhibition game. The memory and hypocrisy of the antigambling stand of Judge Landis was fresh in mind, even though Happy Chandler, recently a senator from Kentucky, of all places, was now Commissioner of baseball and tsk-tsking "racetrack connections." Leo said something like, "Look at what MacPhail gets away with; if they were guests of mine, I'd be barred from baseball."

Since they weren't guests of his, Chandler barred him from baseball for only one year just for saying so.

Previously, that winter, MacPhail had wanted him for the Yankees. Durocher had decided to stay with Rickey, and MacPhail may have been vindictive in urging Chandler to act. Bucky Harris became Yankee manager, Rickey brought in his old Sunday assistant Shotton to manage the Dodgers, and both teams wound up in a 7-game World Series while Leo, now married to actress Laraine Day, spent the year with the Hollywood set, collecting full pay.

Rickey did reinstall him as manager for 1948 but in July pulled off the most startling deal in baseball history.

Leo Durocher, the ultimate Brooklyn Bum who had enabled the borough to lord it over the hated (but I mean *hated*) Giants, was going to replace Ott, the personal protégé of John McGraw, as manager of the franchise McGraw had built. And if Brooklynites hated the Giants, that wasn't even half of the intensity with which Giant fans hated Durocher. It was as if Robert E. Lee were suddenly made commander of the Union Army.

The Little Shepherd of Coogan's Bluff

With the Dodgers, Durocher had been essentially a "game" manager. For all his success and notoriety, his seasoned cast didn't need "direction" except during the game itself. Talent procurement and policy decision making were entirely in the hands of MacPhail and Rickey. Leo's job was to win games with the people they provided.

The situation with the Giants was different. The owner was Horace Stoneham, Charles's son, who had grown up in the Polo Grounds, around McGraw, from childhood. He had succeeded his father as president in 1936, when Terry was in the middle of winning three pennants in five years, and began only then to build a farm system his father had disdained.

Stoneham was only a few years older than Ott, whom he knew from the day Ottie had arrived in New York, and had made him manager when Terry stepped out in 1942. But the war held back the growth of the farm system, and the backbone of the 1930 greatness—Terry, Ott, Carl Hubbell, Hal Schumacher—was irreplaceable. Under Ott, the postwar Giants weren't doing well, sinking into a fatally distant third behind the Yankees and Dodgers in New York's pecking order. Ott and Stoneham, naturally enough from their experience, thought you could win with power, and collected a team that hit a record 221 homers in 1947—yet finished fourth. Ott, the nice guy, wasn't finishing last but wasn't the one to stir things up, either.

Leo Durocher

In getting Durocher, Stoneham was admitting to himself, as well as to the rest of the world, that a different approach was needed.

And Leo, for the first time, was in a position to tell the owner—a receptive owner—that *he* wanted to be able to play winning baseball the way he saw it: the McGraw way, ironically enough, from which the home run oriented Ott had strayed. At Leo's instigation, the Giants were torn apart in 1948 and 1949 and put back together along entirely different lines. Now Leo was a builder and a commander beyond individual ball games, a managerial presence not overshadowed by a larger-than-life owner.

That's why, ultimately, the managerial stream that flowed from his Giant teams was so strongly marked by Durocherism, while those who played for him in Brooklyn were and remained Rickey system products.

What Durocher found in the Polo Grounds, in the middle of 1948, was a team of big bats, no speed, and shaky pitching. What he wanted was pitching, speed, and defense. Discarded were John Mize, Walker Cooper, Sid Gordon, and Willard Marshall, who had accounted for 135 of those 221 homers. Acquired were shortstop Alvin Dark and second baseman Eddie Stanky, who had anchored the pennant-winning Braves in 1948, when Dark was rookie of the year. (Stanky had been Leo's second baseman in Brooklyn, dealt off after 1947 to let Jackie Robinson move back to second from first.) Also added were Sal Maglie, a pitcher who had been exiled for a while for playing in the Mexican League, and Monte Irvin and Henry Thompson from the Negro leagues. On hand, products of the Giants' own system, were outfielders Bobby Thomson and Whitey Lockman, catcher Wes Westrum, and some pitchers. The one quality pitcher available all along, since 1946, was Larry Jansen. Another turned out to be Jim Hearn, abandoned after years of trial by the Cardinal chain.

Here was a team that could hit and run and stay alive in low-scoring games. To outwit the opposition, you have to be close, inning after inning, so that when you do get an edge it decides the game. Only then could Leo's intuition and alertness pay off. By 1950, closing strong, his Giants placed third, only 5 games out as the Phillies beat back the Dodgers on the final day.

And 1951 brought him Willie Mays.

In the Miracle of 1951, climaxed by Bobby Thomson's playoff home run off Ralph Branca, Durocher's stewardship reached full flower. He had gathered a coaching staff geared to his needs.

The Descendants

Herman Franks, who had been a second-string catcher for him in Brooklyn, was his first lieutenant. Freddie Fitzsimmons, who had pitched for McGraw and then for Leo in Brooklyn, and who had managed the Phillies for a couple of years, coached at first, with Leo himself at third. The third coach was Frank Shellenback, a Pacific Coast legend for almost twenty years, still licensed to use the spitball until he stopped pitching in 1938, and subsequently a major league coach in Boston and Detroit. Among these three, the knowledge of pitching and the handling of pitchers was of the highest order. And in running the ball game itself, Leo needed no help.

What also emerged is what Rickey had foreseen: To a younger generation of players, Leo was becoming someone to listen to, not resent. With Mays in particular, he formed a warm and supportive relationship from the first moment. (Leo's detractors would say, "Why not? He could see what Willie could do for him." But the fact is, in this and many other cases, Leo could be thoughtful and considerate and generous and truly helpful—when he wanted to be.) But more than anything, they admired his grasp of the game and his response to situations. They developed absolute faith in his ability to guess right and stay ahead of the opposing manager's thinking. Even those who found his lifestyle and personal manner distasteful, like Dark and Thomson, felt wholeheartedly that his leadership made winning possible.

Leo was known as profane in language, ruthless in competition (he believed in the knockdown pitch and mayhem at second in breaking up double plays), unconcerned about even his own players getting hurt if it might win a game now. But when the 1951 season started out with 12 losses in 14 games, he didn't abuse anyone and kept confidence high—a basic attribute of good managing. He left his mature pitchers, Jansen and Maglie, alone; he babied and urged those who needed it, like Hearn. He switched people around until he got the best combination, moving Lockman from left to first and Irvin from first to left just before Mays arrived; and after Mays had taken over center field from Thomson, put Bobby at third base in July. The great pennant run, which started with a 16-game winning streak from $11\frac{1}{2}$ games behind the Dodgers in mid-August, really began when Thomson, at third, started hitting .357 for the rest of the year. His homer off Branca had been the difference in the first playoff game at Ebbets Field, and the historic 3-run shot with one out in the bottom of the ninth of the third game, erasing a 4–2 Dodger lead, was only the last and crowning blow of a two-month-long fantasy.

In short, all his moves worked, and that's what impressed his players. Stanky, the second baseman and leadoff man who played baseball more with brains and bravery than physical gift, was his delegate on the field. (In receiving an award from the New York Baseball Writers, Stanky thanked them for "recognizing my intangibles.) Eddie called him "Leo the Lion," and tackled him in the third base coaching box as Thomson approached on his homer, to make sure Leo wouldn't make it illegal by grabbing Thomson in celebration. The press, notably Red Smith in his columns and Willard Mullin in his cartoons, started calling Leo "The Little Shepherd of Coogan's Bluff," noting his new role as true leader of the flock entrusted to him, not simply a gambling play caller. (Coogan's Bluff was the cliff that overlooked the Polo Grounds.) And, better still, the "practically peerless leader."

The 1951 miracle could not be repeated in 1952, as the Dodgers won by 4½ games, and whatever else may have been involved, one reason was explanation enough: Mays left in May to serve his time as an army draftee. He was gone all of 1953, too, while Maglie and Jansen were showing signs of age, and Irvin was slowly recuperating from a leg injury that cost him most of 1952. Stanky had gone over to manage the Cardinals in 1952, so a lot of rebuilding was in order.

At this stage, two of Leo's persistent flaws surfaced. His turbulent personal life led to Stoneham's disenchantment with him as a person. And his tendency to lose interest and not pay attention when it was obvious he had no chance to win asserted itself as 1953 wore on. The Giants finished fifth, and Stoneham was getting fed up.

As 1954 began, Mays was back, and a new young pitching leader had been acquired, Johnny Antonelli, from Milwaukee for—hold your breath—Bobby Thomson. A new young, gutsy second baseman was on hand, Davey Williams, and Dark was now the field captain. This team couldn't match the strength "on paper" of the two-time champion Dodgers or the increasingly powerful Milwaukee Braves, but it could have a chance.

In spring training, there was a flare-up between Stoneham and Durocher. The boss was ready to fire him. The players, under Dark's leadership, asked him to relent: With Leo we can win, was their message; without him, we can't. Stoneham listened. Leo

The Descendants

promised to behave (and kept the promise). All was sweetness and light as the Giants did win, beating back the stronger teams and playing textbook "counterclockwise" baseball—hit to right, move the runners, manufacture one run at a time, get tight pitching, and make the plays in the field. With Willie in center, of course, they not only made all the possible plays but a lot of impossible ones as well.

After every victory, Leo would lean back expansively in that center field clubhouse office once occupied by McGraw, grin at the writers, and say, "Don't praise me, praise the players. They're doing it all." His in-game decisions were never sharper, and he made two larger strategic moves that all his budding managers took to heart.

He had, since 1952, a rookie pitcher with an incredible knuckle ball, named Hoyt Wilhelm, who could not only control it but throw it with greater velocity than most. A knuckleballer's problem is that catchers can't hold it, so it backfires with men on base, especially in tight situations when a steal must be prevented. But Westrum could catch Wilhelm's, and Leo made him a relief specialist. If they couldn't hit it, you didn't have to worry about the runner. And Wilhelm had the right cool temperament to work in a crisis.

But Leo also had an old, hard-bitten, power pitcher named Marv Grissom, who had never set the world on fire, but who also had the perfect reliever's mental toughness. So Leo used him too. Sometimes the situation was better for one than the other. Sometimes both helped win the same game. The two-reliever system was fully exploited for the first time by Leo that year.

The other move was remarkable in a different way, and possible only because Mays was the superman he was. By the end of July, Willie had 36 homers and the papers were full of those "He's ahead of Babe Ruth's 1927 pace" stories. But the team hit a losing spell, and the lead was down to half a game by mid-August.

Leo told Willie to stop hitting homers.

Go to right field, he said, and get on more often. You can run when you're on base. You can spread the defense. We've got other hitters who can drive you in. We'll score more runs, when we need them, with you on base more often than we will with your homers. Counterclockwise baseball.

Willie said he'd try. He did. He hit only 5 more homers the rest of the year—2 after the pennant was clinched, and 1 an inside-the-park job—but he raised his average from .316 to .345 and won the league batting title.

Leo Durocher

Here we have the whole story of brilliant managing in a nutshell: You have to figure out the thing that will win for you—and you have to have the player who can do it. And you have to recognize that you have him, and sell him on the idea.

The Giants swept the World Series from the 111-victory Indians. For the first time in more than twenty years, since 1933, the Giants were number one in the three-team New York market.

That was Leo's peak year. In 1955, the breach with Stoneham didn't heal, the Dodgers ran away with the pennant by a huge margin, the Giants finished a distant third, and Durocher was fired. Among other things, Stoneham already knew that his position in New York was untenable and was thinking of moving the team to Minneapolis, just as Walter O'Malley, in Brooklyn, was flirting with Los Angeles and arranging to play some home games in Jersey City. Leo's identity as a celebrity was simply becoming irrelevant, his talents could not help a deteriorating team, and there was no reason to put up with his ego.

Here's an example of just how egotistical Leo really was. One of the big theatrical events of that time was the play *Inherit the Wind*, in which Paul Muni played Clarence Darrow as defense counsel in the famous Scopes trial in Tennessee against the teaching of evolution in the schools. The opposing lawyer is William Jennings Bryan, who quotes from the Bible. In one scene, Darrow picks up the Bible to quote from it himself, and says to Bryan and the courtroom in general:

"All right, now we'll play in *your* ballpark."

Leo attended the play one night in a house seat, right in the middle of the third row.

"Muni looked right at me when he said it," he told me afterward, "so they must have told him I was in the theater. I think they wrote in that line that night just for me."

He really meant it.

Elder Statesman

When Leo left the Giants, he was out of baseball for five years. His home was Hollywood. He remained in the public eye as a television commentator for NBC's game of the week. His name was always mentioned when a managerial opening appeared, but no one hired him.

Finally in 1961, when the Dodgers were starting their fourth season in Los Angeles and preparing to move into their own

The Descendants

Dodger Stadium the next year, O'Malley hired Leo as a coach. It created an awkward situation for Walt Alston, the manager, because Durocher outshone him as a celebrity (especially in the Hollywood environment) and was perceived as calling the shots for the very conservative Alston. Nevertheless, the system worked fine: the Dodgers (who had already won three pennants under Alston alone) won the World Series in 1963. But after the 1964 season, Leo severed his connection with the Dodgers for the last time.

The Cubs, having fallen on evil times and experimented with no manager at all for several years (using a committee of coaches), called him out of retirement in 1966. Leo was now sixty and facing a serious generation gap in communicating with twenty-year-olds of a particularly rebellious era eventually identified as "The Sixties." In 1966, he achieved something unprecedented: His Cubs became the first team ever to finish below the New York Mets, placing tenth and last as his former catcher, Westrum, lifted the Mets to ninth place for the first time as Stengel's successor.

But by the very next year, Leo had the Cubs in third (while the Mets fell back to last) and third again in 1968. The Cardinals dominated the league those two years, and Franks was finishing a four-year run of second-place finishes with the Giants, so Leo was flying high in Chicago—where the White Sox were being managed by Stanky. (Did we mention that baseball is a small world?)

In 1969, the Cubs seemed on their way to a first-place finish in the brand-new two-division setup, only to run into a bigger miracle than 1951: the Miracle Mets under Gil Hodges, who closed with a rush in September and went on to win the World Series.

The Cubs just missed again in 1970, finishing second to Pittsburgh, and were a more distant third in 1971. With the team around .500 halfway through 1972, Durocher's welcome was worn out and he turned the team over to Whitey Lockman. A month later Leo was called to Houston, where the Astros were chasing Cincinnati, to replace Harry Walker with six weeks to go in the season. The Astros did finish second, and went 82–80 while placing fourth in 1973, but that was Durocher's last year in uniform.

He was sixty-seven years old, and the sharpness that had always given him his "edge" was not only dulled by time but less pertinent to a new world where many managers were equipped with charts, visual aides, statistics, research departments, and specialized coaches. For a man who played with Babe Ruth under

Leo Durocher

Miller Huggins, an indoor ballpark with artificial turf in a two-division pennant race seemed centuries removed from his origins.

Still vigorous, still talkative, still a celebrity, Leo settled in Palm Springs, California, made the Oldtimers circuit, and, despite occasional illness, was going strong at eighty-five when he spoke at a New York Writers Dinner in 1991. He told stories about Mays and 1954. He died peacefully later that year.

But the true measure of his impact on baseball is simply the list of names of people who played under him who later managed major league teams:

Cookie Lavagetto. Fred Fitzsimmons. Billy Herman. Herman Franks. Bobby Bragan. Eddie Stanky. Clyde King. Gil Hodges. Bill Rigney. Whitey Lockman. Wes Westrum. Alvin Dark. Bob Elliott. Billy Gardner. Joe Amalfitano. Don Kessinger. Lee Elia. John Felske. Tommy Helms. Doug Rader.

That may not be a complete list. Durocher influenced some much more than others. Some managed a long time, some briefly. But all had teammates who were also affected by Leo, and spread Leo stories by word of mouth and personal contact to other teammates on other teams.

He remains the prototype, in baseball's memory bank today, of the in-game-decisive manager at his sharpest in smell of victory with players capable of executing his flashes of inspiration.

10

Al Lopez

Senor Serenity

If nice guys must finish last, Al Lopez never made it.

That he was a nice guy is beyond dispute. I have never met anyone in baseball who thought otherwise.

Well, in his first twelve years as a manager, Lopez never finished lower than second. In the remaining six years of his "real" career, he dipped as low as fifth once and added three more seconds.

When asked to come out of retirement a few years later, he did spend the second half of a season in charge of a team that was ninth when he got there and ninth when the season ended—but even that's not last in a ten-team league. What nice guys do is favors for friends, and that's the only reason he managed that year at all.

In a rough-and-tumble business, playing the physically most demanding position—catcher—in a record number of games, Lopez not only behaved like a gentleman but induced, by his presence, decent behavior in others. He was the human equivalent of a phenomenon noticed when the Astrodome opened as the first indoor ballpark. Under a roof, moving among theater-type seats with and under good lighting, the customers tended to avoid littering the floor with peanut shells and hot dog wrappers and empty cups the way they did automatically in outdoor stadiums. It just didn't feel right in a theaterlike setting. And Lopez had the same effect: He was so serene, in good times and bad, that you didn't feel comfortable raising your own voice.

Lopez illustrates three interesting points about how the position of manager was changing with changing times. His career began only in the 1950s, and extended into the early turmoil of the 1960s.

Al Lopez

First, dealing with the press became a more standardized aspect of a manager's responsibilities, as more and more radio broadcasting pushed newspapers into greater pursuit of "quotes." At the same time, professional ethics in journalism started to stress the adversarial relationship between reporter and subject. McGraw and Mack and Huggins and even Harris, and the early Durocher, could "own" their writers, enhancing the writer's prestige by acceptance and inclusion, punishing or threatening to punish by exclusion and verbal abuse—all with considerable confidence that both sides had similar ideas about what "should" be kept off the record or unreported. In the 1950s, this tacit compact began to break down, and writers saw their "integrity" compromised by being "too close" to the club they were covering. To the older "us versus them" school, what writers considered "honest objectivity" was "enemy propaganda." The older managers had difficulty handling such relationships. But Lopez, with his innate decency, not only avoided conflict but provided a model of how to do it. If being patient with players was a managerial virtue, being patient with the media—suffering fools gladly—was also a virtue, and an increasingly necessary one.

Second, the gentle element of Lopez's manner fit nicely with the emerging self-awareness players' had about their rights. The blacks coming into baseball still faced an extremely racist environment and had antennae tuned accurately to types of mistreatment most white players didn't notice. Young men in general were less disposed to "take orders" blindly and wanted to be given reasons for what they were asked to do. They were growing up without the pervasive fear of unemployment that was the common experience of the Depression generation and of immigrant families for many generations; and they all had a taste, through the military draft, of authoritarian ways they wanted no part of in civilian life. Again, this meant a serious adjustment for whip-cracking old-school managers (like Hornsby or even McCarthy, in his softer way). But for Lopez, the low-key approach he had anyhow was a perfect adaptation for the new circumstances—and, again, a model others could learn from.

Finally, as media exposure increased, as other sports like football and basketball began to compete for public attention, as the money stakes for all involved became larger and caused increased tension, and as conventional wisdom spread more uniformly throughout the farm system–driven baseball environment, more importance than ever was placed on results. Only winners were worth listening to. Lopez, thanks to the consistent winning records his teams produced, became influential simply by example, not through adulatory writers or self-promoting behavior. This, too, was more in tune with the times.

Conceptually, Lopez was grounded in McGrawism. He came up to Brooklyn while Uncle Robby was still there, played under Stengel (his particular friend) in Brooklyn and Boston, under McKechnie in Boston, and under Frisch in Pittsburgh. And he showed this heritage in a striking way in the two halves of his career. At Cleveland he had great hitting backing up an even greater pitching staff, and no speed; he finished behind only the Yankees (five times) and beat them once. At Chicago, he had little power and good but less stable pitching, and available speed. So he switched style from big-inning-and-hold-them to hit-and-run, bunt, steal, and scramble, with no loss of efficiency. There too, he lost only to the Yankees four times and beat them once, although he also had a stretch of finishing third, fourth, and fifth during the expansion changeover.

This was the McGraw pattern in reverse, the great skill of adjusting to circumstances. McGraw had shifted, faster than anyone, from low-score to power baseball when the ball changed. Lopez shifted from power to low-score when his personnel and home park changed.

Lopez came from Ybor City, the Spanish section of Tampa, Florida, where his father worked in a cigar factory and he did too, as a teen-ager, during vacations. But as soon as he discovered he could play ball well enough to get paid for it, Lopez set his sights on a baseball career.

He was sixteen years old in 1925, when the Senators, training in Tampa, gave him a taste of the real thing. Bucky Harris, the manager, let him catch batting practice and warm up some pitchers—including Walter Johnson, a mind-boggling experience for so humble a boy, which he never forgot. When spring training ended, Lopez got a job with the Tampa team in the Florida State League. After two years, he moved up to Jacksonville. When he got some hits off Dazzy Vance in an exhibition game against the Dodgers, Uncle Robby was impressed enough to buy his contract for $10,000 and farm him out to Macon. In 1929, the Dodgers sent him to Atlanta. But Robby, the old catcher, was not interested in his hitting; he could see, in Lopez, the makings of an outstanding

Al Lopez

receiver: a good arm, a sure glove, and above all a good handler of pitchers, which meant not only brains (to know what to call) but psychological rapport to keep pitcher's emotions on an even keel. Al's good nature was a factor in his success even as a player.

He came to Brooklyn to stick in 1930, worked for Max Carey, and became especially admired by Stengel, who nevertheless traded him to Boston after the 1935 season. There, he absorbed McKechnie's pitching philosophy, and a couple of years later Stengel showed up. And in midseason of 1940, Stengel traded him again (to raise a little cash) to Pittsburgh, where Lopez spent the next six years catching for Frisch, who was as steeped in McGraw training as Stengel. In 1947, winding up his major league career at the age of thirty-nine, he was the reserve catcher for Cleveland, where McKechnie was Lou Boudreau's second in command.

Lopez had caught 1,950 major league games, a record that stood until the 1980s when Bob Boone and Carlton Fisk passed it. The Indians, run by Veeck and Hank Greenberg (who had just ended his own playing career) offered him the managership at Indianapolis, their top farm club. Al won the American Association pennant in 1948 and finished second the next two years.

In 1951, Veeck had moved on to St. Louis and Greenberg, in charge of the Indians, brought Lopez up to Cleveland. Boudreau, no longer able to play shortstop full time for himself—his key asset as a manager—had moved on to Boston (where he would soon resume managing). Lopez then embarked on his celebrated battles against his one-time master, Stengel.

They had a close race right from the start, and in mid-September 1951 the Indians were actually ahead, but the Yankees prevailed in the final week. In 1952, both teams won at a fantastic rate through September, but again the Yankees stayed 2 games ahead. In 1953, the Yankees got ahead earlier and further than usual, on their way to a fifth straight World Series victory, and the Indians had to overtake Chicago for second place with a September drive.

Then, in 1954, the Indians won 111 games and there was nothing Stengel could do about that.

The Cleveland staff Lopez commanded has seldom been equaled: Bob Lemon, Early Wynn, and Mike Garcia won 83, 83, and 79 games, respectively, in the four seasons of 1951–54. Bob Feller, still a 22-game winner in 1951, was limited to 19 starts in 1954—and went 13–3. Backing them up were Hal Newhouser, deferring his retirement, and Art Houtteman. The closers were a relief tandem, Ray Narleski (righty) and Don Mossi (lefty) used in percentage fashion, not in the more creative patterns Durocher was employing with Wilhelm and Grissom the same year. The staff earned run average was 2.78.

None of that mattered against Durocher's hot hand in the World Series sweep. But disappointment or not, Lopez had put together quite a team. The infield was Vic Wertz, Bobby Avila (a second basemen who won the batting title at .341), George Strickland, and Al Rosen; the outfield had Larry Doby, Al Smith, and Dave Philley; and Jim Hegan was the catcher. They loved playing for Lopez, and Lopez, in his forties and not that far removed from his playing days, had an unusual degree of rapport and communication with his players for the standards of that time.

After running second to the Yankees again in 1955 and 1956, Lopez moved to Chicago in 1957, where Veeck had come into control. The White Sox had been built into contender status in the early 1950s by Paul Richards, and had been managed by Marty Marion the last two years. (Richards had moved over to Baltimore when the old St. Louis Browns had become the new Orioles in 1954.) In Comiskey Park, less suited to homers than Cleveland Stadium, Lopez found only Doby, who had preceded him to Chicago, as a power threat. But Luis Aparicio, his twenty-three-year-old shortstop, could run, and so could Jim Rivera, and Minnie Minoso, and Jim Landis. The pitching staff had no dominant figures like Lemon-Wynn-Garcia, but lots of effective arms that could be juggled correctly. Nellie Fox, the little second baseman, developed by Connie Mack, was an artist of bat control.

So Lopez turned his runners loose and juggled six starters and three relievers. Aparicio, preceding the base stealing revolution that Maury Wills would set off in 1962, led the league with 28 steals in 1957, 29 in 1958, and 56 in 1959, when the White Sox won the pennant, fighting off Cleveland and leaving the Yankees far behind. In those three seasons, the White Sox stole 106, 101, and 113 bases—the only team in either league to reach triple digits since the 1949 Dodgers led by Jackie Robinson.

For the next three years, the White Sox simply didn't have the talent to challenge the Yankees (who kept winning) or match the Baltimore and Detroit teams that did challenge them. But in 1963 and 1964, the last two years of the Yankee reign, Lopez was second again and missed by only 1 game in 1964.

Al Lopez

There was, however, a noticeable difference in his relationship to his players in those years. He never lost his calm manner, but as the age gap between him and his players increased, Lopez became less communicative. He had learned what all managers find out sooner or later, that there's a limit to satisfying the craving to be "understood." Older managers stop trying to explain their moves, about putting people in and out of the lineup, and stop discussing particular plays, because they find that too many players too much of the time are simply looking for an alibi. The desire to be told "what's going on" is too often a desire to simply argue and make self-justifying pleas. The explanations that Lopez and Stengel meant to be instructive tended to become raw material for grievance. Stengel never did shut up, and was considered a clown by the less perceptive players in both his Yankee and Met days. Lopez, not exactly withdrawing into a shell, simply found his patience best kept under control by silence.

And his players, in the universal and predictable cry of the 1960s, said, "He doesn't communicate."

Lopez finished second again in 1965, well behind Sam Mele's Minnesota Twins, and that was enough. He retired at fifty-eight, but retained affiliation with the club. His successor was Stanky, a dramatically different personality but not so different in his ideas of how to play. After two stormy seasons, in which Stanky lost out in a four-way race in 1967 that placed the White Sox fourth only 3 games out of first, Stanky had to be replaced halfway through the 1968 season, and Lopez was pressed back into duty, more to soothe the atmosphere than to perform miracles. The team finished ninth, and 17 games into the 1969 season, Lopez turned the team over to Don Gutteridge, his coach through all the Chicago years, and retired to Florida for good.

Lopez, as much as anyone, turned the McGraw principles of winning baseball into common wisdom, standard procedure, ordinary practice—stripped of hype, stripped of melodrama, free of unnecessarily heightened tension. Among his players who went on to manage were Bob Kennedy, Doby, and Lemon, but more of them became highly respected long-term coaches and minor league managers, and Rosen became general manager of three clubs that finished first. All reflected Lopez's central lesson: You can do the job right, with no sacrifice of competitive aggressiveness and daring, without shouting.

But everything has plusses and minuses, and his lack of flamboyance decreased the influence he might have had on the game as a whole, and denied him full credit (not that he cared) for daring and innovation. Maury Wills and the Dodgers of the 1960s brought base running back into the mainstream after forty years of neglect—but Lopez had done that with Aparicio a few years before. Durocher's two-man bullpen pushed the trend toward specialization—but Lopez was already using it with Mossi and Narleski. Because the Dodgers and Durocher were so much in the spotlight, their moves could be models for everyone and could not be ignored. Because Lopez conducted his business so quietly, only the more perceptive people noticed, and fewer were ready to risk imitation. That's one more facet of managing that cannot be glossed over: The squeaky wheel *does* get the grease.

11

Frank Frisch

The Fordham Flash

One can think of Frankie Frisch as McGraw with a sense of humor.

Volatile is too gentle a word for Frisch, a man who bubbled over with ideas and enthusiasm. But *uninhibited* is a good one. He loved to say what he thought, and even to say something that would upset others even if he didn't quite think it. He was stubborn, but not out of resistance to someone else's desire or suggestion; he simply knew absolutely for sure that he was right. He loved competition, and the thrill of victory. He loved the baseball scene the way he knew it—rough, profane, intensely fought, yet full of camaraderie and appetite for fun that diminished as the game got richer, more professionally technical, more genteel, more spread out. *Opinionated,* like *volatile,* is too weak a term for his firmly held, and loudly articulated, opinions on anything and everything. And behind it all was a quick and well-educated mind, combined with a willingness to risk his body recklessly and an expectation that others should too.

McGraw was his mentor and model, but Frisch came from a different background and had a different nature. He was a New Yorker born and bred, from an affluent family. Growing up in the years before World War I—he was born in 1898—he had all the advantages of the well-to-do in an age when the metropolis was entering its most glamorous period. By the time he was old enough to follow the baseball news, McGraw was a New York institution, but not the only one he knew: He was well aware of the museums, the concert halls, the libraries, and the good restaurants too. He prepared for college at Fordham Prep and went on from there to Fordham, not far from the Bronx neighborhood his family lived in, presumably to study chemistry and—his father hoped—to join him and his older brothers in their linen manufacturing business.

The Descendants

But Frankie was a terrific athlete. He was captain of the base-ball, football, and basketball teams, a good enough halfback to be named to Walter Camp's All-America second team in 1918, a good enough shortstop and hitter to be recommended by his coach to the Giants.

Since his Fordham coach was Art Devlin, the third base star of McGraw's Giants during the glory years of 1904–11, the rec-ommendation meant something to Devlin's old boss, with whom he'd been a favorite. When the college baseball season of 1919 and graduation ceremonies at Fordham were over, McGraw magnanimously offered the twenty-one-year old Frisch a minor league contract.

Frisch said, in effect, "Hey, I don't have to do this for a living. Major leagues or nothing." McGraw, always impressed by feisti-ness in a talented player, agreed, and brought him to the Giants right away. He didn't think Frisch had a shortstop's range, so he tried him at second and third and settled on second. Frisch was a switch-hitter, but held the bat the wrong way right-handed (with the left hand on top) and McGraw had to change that. In those famous morning workouts at the Polo Grounds, Frisch got special attention.

"The Fordham Flash," as he was called right off the bat, was spectacular in style as well as result. Any ball he couldn't field cleanly he blocked with his flying body, like a hockey goalie. He was exceptionally fast and would slide headfirst. The cap flying off his head became a trademark thirty years before Willie Mays arrived. And he could hit. He ended a nineteen-year playing career with a .316 average, never having spent a day in the minors.

Of all the managers in this book, he was clearly the best player. A reporter once asked Joe McCarthy to list the composite points of a theoretically perfect player. "What's wrong with Frisch?" said McCarthy. "What can't he do?"

What Frisch couldn't do was take life too solemnly, or accept abuse. For the first six years, he was McGraw's pet, and a key element in those four straight pennants (1921–24). He was made team captain, and McGraw let his friends know that when and if he would ever retire, he intended to name Frisch as his successor. But McGraw had also developed the habit of singling out his captains for his most vicious tirades after defeat, as if the captain was also the talisman for the team's fortunes. The fortunes weren't as good as they were before 1925 and 1926, and the aging McGraw was alienating more people as time went on. He turned the full force of his criticism on Frisch. Finally, one day in St. Louis, Frank decided he'd had enough, packed his bag, checked out, and took the train back to New York.

The umbilical cord was cut.

Frisch finished the season, but it was obvious he couldn't stay. The same year, Hornsby player-managed the St. Louis Cardinals to their first pennant and World Series triumph (over the Yankees)—but alienated Breadon, his club owner. Breadon insisted that Hornsby be traded, the Giants wanted him, Frisch was no longer welcome, and Breadon, a New Yorker, knew all about him since Fordham. The trade was made.

St. Louis was furious. It's a sentimental town anyhow, and has always preferred retaining familiar stars beyond their best playing days to accepting "strangers" in their place; it's still that way. Losing Hornsby was intolerable. There were threats of boycott. There was antagonism to Frisch simply because he wasn't Hornsby. But within a year, Frisch won over the St. Louis public by his play and spirit: He wasn't the hitter Hornsby was—no one was— but he was a better all-around player. The manager in 1927 was Bob O'Farrell, the catcher. In 1928, Bill McKechnie took over, and the Cardinals went to the World Series again.

In the switch, Frisch learned something he took to heart as a manager later. He admired and wanted to match McGraw's toughness—but he didn't have, and understood the harm in, McGraw's sadistic tendencies. He also didn't want, or see the need for, the dictatorial power McGraw insisted on exerting. You could be a leader and even a boss without yielding the right to have some fun—and without depriving others of their right to enjoy what they were doing.

Breadon was his fan, since by his great play Frisch had made the St. Louis public and writers get off the Hornsby question. But Frisch saw, firsthand, the emasculating routine Breadon went through with McKechnie, making him switch positions with a minor league manager (Billy Southworth) before bringing him back out of necessity, so Frisch's lifelong religion of self-reliance became stronger than ever.

In 1930 and 1931, Gabby Street was the manager and the Cardinals won two more pennants, and the 1931 World Series. Frisch was at his playing peak and feeling at home among some flaky

The Descendants

teammates at a time when the word *flaky* wasn't yet in use. He had now played in seven World Series for National League teams, and no one else had done that.

In 1932, when the Cardinals suddenly fell to seventh place, Frisch had slowed up noticeably and was criticized for it. Actually, he was playing hurt, with muscle strains in both legs, and was outraged that Street had refused to tell any of the newspapermen about his condition. "If I was managing, I'd certainly tell the press about a player being hurt," he declared—and set off talk about the possibility of his being a manager. That season, of course, McGraw had passed the baton to Terry at the Polo Grounds, so there was no possibility of going back to New York. And then, when the Cardinals were mired at the .500 mark in late July, Breadon had Frisch replace Street, starting a new phase in his career.

The Gashouse Gang

The team Frisch took charge of was full of what people then called "characters," or less politely, "nuts." There was Pepper Martin, called "The Wild Hoss of the Osage" after getting 12 hits and stealing 5 bases in the 1931 World Series and becoming a national celebrity. He led an improvised country music band using homemade instruments (like a pot) in the clubhouse. There was Dizzy Dean, who utterred outrageous boasts and then made good on them, and who loved practical as well as verbal jokes. Rip Collins, Joe Medwick, Durocher, Burleigh Grimes—these were not what one would call "ordinary" people.

Dean set the tone more than anyone. Many players lied about their age, to appear younger; Diz lied about his name and birthplace as well, giving two versions of the first (Jay Hanna Dean and Jerome Herman Dean) and three states for the latter, explaining that he was doing newspapermen a favor by giving each a scoop. He'd organize a group of players to dress up as painters and, equipped with brushes, paintpots, and ladders, disrupt a banquet in the hotel the team was using. He'd go on strike in midseason for more money, tease and insult opponents, fool around in games—and still win. He'd grown up in a family of itinerant cotton choppers, got no schooling past fourth grade, enlisted in the army at sixteen (where a sergeant gave him the name "Dizzy"), and had delayed his major league career by a year by talking himself back to the minors during spring training in 1931. When his silent and introspective younger brother Paul joined the team in 1934 and was named, inappropriately but unavoidably, "Daffy," Diz did the talking for both of them, predicting 45 victories for "me 'n Paul." They made good, winning 49 (Diz providing 30) and then all 4 World Series games from Detroit (2 each).

This collection of zanies sometimes drove Frisch to distraction, especially Dean, but he also felt at home with them. He could yell, threaten, issue fines, break up fist fights, and tinker with the lineup without creating or holding any carryover grudges. It was almost as if he were two people: inside a ballpark, Frisch was profane, combative, and irreverent, wallowing in the barracks atmosphere and indulging in it wholeheartedly; outside, he was a man who read serious books, went to the opera and symphony, befriended concert pianists (and played the piano himself), and confined his speech to a perfectly respectable vocabulary.

In running the game and making baseball decisions, however, he was pure McGraw: hit and run, run bases aggressively, play hurt, and use the hot pitcher. He let Dean, for instance, in the three seasons 1934–36, make 103 starts (completing 81 of them) and relieve 48 times, logging 951 innings pitched without damage to his arm—which he ruined anyhow the following year by coming back too soon after suffering a broken toe when hit by a line drive in the All-Star Game. (The day he returned, McKechnie, managing the Boston team he was to face, warned Dean before the game not to pitch, because the inability to stride normally would put unnatural strains on his arm. Sure enough, late in the game, Dean's arm popped and the famous fast ball was gone for good.) But those 151 appearances in three years for the Cardinals had produced 82 victories and 23 saves—38 percent of all the games the team won in three close pennant races.

At the same time, Frisch was being exposed on a daily basis to Rickey's ideas and systems. As personalities, they were not congenial and the fact that Frisch was Breadon's bobo while there was friction between Rickey and Breadon didn't help matters. But Frisch understood fully, and absorbed, the virtues of Rickey's analyses and insights, and the kind of talent flow it was producing. The principles being taught systematically through Rickey's organization were, after all, McGraw principles: counterclockwise baseball with emphasis on speed and defense, and in their own way the ultimate authoritarianism. Frisch didn't accept the methods, but he grasped and passed on their significance.

The 1934 Cardinals remain, in baseball lore, one of the most colorful of all teams, and were so perceived at the time. In 1935, they were overtaken in September when the Cubs won 21 in a row. In 1936, they tied the Cubs for second, 5 games behind Terry's Giants. In 1937, with Dean useless after the All-Star Game, they fell to fourth. (At All-Star break, Diz was 12–7 and the Cards were near the top; after it, he was 1–3.)

Frisch, by now, was thirty-eight and essentially a bench manager, with Jimmy Brown and Stu Martin, farm system products, taking his place. In 1938, with the team in sixth place in September, Breadon fired him.

But Durocher, about to start managing in Brooklyn, would carry on his legacy—handling veteran players with individualistic tendencies in an explosive setting—there.

"Oh, Those Bases on Balls!"

In 1939, out of uniform for the first time in twenty years and an authentic civilian for the first time in his adult life, Frisch turned to play-by-play broadcasting for a station in Boston. I used to hear him on the car radio when we drove into Connecticut or Massachusetts. He would say things like "Ball one"—long silence, sporadic crowd noise in the background—"Ball two"—more silence—"Strike one"—long pause—"Double to left!" But he would also, at other times, spout his unvarnished opinions and sharp observations, and the one that became a rallying cry among all his listeners was his bleat after a walk: "Oh, those bases on balls!" They kill you, he'd explain. Let the other side earn what it can, but giving away a base for free was sure to produce disaster, so why would a pitcher do it?

This was, of course, the other side of the coin of basic counterclockwise move-the-runner baseball: If advancing the runner is the way to manufacture runs, don't help the opposition get started by putting someone on or, worse still, walking a man with someone already on first to push him along.

Frisch seemed to enjoy himself, and was in great demand as an afterdinner speaker. But his heart was down on the field. So when the Pirates offered him a chance to manage again, in 1940, he took it, aware that he didn't have anything like the teams he was used to in New York and St. Louis. The club had been inherited in 1932 by Bill Benswanger, a nephew of Dreyfuss, and had remained a contender under Pie Traynor through 1938 (when it lost a lead to the Cubs in the final week). But it had fallen to sixth in 1939 and all its key players had aged: Paul and Lloyd Waner, Arky Vaughan, Ray Berres. It had never built a farm system, it wasn't backed by great wealth, and the war was coming. In competitive terms, the franchise was headed for bankruptcy.

In this milieu, Frisch's talent for comedy flourished. Instead of berating his players (which he did too, from time to time), he concentrated on baiting umpires. Again, unlike McGraw, he did it without viciousness and with a great deal of originality. To McGraw, umpires were the enemy; to Frisch, they were only targets.

And he had a good partner in action. Casey Stengel had been his friend and teammate on the Giants (and his first real exposure to the kind of thinking around corners he would find in St. Louis). Casey was managing in Boston when Frisch was broadcasting there in 1939. He remained with the Bees for the first few years of Frisch's time in Pittsburgh. They entered into an unofficial contest of topping each other in gags, not all restricted to umpires.

So while Frisch's Pirates finished fourth, fourth, fifth, fourth, second (in the deepest war year of 1944), fourth, and seventh, his antics got more attention than his results.

Coaching at third base, he pretended to faint at one of Bill Klem's calls. While he lay prostrate, Klem raced over and yelled, "If you ain't dead, Frisch, you're out of the game." (And if he was, he could stay in? I've always wondered what Klem meant.)

Wanting a game halted because it was raining, he went out to talk the umpire carrying an umbrella. On other occasions he used galoshes and ponchos. He, Stengel, and others used flashlights to remind umpires that it was getting dark, and one of them actually found a Japanese lantern to carry to home plate.

Once Eddie Stanky, playing third base for the Cubs, threw a hip block at a Pirate runner rounding third, and sent him sprawling. The umpire saw it, and awarded the run automatically. But Frisch, as a close witness, decided that wasn't enough. When another runner approached third with Stanky set to make a play on him,

The Descendants

as the runner slid in from one side, Frisch slid in from the other and the confused Stanky tagged Frisch instead.

The umpire (Jocko Conlan) called the runner safe and Frisch out—out of the game, that is.

One hot and humid day, with the team going nowhere, Frisch didn't mind getting thrown out, and tried to provoke an argument. It would cost him a $50 fine from the league, but it would be worth it. But the umpire was on to him. "It's hot for me too," he declared in the face-to-face jawing match with Frankie. "I've got to stay out here and so will you."

But all this was to be forgotten instantly when it was over. Frisch's motto was "Make fun, not war." When Ford Frick, the league president, heard that Frisch planned to pay off a $100 fine in pennies, he sent him a succinct wire: "Don't, Dutchman."

And the exchanges with Stengel, by wire, were in the same vein. When Stengel was hit by that car in Boston and wound up in the hospital with a broken leg at the start of 1943, Frisch wired: "Your attempt at suicide fully understood. Deepest sympathy you didn't succeed."

Then Stengel heard that a Pittsburgh home run had been nullified because a base runner, Frankie Zak, had called time out to tie his shoe. Stengel wired: "Am rushing pair of button shoes for Zak."

Such stories have become standard baseball lore, retold in many books, sometimes with variations and different names. But they do relate to the serious side of managing. Every manager must show his own players he's willing to stand up for them when they think they've been wronged. The vast majority of manager-umpire confrontations out in the open are for calculated effect on the manager's own players, not to change the mind of an umpire (which isn't going to happen anyhow) or to express truly uncontrollable emotion on the part of the manager. Frisch, especially, could make these escapades funny and get two benefits. The message to his players, "I'm sticking up for you," was delivered, but residual animosity in umpires was diluted. Actually, Frisch had friendly off-field relationships with many umpires—as he did with almost everyone connected with baseball—without compromise of integrity on either side. One umpire borrowed his car, then had Frisch pay for the gas to fill it up before he took it—and the next day chased him out of a game and recommended a fine and suspension.

Frank Frisch

Bob Broeg, the St. Louis sportswriter, was a collector of Frisch stories and knew him well. After his retirement, Frisch told Broeg: "I was a better manager with a good ball club than with a bad one. . . . I think managing shortened my playing career, but I was a better manager playing, when I could lead like a platoon sergeant in the field rather than as a general sitting back on his duff in a command post. . . . But I won't apologize for wanting my players to be as good as I was supposed to be." That's what they said about Durocher, of course: better with a good club, bored with a bad one.

Then Frisch added, "If intolerance of mediocrity is a crime, I plead guilty," anticipating Barry Goldwater's famous 1964 presidential campaign theme that "Extremism in defense of liberty is no vice, moderation in combatting tyranny is no virtue."

Of course, no manager can demand that players be more talented than they are, which is why so few of the best managers were great players: the less gifted understood that. Those who could be playing managers, like Mickey Cochrane and Joe Cronin and Frisch and Bucky Harris and Hornsby, didn't have to face this problem while they were on the field themselves. But when they could no longer play, they couldn't deal well with inferior players. Ty Cobb, Walter Johnson, Mel Ott, and Lou Boudreau are examples of Hall of Famers who couldn't cope, and not because of intolerance, which Cobb had in his nature and Frisch expressed. Johnson and Ott in particular were the best-meaning and kindest men imaginable: They simply didn't know how to help lesser players overcome their problems because they'd never experienced inadequacy themselves.

Frisch's time in Pittsburgh ran out at the end of 1946 when, among other things, the first abortive attempt to form a player union disrupted his club. So he was back behind a mircophone in 1947, with the Giants, no less, more garrulous than before, his New York accent sweet in his listeners' ears.

In 1949, he got back into a Giant uniform as a coach when Durocher came over to manage, but by June he was a manager himself again. The Cubs, after losing the 1945 World Series, had bumped down the ladder into last place by 1948, and midway through 1949 were headed for the same fate. Charlie Grimm, their savior in 1945, had been unable to prevent the decline, and the call went out for "The Old Flash," as Frisch now referred to himself.

The Descendants

The change had no visible effect. The Cubs stayed last that year, inched up to seventh in 1950, and were running seventh just past the midpoint of the 1951 season when Frisch gave way to Phil Cavaretta (who completed another last-place season).

Still only fifty-two, Frisch retired to his home in New Rochelle, just a few miles from his native Bronx, and lived the good life. He would make the banquet and Oldtimer circuits, and spout his views about how spoiled the next generation of ballplayers was becoming, how silly batting helmets were, how soft spring training had become, and so forth. Early in 1973, he was critically injured in an automobile crash and died five weeks later, at the age of seventy-four.

Frisch's influence was not based on his record of victories, but on his transmission to a whole generation of players of the McGraw elements of baseball playing. Of the men who played for him, Durocher, Don Gutteridge, Terry Moore, Bob Elliott, Al Lopez, and Cavaretta managed in the majors, and Gutteridge, Mike Ryba, Rube Walker, Hank Sauer, and others became top coaches and/or minor league managers feeding the majors in a farm system age.

But the real line goes like this:

McGraw to Frisch to Durocher to Bill Rigney.

As a Giants infielder when Durocher came over from Brooklyn, Rigney consciously modeled himself on Leo when he went down to the minors to manage. He came back as Leo's successor and moved with the Giants to San Francisco. Subsequently he managed the original California Angels and the Minnesota Twins. The fallout goes this way:

Durocher's 1951 Giants: Stanky, Al Dark, Whitey Lockman, Wes Westrum, Rigney.

And Rigney managed no less than thirteen future big league managers: Lockman, Dark, Westrum, Red Schoendienst, Jim Davenport, Joe Amalfitano, Ken Aspromonte, Buck Rodgers, Jim Fregosi, Frank Quilici, Del Rice, Joe Adcock, and Jim Marshall.

Not all, of course were equally affected by Rig, and Schoendienst, although he played a couple of years for Rigney in New York, is a Rickey Cardinal product through and through.

And it was Schoendienst, when he first became manager of the Cardinals in 1965, to whom Frisch gave his bottom-line managerial advice:

"Don't take a hotel room higher than the second floor, because you might want to jump."

12

Paul Richards

The Answer Man

Paul Richards represents a departure from our pattern, and yet he confirms it. He acquired his ideas less by direct imitation of masters and their disciples than by deduction from observation. He insisted that he learned more from the mistakes made by managers he played for than from their good points. By concentrating on what not to do, he evolved his theories of what should work. In a sense, he was no one's disciple but a counter-disciple, like a reverse print of a photographic negative that comes out white on black instead of black on white.

And yet, he actually played for McGraw and Mack, and modeled his methods on Rickey as soon as he got into position to run an organization. He was, when all is said and done, directly on the McGraw line but with his own applications and a totally different kind of personality. He was analytic and didactic and distant, citing "restraint" as the key quality for a manager, in contrast to McGraw's volcanic approach. He didn't browbeat or intimidate—but he was even more certain of his own correctness than McGraw or anyone else. All his conclusions came from calculation—but he didn't hesitate to try something new, different, unorthodox, or risky when he thought of it, and he spent a lot of his time thinking of things like that. You can win by the book, he'd say, but you don't have to lose by the book; that is, know the percentages but recognize when to go against them. Not everyone responded to his teaching, which was a distillation of McGrawism, but those who did became dedicated followers.

Richards stressed two points above all others. He was an expert on pitching techniques—the mechanics of gripping and releasing various pitches, not just pitch selection—to a degree all our other managers left to their pitching coaches. And he believed that the tiniest details had to be noted, worked on, analyzed, and reviewed at all times: batting stance, defensive position, taking a lead, and so forth. These, he preached, were more important than grand strategic designs—and the point is, he *preached* this. Others may have believed in the details as thoroughly (Mack did), but Richards talked about them more than they did.

I never enjoyed talking to him, but that's my personal problem, not his. He thought he was smarter than anyone else, which in itself is neither unusual nor necessarily unpleasant. But he gave you (or at least me) the impression that he thought you were too dumb to understand how smart he was. His baseball intelligence was certainly far above average among his peers; but he wielded it with a certain intellectual arrogance, conveying the idea that such-and-such a profound point was not just known by him, but only by him. My favorite story along those lines comes from Eddie Lopat, who had been a mainstay of the Yankees in the years they were finishing ahead of Richards's White Sox, and finally wound up at the end of his pitching career on Richards's staff in Baltimore.

Richards suggested that he try holding a palm ball a certain way, to add to his pitching repertoire.

"I've got that pitch," Lopat told him, "here, here, here, and here," indicating four different release points. "What do you think I've been getting you out with all these years?"

The fact is, however, that Richards *was* an expert on all these things, and his influence and importance lay in how much of them he passed along rather than in his own record of success.

And his background was significant.

Remember Waxahachie, Texas? Richards was born there on November 21, 1908. It's about twenty miles south of Dallas and about sixty miles north of Marlin, where McGraw established his spring training base for the Giants in the spring of that year. The Giants would play exhibition games in and around the area. Richards was the son of a schoolteacher and, learning to read at an early age, devoted a lot of that skill to studying box scores and stories in the Dallas papers. Waxahachie was a small town, but loaded with good ballplayers. Its high school team, as soon as Richards joined it, won 65 straight games and three consecutive state championships, and five of his teammates also made it to the majors. So it was well scouted, and Richards, tall and thin, was

Paul Richards

the best of them all, playing third base and shortstop and pitching—with both hands.

That's right, both hands. He was ambidextrous, and this got him some national notoriety even while he was still in high school. He did use the ability, changing according to the hitter, a couple of times in the minors, including an incident that represents the ultimate standoff: A switch-hitter came up, and when Richards switched hands, he switched batters' boxes. Richards responded by standing with both feet on the rubber and his hands behind his back, so that the hitter had to commit himself first. Thus Richards won the mind battle, but he lost that time-at-bat war by walking the hitter.

But his baseball heritage was even richer than that. In 1917, when he was only eight years old, the Detroit Tigers trained in Waxahachie (under the direction of Hughie Jennings), and McGraw brought his Giants over for an exhibition game. In it, Ty Cobb dropped an easy fly ball. This made an indelible impression on the boy in the stands, as he told Donald Honig sixty years later. That the greatest player in the world could make such an error was something he could never forget, while he could forget all sorts of positive accomplishments because they were supposed to happen. So this frame of mind—learn from the unusual and the errors—was part of him from the beginning. Eventually, he became very friendly with the retired Cobb, and in discussing baseball with him acquired intensification of the idea of the winning detail, of which Cobb was a master.

His high school exploits got the attention of Wilbert Robinson, back in Brooklyn, and Robinson sent his ace pitcher, Nap Rucker, to take a look. It was Rucker who signed Richards to a professional contract and who told him stories about Cobb, whose roommate he had been. This was 1926, and the seventeen-year-old Richards spent a couple of months on the bench without getting into a game before being sent down to the minors in Crisfield, Maryland. With typical Daffy Dodger inefficiency, he was left unprotected in the minor league draft and was taken by the St. Louis Browns. Uncle Robby's protest was rejected by Judge Landis, and the Browns returned him to the same minor league club as their property. He was primarily an infielder, and in 1928 was sent to Muskogee, Oklahoma, where he pitched too. But by the end of the year he was in Macon, Georgia, in the Sally League

The Descendants

(South Atlantic League), and that had a Dodger affiliation. The manager there, Charlie Moore, was the team's only catcher, and in spring training in 1930, Richards was in danger of being sent further down (to Jacksonville) because other infielders were doing better than he was. So he volunteered to catch, and became a catcher for the rest of his career. His arm was a good one, and his brain was the best.

He spent 1931 at Hartford, got a brief glimpse of Brooklyn (3 games) in 1932, but was sold in June to the Giants, who sent him to Minneapolis. (The Dodgers, after all, had Al Lopez catching every day.) There the manager was Donie Bush, and Richards—who had been unimpressed by Uncle Robby's easygoing ways even as a teen-age observer—was greatly influenced by Bush's strictness in handling players, many of whom were former major leaguers. And Bush, of course, had been Detroit's shortstop under Jennings, and a direct inheritor of Old Oriole baseball.

The Giants brought him up as their reserve catcher (behind Gus Mancuso) in the first full year of Terry's regime. Among the pitchers he caught were Carl Hubbell, Freddie Fitzsimmons, and Dolf Luque, sophisticated veterans who quickly increased a rookie catcher's awareness of pitching intricacy. Also on the team was Lefty O'Doul, whose dissertations on hitting were an invaluable education. And at twenty-four, with seven years of professional experience behind him, Richards did not hesitate to judge the managerial skills of Terry, which he found effective but one-dimensional. Terry, he thought, was totally committed to pitching and defense with little creative offense, relying on the individual ability of good hitters to provide necessary runs. The first part, Richards thought, was perfect, as long as you had good pitchers and fielders, but he would not neglect the second when he managed. Also, Terry, like Robinson, seemed to care little for instruction and experimentation aimed at improvement. When Richards suggested that one of the pitchers could improve a certain delivery by changing his grip, Terry told him to leave matters alone, the pitcher was doing all right; and Richards made no more suggestions.

The Giants won the 1933 World Series and lost the pennant race on the last day in 1934. In June of 1935, Terry sold Richards to the Athletics. Mack was in the final stages of dismantling his great team—he still had Foxx—and again Richards was not impressed. Mack, at seventy-two in his forty-first year as a manager,

Paul Richards

was unreceptive to suggestions from a twenty-six-year-old reserve catcher in his third big league season, and Richards didn't think he was driving his team as hard as it should be driven. Mack was unimpressed too. He sent Richards down to Atlanta in 1936.

In Atlanta, Richards found a home. He played there for seven years and managed the last five, winning two pennants and building a reputation for developing players. This was the Southern Association, Double-A, one notch below the International League, American Association, and Pacific Coast League, but in those days a level of play comparable to today's Triple-A. Among the pitchers he sent to the majors were Tom Sunkel, Luman Harris, Frank Gabler, and Bob Chipman, none of them "great arms" or terrific talents, but so well schooled that they had productive careers.

But even before he became the manager, he helped pitchers in Atlanta. Emil Leonard, called "Dutch" because that had been the nickname of a famous Red Sox pitcher twenty years before, had failed with the Dodgers for four years because catchers couldn't hold his knuckle ball and wouldn't call for it. At Atlanta, Richards told him to throw it as often as he liked, he'd catch it. Leonard had two season of 13–3 and 15–8 and went back up to the majors (to Washington first) for the next sixteen productive years.

As the wartime shortage of major leaguers developed and the continuation of minor league play was in doubt, Richards took the opportunity to return to the majors as a player with the Tigers in 1943. The manager was Steve O'Neill, a catcher who understood what good catching was, and one of the first projects was to help straighten out a left-hander of enormous promise named Hal Newhouser. "Prince Hal" had joined the Tigers in 1939, at the age of eighteen, a Detroit native son, much admired. But in five seasons, he'd never had a winning one and his career record stood at 34–52. He had a great fast ball but couldn't control it. Richards showed him how, and in 1944–46, Newhouser won 29, 25, and 26. And he was the winning pitcher in the seventh game of the 1945 World Series when Richards helped him to a 5-run lead before he took the mound by stroking a 3-run double in the top of the first.

With the regulars back from the war, and approaching forty, Richards went back to the minors for the Tigers as manager and general manager of their top farm club at Buffalo. He had future big league pitchers like Ted Gray and Saul Rogovin. In 1950, with

The Descendants

the Detroit organization making changes, he moved on to Seattle in the Pacific Coast League, where the roster was full of former major leaguers and he got a chance to apply his people handling skills noted under Bush back in Minneapolis almost two decades before.

Boss

The Chicago White Sox, by 1950, had fallen on hard times. After the Black Sox scandal wrecked them, they spent fifteen consecutive years in the second division. Jimmy Dykes got them up to third a couple of times in the 1930s, and again in 1941, but the rest of his regime (which lasted into 1946) was spent in the bottom half of the league. Attendance was poor, even after the addition of lights just before the war and during the postwar economic boom of 1946–48. The Comiskey family still owned the team (the "Old Roman" had died in 1931) and in 1949 brought in Frank Lane as general manager in an attempt to revive the franchise.

Lane was a dynamo, trained by a bigger dynamo. He was refereeing basketball and football games and running a semipro baseball league in 1934 when Larry MacPhail arrived in Cincinnati, Lane's home town. MacPhail made him business manager, then sent him down to run their minor league club in Durham, North Carolina. When MacPhail went to Brooklyn, Warren Giles brought Lane back to Cincinnati as his assistant. Then Lane spent World War II as a navy officer, even though he was forty-five years old before Pearl Harbor.

Returning to civilian life, he hooked up again with MacPhail, who had bought the Yankees, and was put in charge of the Kansas City farm operation.

That was in 1946. The next year he succeeded Roy Hamey as president of the American Association, and after two years in that post was hired by the White Sox. Lane's first choice for manager was Jack Onslow, a fifty-eight-year-old longtime minor league catcher and manager, who had been a big league coach under McKechnie and Mack. His 1949 White Sox finished sixth, and early in the 1950 season, Lane—who liked to sit in the stands among the fans and shout unflattering opinions about his own players and managers as well as about the opposition's—fired him. Red Corriden finished the season, sixth.

Paul Richards

Lane knew everyone in baseball at all levels, and, aware of the abilities Richards had, brought him to Chicago. Their personalities were opposites: Richards tight, controlled, consistent in his thinking, careful of everything he said in public; Lane loud, profane, uninhibited, mercurial in his emotions and thinking both. Richards kept writers as well as players at arm's length; Lane sought them out. But Lane knew enough to put baseball-decision authority in Richards's hands, to a greater extent than Richards had ever enjoyed before.

And the results were immediate. The White Sox jumped to fourth and three straight thirds behind the Yankees and Indians, winning 81, 81, 89, and 94 games, averaging 1.2 million in attendance.

These were teams built on pitching and speed, still a relatively new idea (or rather a return to the old idea) in the early 1950s. Durocher was doing it with the Giants, and the Cardinals had started to go that route at Rickey's urging in the 1940s, but the dominant Yankees, Indians, and Dodgers were still functioning along power lines.

The trick that got Richards the most attention was one he had used in the minors. He had a right-hander, Harry Dorish, pitching when Ted Williams came up with men on base and the game on the line in Fenway Park. A left-hander was the best bet against Ted, but the following hitters were right-handers aiming at the Wall. So he brought in Billy Pierce to pitch, took out the third baseman, moved Dorish to third, and thus kept him in the game. Pierce got Williams out, and Dorish returned to the mound, with a new third baseman going to Pierce's slot in the lineup. The danger of Williams hitting a hard grounder at Dorish was nonexistent, so it was a safe, sound move, all the more brilliant because others could have done it and didn't. He used that maneuver other times too, not just against Williams. I remember him doing it against the Yankees in Yankee Stadium, and don't remember the hitter, but if it was Joe Collins, I wouldn't be surprised.

In his attention to teaching detail, as well as noticing it, he was following the Rickey formula, which he had seen in action so extensively during his minor league years. And he was about to get a chance to put it into practice system wide.

In 1953, the Boston Braves shook the baseball world by moving to Milwaukee, the first change of venue in the American and National leagues since the Yankees had come to New York from

The Descendants

Baltimore in 1903. To the fans at that time, it was as if one of the planets in the solar system had changed orbits.

That opened the floodgates. Four more teams moved in the next five years, ending up with the Giants and Dodgers going to California in 1958.

The second team in the sequence was the St. Louis Browns. They were the least successful of all twentieth-century baseball teams, having finished first only in 1944, at the deepest point of wartime talent shortages, and second only twice in fifty-two seasons. They had been sixth, seventh, or eighth thirty-two times. But that was not the reason for the move to Baltimore in 1954.

They had been acquired, in 1951, by Bill Veeck, who had cashed in his enormous success in Cleveland. The significance of his purchase lay in his invention of a new form of partnership financing, which took full advantage of capital gains tax laws (as they then existed) in an original way. He knew that the club had no prospects of improvement: few established players, no farm system, no attendance. Its one asset was Sportsman's Park, where the Cardinals were the tenants. What Veeck really wanted was to sell the ballpark and move the team to Los Angeles, the West Coast gold mine.

But he had two problems. One was that he was still a bit premature in practical terms, since jet air travel was still on the drawing board, seven years away. The larger one, however, was that the other club owners disliked his showy promotions, didn't want to meet the level of competition he had thrown at them in Cleveland, and did want him out. He had alienated the ruling powers—that is, the Yankees—by daring to suggest that visiting teams (like his) should share in the radio-television income of home teams (like the Yankees in the New York market) as they had always shared gate receipts. There was, as yet, no national radio or television package in any sport, on a leaguewide basis, so the Yankees instantly interpreted this proposal as pure communistic bolshevism aimed at their own treasury.

In St. Louis, Veeck would go broke, especially after the overwhelmingly powerful Anheuser Busch Brewery bought the Cardinals (for $3,750,000) in January of 1953. It was Veeck's threat to move to Milwaukee that forced the Braves to move there when they did, since they "owned the territory" containing their top farm club. So Veeck asked to be allowed to go to Baltimore instead. His fellow club owners said no, forcing him to sell the Browns. As the 1953 season ended, they then approved the switch of the franchise to Baltimore under new, Baltimore-based owner-ship.

The transferred club was put into the hands of Mack intimates: Art Ehlers as general manager, Jimmy Dykes as field manager. It duplicated the 1953 record of the Browns, 54–100, but finished seventh instead of eighth because the A's lost 103—which was enough to convince the Mack heirs to sell the team to Kansas City, where it opened in 1955.

But even with 100 losses, the new Baltimore Orioles had drawn over one million customers and revived a civic baseball enthu-siasm dormant since McGraw left. The new ownership had the money and will to build something worthwhile, and the most visible example of an effective rebuilder was Paul Richards, in Chicago. They offered him the general managership and the man-agership as a package, and he grabbed the chance to have full authority. In September of 1954, he made the shift.

He knew exactly what he wanted to do. He launched a long-range plan for a Rickey-style farm system, based on signing a large number of prospects and a unified, intensive teaching sys-tem. He traded for quantity with existing systems, notably a seventeen-player deal that sent Baltimore's only two promising pitchers, Bob Turley and Don Larsen, to the Yankees with six others for seven players he could use immediately (including three catchers: Gus Triandos, who became his regular; Hal Smith, who would help Pittsburgh win the 1960 World Series; and Darrell Johnson, who would manage the Red Sox into the 1975 World Series).

Richards built slowly but meticulously. He knew talent. He knew how to lead. He could teach and spot other good teachers. He could organize scouts and paper work. He sought to develop pitching first of all, but also a mix of speed and power. He made Harry Brecheen, a clever pitcher who had starred with the Cardi-nals, his pitching coach. He brought in Luman Harris, whom he'd managed back in Atlanta, as his second-in-command in the dugout.

Richards started to build a farm system of such scope and size that it remained one of baseball's best for more than thirty years. It was the foundation of all the notable Oriole success from the middle 1960s to the middle 1980s.

The immediate results weren't as striking: seventh, sixth, fifth, sixth, sixth. But in 1960, the "Baby Birds" were ready to fly. They pushed the Yankees all season long in the year that Stengel won

The Descendants

his last pennant, challenging a team that had Mickey Mantle, Roger Maris, Whitey Ford, Bobby Richardson, Elston Howard, Yogi Berra, Tony Kubek, and Bill Skowron—household names— with a collection of names that would become familiar to baseball fans only later. His starting pitchers in 117 of the 154 games were twenty-one or twenty-two years old: Chuck Estrada, Milt Pappas, Steve Barber, Jack Fisher, and Jerry Walker. His twenty-two-year-old shortstop, Ron Hansen, also led the team with 22 homers. His third baseman was a twenty-three-year-old who had been trying for five years to overcome a "questionable" label and finally did so that year: Brooks Robinson.

But Richards also got into trouble at the front office level. In signing bonus rookies, under the complex rules of that time, and shifting players around, he violated some regulations and got caught. In 1959, the Oriole ownership brought in Lee MacPhail, who had been running the Yankee farm system under Weiss, as general manager and promoted him to club president in 1960. Richards retained absolute authority on the field but not in the front office.

So he was receptive when the next offer came. It seemed tailor-made. The first expansion was bringing Los Angeles and a new Washington team into the American League in 1961. The National was adding a new New York team and Houston, although they wouldn't begin play until 1962. For the first time, Texas would have a major league team. Who better to build it from the ground up than the tall Texan, Paul Richards?

The new teams were to be stocked with major league castoffs and given only slight access to existing farm systems. The Mets (George Weiss president, Casey Stengel manager) opted for recognizable names (Gil Hodges) and others who would be, presumably, immediately useful. Richards chose the younger-player route. The 1962 Houston Colts finished 24 games ahead of the Mets, and 5 ahead of the Chicago Cubs, who were operating under a committee of coaches instead of a single manager.

In Houston, Richards took the front office role completely. His manager was Harry Craft, plucked by Richards from the Chicago coaching board. Harry was an outfielder who was Cincinnati trained in the McKechnie era of the late 1930s, then an aging player at Kansas City and, starting in 1949, a minor league manager in the Yankee system. (That year, at Independence, Missouri, and the next year at Joplin, his scatter-arm shortstop was the teen-age Mickey Mantle.) Craft had managed the A's in Kansas City before going to Chicago. He knew the talent situation throughout baseball inside out, and was good with young players.

The first three years, the Colts played in a hastily built, mosquito-infested outdoor park while the Astrodome was being built. The revolutionary building wasn't ready for 1964, but Richards wanted one of his own people in charge when it would be. The Colts slipped back to ninth in 1963 and 1964 (because the Cubs had come to their senses and put a single manager, Bob Kennedy, in place), and as the 1964 season wound down, Richards replaced Craft with his most trusted aide, Lum Harris.

In the new building, with the team's name changed to Astros, pitching was at a premium. The outfield fences weren't close, the ball didn't carry, and an artificial surface had to be installed because the sun's glare through glass skylights meant they had to be painted opaque, and that killed the grass. Indoors or out, the Astros finished ninth again, but they were still playing with a stacked deck, denied access to existing talent—as were the Mets. In the first four years of National League expansion, the Mets won 194 games, guided by the two great brains of the Yankee dynasty, Weiss and Stengel. Houston in the Richards regime won 261.

But baseball's game of musical chairs was still going strong. The Braves, having milked Milwaukee, were sold to a group of young Chicago investors who decided to move the team to Atlanta, where a fat radio-television deal was available. Law suits prevented the move in 1965, but it was cleared in 1966. Meanwhile, the ownership of the Astros was shifting into the full control of Judge Roy Hofheinz, and in December of 1965 Richards was fired. So he was available when the Braves, loaded with talent (Hank Aaron, Eddie Mathews, Joe Torre) got off to a bad start in Atlanta and the carpetbagger owners decided they'd better put a seminative son in charge. No one had a better reputation in Atlanta than Richards, even more than two decades after he'd managed there. They hired him as general manager on June 25 and made him "vice president in charge of baseball operations" on August 31. Richards fired Bobby Bragan, the manager who had come with the team from Milwaukee, on August 9 in favor of Billy Hitchcock, a Yankee-system trained, much-traveled infielder who had followed Richards as manager in Baltimore.

Here Richards was not dealing with building up anything or youth movements. The Braves had a well-functioning farm system, big stars, and major league talent aplenty. What they didn't have was good pitching, and they had moved into an Atlanta stadium that turned out to be homer heaven (because the ball carried so well; atmospheric conditions have more to do with home run production than the distance to a fence). Hitchcock presided over a late-season spurt in 1966, but placed seventh in the ten-team league in 1967, and Richards turned to his old standby, Lum Harris, who had just won the International League pennant with Richmond, Atlanta's top farm club.

In 1968, the last year of the ten-team league, the Braves broke even and finished fifth. But in 1969, with the league split into six-team divisions, they won the first Western Division race, only to be swept in the first three-of-five League Championship Series by the Miracle Mets. Their leading pitcher, interestingly enough, was Phil Niekro, knuckleballer par excellence, reflecting Richards's continued acceptance of that difficult pitch. Years before, he had invented an outsized floppy catcher's mitt to help receivers knock down the unpredictable delivery, but that was eventually outlawed.

Richards stayed in Atlanta into 1972, with Harris as manager but without success. A different sort of problem had arisen. The Players Association had emerged as a true labor union in the late 1960s, under Marvin Miller, and the autonomy of club managements and the commissioner's office was being restricted. Richards was one of the most vociferous and intemperate opponents of the changing bargaining-power position, fighting the union in grievance cases and speaking out against its "demands" and leadership. Modern as he was in technical baseball matters, he could not accept what was, to him, the prospect of the inmates running the asylum—as if the evolution of twentieth-century labor relations had never existed.

Midway through the 1972 season, Richards was asked to change places with Eddie Robinson, his own choice as farm director, and at the end of the season his contract simply wasn't renewed.

In 1976, at the age of sixty-five, he came back to the dugout for a year with the Chicago White Sox. Veeck, who had owned the team in 1959–61, when it won under Al Lopez, had just reacquired it in the face of talk about moving it out of Chicago. His idea was to move the fences back as far as possible and depend on pitching, and he persuaded Richards, the acknowledged expert on such matters, to take over. It didn't work. The Sox got shut out 21 times, won only 64 games, and finished with the worst record in the twelve-team league. They would have done better, but Wilbur Wood, who had won 106 games averaging more than 300 innings a season for the past five years, was through for the year on May 9 because of a fractured kneecap, and Clay Carroll, their relief ace, broke a bone in his pitching hand in July.

The impact of Richards on the baseball scene of his time should not be underestimated. Among the players who worked under him were Joe Torre, Sam Mele, Dick Williams, and Whitey Herzog, who become pennant winning managers, and Billy Gardner, Bob Lillis, Ed Kasko, Jim Marshall, and Bob Elliott, who also managed. On his 1976 White Sox were Bucky Dent, who wound up as a Yankee manager for a while, and Jim Essian, who got his chance with the Cubs in 1991. Two others, Robinson and Woody Woodward, became general managers of more than one club.

He belongs, ultimately and with qualifications, in the McGraw line with a strong Rickey overlay. But to a greater extent than any of the others in this "Descendants" section, he developed his own ideas and methods on top of the firm foundation he acquired through such a sharp and critical eye.

My pet formula applies to him. The nature of baseball is such that hitters fail 70 percent of the time, which means that pitchers succeed 70 percent of the time. Which sort of director would you rather have for your club, the one who's an expert in the 70 percent failure department or the 70 percent success department?

13

Loose Ends

The year 1960 is as distinct a dividing line in baseball history as 1920. The game became entirely different when the lively-ball era began, and it became entirely different again when expansion began, ending for all time the neat patterns of the eight-team 154-game leagues.

From 1921 through 1960, there were eighty pennant races, and forty-two of them were won by the managers we have just discussed—even though Rickey and Richards didn't win any. If you add in those who can be traced directly to Rickey, McGraw, and Mack influence, you get up to sixty-one—and even then, most of the remaining nineteen have ties to the originators.

There is also, however, another branch that we have glossed over so far—not quite thick enough to be its own tree, but very similar in effect. It stems from Clark Griffith.

Griffith's place in baseball history tends to be underestimated, but it adds a dimension to our theme. If, as we've said, the key word for McGraw was "dictator," for Rickey "organizer," and for Mack "talent scout," the term for Griffith was "pragmatist." He was one of the first "smart" pitchers, dubbed "The Old Fox" when he was only twenty-five years old and known as that to sports-page readers for the next fifty years. He helped launch the American League, managed its first pennant winner and its first New York entry (the Yankees), managed in the other league at Cincinnati, then settled in Washington where he became the club's owner. In his boldest stroke, he made his twenty-seven-year-old second baseman, Bucky Harris, manager in 1924, and Harris promptly won two pennants, interrupting the reign of the Huggins-Ruth Yankees. Then, in 1933, Griff did it again, appointing as manager a twenty-six-year-old shortstop who was also his son-in-law,

Joe Cronin, and won another pennant. Those were the only three championships in the seventy-one-year history of American League baseball in the nation's capital.

Since Harris went on to manage for twenty-nine years in Boston, Detroit, and New York as well as Washington (three different times); and since Cronin went on to become manager of the Red Sox, then general manager, then American League president, the fallout influence of just these two protégés was immense. And there were others.

Griffith was born on the frontier in 1869, in western Missouri. He was six years old when the National League was formed (and General Custer got wiped out at Little Big Horn). When he started to pitch professionally, in 1887, the pitching distance was still fifty feet (from a box) and overhand pitching had just recently been authorized. When he reached the majors, with Cap Anson's Chicago National Leaguers in 1893, the present distance and pitching rubber were in use for the first time, and he had just recovered from a sore arm.

He was a small man, about five feet eight inches, weighing 150 pounds. He wasn't going to blow anybody away, so he mastered control, changes of speed, and tricks. Anything that could be done to a baseball, he did: scuff it, scratch it, rub mud on it, squirt tobacco juice on it, treat it with all sorts of arcane substances. With one ball in play most of the game, and with few explicit rules against tampering with it, his technique was brilliantly effective—and at the longer distance, all those changes of speed and tricky trajectories had more time to take effect.

So for seven years, starting in 1894 he became Chicago's star pitcher, winning 21, 25, 22, 21, 26, 22, and 14 games for teams that were never in pennant contention. That's why they called him the Old Fox.

When Ban Johnson decided to make his minor Western League the major American League, during 1900, Griffith joined Mack, McGraw, and Comiskey in recruiting National Leaguers for it. Seventy years later, in the Curt Flood antitrust trial, Cronin, as American League president, was on the witness stand defending the sanctity, morality, and necessity of the reserve clause, and the unthinkability of "jumping a contract." Didn't he know, attorney Jay Topkis asked him, that his revered father-in-law and mentor had helped start the American League by jumping his National League contract and urging others do so, as an explicit blow for a worker's freedom to seek better pay wherever he could get it? The stunned Cronin didn't know what to say.

But to Griffith, this was simply in line with everything else he ever did: Be practical and survive. In 1901, he managed the newly formed Chicago White Sox to the league championship, enjoying a 24–7 season as a pitcher himself, and establishing the north-side-southside rivalry that has animated Chicago baseball ever since.

But in 1902, of course, all was turmoil. McGraw went from Baltimore to the New York Giants, and the deal was struck to allow creation of the Yankees in 1903, and Johnson needed his most capable lieutenant to run this vital enterprise. Griffith became the first manager of the Yankees and in 1904 almost won the pennant. The Yankee owners, however, were Tammany Hall hacks (Frank Farrell was a bookie who ran a poolroom syndicate and flashy gambling house, while Bill Devery was an ex-cop constantly being investigated for graft and corruption as a bagman for the Tammany machine). What's more, they didn't get along with each other, giving conflicting orders, creating the kind of chaos as a tandem that George Steinbrenner would someday manage to create all by himself. Griff took it as long as he could, but quit midway through the 1908 season.

He wanted to manage Washington, but the job wasn't available, so he moved to Cincinnati as manager for 1909–11. Two facets of his regime there displayed his pragmatism. On the field, the Reds stole more bases than even McGraw's Giants, because Griff, as a pitcher, knew the difficulty of holding runners on—and that most pitchers couldn't. And in 1911, he started to scout seriously and sign Cuban and Caribbean players. A good player was a good player, regardless of origin—and if those coming out of the impoverished Caribbean economy would play for less money, what was wrong with that?

In 1912, Griffith got his chance in Washington. He could buy 10 percent of the Senators for $27,000 and step in as their field manager. (Only nine years before, 100 percent of the Yankees cost only $19,000.) He mortgaged the ranch he'd been able to buy in Montana and made the deal.

One of the first things he did was to persuade William Howard Taft, the president of the United States, to throw out the first ball at the season opener, boosting baseball's prestige by establishing that tradition. He kept Walter Johnson, baseball's best pitcher and a national hero, from going to the Federal League in 1914 and 1915, but the team had few other assets and was always short of capital.

In 1919, however, he got his break. With the war over, a successful grain dealer from Philadelphia, William Richardson, joined him in a partnership that let them buy 80 percent of the Senators, and Griff moved up to club president. He could see the prosperity Ruth could generate, and supported all the lively-ball and pitching-restriction changes, even though trick pitches had been his own stock in trade. He staffed the whole operation with family members, became a Washington institution, and in the prosperity of the 1920s produced winning teams.

When the Depression came, he found himself in the same boat as Mack in Philadelphia, and sold off assets—including Cronin to the Red Sox for $250,000 (on the condition that he would manage there).

Meanwhile, he had pioneered another innovation: a true relief specialist. Although Harris was his manager, Griff was still making primary strategic decisions in the 1920s. A decade before others started using the idea regularly, he turned a twenty-five-year-old right-hander who seemed only ordinary as a starter into a terrific finisher. Fred (Firpo) Marberry, in three years, relieved 149 times and posted 52 saves and 23 victories in those games.

His Cuban and Caribbean scouting balanced, at least to a modest degree, some of the advantages others were getting through farm systems (with which he couldn't keep pace any more than Mack could). And then there was the color line.

The Negro National League had a team called the Washington-Homestead Grays, which played half its home games in Pittsburgh and half in Griffith Stadium, from 1937 through 1948. Parts of the Negro League World Series were played there in 1942 and 1943. Griffith saw those players. During the war, national social pressure for integration was growing, started by the New Deal and increased by the military draft. In 1943, Griffith asked Josh Gibson and Buck Leonard, two black superstars (eventually enshrined in the Hall of Fame) if they wanted to play major league ball. They said yes, of course; but he never got back to them. Landis was still commissioner, and had quashed a plan by young Bill Veeck to buy the Phillies and stock them with Negro league stars. Griff was now seventy-one, undercapitalized, in no position to push against resistance, so he didn't do what Branch Rickey in Brooklyn was already figuring out how to do after the war. But in his mind, there was no question: Good ballplayers are good ballplayers, wherever you find them.

To win, you do whatever it takes. If you can't win, survive. To survive, you have to think fast and not be afraid to try anything you think might work. But don't forget you're part of a larger whole—club, league, industry, country—and if you have to choose between your own immediate advantage and the welfare of the whole, don't make the selfish choice—at least not too selfishly, not too often.

It's this frame of mind that Griffith passed on to those who played for him and managed in turn, especially through Harris and Cronin. It wasn't nearly as specific as McGraw's precepts or Mack's details but an important middle ground. He shared McGraw's aggressiveness without McGraw's egotistical insistence on power. He didn't have Mack's degree of personal warmth and technical expertise but plenty of the loyalty and concern for his players that both men showed. All three had exceptional capacity for grasping and responding correctly to baseball reality. But in McGraw, determination took precedence over everything else; in Mack, civilized decency was never to be abandoned; and in Griffith, fresh thinking was a constant goal—sharp, quick, sly (foxlike, after all), consider-the-consequences thinking, with the willingness to dare unhesitatingly to act upon the promising thought.

Whatever works.

Let's sum up, then, the managerial profile of the 1920–60 period and cite some of the other significant figures.

The most important is *Billy Southworth,* who managed the Cardinals to three straight pennants in 1942–44 and the Boston Braves to their 1948 flag. In 1924, he was a thirty-year-old outfielder who had played six years at Pittsburgh and Boston when McGraw traded Stengel and another outfielder to get him. Two years later McGraw traded him to the Cardinals, a move he later called "one of the worst decisions I ever made." In St. Louis, Southworth was nearing the end as a player, but Rickey and Breadon quickly grasped his potential for leadership. They made him the manager in Rochester for 1928.

Loose Ends

His premature promotion to the Cardinals, replacing McKechnie, has already been mentioned. He was back in Rochester in time to complete a run of four straight championships (1928–31). As a player, he had been known for fire and hustle and acquired the name "Billy the Kid," popularized by gunfighter legends. As a manager, he still carried the designation although his strength was exactly the opposite: conciliation inside the clubhouse and careful handling of diverse personalities.

He absorbed the Rickey development system as it was evolving, contributed to it, and found in it the answer to what had alienated him from McGraw. He believed in the daring game decisions McGraw used but couldn't stand the stifling dictatorship and verbal abuse that McGraw combined with it. So tactically, as a manager, he remained "Billy the Kid," and the hallmark of his teams became late-inning rallies and higher finishes than pre-season form predicted.

In the middle of 1932, Larry MacPhail hired him away from Rochester to manage Columbus, which MacPhail had just taken over. In the spring of 1933, Southworth returned to the majors as a coach for Terry with the Giants, but he couldn't get along with him any better than he had with McGraw, and left before the season started. He went into business in Columbus and was out of baseball for two years.

In 1935, Rickey asked him to come back into the minor league system further down, at Asheville, North Carolina, to train the increasing number of hot prospects the farm organization was turning up. Halfway through 1936, with no openings higher in the St. Louis hierarchy, Rickey got him a better job managing Memphis, with the promise that he could come back to the Cardinal family at the first opportunity. It came up at the end of 1938. Ray Blades was promoted from Rochester to replace Frisch with the Cardinals, and Southworth returned to Rochester for 1939. In July of 1940, he was chosen by Breadon—who had stripped Rickey of most control by then—to replace Blades.

At St. Louis, Southworth had all the products of the farm system he had dealt with on the way up. The Cardinals lost out in a great stretch run to the Dodgers in 1941, but made up a 10-game deficit and beat them in 1942. Then, after losing the first game of the World Series to the Yankees, they swept the next 4, becoming the first National League team to beat them in a World Series since

The Descendants

the 1926 Cardinals—for whom Southworth had played an important role after coming to them from the Giants in midseason.

Southworth won the next two pennants also, losing to the Yankees in 1943 and beating the Browns in 1944.

Then a personal tragedy struck. His son, Billy Jr., had developed into an outstanding minor league player but in December of 1940, enlisted as a flying cadet, the first professional player to join the armed forces. By early 1945, he was a much-decorated major, back in the United States after many bombing raids over Europe. Then, on a routine flight, he was killed in a plane crash trying for an emergency landing at LaGuardia Field in New York.

It was an emotional shock from which Southworth never fully recovered. His son had survived years of combat—now this. The father's skill was intact, but some of the fire inside him was quenched for good. The 1945 Cardinals missed by 3 games making it 4 in a row, and for 1946 Southworth was replaced by Eddie Dyer—who won the World Series (against Cronin's Red Sox) with the players Southworth had trained. Southworth was immediately hired by the Braves, who had been no higher than fifth for twelve years, and in three years, Southworth got the team to fourth, third, and first. He had Warren Spahn and Johnny Sain winning 81 games between them in 1947 and 1948, creating the refrain, "Spahn and Sain and two days of rain." His infield had Dark and Stanky in the middle, Bob Elliott at third, and Earl Torgeson at first. Finishing 6½ games ahead of Dyer and the Cardinals in 1948, with Rickey's Dodgers third, was vindication of the purest sort.

But in 1949, some of the players turned against him and Southworth's morale crumbled. He took a leave of absence and the team finished fourth. When he returned in 1950, Dark and Stanky had been traded away, and the Braves were fourth again. Midway through 1951 he was replaced by Tommy Holmes.

Southworth represents the early Rickey system line in its broadest form: loads of talent flow but not fully unified training control. Of his St. Louis players, Marty Marion, Terry Moore, Harry Walker, and Lou Klein became managers. His Boston alumni included Dark, Stanky, Elliott, Holmes, Roy Hartsfield, Del Crandall, Gene Mauch, and, briefly, Billy Herman and Danny Murtaugh.

Rogers Hornsby, who has been in an out of our story so many times, was a winner only with the 1926 Cardinals and managed the Cubs the first half of 1932, which Grimm finished by reaching the World Series. In all, he managed four National League teams and the St. Louis Browns (in his longest stint, 1933–37, and again in 1952 for Veeck). He simply couldn't get along with anybody for any length of time.

As for the rest:

Charlie Dressen. A remarkable man whose only two pennants were with the 1952 and 1953 Rickey-produced Dodgers recently taken over by O'Malley—who dismissed him when he asked for a three-year contract. But Dressen, associated with Durocher through much of his career, had his own sterling qualities. He came from Decatur, Illinois, where he was born in 1898, and got no schooling past the age of fourteen. At nineteen, although he was only five foot six and weighed 150 pounds, he was playing quarterback (a blocking position then, but the "brains" who called the signals) for a professional football team about to become the Chicago Bears—[the Staleys of Decatur, a starchworks that had hired George Halas to run the football and baseball teams it sponsored for publicity.]

Turning to baseball, Dressen kicked around the minors and decided early on (as he told Harold Rosenthal, who covered him in Brooklyn) that "I'd better learn something. A lot of older guys would start to lose it and then what? I started studying the game, percentages and things like that. I figured my chance to hang on was to be a manager."

He got his chance in 1934 when MacPhail, taking over Cincinnati, promoted him in midseason. One of the coaches was Shotton, so Dressen was moving into the sphere of Rickey disciples. The Reds were a total flop in those days, and Dressen wound up back in the minors, but when MacPhail brought Durocher to Brooklyn and made him the manager, he also hired Charlie as Leo's third base coach.

In the success of the next four years, Charlie played a significant role and didn't mind letting it be known that a lot of those "brainy" moves were his rather than Leo's. He boasted he could steal signs, read pitches, tip off his own hitters by whistling, and suggest plays and pitches to call. Leo didn't object strongly—he didn't care where good ideas came from if they worked; he appropriated them cheerfully and reaped the benefit, and as manager he was getting all the credit anyhow. (One thing about Leo, he wasn't the jealous sort.)

But in 1943, when Rickey took over from the war-bound Mac-

The Descendants

Phail, he fired Dressen, presumably because he disapproved of his betting on the horses, and because he had more confidence in Durocher's judgment than MacPhail did. But Charlie the Survivor pleaded his case and by July, Rickey let him come back—at less money. Dressen stayed with Durocher through 1946.

Now MacPhail had the Yankees and created a fuss by brining Dressen in as a coach. Rickey complained that this was a preliminary move to get Durocher and constituted tampering. But the upshot was that Dressen coached third for Bucky Harris for two years and against the Dodgers in the 1947 World Series. After 1948, Harris was gone and so was Dressen.

Charlie went to Oakland, replacing Stengel, who came up to the Yankees. He finished second (with Billy Martin as his second baseman), first in 1950, and was brought to Brooklyn by O'Malley to replace Rickey's man Shotton. That year, 1951, started in glory and ended in the disaster of Bobby Thomson's homer, but the next two years brought pennants and frustrating World Series losses to Stengel's Yankees.

Always bursting with confidence, Dressen was constantly teased about his ego, which wasn't as big as he made it sound. ("Stay close for seven innings and I'll think of something.") Always compared to Durocher, he was actually less self-centered. I found him, at the core, a kinder and friendlier person, all the easier to make fun of because he took it so well. His remarks about being always right were simply the truth as he saw it, not an effort to impress you. He wasn't trying to exert dominance; he just wanted you to know he was right because he knew he was right—whether he was or not. And if he figured something out, why not speak up? How could his knowledge help you unless he told you?

The key distinction, it seemed to me, was this: Leo wanted you to do well because that would win for Leo; Charlie wanted you to do well because he honestly wanted you to do well for your own sake—as well as his, of course.

When O'Malley dropped him, Dressen went back to Oakland. But he had made friends and a reputation. The Griffiths brought him to Washington, to a failing situation. Then he coached for Alston, his successor with the Dodgers, in Los Angeles. Then he was called in to manage the Milwaukee Braves until deposed by the vice-president who had hired him, Birdie Tebbetts, who decided to manage the team himself. Back to the minors at Toronto (where his second baseman was a Dodger system discard named George Anderson, better known later as Sparky). Then he was asked to bail out a fading Detroit Tiger team and was in harness, early in 1966, when he died of a heart attack.

He was a Rickey-system person without ever absorbing the organizational aspect of that philosophy, but had its essence in his head and heart. For every baseball problem, there was a "right solution," and he was sure he knew it. Those who played for him found themselves more influenced by his thinking after he was gone than while they were with him.

Bill Terry. Winning with the 1933, 1936, and 1937 Giants, he consciously avoided McGraw's mannerisms as his successor. He was a conservative and orthodox strategist, sound but noninspirational. His effectiveness decreased as his own playing effectiveness waned.

Gabby Street. Manager of the Cardinals in their 1930 and 1931 winning years, he had been Walter Johnson's catcher in Washington. He doesn't really fit any of the categories we've set up.

Donie Bush. The 1927 Pirates were his pennant winner. His credentials were Old Oriole through Hughie Jennings, for whom he had played at Detroit.

Charlie Grimm. He had a hand in four Cub pennants, managing all of 1935 and 1945, the second half of 1932 and the first half of 1938 (which Gabby Hartnett finished). All his playing experience was under McKechnie and McCarthy, so he was in the McGraw line as a tactician but at the opposite end of the scale in genial warmth, his best characteristic.

Burt Shotton. Rickey's "Sunday manager" with the Browns, he answered Rickey's call again and again. He took the Dodgers to the World Series when Durocher was suspended in 1947, and again in 1949 after Durocher left, and missed in 1950 only on the last day. His kindly manner overlay a streak of toughness, but he was well liked.

Fred Haney. Before managing the Milwaukee Braves to pennants in 1957 and 1958, he presided over two of the worst teams in history—the 1939–41 St. Louis Browns and the 1953–55 Pittsburgh Pirates. As a small, tough, fiesty infielder he had played for Cobb in Detroit; but in many subsequent years as a player-manager in the Pacific Coast League, he became closely associated with the Rickey system. Rickey brought him back to the majors at Pittsburgh, setting up his Milwaukee opportunity. Later he became general manager of the expansion Angels. He was a book manager who belongs in the Rickey column, a great talker who had done a lot of radio broadcasting. One can consider him, in that respect, a toned-down Frisch.

Mickey Cochrane. Of the forty American League pennants in this period, thirty-four were accounted for by Huggins, Harris, Mack, McCarthy, Cronin, Stengel, and Lopez. Cochrane, a Mack protégé, was manager and catcher for the Detroit Tigers in 1934, losing the World Series to the Gashouse Gang, and 1935, beating Grimm's Cubs in 6 games. His career effectively ended in 1936 when a pitch fractured his skull, although he did return to managing.

Del Baker. A coach under Cochrane, he was the Tiger manager when the team won again in 1940. His experience was enormous. He had caught for Jennings in Detroit, enjoyed a long career in the Coast League, managed in the Texas League, and became a Detroit coach for Harris before Cochrane arrived. After the Tigers dropped him in 1942, he managed three more years in the Coast League, then served as a coach with the Red Sox, under Cronin's general managership, on and off through 1960. He can't be classified as other than "knowledgeable" in a fifty-year career.

Steve O'Neill, Detroit's winning manager in 1945, and *Luke Sewell,* manager of the only pennant-winning Brownie team in 1944, had both been catchers under Tris Speaker in Cleveland, but Sewell also absorbed a lot of Griffithism from Cronin in Boston and Roger Peckinpaugh in Cleveland.

Lou Boudreau, as a Cleveland player before being named manager, broke in under Ossie Vitt, who had managed high in the Yankee system of the 1930s.

And although he never finished first, *Jimmy Dykes* must be mentioned. He was an admirer of Mack, for whom he played on the great 1929–31 teams, and a favorite of his. In the course of twenty-one years as a manager, Dykes spread the Mack influence. Future managers who played for him included Ted Lyons, Sewell, Joe Kuhel, Luke Appling, Bob Kennedy, Ben Chapman, Ed Lopat, Kerby Farrell, Eddie Joost, Billy Hitchcock, Billy Hunter, Sam Mele, Roy McMillan, Frank Robinson, Alex Grammas, and Harvey Kuenn.

He managed the Chicago White Sox for 13 seasons, the Philadelphia A's for 3, Baltimore 1, Cincinnati 1, and 1½ seasons each at Detroit and Cleveland. The final switch was one of baseball's most bizarre developments, and a fitting end to the sixteen-team era.

In 1960, Dykes was managing the Detroit Tigers for Bill DeWitt, whom we met as a teen-age office boy for Branch Rickey with the Browns in St. Louis in 1915. He followed Rickey to the Cardinals, became a lawyer, served as Cardinal club treasurer and then as business manager for Pepper Martin and Dizzy Dean, bought a part interest in the Browns in 1936 and was their general manager when they won their pennant, bought the rest of the club in 1949 and sold it to Veeck, worked for the club after it moved to Baltimore without Veeck, spent a couple of years as assistant general manager of the Yankees under Weiss, and wound up as president of the Tigers in 1959. Later he would buy and sell the Cincinnati Reds. He was, one might say, a well-rounded baseball man.

Joe Gordon was managing Cleveland, whose general manager was now Frank Lane, who had been hired and fired by the Cardinals.

Dykes had Harvey Kuenn, the 1959 batting champion (at .353). Gordon had Rocky Colavito, whose 42 homers had shared the league lead with Harmon Killebrew. Both players were immensely popular with their home fans.

The day before the season opened, DeWitt and Lane made a blockbuster trade: Kuenn for Colavito, even up, altering the character of both lineups.

This caused so much fuss and conversation that the two uninhibited operators, ever sensitive to the value of getting attention, decided to top it.

In August, they swapped managers.

Dykes went to Cleveland, taking his top coach, Luke Appling, with him. Gordon took Jo-Jo White along to Detroit.

And Kuenn and Colavito, of course, were back with their old managers.

The net effect wasn't exactly a success. The Indians, second in 1959, fell to fourth; the Tigers, who had been fourth, fell to sixth; Kuenn dropped to .308 and finished fifth in a season when .320 was good enough for Pete Runnels to win the batting title; Colavito's 35 homers left him 5 behind Mickey Mantle's 40. Detroit's attendance was off 50,000, Cleveland's 500,000. Before 1961 was over, DeWitt owned the Cincinnati Reds, Lane had been hired and fired in Kansas City, and Dykes and Gordon were no longer managing. Kuenn was with the San Francisco Giants and only Colavito, still in Detroit, got back to 45 home runs under the new manager, Bob Scheffing.

But that left him 16 behind Roger Maris's 61.

An era had ended in more ways than one. And the Dykes-Gordon trade drove home the devalued status of managers in general. Not only were there no longer any Little Napoleons or owner-managers, but policy was in the hands of general managers who saw field managers as just one more cog in a complicated machine.

To be a good manager in the future, one would have to function in accordance with these new realities.

Part Four

The Moderns

14

Walter Alston

Company Man

When Walter Alston was made manager of the Brooklyn Dodgers in 1954, he was exceptionally well trained for that specific job. He then kept it for twenty-three years, working under twenty-three consecutive one-year contracts, so he must have done it well. He was never perceived, however, as *the* boss of the Dodgers, in his own eyes or anyone else's; the boss was Walter O'Malley, who owned the team, hired him, took him to Los Angeles with it, kept rehiring him, and let him do the specific organizational task assigned to him: manage the team on the field and in the clubhouse, with no hint of larger responsibilities.

This suited Alston fine, and served the organization well, and produced a stability unique in baseball annals. Only two men have ever managed a single team for more than two decades: Connie Mack, who was his own club owner, and John McGraw, whose own stature overshadowed the three club owners he worked for and who was, in effect, his own general manager. But Alston was purely an employee—the most loyal, low-key, untroublesome employee any employer could wish for—and neither craved nor sought any authority beyond the carefully delineated duties assigned to him. Within the parameters of his job, he executed all necessary authority with confidence and dispatch, but anything they wanted upstairs, he did their way.

For such a position, Alston was perfectly equipped by background and personality. In two of the world's greatest venues of the cult of the personality—Brooklyn of the 1950s and Hollywood—he displayed absolutely no charisma nor the slightest desire for the trappings of a Big Ego. He didn't dodge the spotlight; he simply paid no attention to its presence. His strong ego—no one can be a manager without one—was content with success itself and appreciation within the Dodger family, and he honestly disliked calling attention to himself.

Such a man, given sound technical knowledge, was the ultimate embodiment of "system" the way Rickey had conceived it. The irony was that it came to fruition only when Rickey was out of the way.

Let's take the story from the beginning.

Alston was born December 11, 1911, in Venice, Ohio, in farm country just north of Cincinnati. He grew up in a farm family and went to high school in Darrtown, which can be called a suburb of Hamilton, which is fifteen miles north of Cincinnati and well within the metropolitan Cincinnati orbit. When it was time to go to college, he enrolled at Miami of Ohio in Oxford, about five miles the other side of Darrtown. He grew big and strong, about 6 feet 2 inches and close to 200 pounds, was an outstanding athlete and a good student, and played semipro baseball in the area. But in 1935, with the Depression grinding on despite Roosevelt's New Deal, times were not promising for farmers or anyone else, so an offer to play baseball professionally for $125 a month was welcome indeed.

The offer came from Rickey's brother Frank, who was working in the St. Louis Cardinal system Rickey was still building. Alston was a right-handed hitting first baseman and played out that first year at Greenwood, Mississippi, in the East Dixie League, hitting .326.

That earned him a promotion to Huntington, West Virginia, in the Middle Atlantic League, where he hit .326 again and led the league with 35 homers in 120 games. Such a prospect, today, would be banking millions, but the world was different then. To put his batting average in perspective, one must note that the two leading hitters in that league were Barney McCosky at .400 and Jeff Heath at .383, both of whom went on to solid but not spectacular major league careers, and that a Portsmouth infielder named Eddie Stanky hit .337.

What's more, Alston was in a blind alley within the Cardinal system itself. First of all, it preferred left-handed hitters for first base, on principle and because of the contours of Sportsman's Park in St. Louis. Second, the Cardinals already had a left-handed rookie first baseman, two years younger than Alston, about fifteen pounds heavier, and just as tall, named John Mize. In 1936, when

Walter Alston

Alston was hitting .326 in Huntington, Mize was already hitting .329 in St. Louis, against major league pitching.

So although his good season was rewarded with a trip to the parent club's bench in September, for the proverbial "cup of coffee" in the majors, it was clear that his future lay elsewhere.

On the last day of the season, he got into a game. Mize was ejected for arguing with an umpire, so Alston played in the late innings. He got to bat once, against Lon Warneke of the Cubs. He struck out.

When Alston went back to the minors in 1937, in higher level leagues, it developed he couldn't hit that pitching either. He split that season between Rochester (.247) and Houston (.212), so his sales value wasn't much. In 1938, he found his level at Portsmouth, back in the Middle Atlantic League, and hit .311 there and .323 at Columbus, Georgia, in 1939.

So he was making a modest living by teaching school in the off-season and, approaching thirty, accepting the reality that he wasn't going to make the majors. But the Cardinal system was also set up to notice intelligent, dedicated workers, and in 1940 made him player-manager at Portsmouth. His team finished sixth, even though he led the league with 28 homers (the Hornsby-Boudreau style of managing), but he kept his job as the franchise was moved to Springfield, Ohio (near Columbus), for 1941. He led the league in homers again, and even pitched in 3 games (anything the job required) as the team finished fourth. In 1942, he hit fewer homers, pitched more often, and finished fifth. But the Cardinal chain didn't care where the minor league team placed; it cared about the instruction and development its chain gang members were getting, and Alston had the teaching skills.

With playing talent thinned out by the war, the Cardinals moved him to Rochester in 1943 to serve strictly as a player. But early in the 1944 season, he injured his back and knew he was finished as a player. He was released.

Rickey, by now, was in his second season in Brooklyn. Within a week, he called Alston and offered him a playing-managing job at Trenton, New Jersey. At that level, by midseason, he could play— the economics of minor league baseball required a player-manager—and put in a full season in 1945.

For 1946, Rickey moved him to Nashua, New Hampshire, at the same Class B level, because he had such confidence in Alston's handling of young players, so many of whom were coming back out of the military.

And it wasn't just a matter of "young" players. Rickey had broken the color line and had Jackie Robinson at Montreal. To Nashua he sent Roy Campanella and Don Newcombe. That situation, at that time, required a strong, unflappable leader capable not only of smoothing over conflicts that were bound to arise but guaranteed not to stir up any conflicts himself. The entry of Campy and Newk into organized baseball got little publicity (which was all focused on Robinson) and proceeded without incident.

In 1947, Rickey sent Alston to Pueblo, and in 1948 to St. Paul. This was the highest level of the Rickey system, the American Association Triple-A outlet on a par with Montreal in the International League, both owned outright by the Dodgers. Including working agreements, Rickey had twenty-five teams in the chain, and the Vero Beach operations let all of them start each year with an exchange of information and evaluations.

Alston was now a company man, a middle-level executive, in the truest sense, all but invisible to the outside world (except where he was actually managing), but completely steeped in the methods and traditions—and goals—of the Rickey enterprise. He managed St. Paul in 1948 and 1949, and Montreal the next four years.

But in 1951, we know, the political structure of the Dodgers changed completely, and part of the fallout led to Alston's opportunity.

O'Malley won the battle for ownership control and forced Rickey out—but the entire organization was Rickey-built, and O'Malley, being the astute businessman he was, understood the value of the assets he inherited. Many a club owner has made the mistake of applying his unquestioned authority to the right to make baseball decisions; O'Malley was smart enough to use his authority to leave baseball decisions to the experts he was paying. While he wouldn't leave Rickey's man Shotton in the dugout, replacing him with Dressen, he didn't tamper with the rest of the structure. Fresco Thompson had been Rickey's director of the farm system. He now became, in effect (and later by title) director of baseball operations. Buzzie Bavasi, acting as general manager of the Montreal team, moved up as O'Malley's front office chief, negotiating contracts with the players and serving as the field manager's direct supervisor. All the way down the system, the scouts and minor-league managers were kept in place or moved around: Alex Campanis, Clay Bryant, Andy High, Greg Mulleavy, a bunch of others. Some who followed Rickey to Pittsburgh eventually drifted back. What we now call the "Dodger system" is, in its content, the pure Rickey system, and O'Malley deserves full credit for enhancing as well as maintaining it.

What did this mean for Alston? Well, when Dressen made the mistake of asking for a three-year contract after 1953, and O'Malley decided to let him go, O'Malley looked inside the organization for a replacement—and all the people he turned to for advice were Rickey-trained individuals who knew Alston and had worked with him. (An "established" manager, with his own reputation, was the last thing O'Malley could tolerate.)

Alston's self-effacing manner fit everyone's needs. The basic consideration, of course, was that they knew his abilities and had high regard for them. But it was not coincidental that he would present no personality challenge to those already in place in the blinding New York limelight. O'Malley clearly wanted to be perceived as boss as well as to be one. Bavasi and Thompson didn't need outsiders, with their own reputations and constituencies, coming in to shake things up, as even Dressen had done to a degree. Whatever else Alston might do, he wouldn't upstage anybody.

And if he failed, firing him would be the easiest thing in the world.

So Alston took over a team that had just won two straight pennants, beating the hated Giants of Leo Durocher, and losing the World Series only to Stengel's Yankees. It was, in the true sense of the word, "America's Team" long before the Dallas Cowboys. Anything less than another pennant would be failure.

But if Alston was a total stranger to most of the baseball public, and especially in New York, he was not a stranger to most of the players on the spring roster, seventeen of whom had played for him in the minors. After Campy and Newk, he'd had Joe Black, Carl Erskine, Clem Labine, Johnny Podres, Jim Gilliam, Don Hoak, Jim Hughes, Dick Williams, and Don Zimmer at St. Paul or Montreal.

He was, however, only one of the Vero Beach crowd to Robinson, Pee Wee Reese, Gil Hodges, Duke Snider, Carl Furillo, Preacher Roe, and Billy Cox—pennant-winning regulars all—and that *was* a problem.

Everything that happened in 1954 was permeated by the consciousness of what had occurred in the three preceding seasons. The trauma of the 1951 playoff ending was assuaged but not erased by the Dodger pennants of 1952 and 1953, because these had led to World Series frustrations. World Series losses had intensified, by their very frequency and the exploding publicity mechanism of that time, the obsession. The Dodgers were never allowed to forget for a moment that "Brooklyn had never won a world championship." Dodger teams had reached the World Series and lost in 1916, 1920, 1941, 1947, 1949, 1952, and 1953—the last five times to the all-too-proximate and infuriatingly aristocratic Yankees. They had also lost pennant playoffs in 1946 and 1951, and a chance for a pennant tie on the last day in 1950. No longer was winning day to day enough, and sitting in first place through most of a season only made them more apprehensive rather than more confident. Nothing less than World Series victory would do.

At the same time, in a realistic sense, they had matured into what everyone considered the strongest team in baseball, Yankees or no Yankees, and it was Dressen who had led them that far. Now—as far as the veteran players were concerned—Charlie had been summarily dismissed and their fate was being put in the hands of this nobody, whose major league career consisted of one strikeout, who was a lifelong busher and—from what they could tell—not very clever and not particularly friendly. They (the older players) knew they weren't getting any younger; their quest for the world championship could not be deferred. What was O'Malley doing by risking their chances in such a way, replacing a known quantity (Dressen) with this minor league schoolmaster?

What Alston was walking into was a typical baseball situation, McCarthy and McKechnie had faced it before they won their first pennants. The caste system in player mentality is rigid and universal. How can anyone who wasn't a major leaguer himself know what major leaguers needed?

Going into the 1954 season, the Dodgers were clearcut favorites to repeat. The Giants had come completely apart in 1953, falling to fifth, and even though Willie Mays was coming back from the army, he couldn't make *that* much difference. The other team loaded with talent was in Milwaukee, where fan enthusiasm for the transferred Braves helped pump up the players, but it still didn't seem to be a match for the Dodgers, who had so many great players still at their peak.

Walter Alston

Nothing much happened until June. Then the Giants and Dodgers both pulled away from the pack, stride by stride. But in July the Giants kept winning and the Dodgers started to hang, winning a couple, losing a couple. The grumbling among the older players became vocal and started to get into the papers.

Still, the second-place finish was not reason enough to discard the company man the front office found so comfortable to work with. Campanella had a hand injury that ruined his season. Newcombe, back from a two-year army hitch, couldn't find himself and won only 9 games. The Giants had pulled off Leo's second miracle. If some of the Dodger stars, in a position to ask for more money, didn't like working for Alston, that didn't necessarily make O'Malley unhappy; and Bavasi, who liked running things to the extent of saying who should play, who should pitch, and who should be traded or promoted, just loved an acquiescent manager.

So Alston came back in 1955, and hit the jackpot. The Dodgers won 22 of the first 24 games, were 30 games above .500 by mid-June, were never threatened and finished first by 13½ games. As had become usual, they split the first 6 games of the World Series with Yankees, but then—on October 4 at Yankee Stadium—won the seventh game, 2–0, behind the young left-handed Podres.

Brooklyn finally had its first (and as it turned out, its last) world championship, and one might think that this alone would establish Alston as certified genius and folk hero. But it didn't work that way at all. The triumph was seen as a tribute to the great Dodger lineup, which long preceded Alston's arrival, and to the O'Malley regime. Alston's role was given a polite nod (and even his choice of Podres for the final game was being second-guessed until the result was in). As far as the Dodger steadies were concerned, they had won on their own merit, with Alston performing the mechanical functions any manager must. Who wouldn't win with a team like that?

So when 1956 began, the simmering antagonism between the "true" Dodgers and Alston was still there. Alston insisted on off-field rules, like curfews; he had the nerve to make suggestions about hitting to people like Snider; he was too obviously in Bavasi's pocket in making decisions about players, and the players (who liked Buzzie well enough on a personal basis) knew he was their archenemy when it came to dollars on a contract. They had learned to live with the schoolmaster, and had accomplished their long-sought goal, confirming their previously frustrated superiority. But they certainly didn't ascribe any of their success to Alston's presence.

Now, any manager, to some degree, must generate at least a little healthy fear to maintain control. It can have only three sources: job security, psychological dominance, or physical strength. The players are, after all, athletes, not intellectuals; and especially in the first half of this century, they understood a potential punch in the nose better than a logical disputation as a definitive settlement of conflict. In Alston's case, he had no leverage on job security—clearly it was the front office, not he, who decided who would play when and when someone might be sent away and how much he would be paid. So his fear factor in that regard was zero. Psychologically, players respond to reputation (my manager was an outstanding player himself, so he must know something) or convincing tactical brilliance (as proven by results even when the manager was disliked personally, as with Durocher and Stengel and McGraw). On this score, Alston was also a zero, since he put on few plays, handled pitchers conservatively, expressed the most orthodox ideas and attitudes, and didn't talk much.

But he was large and obviously strong, and although slow to anger, ultimately explosive when his long fuse finally burned down. His response to challenge, explicitly as well as implicitly, was "Let's step outside" and settle it with fists. Any player is reluctant to reach that point of conflict with any boss, under any circumstances; but when it seems likely that the boss really can punch you out if it gets to that, the reluctance becomes healthy fear.

On that point, Alston had something going. Those who didn't respect his mind respected his physique.

Even this reaction, of course, is largely sublimated in practice to exchanges of nasty words. What the believeable threat of fists really does is make listeners tolerate inflammatory insults more than they would if they were sure they could answer with a punch. Verbal aggression is real: It drove Frisch away from McGraw. But it can also make the hearer face up to deficiencies otherwise shrugged aside, which is why leaders use it.

A turning point occurred halfway through the 1956 season.

The Dodgers were expected, of course, to win again. At All-Star break, they were running a close third to the Reds and the Braves and resumed play with a 4-game series in Milwaukee. The Dodgers lost all 4, including a Friday night double-header, and moved on to Chicago.

The dean of the beat writers covering the Dodgers at that time was Dick Young, of the *Daily News* (in my opinion, the best daily baseball coverage reporter ever). Young's influence was enormous, not only because his paper had a circulation of about two million in New York, but because he had a nationally circulated column in *The Sporting News,* then fully deserving its reputation as "baseball's Bible" and a trade paper read intensively within the industry. He had been covering the Dodgers since the middle 1940s, was closer to the players than anyone else, and was aggressively definite in his opinions, pulling no punches. He could be, and sometimes was, wrong; but nothing he wrote could be ignored.

Dick wrote that between games of the Friday double-header, Alston had chewed out the team in no uncertain terms, calling them "gutless," one of baseball's most inflammatory words.

Naturally, all the other papers had to jump on the story.

Alston denied everything, offering as proof: "Gutless is a word I never use."

I was on that trip working for the *New York Post.* There were still seven major daily papers in New York City itself in those days, and about four major suburbans, so the writing corps was large. We all had to follow up the dissension angle, and the result was universal dissemination of a clubhouse situation that had been essentially kept within the family for two years.

The bottom line was the collective attitude of the established players: "When we're going good, we don't need him; when we're going bad, he can't help us." And in that case, where did he get the right to insult us, and to what end?

I wrote more or less what everyone else wrote, but I felt awkward about it in one respect. I didn't know Alston well, he didn't know me, and I had been with the club only sporadically in the last two years. We were on the road, where he could not see my stories even if he wanted to, and I felt funny about talking to him as if everything were normal while I knew, and he didn't, that my stories back home constituted the most damaging criticism possible (by players who refused to be named) of his managing.

So when we reached Cincinnati the next day, I sought him out during batting practice and said: "Walt, I think you ought to know what's been in my paper, which is pretty bad stuff, so that I don't seem two-faced talking to you now."

He said: "I don't give a damn what you write, or anyone else writes."

Fine, I thought. That's that.

But the last stop was St. Louis, and by that time, someone had come from New York with a week's worth of New York papers, including mine. And now he finally read the story he didn't give a damn about.

I don't know what he said or didn't say to anyone else, but as we were leaving for the airport that Monday morning, he started to shout at me in the hotel lobby, objecting to what I had written days before and to me in general.

And the first word out of his mouth was "gutless."

The point of this anecdote is not the personal run-in, which was temporary and soon forgotten as we dealt with each other for twenty more years, nor the self-refutation in choice of language, nor even the example of his "step outside" mentality.

It's that the entire incident, starting with his tirade in the clubhouse, did mark a significant difference in his assertion of control. His chief antagonist, Jackie Robinson, was gone at the end of the year anyhow. (And there was no racist element in that conflict; it was the same sort of king-of-the-mountain test Miller Huggins had from Babe Ruth.) But the others came to see some truth in his criticism, gained respect (in a perverse way) for his contempt of the press and (more to the point) his refusal to be swayed one way or another by the remarks of his players, the writers, or anyone else.

The fact is that after that series in Milwaukee, the Dodgers won 12 of the next 15 games and 29 of 41. They didn't reach first place until mid-September, but did win the pennant on the next-to-last day, having won two-thirds of their games after the Milwaukee blow-off.

Then they lost the World Series to the Yankees in 7 games.

At that point, O'Malley was well into his plans to move the team to Los Angeles if he couldn't get the domed stadium he wanted in downtown Brooklyn, so there was no point about even thinking of changing managers. Besides, the stars were aging, and the 1957 Dodger team would be a transitional one in any case.

In 1958, and for the three seasons after that, the Dodgers played in the lopsided Los Angeles Coliseum, with its 250-foot left field screen and limitless acreage in center and right, even inside a false fence. They were seventh in 1958, won the World Series (from the Chicago White Sox) in 1959, finished fourth in 1960, and second in 1961.

By the time they moved into Dodger Stadium in 1962, Alston was a completely different manager in a completely different situation.

The Old Guard was long since gone. Even of the players he had managed in the minors, only Gilliam was left. The team now consisted of a new generation of Dodger system products, with one key trade acquisition (Wally Moon), and these players, as they arrived, had no trouble accepting Alston as a wise father figure and entrenched Dodger boss. First of all, he had his own reputation: twice a World Series winner, three times a pennant winner, so he must know what he's talking about. Second, he was teaching and demanding all the same stuff they had absorbed on their way up the system. Third, there were no veterans around to give a contrary impression. Fourth, whatever orders he may or may not have been following from upstairs were of no concern to ambitious youngsters who had no other major league experience. Fifth, he still looked like a guy who could punch you out if you got him mad. Sixth, there was no question that if you didn't do it his way, you wouldn't play.

Therefore, many of Alston's characteristics that had been seen as drawbacks now emerged as assets. What was "unimaginative" was now properly "conservative percentage play." What were chafing rules of behavior were merely systemwide common-places. What had been "criticism" was now "instruction." And what was the Rickey-system approach to playing baseball— overpowering pitching, good defense, speed—was the right way to play in the new Dodger Stadium, because the structure had been designed that way—to be a pitchers' park. In Ebbets Field, waiting for the homer made sense (although alas, there were many enemy homers too). Here it didn't.

Alston was, in my opinion, fortunate in two respects. If the team had remained in New York, no matter how it did, he could not have survived in that media climate. He was simply too rigid and private a person, and too tempting a target. In coming to Los Angeles, however, he found an adulatory local press delighted to get its major league team (and what a team!), and not only not looking for trouble but with no basis for comparison. The Holly-

The Moderns

wood crowd, cultivated by O'Malley, was only too happy to focus on the owner and the glamorous players, and if Alston wanted to remain self-effacing, they had plenty of other material and could let him set his own terms. And his stoicism stood him in good stead as Bavasi didn't make it easy for him in one respect: In 1958 and 1959, he hired Dressen as a coach, and in 1961–64, Durocher. The baseball world kept making cracks about who was really doing the "thinking," and that each was about to replace Alston as soon as anything went wrong; and Cholly and Leo didn't hesitate to make modest denials that sounded like confirmations.

Bavasi, of course, had no intention of replacing Alston, his man, with Dressen or Durocher. They were significant assets to the team, and Leo was a Hollywood personality of the first magnitude, but Alston was the manager. A man less stolid than Alston could not have functioned very long in such circumstances, but Walt didn't let this bother him any more than he let other things bother him.

The second way in which he was fortunate was in the character of Sandy Koufax and Don Drysdale. Both had started in Brooklyn and, as rookies, had been exposed to the views of the disgruntled veterans there, who were their role models when they arrived. They could have carried on the schism and infected the newer arrivals, if they had been so inclined, and by the leadership positions they attained in Los Angeles, could have made serious trouble for Alston. Instead, they functioned as loyal employees, keeping to themselves whatever private reservations they had about Alston's managing skills (and they had plenty). They exhibited the best aspect of "team play" by their behavior, in a way that's even more important than hitting the cutoff man or giving yourself up to move the runner: they didn't second-guess the manager.

In 1962, the first year that the National League expanded to ten teams with a 162-game schedule, the Dodgers could not hold onto the lead in the last few days in their new stadium in Chavez Ravine, and finished in a tie with the Giants. And, as in 1951, they lost the third game of the playoff in the ninth inning. (Only Duke Snider was left from 1951 to endure that agony again; but the Giants had not only Willie Mays in uniform but manager Alvin Dark and coaches Whitey Lockman, Larry Jansen, and Wes Westrum as their brain trust; and Leo, as a Dodger coach, experienced the other side of the coin.).

Walter Alston

To the Los Angeles media and public, however, 1951 was ancient history on an alien planet, so again, Alston was not subjected to the kind of abuse any manager would have received if the same thing had happened in Brooklyn.

However, the Dodgers swept the Yankees in the 1963 World Series, with Koufax and Drysdale dominant. They failed to win in 1964 when Koufax was injured half the season, but won pennants again in 1965 and 1966, beating Minnesota in a 7-game series the first time and being swept by the Baltimore Orioles in 1966.

Alston's managing style was now perfectly suited to personnel and ballpark. He was a stickler for giving pitchers proper rest, but let Koufax and Drysdale work on a four-day rotation, which they could handle but which conventional wisdom was turning against. He built a strong bullpen and used it well. He let Maury Wills run, and Wills stole 104 bases, shattering a Cobb record considered as inviolable as Babe Ruth's 60 homers had been before Roger Maris hit his 61 the year before. And Alston maximized Maury's chances by having Gilliam bat second. Walt recalled, in later years, that he was astounded to find out that Gilliam could actually see, while at bat, whether Wills had broken from first or not, and could hold up his swing on a hit-and-run play if Wills had not gone.) He believed in a daily lineup as much as possible, and platooned less than most managers were starting to. And he never stopped instructing, correcting, paying attention to fundamentals, fundamentals, fundamentals, fundamentals.

Within a game, he managed the same way he always had. In training and conditioning, he kept to all the Dodger system methods. But he did learn to lighten up on discipline. "The fewer rules you have, the better off you are," he said late in his career, but it was as much a change in circumstance as in thinking. Having established his own reputation and authority, he didn't need as many rules to be obeyed as he did when he was a nobody taking over the direction of big shots.

After 1966, the Dodgers went through another wholesale rebuilding of the parent club from their farm products. They dropped to eighth and seventh, struggled back to fourth, and then ran second three times and third once to the emerging Big Red Machine in Cincinnati. In 1974, however, they won the pennant again—Alston's seventh in twenty-one years—with an entirely new generation: the infield of Steve Garvey, Davey Lopes, Bill Russell, and Ron Cey, an outfield of Willie Crawford, Bill Buckner,

and Jimmy Wynn (the only nonsystem product), Don Sutton and
Andy Messersmith and Tommy John as starters and Mike Marshall making 106 relief appearances, Steve Yeager and Joe Ferguson sharing the catching. His top coach now was Tommy Lasorda,
who had managed most of those players in the minors.

Then, after finishing second, by big margins, to the mighty Reds
again in 1975 and 1976, Alston retired and passed the baton to
Lasorda.

In retrospect, I have a higher opinion of Alston as a manager
than I did while he was active. Part of this is my prejudice: I kept
hearing about his shortcomings from players and rivals I knew
well and had reason to believe, and he certainly was the kind of
"book manager" Stengel and others had taught me to put down.
But as the years went on, even while Alston was still managing, I
came to understand better certain phases of baseball life, such as:
Players often underrate a manager in finding alibis for themselves; rivals talk down opponents partly as a competitive ploy
and partly to keep their own fires burning; stability of atmosphere
and quiet authority have values of their own, apart from intuitive
leaps and cleverness; managing an effective pitching staff is not
as easy as, and even more important than, it looks, even when the
pitching talent is outstanding.

Nevertheless, he was not a "smart" manager in the sense that
McGraw, Martin, Weaver, Durocher, and others were. His place in
the Hall of Fame, to which he was named in 1983, rests on his
record, compiled by consistency, longevity, and ability to win in
so many different circumstances with so many different sets of
players.

In some ways, he was ahead of his time. He was the ultimate
organization man who makes organizations function effectively
and who needs that organization to function himself. In an earlier
day, he might not have been a successful manager, dealing with
talent procurement and a rowdier population and less systematized procedures to lean on. But his devotion to, and mastery of,
system and basics, his ability to work within the overall structure
with minimum ego, and his maintenance of calm climate without
loss of alertness were qualities that became more and more
important—and sought after—as every club developed further
and further along farm system organizational lines. His stern but
fair approach, never causing public embarrassment but willing to
explain in private while taking no guff, fit well the emerging

Walter Alston

population of post-1950 players, who had more schooling and middle-class backgrounds than so many of their pedecessors.

Would his style have worked in the 1980s (apart from his own aging, that is)? I doubt it, because the big money that followed free agency in 1976 created a new situation altogether. Players earning ten times what the manager earned might react to him the way the original Dodger veterans did for other reasons: "Who's he to tell *me* what to do?" And management, which under Walter O'Malley always made it clear that players were "merely" employees and gave the dugout boss absolute backing, does not operate that way anymore. Teams pamper the $4 million player more than their own executives.

So Alston was a perfect example of the right man at the right time in the right situation, who had the capacity to make more of it and who avoided pitfalls awaiting anyone less able than he to ignore annoyance and sniping.

He died in 1984, and the following anecdote sums up for me the kind of impression he made on the people around him. The allegation on which this story is based may or may not be true—I have no idea—and its factuality has nothing to do with the sense of the point I'm making. It's a common enough allegation in sports and show business and not intended to portray anything about the man himself, but only the reaction of others to him.

A longtime baseball writer was typing a story in the pressroom at a World Series and had just tapped out, "Walt Alston, a fine family man" when a colleague looked over his shoulder.

"How can you call him a fine family man?" said the second writer. "Don't you know about the girlfriend he's had on the road with him for years?"

"Is that right?" said the first writer. "I never heard that."

"Everybody knows about it," the second writer assured him.

"Well, okay," said the first writer, trusting the colleague he had known as a good friend and a reliable source for twenty years, but still doubtful.

So he crossed out *fine* and substituted *good.*

15

Ralph Houk

The Major

If Walter Alston was a 100 percent pure product of a single organization, so was Ralph Houk—but it was a different organization and he was a different type of person. The Rickey-Dodger system stressed uniformity of teaching and development, the collection of hundreds of applicants exposed to instruction so that the cream could rise to the top. The Yankee system, even more successful, focused on individual talent. It sought to identify and sign outstanding prospects as early as possible, and in their early experience to let them maximize their special skills (along with teaching them the basics, of course). The Yankees didn't intend to wait for cream to come to the top, they intended to skim the cream wherever they could find it, from high school on up. Rickey had a master plan—an excellent one—and sought players who could fit it. The Yankees had stars and wanted more stars, and had the money to spend and the record of perpetual victory to attract competitive personalities. The Rickey system taught: Do things the right way and victory will be your reward. The Yankee system taught: Beat the opposition any way you can simply because you're better, and if you're not better, we'll get somebody who is.

Alston, then, was well suited to rise in a system that stressed cooperation and smooth working together. In the Yankee system, more assertive personalities thrived.

And Houk had an assertive personality.

They called him "Major" because that was the rank he held when discharged from the army after infantry combat duty in Europe during World War II. He had entered as an enlisted man and won a battlefield commission. In various heroic exploits, he won decorations, most while a second lieutenant, the most hazardous position any soldier could have in the kind of war he fought.

This experience and the personal qualities that enabled him to survive it were a basic element in his eventual baseball success. He was what the military calls "a leader of men," not by authority vested in him officially, but by his capacity to make men follow. It was his prime talent in managing ball clubs.

When he managed his first World Series game, in 1961, Houk was forty-one years old and had worked for the Yankees, except for his four years in the army, since he was nineteen. On the bench, one of the six hundred or so media people milling about before the game asked him if he felt nervous at this peak moment of a professional career. How would he feel if he had to go out and change pitchers?

Houk laughed.

"Nervous?" he repeated. "Why, is someone going to be shooting at me?"

This was, he reminded everyone, only a baseball game, and how could life be better than that?

He took it seriously enough, of course, but he never forgot that it's supposed to be a joy as well as a job for those doing it. Nervous is what you felt when people shot at you.

His outstanding quality, then, was positive thinking. His primary task as a leader, he felt, was to keep up the morale and confidence of his men. He could pump players up—blow smoke up their rear ends, as the saying was then—to the point of overachievement. He didn't teach technicalities, leaving that to coaches. He didn't have elaborate behavior rules. He didn't tinker with lineups any more than necessary, played the game largely by the book, didn't make a fetish of conditioning, and knew all about the care and feeding of pitchers. But most of all he subscribed to and practiced faithfully the New Commandment that came to be considered baseball law in the 1960s: Thou shalt not speak ill of any of your own players, under any circumstances." And the only permissible answer to any question about the future was, "Things are getting better."

If the key description of Alston is "even keel," the key description of Houk is "upbeat."

However, that's not the whole story by any means.

Houk grew up on a farm outside of Lawrence, Kansas (where the University of Kansas is located), in a family that was doing fairly well even in the Depression years. He had uncles and brothers with whom he played a lot of semipro ball (as Alston had in Ohio). His birth date was August 9, 1919.

He was a catcher from the start, stocky, strong, smart, tough, a so-so right-handed hitter. The Yankees signed him in 1939 (when Weiss was running the farm system for Barrow) and placed him in nearby Neosho, Missouri, at the bottom of the chain. In 1940 he was at Joplin, a few miles away but a classification higher, and in 1941 at Augusta, Georgia. Then, for the four years he was in service, he was carried on the Binghamton roster. When he came back, he was sent to Triple-A Kansas City, but after a few games it was determined that this was too high and he played out the year one notch lower, at Beaumont in the Texas League.

In spring training of 1947, at St. Petersburg, with Bucky Harris just taking charge, he made the team as the third-string catcher, behind Aaron Robinson, the regular, and the rookie Yogi Berra, who was so green at the position that he played the outfield part of the time so that his bat could be in the lineup. Houk got to bat in the World Series and got a hit.

But in 1948, he was back at Kansas City for the whole season, because Gus Niarhos shared the regular job with Berra and Charlie Silvera beat him out for the third slot. Late in 1949, he was called up by the Yankees and found himself in the spotlight for the first time.

The 1949 season was so eventful that whole books have been devoted to it, and the events of the final week have become legendary. It was Stengel's first Yankee season, and after clinging to first place all season long, the Yankees were being overtaken by the more talented Red Sox. On the next to last weekend, they went into Boston with a 2-game lead, lost twice, and fell into a tie. On Monday, they lost again, 7–6, on a hotly disputed game-ending squeeze play. Houk was the catcher and screamed that he had made the tag, and might have ended his baseball career right there if his inclincation to kill the umpire—literally—had not been checked in the general confusion.

Six days later, the Yankees won the pennant anyhow, by beating the Red Sox twice at Yankee Stadium, but for the next few years Houk's identity in the minds of Yankee fans was encompassed in that one wild game in Boston.

Stengel liked Houk's brains and aggressiveness, and kept him as his third-string catcher for the next five years. Yogi was catching virtually every day now, and Silvera was his replacement when necessary, so Houk actually got into only 31 games in five years. He spent his time in the bullpen, getting to know the steady stream of veteran pitchers (as well as rookies like Whitey Ford) who passed through, absorbing the pitching theories of Jim Turner, Stengel's pitching coach.

In 1955, when the Philadelphia Athletics moved to Kansas City, the Yankees had to move their farm team to Denver. It was, now, the unadulterated top of their chain, Newark having disappeared. They made Houk the Denver manager, and he stayed there three years, with considerable success, winning the Junior World Series in 1957 and sending along to Yankee Stadium Tony Kubek and Bobby Richardson (and Marv Throneberry, who would become the quintessential Original Met in 1962), Norm Siebern, Ryne Duren, and Don Larsen, among others. And also playing for him there were Darrell Johnson (catcher), Whitey Herzog (outfield), and Tommy Lasorda (pitcher), all of whom would manage in the World Series some day.

In 1958, he was brought back to Yankee Stadium as a coach, joining Frank Crosetti and Turner and replacing Bill Dickey. He was certainly less visible, to fans and press, than any of them, but very highly regarded by Dan Topping, the resident owner, whose opinions were carrying more weight than those of Del Webb, who was seldom around. Stengel was sixty-eight, Weiss a year younger, and Topping was already thinking of replacing them. In Houk he saw an heir apparent, not only because of this fine record in Denver and the respect he commanded within the Yankee family but because he liked him personally as well.

And Houk was certainly well prepared. The Yankees were still winning, but not as decisively as before. In 1957, they had lost the World Series to Milwaukee in 7 games. In 1958, they were down 1–3 to the Braves before they came back and won. And in 1959, with injuries and age and other problems, they had the worst season of Stengel's regime, finishing third only 4 games above .500, out of first place by 15 games.

Speculation that Houk would succeed Stengel gained momentum. Other clubs, notably the Red Sox, made it clear they'd like to have Houk if the Yankees didn't want to promote him. Stengel didn't like it and wondered if Houk, so visibly a favorite of Top-

ping's, was undermining him. The players, those who had played
for Houk in Denver and the older ones who had known him as a
teammate, liked him and found him the most accessible of all the
coaching staff. Crosetti was old-fashioned crabby (and never
missed a trick), not much in sympathy with the emerging youth of
America. Turner was sixty-five and strictly a mother hen for his
pitchers. Stengel was Stengel. Ralph was a man you could talk to
and, invariably, come away feeling better. At the same time, no
one doubted his toughness, and (not unlike Alston) when he did
lose his temper you didn't want to be the target. If it came to a
fight, you were pretty sure you wouldn't be the one to walk away
in one piece.

So Houk was in a tough spot. What could he say? That he didn't
want his shot at managing? That he'd wait forever? Could he turn
aside players looking for help and support by taking a "sorry,
that's not my department" stance? Could he reassure Stengel of
his loyalty, or even bring up the subject? Could he tell other clubs
not to drop his name? His best efforts were devoted to helping the
club win—which would prolong Casey's regime; anything less
would be perceived as undermining Stengel, and if the club lost
would be interpreted that way no matter what Houk did. It was
not a comfortable position.

In 1960, the Yankees did win. They lost the World Series in 7
games to Pittsburgh, almost certainly because Stengel made a
bad mistake—as he himself described it later. Instead of starting
Whitey Ford in the first game, so that he could pitch three times if
necessary, he held him out until the third, back at Yankee Stadium (favorable to lefties). When Ford did pitch, he produced 2
shutouts, but the Yankees lost 3 of the other 4 games up to
3–3—and in the seventh, with Ford unavailable, they were beaten
10–9.

Topping, however, had made up his mind even before that:
Stengel and Weiss had to go. He tried to get them to retire
gracefully, but Stengel would have none of it. Weiss was forced
into retirement because Topping had Roy Hamey, a congenial
man with an extensive administrative baseball background, ready
to step in as general manager. And Houk was manager of the New
York Yankees at the age of forty-one, just old enough to take
charge of stars like Mantle, Ford, Elston Howard, Roger Maris, and
Moose Skowron but young enough to be in touch with their
feelings. And he was just old enough to be the wholly accepted

company commander of the new platoon of younger stars in the making.

They had, in 1961, one of the most successful seasons any team has ever enjoyed: They won the World Series, Maris broke Babe Ruth's record by hitting 61 homers (while Mantle hit 54), Ford posted a 25–4 record when given a four-day rotation for the first time in his career, and the new infield of Richardson at second, Kubek at short, and Clete Boyer at third was a defensive marvel. And with Stengel sitting in California, Weiss in Connecticut, and the officially born but not yet active Mets in the preliminary stages of organization, the Yankees had New York all to themselves. In one year, Houk had gone from respected obscurity to full-bore celebrity.

And the success continued. They won the World Series in 1962 and the pennant in 1963, although this time the Koufax-Drysdale Dodgers swept them in 4 games. No manager had ever done what Houk had just accomplished: win pennants in each of his first three seasons.

Life would never be that sweet for him again, professionally. But before we go on with the story, let's pause for some analysis.

Houk, by his own testimony, learned everything he knew about managing from Stengel, who, by his own testimony, tried to emulate McGraw as much as possible. But Houk, being his own man, also learned from Stengel what he *didn't* want to do as a manager. There were three main points.

1. Evaluating talent correctly is the most important thing, to get the right man in the right spot at the right time. You can do that only if your judgment of his—and the opponent's—capability is objectively correct. But this includes evaluating yourself, and the need to conform to your own capabilities. Houk knew that he didn't have Stengel's mercurial mind or knack of the inspired guess; he understood thoroughly which of Stengel's actions, when they succeeded, were in line with the "percentages" and which weren't. So he, Houk, would stick to the book as much as possible, since guessing will undermine the percentages unless you're dead sure you're guessing right. (We saw McKechnie come to this conclusion long ago.) He wasn't repudiating the "hunch" element Stengel had taken from McGraw; he was merely being true to himself, applying all the orthodox basics. He didn't lack nerve to act on a hunch when he had one; he just didn't get many hunches.

The Moderns

We teased him about it right from the start. In the very first game he managed, on April 10, 1961, against Minnesota at Yankee Stadium, Richardson, the first Yankee batter, hit a grounder to the second baseman.

I stood up in the press box and made the announcement I had prepared weeks before: "Casey would have had him taking."

Houk gave it his high-pitched cackle laugh when we told him about it afterward. He knew as well as anyone that the comparisons could not be evaded until his own regime created its own record. He could handle the inevitable second-guessing and was ready to start.

2. Player relations in the 1960s could not be what they were in the 1920s. Stengel didn't display McGraw's dictatorial meanness, but he had the old-time view of boss-worker interaction. Whitey Ford, in the book he wrote after retirement, has the following passage:

> The thing about Stengel is that he never showed what he felt. He was just not an emotional man. He never would hug you after a game the way Tommy Lasorda does. He wouldn't fit in now the way these guys hug and kiss one another after a game. If you pitched a particularly good game, he might come over and wink at you, but he'd rarely say anything. It wasn't that he didn't appreciate what you did, but he was kind of remote and it must have been difficult for him to show what he felt. Casey never went out of his way to say "Nice game" to you. I guess his approach was that you were a professional and you were being paid to do a job and you did it. If you didn't do the job, you were gone, so the fact that you were there, and he was playing you, was compliment enough. Even when he took me out of my first World Series game in 1950 when Gene Woodling dropped the fly ball that would have been the third out, he never came to me afterward and said he was sorry he had to take me out. A guy like Ralph Houk would have said something like that. Most managers would, but not Casey. It just wasn't his way.

Casey's was a way, Houk felt, that had to be changed.

Ford, one of the sharpest observers of a person's mannerisms and character I've ever come across (which helped him be such a good pitcher), read Stengel perfectly. The only thing he didn't grasp was that Stengel, in his sixties, had a reason for withholding overt praise. He had learned from experience what almost all older managers do. If you say, "Nice game" today and fail to say it, for whatever reason, next time and every time, you imply criticism by silence. It's like the old joke about a mother sending her son two neckties for Christmas and he wears one of them to dinner that night. "What's the matter," she says, "you didn't like the other one?" It's better to let silence imply praise than the other way around.

But that's the sixty-year-old view. Houk still had the forty-year-old view and he saw, correctly, that the twenty- and thirty-year-olds of 1960 wanted—and needed—more explicit encouragement. His leadership quality, rooted in a personality so different from Stengel's and shaped by the under-fire experiences of war, took the form of perpetual encouragement. He wanted to decrease tension, not add to it. Particularly in the Yankee situation, where winning was such an ingrained habit, the younger men (and particularly newcomers from trades or just up from the minors) had to be constantly convinced that they could keep up the standard. The fear factor in Stengel's directorship was fear of disapproval: If you didn't do it right or try hard enough, he'd get down on you. Houk had a way of arousing the fear in your own conscience: If you failed, you felt you were letting him (and the team) down, and you were afraid of losing his respect for you, rather than afraid he would punish you. To generate that, Houk had to make the player feel that he (the leader) was on the player's side at all times in all circumstances, and that he had belief in the player's ability even when the player's confidence flagged. If a bawling out were needed (and players know when they misbehave), it would be administered in private; Houk, you felt sure, would never embarrass you in front of others or in print.

3. Stability and empathy deserve more attention than traditional managerial procedures gave them. Stengel juggled lineups, played people out of position (he had Kubek try center field), platooned heavily, urged men to "play hurt," didn't hesitate to overuse a hot pitcher—all McGrawisms—and steered clear of involvement in the personal lives (and personal problems) of his players. Houk wanted to be a friend—paternalistically, to be sure—to any player who needed help or reassurance even in a nonbaseball matter. He was more scrupulous about pitcher's arms, less demanding about return after an injury. Above all, he wanted a set lineup in which each player, including the bench players, knew his role, and he spelled out that role in so many words (in private). On the one hand, this was part of the innate conservativism of his approach, optimizing the conditions under which the "percentages" would work in your favor. On the other, it was part of the technique of generating loyalty and desire to please the leader, not simply to avoid his wrath.

On the first of these points, Houk was absolutely right, following the fundamental precept of "be yourself."

On the second, he was also absolutely right, getting in step with the psychological and social climate of the time.

On the third, he was right in the short term and wrong in the long term, as we shall see.

Of all the managers in this book, I knew Houk best in terms of how he operated. I spent more time with him, and had a more open relationship for discussion, than with any of the others because I covered the Yankees so much of the time he was manager there. He was invariably honest in answering any question, because we established working ground rules right at the start. If there was something he didn't want to tell me about, he'd lay that right out: "I can't discuss that now." But under no circumstances would he mislead me by an outright lie or try to manipulate the information I got. For my part, I would observe the confidentiality of anything that wasn't explicitly a part of my story, unless it came to me from another direction or got out elsewhere. I would be conscientious about not embarrassing him or his club needlessly (the key word being "needlessly"). He would be conscientious about giving me the straight dope about any situation that had to be kept off the record or unattributed, so that I wouldn't be trapped into misinformation.

It is an axiom of sports coverage that the more you know, the more certain you are to be "scooped" occasionally, and that your best friends have to "lie" to you sometimes (about injuries, planned tactics, steps not ready to be announced, private negative thoughts that require positive public expressions). You learn, in time, what's "fair" to ask and what isn't. And the people you have to cover regularly learn, in time, what's "fair" to withhold and what isn't. "Honesty," in this context means "don't give me a bum steer or let me pursue a mistaken lead when I ask you something specific."

Houk, in the thirty years I dealt with him on and off, was thoroughly honest in this respect. He wasn't the only one, by any means; but there was none better.

He is also the only manager in this book who had extensive combat experience in war. I think that gave him a sense of perspective about baseball (and life) that many others lacked. And I think it added a dimension to his relationship with his players, in that in addition to figuring out ways to get them to perform under pressure (which every sports coach has to do anyhow), he felt a "responsibility" for their welfare analogous to an officer's concern for the safety of his troops.

He was not, however, universally popular with the media. He was cooperative, but certainly not witty, and so dedicated to saying the "right" thing (according to his purposes) that he was often dismissed as Pollyanna-ish and hopelessly uncontroversial. Writers, after a game, would try to anticipate his "all's for the best in the best of all possible worlds" observations: The Yankees got whipped, 13–3, but the fourth pitcher looked good pitching a scoreless seventh; Mickey Mantle tore a muscle and would be out for two weeks, but he needed the rest and it would help his hitting when he came back; true, we've lost 5 straight, but we were hitting the ball better today, even if it was right at someone.

And that violent temper, which he had learned to control so well after his playing days, wouldn't let him accept whatever he felt (rightly or wrongly) was an "unfair" story. He would freeze up and avoid talking to the offender, until and unless he could actually tell him off (which happened rarely). Then he could forget it. But there was no guarantee the writer would.

Out of uniform, he was good company, at ease in any society, a good storyteller when relaxed, gregarious, with an infectious laugh.

At the end of the 1963 season, Houk sat atop the baseball world as few men ever had. He was forty-four. In three seasons, his Yankees had won 309 games, three pennants, two World Series. Stengel, back in New York with the Mets, had lost 231 games in two years at the Polo Grounds, so those who had been impatient to have Houk replace him had additional evidence for their opinion. The all-star Yankee lineup was still relatively young (Mantle was thirty-three, the infielders in their twenties). Houk's coaching staff was outstanding. Crosetti had remained as his third base coach. When Turner retired with Stengel, Houk brought in Johnny Sain as pitching coach, having learned to appreciate him in the early 1950s in the Yankee bullpen when Sain was helping Stengel win those pennants. To teach and help the hitters, he hired Wally Moses, who'd been a fine outfielder for Connie Mack's A's and two other American League teams for seventeen years, and who had coached in Philadelphia and Cincinnati afterward; and he added, as bullpen coach, Jim Hegan, who had been Cleveland's catcher in the 1950s for all those great pitchers.

The Moderns

There was no reason to think Houk couldn't go on and match Stengel's record of five straight pennants.

In actual fact, he managed seventeen seasons, in three cities, without ever winning again.

A sequence of historic events and bad decisions in 1964 changed the course of baseball history, ending four decades of Yankee dominance.

Dan Topping was the instigator. Since Weiss's departure, the front office had been run by Roy Hamey, who had a wealth of experience as a minor league executive and general manager in Pittsburgh (the 1940s) and Philadelphia (the 1950s). By the end of 1963, he was sixty-one and in poor health, and wanted to retire to Arizona. Topping wanted someone he could be comfortable with to take his place, knowing that he (with Webb's approval) was planning to sell the club without giving up operative control. Their idea was that Hamey would retire, Houk would become general manager, and the dugout manager would be— Yogi Berra.

It was bad thinking on several levels. Houk was no more equipped, by background and temperament, for front office duties than Gen. George Patton would have been to be head of the quartermaster corps. Making Yogi manager of his teammates—he was still playing in 1963—was the wrong thing to do, not because Yogi couldn't manage (he proved he could) but because Topping and Houk didn't really believe in him and because it shook the confidence of the players Houk had won over so convincingly while simultaneously leaving Houk accessible to them to take grievances upstairs over Yogi's head. (Encouraging them to believe that he could help and support them had been the chief plank of Houk's managerial policy.) And the reasoning that went into the choice of Berra was flawed in its own terms. Stengel, for all the Met losses, was monopolizing media attention and the Mets were about to move into their new stadium in Flushing. The battle for attendance and local TV ratings was about to be engaged, and the Topping-Hamey-Houk triumvirate had the wrong-headed notion that since Stengel was getting laughs, and Yogi was supposed to talk funny, they could somehow match the Mets in the clown department while maintaining their field supremacy.

And that, of course, was the real hubris: They thought the Yankees were so good, it didn't matter who managed in the dugout; and if Berra needed help, Houk was right there to provide the answers wasn't he?

Ralph Houk

But the Yankees weren't that good. Weiss, a couple of years before he left (reading the handwriting on the wall), had started starving the farm system to maximize profits (in which he and other employees shared), and the talent flow wasn't what they thought it was. Besides, the very managerial methods that had worked so well for Houk depended entirely on his presence and personality, not on the pedestrian strategy he used. Yogi had first-rate baseball judgment and was, in fact, a less conservative tactician than Houk; but he wasn't very verbal, was not at all a disciplinarian, and was unable to provide the one thing at which Houk excelled: the positive-thinking magic conveyed by an endless stream of uplifting pep talks (one on one) delivered with originality and good timing.

The fact was, Topping didn't have much respect for Berra, and expressed it, further undermining Yogi's authority with the players. Even before spring training ended, it was clear that the front office didn't think Yogi was terrific, but that the team could win anyhow.

The 1964 Yankees got off to a slow start and were trailing Baltimore in July.

In August, Topping and Webb sold 80 percent of the team to the Columbia Broadcasting System, with Topping remaining in charge.

In late August, with the Yankees about 6 games out in third place, Topping and Houk decided Berra would have to be replaced at the end of the year. They were interested in Alvin Dark, but he suddenly became unacceptable (we'll see why in the next chapter). Houk then thought of Johnny Keane, whose St. Louis Cardinals were also floundering (in fifth place) and whose job was in jeopardy because Bing Devine, his boss, had become embroiled in the power struggle that developed when Branch Rickey was brought back to "advise" Gussie Busch. Houk, while in Denver, had managed against Keane, then in Omaha (the top Cardinal farm), and had great respect for his low-key style.

In short, the management of both clubs was in a mess.

But the Yankees made a great September drive and won the pennant, thanks to the best move Houk made as a GM: He acquired Pedro Ramos to pitch relief. And the Cardinals also emerged as champions of the National League in a wild race that saw Philadelphia blow a 6½-game lead in the last 12 games.

The Moderns

So the teams faced each other in the World Series, both secretly committed to discarding their managers, who had just become public heroes.

The Cardinals won the World Series in 7 games.

The Yankees went ahead and dismissed Berra.

The embarrassed Cardinals offered Keane a raise (with Devine already gone), but he said no thanks—and signed on with the Yankees.

And Yogi signed on as a player-coach for Stengel with the Mets—who had finished last again with 109 losses, but had outdrawn the Yankees, 1.7 million to 1.3 million.

It was crazy, all around.

Keane was a terrible choice to manage the Yankees. The contempt Dodger veterans had shown the unknown rookie Alston was nothing compared to how the even-more-victory-sated veteran Yankees responded to Keane's prissy schoolmasterish ways. There was nothing wrong with his understanding of baseball, but he was a small-town person, coming off a humiliating experience in St. Louis, totally unequipped for the New York media zoo—whipped to fever pitch by the events of 1964. But Alston, at least, had had those seventeen younger players who knew him from the minors. None of the Yankees knew Keane, nor the two new key coaches he brought along. (In 1964, the trauma for the Yankee players of Houk's promotion had been aggravated by the departure of Sain and Moses. Yogi had made Ford, still pitching, his pitching coach and had chosen an old friend from his minor league days, Jimmy Gleeson, to replace Moses.) Crosetti and Hegan were still in place, but Keane's real lieutenants were Vern Benson and Cot Deal, also strangers.

The 1965 Yankees, on top of other things, had a string of injuries. They finished sixth in a ten-team league, the lowest the franchise had been since 1925.

The 1966 Yankees got off to a 4–16 start, with player morale at rock bottom. The situation was clearly unstable.

The team was in Anaheim when Houk fired Keane and came back to the dugout himself. For about a month, the team seemed to revive, but then settled into complete deterioration and finished dead last. Tenth. To add to the embarrassment, that year the Mets finished ninth for the first time.

Before it was over, however, Topping completed the sale of the rest of his holdings to CBS, and the new club president was a CBS appointee, Mike Burke. Lee MacPhail joined them as general manager, and the Burke-MacPhail-Houk troika developed a good working relationship for the next few years. MacPhail, one of Larry's sons, had run the Yankee farm system for several years under Weiss in the 1950s, before becoming president of the Orioles in 1958. In 1965 he had become administrative assistant to the new and totally unprepared commissioner William D. Eckert, a retired air force general, and left that post a year later to return to the Yankees.

But the farm system was beyond repair, and the old Yankee heroes were old and crippled, and the new amateur draft rules just adopted precluded any reconstruction of the farm system along former lines. The Yankees were simply out of talent.

And in this circumstance, in my opinion, Houk developed into a better manager than he had been when the Yankees won.

All his personal-relations and confidence-building skills were intact. But his by-the-book and set-lineup methods worked only when you had superior talent. Now he was forced to be more original, to experiment, to take chances—and to exercise day by day and player by player his evaluative judgment, which was always excellent. He also started, gradually at first, to do more teaching. He learned, in short, how to play the hand he was dealt when the hand was not brimming over with aces.

The 1967 Yankees were ninth, but in 1968 they climbed over .500 and finished fifth. The 1969 season was the first in which the league split into two divisions, and the Yankees, 1 game under .500, were fifth but within 6½ games of third. In 1970, they won 93 games, which was 15 less than first-place Baltimore's 108, but they had second all to themselves and had clearly regained respectability. In 1971, they slipped to fourth, at 82–80, but in 1972 were part of a close four-team race into mid-September before finishing fourth again, 79–76.

And then CBS finally unloaded its bad investment. In January 1973, it sold the team to a group headed by George Steinbrenner and, presumably, Burke. But Burke was out in no time, and Mac-Phail left to become president of the American League; and at the end of the season (another fourth-place finish), Houk resigned. Just a few weeks of contact with Steinbrenner had convinced him that he wanted no part of that operation.

Houk was, at this point, highly respected despite the Yankee record. He was seen as a fine handler and developer of young players, a patient teacher, a good motivator. Within two weeks, he was hired by the Detroit Tigers, who had fired Billy Martin a month before.

Houk spent five years in Detroit, bouncing between fourth and sixth, but laying a foundation with young players who would blossom later under Sparky Anderson (including Alan Trammell and Lou Whitaker). He retired to Florida after the 1978 season, then answered a call from the new owners of the Boston Red Sox in 1981, the year marked by a two-month strike. His 1982 team was a strong third, and his next two finished sixth and fourth, but again he was laying a groundwork that others would benefit from. He left after the 1984 season and the Red Sox made the World Series in 1986 and won division titles in 1988 and 1990.

Houk never managed again, but his constructive influence played a role in one more success. When the Minnesota Twins won the 1987 World Series under rookie manager Tom Kelly and rookie general manager Andy MacPhail—Lee's son—Houk was part of their brain trust, listed as a "special consultant."

In our family tree, Houk is a McGraw offshoot, through Stengel, all the way. But his long career illustrates three of the deepest truths about managing, that apply to all:

1. When you have the players, you're supposed to win, but when you don't, thinking won't do the job.

2. The quality of managerial performance cannot be judged simply by a team's won-lost record.

3. The "intangibles" of handling people mean more than all the game plans, analysis charts, and computer printouts put together.

16

Alvin Dark

The Captain

Alston didn't talk much, perhaps because he didn't have much to say. Houk talked a lot, but didn't say much, because he was so careful to let only positive and upbeat statements pass his lips.

Alvin Dark couldn't keep his mouth shut, and it ruined his career. Many times.

In managerial terms, Dark was one of the "smart" ones, much more so than Alston or Houk, in the sense that McGraw and Durocher and Dressen were "game smart." He had a restless and perceptive mind, keenly analytic, sensitive to detail, deeply competitive, obsessed with trying to figure out every possible way to get even a small edge.

He was, it turned out, too smart for his own good.

Because he grasped baseball's intricacies so thoroughly, and thought fast enough to make instantaneous decisions, and was convinced his conclusions were correct (which they were, objectively), he was sure he could make his views prevail in any situation, and that his views would lead to victory.

He was right about the second point: His views would and did produce victories. But he was wrong about how to make people accept them. He depended on verbal and logical persuasion, manipulation, and accumulating formal authority. The persuasion did work with those who were receptive; the manipulation worked sometimes but often backfired; but the ambitious grasp for more authority brought disaster.

But his biggest problem was that he insisted on trying to articulate his thoughts on complex subjects beyond baseball technique, in words and circumstances that were bound to be misunderstood. He was a born preacher, and preached whatever he believed with fervor, and tried to explain why and how he believed as he did—and wound up handing ammunition to those who either resented his manner or believed differently, or had other reasons for wanting to shoot him down.

So he got shot down again and again. But before he did, he produced some brilliant successes. Ultimately, in an autobiography he wrote (with a collaborator) in 1980 after his five managerial stints with four clubs were behind him, he recognized and openly discussed his mistakes. In the process, he made an observation that the stories in this book confirm and that goes to the heart of baseball's managerial process. When a manager is fired, he noted, it's almost always for the wrong reasons; yet what a manager really does do wrong is seldom noted or results in dismissal.

He was one of the best teachers I ever came across in baseball, better for me than Stengel because he would talk so much more in greater detail, better than Houk because he went deeper into baseball questions, and better than anyone because we first began these seminars while he was still an outstanding player with the Giants—the "Captain," as Durocher had appointed him in 1951, often referred to as "Cap." And we became good friends.

One day, when he was managing the A's in Kansas City, he fed me a line I've never forgotten and have applied to all sorts of situations beyond baseball because it's such a profound insight— not original with Alvin nor peculiar to him, but expressed with remarkable conciseness.

"Remember," he said, "there's no such thing as taking a pitcher out. There's only bringing another pitcher in."

It sums up the central facet of effective management in all aspects of life. The only thing that matters is the *next* pitch. Whatever has happened has already happened and cannot be undone. When you decide to take a pitcher out, it's not as retribution for the hit he gave up, but an attempt to get the next man out. If you don't think the man you bring in has a better chance to get that out than the man already out there, don't make the change, no matter how it looks to anyone else. The whole purpose of every decision is to maximize your chances—in your own opinion—of making the *next* thing succeed.

Dark was a master of this kind of thinking, which, one way or another, all the managers in this book practiced. It's the essence of the first guess, which managers must make, as distinct from the second guess, which anyone can get right after they see what has happened. The past is a guide—the only available guide—to what you should expect; but once you've decided what you do expect, the past doesn't matter: You can win only by guessing right about what *will* happen. McGraw's aggressive offense and hunches, Mack's positioning of players, Griffith's eclectic opportunism, Rickey's systematics—all were directed at improving the chances that the *next* move would be successful. It's that judgment, right or wrong, that dictates making out a lineup, sending up a pinch hitter, changing pitchers, or calling for a hit-and-run play. If you don't think it will give you a better chance than the one you already have, don't make the change; or, if you make it, don't kid yourself that you've done something that can help.

In Dark's case, he was already thinking this way as a player. He grew up in Louisiana, although he was born in Oklahoma (on January 7, 1922), into a passionately devout Baptist family. His father worked at supervising the drilling of oil wells. His mother, who married his father when she was fifteen, was a small, strong-willed, loving woman who had to handle a family constantly on the move. There were an older sister and an older brother (nine years Alvin's senior) and a younger sister. The father encouraged the boys' athleticism from the start, and Alvin seemed exceptionally gifted at an early age. At ten and eleven, he was playing on baseball teams with sixteen- to nineteen-year-olds in Lake Charles (an oil port town in Louisiana, thirty-five miles from the Texas line). He became one-track-minded about sports: He'd talk about little else, listed "professional baseball" as his only career goal, and, as a high school senior, made all-state as a football halfback. He was also the basketball captain (a play-making guard), but the school had no baseball team so he played American Legion ball during baseball season.

He accepted a basketball scholarship to Texas A&M, but when Louisiana State offered him a scholarship for basketball and baseball after he turned down one strictly for football, he went to Baton Rouge instead. Of course, football was the sport that counted then (this was in 1941) so he won letters in all three sports and squeezed in his greatest passion—golf—when he could. In the 1941 and 1942 football seasons, he was an outstanding kicker (punting was important then, in one-platoon days) and also able to score touchdowns running and to pass for them. His blocking back was Steve Van Buren, eventually a great National Football League running back.

The Moderns

But Pearl Harbor had happened, and being drafted was a certainty, so in 1943 Dark enlisted in the marine corps V-12 program, which sent officer candidates to college. Stationed at Southwest Louisiana, he played on an outstanding service team there, and got All-America mention. Earl Blaik, coaching army's wartime powerhouses at West Point (the Glenn Davis–Doc Blanchard teams) wanted Dark to come there in 1944, but that would have entailed a four-year military commitment even after the war, and Alvin turned down the invitation. Nor was he interested in pro football. Baseball was his goal.

Dark was commissioned early in 1945. The marines sent him to Pearl Harbor, and after sending him to Saipan with a machine gun unit, yanked him right back to play on the service football team. That December, with the war over, they sent him back to the Orient, to China, theoretically as part of an occupation force but actually to help the Nationalists in their civil war against the Communists. His unit guarded a railroad supply line south of Beijing (it was Peking then), but did no serious fighting. A month after he was rotated back to the States, in March 1946, that marine unit was ambushed and wiped out.

When he got home, Ted McGrew, scouting for the Boston Braves, was waiting for him. The Buffalo Bisons of the new All-America Football Conference (the one that contained Paul Brown's Cleveland Browns) were after him too. Dark was twenty-four years old and had played no baseball for four years. McGrew asked him how big a bonus he wanted. Dark wrote down a figure that was double the most he dared ask for (always think ahead): $50,000. McGrew said, "You've got it." Why? (Alvin asked only after he had signed). "Because we like the competitive spirit you showed in the other sports," said McGrew, who had also spotted the special qualities of Pee Wee Reese and Pete Reiser when he was scouting for the Dodgers.

He reported to the Braves the same day as Warren Spahn, got into a few games, went back to get his discharge, and then spent the whole 1947 season at Milwaukee, the top of the Braves' farm system. They decided he should be a shortstop, and he had a big year, hitting .303 and leading the team to victory in the Little World Series (against International League champion Syracuse). He led the league in at bats, runs scored, doubles, putouts, assists—and errors.

So in 1948 he was with the Braves to stay. The manager was

Alvin Dark

Billy Southworth, but the man who really had an influence on him was the second baseman and his roommate on the road, Eddie Stanky. They became close friends (Stanky was six years older), but their main bond was a shared obsession with talking about, analyzing, and brainstorming baseball techniques and situations.

Dark hit .322, was Rookie of the Year (an award instituted only the previous year and won by Jackie Robinson), and an instant hero as the Braves won the pennant—their first since the 1914 Miracle Braves.

But 1949 was different. The team deteriorated, and firebrands like Stanky took a dim view of Southworth's laid-back managing. Never fully recovered from his son's death, Southworth had developed a drinking problem, but what players felt to be a more serious shortcoming was his refusal (in their eyes) to stick up for them in salary disputes or to take responsibility for plays that went wrong. By the end of the year, Southworth had retired, the Braves had finished fourth, and "troublemakers" like Stanky and Dark were considered expendable.

Durocher, starting his second full year with the Giants, just loved troublemakers with that kind of ability. He persuaded Horace Stoneham to make the trade that changed the character of his club: power-hitting Willard Marshall and Sid Gordon, shortstop Buddy Kerr, and a pitcher, Sam Webb, for Stanky and Dark.

Among the things Dark had always been outspoken about were his militant Christian beliefs. He didn't drink, didn't smoke, and felt guilty when he cussed (which, however, he did do). When he turned down $500 to lend his image to the cigarette ad on the Polo Grounds scoreboard, Leo got him $500 by appointing him team captain, even though he was the junior partner of the second base combination. Leo knew what he was doing, because if a captain's job includes providing verbal inspiration to his teammates, choosing a born preacher was a good way to go.

Durocher became Dark's model for how to manage a baseball game—not a team, necessarily, but the game. In this aspect, Durocher was in the McGraw line (through Frisch and his own nature), and Dark absorbed it completely. Poles apart in philosophy of life and upbringing—one a volubly pious churchgoer, the other a riverboat gambler and flashy braggart dripping profanity at every pore—Dark and Durocher had one deeper quality in common: They wanted to win, at any cost, whatever they were doing, and never tired of thinking up ways to prevail—in baseball, in card games, in arguments.

But Dark was acquiring another mental weapon, even as a player. For all his native athletic ability, he was slow afoot. He had to cover shortstop territory with his brain, not his legs: He had to know just where to play every hitter, which meant he had to know the intent and quality of every pitch his own pitcher threw. (Lou Boudreau was the same kind of shortstop.) He could throw well enough, but he couldn't depend on range. And, as a hitter, he was also cerebral rather than a free-swinger. All the things he had to figure out to get results as a player were going into his data bank for managing some day.

At the Polo Grounds, of course, Dark hit more homers than he would have elsewhere, because of the 279-foot left-field line and the 250-foot right-field line—and he believed, most of all, in hitting to right (he was right-handed). Counterclockwise baseball was right up his alley. After his playing career was over, and he was returning to the Polo Grounds for the first time as manager of the San Francisco Giants to play the Mets, I asked him what the hallowed place made him think of: 1951? 1954? Willie's World Series catch? Some special hit? The pitching of Maglie and Jansen? The days with Durocher?

Without hesitation he replied. "The Polo Grounds? Don't hit the ball to center field."

Sure. Not only was it five hundred feet deep but the odd shape let the three outfielders bunch up and close the gaps. Sentiment, schmentiment; remember what gives you an edge.

In 1951, it was Dark's ground single to right that opened the ninth-inning rally Bobby Thomson's homer ended. In 1953, with the fifth-place Giants playing out the string, Durocher let him "manage" a game (and also let him pitch). In 1954, he took the lead in the rescue plan the players used to save Leo's job when Stoneham was about to fire him, because Alvin felt they could win with Leo—and, of course, they won the World Series.

By 1956, when Bill Rigney replaced Leo, Alvin was thirty-four and slowing down, and the team was going nowhere (because its pitching had worn out). Stanky had left after 1951 to manage the Cardinals. The financial situation of the Giants was obviously precarious, and Stoneham was weighing the possibility of moving the team. The Yankees and the Dodgers were winning more than ever. And in August of 1955, Alvin had injured his shoulder. It was time for a change.

Alvin Dark

The Cardinals were being run by Frank Lane, the man who hadn't hesitated to trade Colavito for Kuenn and then trade managers (Gordon for Dykes). He now didn't hesitate to trade away one of the most popular players the sentimental St. Louis fans ever had, Red Schoendienst. It was a four-for-four trade early in 1956, but basically Dark for Schoendienst. The Giants had a good shortstop coming up and needed a second baseman; the Cardinals had a good new second baseman and no shortstop. Neither veteran was of much help to his new team that year, but in 1957 Dark helped the Cardinals chase the Milwaukee Braves down to the wire before finishing second; the Braves made it because they had acquired Schoendienst from the Giants as the final piece of their championship puzzle.

By this time, Dark's characteristics were known throughout the baseball world. He was an evangelical Christian, willing to help anyone convert, and at the same time a man with a legendary temper. He was famous for ripping up uniforms: After a loss, he would tear off his shirt, scattering buttons like buckshot. He fought to control his anger and succeeded 99 percent of the time—but you could see the struggle 50 percent of the time. As his physical skills receded, teams were interested in him as an elder-statesman teacher-leader, an unofficial coach, even when he could play only part time. He was now playing third base as often as short. Midway through the 1958 season, the Cardinals traded him to the Cubs. At the end of 1959, the Cubs traded him to Philadelphia, and in June the Phillies traded him to Milwaukee, back to his original team, the transplanted Braves. And at the end of 1960, the Braves traded him to the transplanted Giants, in San Francisco.

But this last transaction was no ordinary trade. The Giants wanted him as a manager, not a player.

The Giants, in 1960, had moved into their new ballpark at Candlestick Point—a huge field area with swirling winds, most of them blowing in against right-handed hitters, exactly what a club with Willie Mays, Orlando Cepeda, and a bunch of other power hitters didn't need. Halfway through the season, Stoneham had fired Rigney and installed Tom Sheehan, nicknamed "Superscout" because that has been his second task with the Giants (the first was being good company for Stoneham over a bottle). Even Stoneham knew this wasn't the answer. He had learned to appreciate Dark as a player, although he didn't like his sanctimoniousness, after making the 1950 trade for him with reservations. He hired him again, again with reservations but with more confidence.

Alvin was ready. Those early years with Stanky had focused on game mechanics: If the situation is such and such, what do you do? What's the best way to make certain double plays? How do you figure out a pitcher? But Durocher had been a terrific tutor of the whole game, and Rigney, who patterned his thinking and even some of his mannerisms on Leo, had tried to play the same game with a totally different (and thoroughly nice) personality. At St. Louis, his manager was Fred Hutchinson, whose monumental rages of frustration at defeat were more legendary than Dark's, but who had the mind of an intellectual and the ability to command affectionate respect. At Chicago, his manager was Bob Scheffing, a former catcher who knew pitching. At Philadelphia, a rookie manager, Gene Mauch, dazzled Dark with his baseball intellect. At Milwaukee, he found Spahn still pitching and a laid-back atmosphere under Dressen. All this had gone into his managing file, and he knew for sure exactly what he wanted to adopt or reject from each case study.

As a player, his words didn't make much trouble. His talk about God inspired some, annoyed others, and was ignored by those who didn't care. As a manager, however, everything he said was fodder for the press, and every expression subject to interpretation. Since more were annoyed than inspired by religious views they didn't share, both writers and readers often reacted badly to what Dark thought was a simple, sincere expression of his beliefs.

More important, however, was a tendency to manipulate that now came into play. As a player, if he thought something could improve the club's performance, he could say so to a fellow player, a coach, or even the manager as a matter of gratuitous advice and let it go at that. If they ignored it, fine. As a manager, he had authority as well as responsibility. If he thought this one should tinker with his stance, that one should lose weight, this one shouldn't stay out late so often, that one should not play as much as he'd like, this one should pitch a certain way, that one should pay more attention, he could try to enforce all these changes—not by edict, but by being smart enough to figure out a way to maneuver the object of his attention into doing things his way.

His self-confidence was part of the problem. He not only knew he had the right answers (and he did, most of the time; we've seen that in several managers). He knew in his heart that his motivations were absolutely pure and devoted to the success of the enterprise. When he would say something was "in God's hands," it sounded to most people like an alibi or an arrogant assertion of a pipeline to higher powers. To him, it was simply what he'd been taught to believe all his life beyond the tacit assumption that God helps those who help themselves. And precisely because he didn't try to force his faith on anybody—he was scrupulous about not being a proselytizer—his verbalization of it promoted misunderstanding. He was speaking the language he knew, Bible-quoting reverence in which terms had unquestioned connotations that weren't shared by his listeners. If he hadn't tried to explain, he'd have been all right; since he did, he was constantly being pressed for more explanations, which only made things worse.

So while another manager might tell a player outright, "Don't try to pull; the next time you do, it'll cost you fifty, and the time after that you're gone," Dark was sure he could get the player to do it by indirection, maneuvering him into wanting to do it, as if it were his own idea; by persuasion, parable, exhortation, or some clever ploy that would have the desired effect. Very often that worked; very often it didn't; but when it didn't, the player would feel that the manager had been playing mind games with him; and Alvin kept overestimating how often it would work, and his ability to prod people in the right direction.

Nevertheless, he was a terrific manager, as events would prove.

The Swamp Fox

Being the general instead of just a captain gave his imagination full rein. He surrounded himself with former teammates of the 1951 team: Larry Jansen to coach the pitchers, Whitey Lockman, and Wes Westrum. I've never been around a dugout brain trust that was any more comfortably on the same wavelength as that Giant group of 1961–63.

A power-laden lineup already had Willie McCovey, added to Mays and Cepeda. What was needed was a pitching staff, and Dark pieced one together. His 1961 team, which finished a strong third behind Cincinnati and the Dodgers in the National League's last eight-team season, had no starter winning more than 13 games—

and the biggest winner, with 14, was Stu Miller, the relief pitcher who specialized in tantalizing slow, slower, and slowest stuff. In 1962, in winning the pennant, Jack Sanford won 24 (including 16 straight) and Billy Pierce, the left-hander acquired from the White Sox, was 12–0 at Candlestick while winning 16. Billy O'Dell won 19 and Juan Marichal, in his second full season, went to 18–11 after 13–10 despite a late-season injury.

The end-of-season drama was tremendous. Two games behind with 3 to play, the Giants finished in a tie with the Dodgers by winning 2 while the Dodgers lost all 3. In the playoff, they bombed Koufax, 8–0, in the first game at San Francisco, and lost a four-hour struggle, 8–7, at Dodger Stadium in the second. Now it was October 3, the eleventh anniversary of the Bobby Thomson game, and this time the Dodgers were the home team. They had led, 4–2 in the ninth inning, when Thomson connected; and they led 4–2 in the top of the ninth this time. But the Giants scored 4 runs, Pierce came in to set down the Dodgers 1-2-3, and they were in a World Series.

Against the Yankees, of course.

This was the one in which the teams split 2 games in San Francisco, and the Yankees won 2 of the next 3 at New York. But returning to California, they ran into a four-day rainstorm. The first one was a travel day anyhow, but the next three entrapped the flower of American journalism into a protracted drinking party in a city made to order for such activity. Finally, the Giants won the sixth game, and came within a foot—literally—of winning the seventh. Trailing 1–0 with two out in the ninth and runners on second and third, McCovey hit a fierce line drive off Ralph Terry right where second baseman Bobby Richardson could catch it. (Months later, Charles Schulz, whose home was in the Bay Area, published one of his greatest Peanuts cartoon strips: For three panels, Charlie Brown and Linus, or maybe Schroeder, sit silently on the curb, looking glum; in the fourth panel, Charlie Brown says, "Why couldn't McCovey have hit it one foot higher?")

Less remembered about this notable game was an ironic twist about the way Houk and Dark managed. Dark, the free thinker, went by the book in the top half of the fifth inning. The Yankees filled the bases with nobody out in a scoreless game, and Dark made the universally accepted percentage move: He played his infield back for a double play, conceding one run to prevent a big inning, counting on his own strong hitters, who still had five innings to bat, to produce at least one run themselves. He got the double play—but the run that scored turned out to be the only one of the game. Then, in the ninth, McCovey came up with first base open, a left-handed monster-hitter against right-handed Terry, and Houk went to the mound to talk to his pitcher. Mr. Conservative would have had every right to walk McCovey and face the right-handed Cepeda (since the winning run, in the person of Mays, was already on second), or at least bring in a left-hander to face McCovey. Instead, Houk let Terry stay (as I recall, he asked Terry which he preferred to face, and Terry said, "I'd just as soon get it over with now"). So in the championship showdown, Dark went down with the book and Houk emerged as champion—for the last time in his life—by going against it.

But most of the time, Alvin was thinking up clever plays, and they worked. The most fascinating exchanges were with the Dodgers. In 1961, when the Dodgers were still in the coliseum with it's short left field, their most fearsome right-handed slugger was Frank Howard, six feet seven inches tall, appropriately bulky, and Rookie of the Year the previous season. But he flat out could not hit Stu Miller's soft stuff, nor even make contact with it.

In one extra-inning game, as the Dodgers batted in the home half, Alston had Howard available to pinch-hit and got him ready. As soon as Howard stood up, Dark waved to Miller to start warming up in the clearly visible bullpen. Alston took one look at Miller and told Howard to sit down. So Miller sat down too. A couple of hitters later, Howard got up again and so did Miller. Neither one ever actually got into the game, but Dark had trumped the Howard ace with his Miller deuce.

But that wasn't the famous case. The famous one happened at Candlestick Park and earned Alvin the title of "the Swamp Fox," with its connotation of the Revolutionary War general.

Maury Wills, the Dodger shortstop, was revolutionizing the game with his base stealing. He was the key offensive weapon for Los Angeles. The new infield at Dodger Stadium was hard-packed, on purpose, to benefit running, and, of course, in California it never rained during the summer months.

What slows a base runner down is soft footing, especially in that all-important first stride. So when the Dodgers came to Candlestick, Alvin had the infield dirt around first base soaked thoroughly—flooded would be a better word. (Elsewhere too, but first is where it mattered.)

The Dodgers, coming out for practice, saw the mud bath created around first, and complained to the umpires. Their objection had merit, and the umpires ordered sand brought out to spread over the soaked area and sop up the excess water.

But that, of course, was exactly what the Swamp Fox wanted.

"No matter how wet it was," he chortled later, "the wind would have dried it out by the fourth or fifth inning. But once they put the sand down, it was there for the whole day, and even harder to run out of than mud."

There was a terrible fuss, and Stoneham didn't like it. He felt his club had been embarrassed by attempting a sharp practice.

Too smart for his own good.

That, however, was not the real problem between Dark and Stoneham.

In 1962, Alvin and his wife, Adrienne, who had been his sweetheart back in Lake Charles, were living in Atherton (south of San Francisco) with their four children. Early that year, Dark met an airline stewardess he couldn't forget. He didn't see her again for a year, but early in 1963 he began seeking her out on the road. They were in love.

Baseball, as I've said, is a small world, where little can be kept secret. That Alvin Dark was having an affair would not be worth even the mildest gossip in ordinary circumstances: Infidelity is as common among athletes as excessive drinking (a characteristic of most professions entailing constant travel), generally considered nobody else's business and a far less serious transgression than (for instance) merely talking to a known gambler.

But Dark was the one who spoke of God and Christ and his devotion to orthodox Christian morality. In his case, it was blatant hypocrisy.

And Stoneham, when he found out about it, didn't like it. It made Dark a fraud, as a person, in his eyes.

It didn't do much for Dark's image with players or writers, either. If he was violating his own most frequently asserted moral standards this way, perhaps he was a phony in other ways too. One wasn't quite sure what to believe.

The deterioration of his position didn't happen all at once, and was capped by a different issue. This was the era of the flowering civil rights movement, the ascendancy of Martin Luther King, Jr., the acceleration of desegregation under President Lyndon Johnson after the assassination of John F. Kennedy. To be accused, publicly, of racism was to be condemned out of hand. Suddenly, Dark was.

Alvin Dark

Now, as a matter of fact and documented record, there wasn't the slightest tinge of racism in anything Dark ever did, especially as a manager. His judgments, decisions, and actions were totally unaffected by any sort of bias, because his true religion was "win." His roster actually had an unusually large mix of blacks, Latinos, and whites—Catholics and Protestants, devout and profane—and many of the writers he knew best were Jewish. Not only was he entirely fair and uninfluenced by prejudice in what he did as a manager, but he was remarkably successful in creating a team unity out of an exceptionally diverse group.

But when he spoke, he fit all the wrong stereotypes.

First of all, he had a distinct Southern accent and was identified as a product of Louisiana.

Second, the religion he had been taught all his life, and whose principles he tried to espouse in so many talks, *did* contain a philosophy of difference based on race.

Third, his political views, as conservative as most baseball people's were, were couched in shallow and old-fashioned rhetoric traditionally inflammatory to the liberal-equal-rights majority of that time.

Fourth, he was not, in truth, a philosopher or interested in politics. He was interested in sports—as nonphilosophic and reality-based an activity as one can find—and had been, almost exclusively, since childhood. (One of the cracks that developed in his first marriage was his total absorption in sports to the exclusion of everything else, while Adrienne had broader interests in life.)

But he couldn't keep his mouth shut.

He insisted on trying to explain his "views," when doing this was unnecessary. He had ideas about how and where to play Cepeda and McCovey, based entirely on baseball considerations. When he tried to lay them out to listeners who had a different orientation, they came out as sweeping generalizations that seemed like bias.

One such interview, in July of 1964, blew the lid off.

In 1963, the Giants had finished third behind the Dodgers and the Cardinals, playing roughly .500 ball from June on. In 1964, they started well and were in first place, being challenged only by the Phillies, well into July. But by now, Dark's affair with Jackie Rockwood was so visible that Stoneham was offended. He was ready to fire Dark (as he had been ready to fire Durocher early in 1954) without regard to the consequences for the ball club.

The Moderns

At that point, Dark had a long conversation with Stan Isaacs, of *Newsday,* who just happened to be passing through San Francisco. They had known each other since 1951 in New York. Dark lectured on his team's problems, and what came out—when Isaacs wrote a column a couple of weeks later—was, in essence, "the blacks lack intelligence and the Latins lack guts and work ethic." (That's my summary, not the exact quote.)

The storm lasted about three weeks, producing denials, amplifications, expressions of support on many sides, condemnation elsewhere, and confusion among his players, who couldn't help wonder, "What does he *really* think?"

The immediate consequences were:

1. Houk and the Yankees, who knew that Stoneham was likely to let Dark go and thought he'd be the perfect replacement for Berra, dropped the idea instantly. You certainly weren't going to bring that bag of worms into New York.

2. The Mets, whose ownership had its eye on Dark as a successor to Stengel, abandoned that idea for the same reason.

3. Stoneham, a decent man, abandoned his plan to fire Dark then, because it would seem to give substance to the prejudice issue, which Stoneham knew had no substance. Firing him in the middle of that controversy would have seemed to confirm the accusations and thus brand him for life. So Dark remained in charge.

4. The club's performance began to suffer—not dramatically, but enough to help cause the five-team scramble that developed in the season's final month.

In the end, the Phillies blew their lead and the Cardinals slipped through and won, beating out the Reds. The Giants wound up fourth, only 3 games out and not eliminated until the final weekend.

And at that point, Dark's dismissal became official.

The prejudice story had been an irrelevancy and a killer. The personal situation was still largely private but complex.

Alvin and Jackie really were in love. She, too, had strong orthodox Christian beliefs, although she was divorced with two school-age children. By 1965, they were thoroughly committed to each other. Dark's divorce process from Adrienne was begun in 1968 and when it became final in 1970, Alvin and Jackie were married within two weeks. He eventually adopted Jackie's two children, and twenty years later their marriage was going strong. It was a

Alvin Dark

midlife shift, with plenty of pain for all involved, entirely typical of American life in the twentieth century, but played out in a spotlight (on a major league manager) few Americans are exposed to.

And within baseball, no one doubted Dark's value as a baseball man. For the 1965 season, he signed on with the Chicago Cubs as coach under manager Bob Kennedy, with the explicit understanding that he would not be a candidate to replace him (on the theory that this would constitute disloyalty and an undermining of the manager). Sure enough, in midseason, Kennedy was fired and replaced by Lou Klein, but Dark remained as coach only.

The Play Doctor

However, Chicago was the home town of Charles O. Finley, who had acquired the Kansas City Athletics in 1961. Finley had a terrific nose for talent, and in the course of his tumultuous twenty years in baseball, hired dozens of the best baseball brains alive, made good use of them, discarded them at whim, and got a lot of results. He appreciated Alvin's baseball brain.

Finley hired him, at the end of the 1965 season, to be a sort of superscout–advisor–administrative assistant. Within a couple of months, his manager, Haywood Sullivan, quit to go back to his roots with the Boston Red Sox in a front office post. (Finley had made Sullivan the manager only during the 1965 season, his fifth manager in five seasons.) So Finley said to Dark, "Go manage," and Alvin was only too happy to resume the one job he truly loved.

In the five years Finley had owned them, the A's had lost 487 games. But he had been accumulating, with great skill, young talent, especially pitchers: Catfish Hunter, Blue Moon Odom, Chuck Dobson, Lew Krausse. There was something here well suited to Dark's talents and methods. He could teach, manipulate, be daring, foster development without the pressures of a large media corps or pennant race obligations. And he had learned one important lesson in San Francisco. His trouble there, aside from the hypocrisy and political correctness issues, had started when he tried to be too clever regarding the Willie Mays situation. When the club moved from New York for the 1958 season, Willie was, beyond any dispute, the best ballplayer in the world. (Some thought the best ever.) But the San Francisco community, ultrasensitive about any comparisons to New York, wanted its own hero, and settled upon Cepeda and other new players who had never been part of the New York Giants. In Seals Stadium, the first two years, there wasn't enough outfield room for Willie's true fielding capacities to be visible (to home fans). At Candlestick in 1960, there was the wind tunnel and distant left-field bleacher, which cut down his home run production. Mays was getting a cold reception in San Francisco, and it bothered him, and as the new manager, Dark was determined to do something to help his key man. So he talked up the greatness of Mays at every opportunity, knowing how well Durocher had helped Willie's confidence back in New York by proper praise. But in trying to give Mays his due, he was indirectly putting down Cepeda—and therefore the judgment of the San Francisco establishment, which was being told that it was too dumb to appreciate the full glory of Mays and wrong in worshipping Cepeda above him.

This was one of those manipulations that backfired, and by the time he got to Kansas City, Dark knew more about handling people and the limitations of manipulation. No comparable situation existed there, but his realization that in San Francisco he hadn't quite known absolutely everything as completely as he thought he did made Dark a better manager (and better communicator) with his young club.

He won 74 games and finished seventh, the team's best record since moving to Kansas City—the same year that Houk's Yankees finished tenth. But that was almost incidental for Finley, who had other problems. He was fighting with Kansas City authorities about getting a new ballpark, losing, and trying to move the team somewhere else—Dallas, Seattle, Oakland, somewhere. He was settling on Oakland, where a new stadium had been built. And he was also confronting, with the other club owners, a cloud on the horizon called the Major League Players Association, which had hired Marvin Miller and was starting to act like (horrors!) an authentic labor union.

In 1967, Alvin talked himself out of another job, or maybe failed to talk, or something. An allegation that one of the young pitchers, Lew Krausse, had become drunk and rowdy on a commercial flight led to an incredible blowup with comic-opera aspects. The details no longer matter, but the situation was this: The allegation was false; Finley, choosing to believe it, ordered Krausse to be suspended; Dark tried to talk him out of it, and failed; the players, rallying behind Krausse, got up a petition to present to Finley, and

Alvin Dark

Dark didn't tell Finley (at least not soon enough) that he knew it was in the works; Finley fired Dark; two hours later, he rehired him, with a raise; meanwhile, the players went public with a threat to strike, supported (or egged on, according to Finley) by Miller and the fledgling union; again, Finley felt that Dark hadn't told him everything he knew, or that he was siding with the players, or that he had misled him, or something; so Finley fired him again and that was that.

It was quite a blow for Dark, who knew what possible glories lay ahead. Bert Campaneris and Dick Green had been there when he came; Sal Bando and Rick Monday had just arrived; Reggie Jackson and Joe Rudi were on the way. The backbone of what would be (to date) the last team to win three straight World Series, in 1972–74, was being built, and now he wouldn't be part of it.

Well, not quite. But nobody knew that yet.

Dark wasn't out of work long, however. His reputation as a baseball technician was higher than ever. (I had teased Houk when the Yankees split a 4-game series in Kansas City: "Look at the players you've got—Mantle, Maris, Howard, Richardson, Tresh, Boyer, Pepitone—and look at the players he's got; you won two games with yours, and he won two with his, so he must be much smarter.") Gabe Paul, general manager of the Cleveland Indians, had approached him in 1966, just after Dark had signed on with Finley. Now he called him again, with the team under new ownership. When the 1968 season began, Alvin Dark was the new manager of the Indians.

Like a general who keeps preparing for the last war, Alvin now outsmarted himself in a new way. Reacting to Finley's autocratic ways, he decided the way to have full control was to be general manager as well as field manager, and went after Paul's job.

When he had managed the Giants, he was applying some of the Durocher-style psychological tricks (as he saw them), and that created problems. In Kansas City, that situation didn't arise, but he was working for an owner-general manager who was constantly interfering and telling him what to do, what not to do, and changing his mind. Dark saw—as so many managers had seen before him—that a manager who doesn't have full control, and the *appearance* of full control, can't win. And in both places, he had seen how a manager can be undercut. But the new owner of the Indians, Vern Stouffer, seemed to have tremendous respect and affection for Dark, while Paul, who had a rich baseball background of his own, was used to exerting standard general-manager autonomy. Dark had nothing against Paul personally, but he figured the best way to be boss himself was to have no one between him and an owner who (unlike Finley) had no delusions of baseball knowledge himself.

Dark was, of course, wrong. Aside from the dishonorable aspect of what he was doing to the man who had actually hired him, he was embarking on a self-defeating course. Baseball, entering the 1970s, had become much too complex an operation for the kind of one-man-dictatorship McGraw, Mack, and others had been able to maintain half a century earlier. Worse than that, however, Dark had no qualifications whatever for being a general manager: he knew absolutely nothing about the business, promotional, economic, and public relations aspects of that job—and Paul did, more than most. Gabe was a Rickey product once removed: A Giles protégé in Cincinnati after beginnings in Rochester, in the Cardinal system, he settled in Cleveland after a brief unhappy start with the expansion Houston team before it actually played a game. By usurping Paul's role, Dark not only exceeded his own capacities but lost the services of a great asset.

Nevertheless, he was able to convince Stouffer to make the move, and his career hit bottom. The fact that his divorce was in progress at this point and his personal life was more and more public didn't help.

In the dugout, though, he was still a terrific manager. The 1968 Indians won 86 games and finished a respectable third, the highest the team had been since 1959. In 1969, when Dark persuaded Stouffer in midseason to kick Paul upstairs, Cleveland was sixth and last in the newly formed Eastern Division, with a 62–99 record. In 1970, the record was 76–86, good enough for fifth. In 1971, by July 30, the team was 42–61 and Alvin was gone, although this was only the third year of his five-year contract.

It was a time of great personal crisis for Dark. The divorce and remarriage, and his adoption of Jackie's children, did not go smoothly. As he describes in his own book, all concerned were emotional wrecks and, in 1973, the money was running out too. He became obsessive about golf and gambling on his golf and card games. Then, Jackie found a Bible-reading class, persuaded Alvin to join it, and they both found born-again religion on a new basis. What had been, in Alvin's life, lip service contradicted by his actions became a wholehearted commitment that gave both of them inner peace and security.

Alvin Dark

But the baseball community had had it with Dark. The racism accusations were sort of a background noise, refuted thoroughly enough by his behavior to those he worked with; but the unreliability, the undermining of Paul, and the charge of hypocrisy were enough to make him unemployable.

By anyone but Finley.

The A's had developed the way Dark had foreseen. They moved to Oakland in 1968, finished first in ther division in 1971, and won the World Series in 1972 and 1973 with Dick Williams as manager. Williams couldn't live with Finley any more than anyone else could, and right after the World Series he quit. He expected to become manager of George Steinbrenner's Yankees, but that's another story, which we'll come to in the Williams chapter. The upshot was that Finley tried to hold him to his contract and blocked his path to the Yankees, but wound up approaching spring training in 1974 with no manager.

So he called Alvin.

The new Alvin—humble, contrite, able to turn the other cheek but never fully alive unless he was in a major league uniform—accepted the job with his eyes open. For months, he followed every whim and order Finley issued, bearing the open contempt of the players who disliked Finley themselves and wanted a manager to resist him in ways they couldn't. The club was so good that it was in first place in mid-July, but it was sputtering, and everything Dark did or said was being second-guessed mercilessly.

Finally, in New York, he called a team meeting and told everyone off. The gist of the speech was that they were behaving like bushleaguers, and that was no way for champions to act. He piqued their self-respect. In his new frame of mind, he wasn't trying to manipulate anybody, and saw his meek acquiescence to Finley's orders as his obligation under the servant-master relationship as he now understood it to be defined in the Bible. His job wasn't to defy his boss, but to figure out ways to win in spite of the boss.

The scolding had its effect. The players, somewhat chastened, started to listen. And Dark's in-game tactical skills started to pay off. So did his teaching, now that there were receptive ears. The A's did finish first, they did defeat Baltimore in the League Championship Series, and they polished off Alston's Dodgers in the World Series in 5 games.

Off the field, Finley's verbal abuse of Dark's family, as well as of

The Moderns

Dark himself, drove Alvin to the point of quitting. But he came back in 1975 and produced the most brilliant managing job of his career. Catfish Hunter had been lost to the club because Finley had reneged on a contract provision. This allowed him to become a free agent (before the whole reserve clause system was breached, a year later), and he signed a five-year $3.2 million deal with the Yankees. Alvin pieced together a pitching staff, leaning heavily on Wes Stock, his pitching coach, and the A's finished first again. This time, though, they lost 3 straight to the Red Sox and didn't make the World Series.

Two weeks later, Finley fired him. Again, words did Alvin in, although the context was somewhat different this time. Since 1971, he had increased the number and fervor of his talks to church groups and, in 1973, had made his livelihood from them. He preached God's love, dedicating oneself to Jesus Christ, and that one's life was in God's control whatever happened. In these talks, he would cite personal experience and often refer to Finley (and others). On one occasion, just before the 1975 playoffs, he told a group that unless Finley accepted Jesus Christ as his savior, Finley—like anyone else—would wind up in hell. The newspaper headline the next day read: "Dark: Charley Finley Going to Hell."

This was not, in and of itself, the reason for firing Dark. It may have been a last straw, but another one would have been found within days. But this time, Dark left with his baseball reputation intact. Finley's tantrums were well known. It was a badge of honor, in a way, to be fired by him a second time.

So Dark sat out the 1976 season and started 1977 as a coach with the Cubs, who had hired Herman Franks as their manager after running through Whitney Lockman and Jim Marshall in Durocher's wake. This was a resumption of old ties. Franks had been Leo's chief lieutenant on the 1951 Giants, and had followed Dark as manager of the Giants in 1965. They had been off-field business associates as well as baseball friends. Alvin was now fifty-five and satisfied to be a teacher—but not so satisfied that he wouldn't answer the fire bell when it rang again.

The San Diego Padres were one of the expansion teams created in 1969, and had finished last in their first six seasons. They had been acquired, in 1974, by Ray Kroc, the man who had made McDonald hamburgers a great success. The first thing Kroc did was grab the public address microphone and apologize to the customers for the quality of his club. In 1975, in John McNamara's second year as manager, the Padres clawed their way all the way up to fourth, but then fell back to fifth in 1976.

The operative head of the Padres, with a small ownership interest, was Buzzie Bavasi, O'Malley's general manager with the Dodgers who had been given an opportunity to improve himself when the new team was created (under the ownership of C. Arnholt Smith, a banker eventually in terrible trouble with tax authorities). Under Kroc, Bavasi still had his position, but Kroc was a lot more like Finley than like Smith, and Buzzie was on his way out. (He would move to the California Angels soon). Early in the 1977 season, Kroc had enough of McNamara and told Bavasi to hire Dark.

Talk about lack of rapport between manager and front office, here it was again in spades. Dark's mission was to rebuild a team that had never been built. He wasn't Bavasi's choice, and the coaches he inherited—Roger Craig for the pitchers, Bob Skinner, and Joe Amalfitano—were not his choices. The team finished fifth again, and before the next season Bavasi was gone anyhow. His successor was Bob Fontaine, another Dodger system veteran. During spring training in 1978, Dark was abruptly dismissed and replaced by Craig.

That was it. Dark worked as an instructor in the White Sox system after that, played a lot of golf, spoke to church groups, and accepted the fact that his managing career was over.

How had he talked himself out of the last job so quickly? Well, he told Fontaine that he wanted to replace Craig as pitching coach with Chuck Estrada, who was working with the minor league pitchers in the Padre system. Instead, Fontaine replaced Dark with Craig—and made Estrada the pitching coach.

I've kept calling Dark's managing "brilliant." What do I mean?

He was a master of noticing the detail that gives an edge: how to read the opposition's intentions; how to bunt, steal, and hit-and-run at the most opportune moments; how to maximize a player's abilities and keep him out of unfavorable situations; what pitch to call; when to pitch out; how to position fielders; how to organize a pitching staff. He was one of the early converts to the five-man rotation (that is, four days off between starts) when the four-man rotation was still standard, because he was convinced the extra rest made the good pitcher stronger in September, when it counted most. He used multiple relievers, played men out of position, employed the double switch, platooned in unorthodox ways (for rest and for particular pitchers, not simplistic lefty-righty alternations).

And he did know how to handle people in the vast majority of cases. The sure sign of that was that so many players who complained while he was their manager spoke so highly of his abilities afterward, as with Stengel and Durocher.

He was, then, a direct descendant of the McGraw-Stengel-Durocher line, with just a touch of Rickeyism in his penchant for intellectual analysis rather than hunch.

When Dark got to Cleveland, in 1968, baseball was in its Death of Offense era. The strike zone had been enlarged in a rewriting of the rules in 1963, and overall batting averages in both leagues fell to pre-lively-ball levels. (Carl Yastrzemski won the American League batting title at .301, and the scoring average for all twenty teams was less than 3.5 runs a game.) In practice, the umpires were calling the low outside pitch a strike, the one that's hardest to hit anyhow, and the official seventeen-inch wide strike zone had become, in effect, twenty inches wide.

Dark ordered his pitchers: Do not throw the first pitch inside the strike zone, because half the time the umpire will give you a strike anyhow; and a lot of hitters will swing at it because they're afraid he might call it a strike. Until he proves he won't, by calling ball one, don't throw hittable pitches.

They changed the rules again in 1969, lowered the mound, and hitting started to come back (although never to pre-1962 levels). So Dark abandoned that policy, and sought some other edge.

I ran into Alvin at an Oldtimers Game at Oakland in 1990. He'd been working with minor league players.

"The best thing to throw with the count two strikes, no balls, is a fast ball just off the plate," he started to tell me. "For most pitchers, a fast ball is the one they can spot most reliably. An anxious hitter may go after it—or the umpire may give you strike three. So there's no sense 'wasting' it too obviously, or missing with a breaking ball that will be too obviously a ball or a curve that hangs if you don't control it just right. A fast ball just outside is your best bet."

I'm not sure I understood (or am reporting) fully and correctly what he meant. But that's the way his mind worked, and in that aspect of managing, no one's mind ever worked any better.

The final phase of his career, therefore, was analogous to what the theater calls a "play doctor." When a show headed for Broadway gets into trouble for some reason—the director, the script, the casting, whatever, but usually script—an expert who was not connected with the project when it started is brought in to straighten things out. This is someone who has had lots of experience, his or her own successes on record, and the knack of noting what's wrong and how to correct it. A play doctor can't make a silk purse out of a sow's ear, and as often as not can't prevent ultimate failure. But he makes the enterprise as good as it's going to get under the circumstances. It's a thankless job, but a valuable one, and only people inside the business—and only a few of them, at that—know who the really good play doctors are. Those are always in demand.

Finley turned to Dark, in Kansas City, to start good talent on its way to development after a succession of managers who didn't have that particular ability. At Cleveland, Alvin's third-place finish in 1968 was not only the highest in nine years, but hasn't been matched since, twenty-five years later. With the A's in Oakland, he stepped into a situation where anything less than total victory would be failure, a championship team suddenly directorless, and delivered. In San Diego, he took over a thorough flop and didn't stay long enough to determine whether or not he could do anything about it. After that, he was used to help players in minor league systems. Whatever his public image, insiders knew what he could do, and benefited from it.

Baseball brains don't come any better than his.

17

Billy Martin

Billy the Kid II

If Dark, in various ways, was his own worst enemy, his problems were clearly self-generated. Billy Martin was a man who made plenty of problems for himself too, but got even more outside help. His public persona as a troublemaker was not entirely unearned, but the price he often paid was disproportionately severe because of other people's purposes. He had his faults, but he was ultimately more victim than culprit.

I knew him longer than any of the others, because when he arrived at Yankee Stadium in 1950, I was in my second season of covering baseball, and when he managed for the last time in 1988, I was still visiting his clubhouse. And he was, in my opinion, the best manager of the 1970s and 1980s, for all his tragic flaws and with all due respect to the others. I base that on one fact: In a twelve-year span, he turned five different clubs from losers to winners. No one else ever did that.

Our original bond was Stengel. In the first half of the 1950s, Stengel as Yankee manager was my primary baseball teacher, during the same period that Stengel and Martin had a deep father-son relationship. Our response to Casey was a path to responding to each other. Our backgrounds and personalities could not have been more different, but in baseball terms, we lived through the same experiences in those formative years and had many of the same unspoken assumptions when we talked in later years. I felt we understood each other.

Martin's size and upbringing were the key to his character. He grew up poor in a tough neighborhood in the San Francisco Bay Area, West Berkeley. It's between the eastern shore of the bay, with a clear view of the San Francisco skyline (much more modest and quaint then than now) on one side, and the hills that

Billy Martin

contain the University of California and more affluent districts on the other. He was born on May 16 (a significant birth date, as we shall see) in 1928, in his grandmother's house. Rafaella Salvini, who had come from Italy (near Foggia) as a young girl, brought up fourteen children and several grandchildren in that house, and her daughter Joan—Martin's mother—was still living in it when Martin returned to Oakland as a manager in the 1980s.

"My grandmother called me 'belli,' Italian for beautiful, and it came out 'Billy.' " Martin recalled one day. "I was in grade school before I knew that wasn't my name. The teacher asked for Alfred Martin and I didn't answer because I didn't know who that was."

His mother's first husband, Frank Pesano, was killed while fishing off Alaska, leaving Joan with a son. Then she married Alfred Manuel Martin, a Portuguese from Hawaii, who left about eight months after Billy was born. So actually, he was Alfred Manuel Martin, Junior.

"That's funny," mused Martin, in talking about his childhood. "I've never used the 'junior,' never even thought of it that way."

And with good reason, because his mother then married Jack Downey, and he was the man Billy considered his real father. Both these affectionate parents lived to share his World Series triumphs as a player and manager.

But it was the grandmother who made the biggest impression. She made a living selling homemade wine, and the large family all helped with the work. At that time, Billy's mother lived in the house next door.

"It was a rough neighborhood," Billy said. "I've told stories about it, but I usually tone them down. In the 1940s, it was the time of street gangs—big gangs, hundreds of guys. If you fought enough of them well enough, eventually they'd leave you alone."

He went to Franklin Grammar school, Burbank Junior High, Berkeley High. And he had only one thought.

"I was going to be a big league ballplayer," he said. "People would tell me I was too small. I'd say, that's all right, I'll make it, I just know I'll make it."

He played American Legion baseball at thirteen and local semi-pro all the time (often in the outfield on a team run by one of his uncles). He played high school basketball, but his mother wouldn't sign the papers to let him play football—so he played semipro football around Oakland, as a running quarterback.

The Moderns

But baseball was his game. At that time, the Pacific Coast League was at the top of baseball's minor league structure, with teams independently owned. The Oakland team, owned by Brick Laws, had its own farm teams in the lower minors. People who saw Billy play got him some workouts with the Oaks, but when he finished high school in 1946, no one was interested in signing him. He was too small, too scrawny. The only thing big about him was his nose, but unlike Cyrano de Bergerac, and like Rodney Dangerfield, he got no respect.

Martin kept plugging away at semipro ball. One day he got a call. Would he go to Idaho Falls, to one of the Oakland farm teams? Sure. Did he have a suitcase? No. Did he have any decent clothes? No. Okay, here's $300 to buy some clothes and a suitcase. Poof! He was a professional ballplayer.

He played there only a few weeks (32 games) and showed enough to be hired for the Phoenix club, in the Arizona-Texas League, at the same Class C level, for 1947. And there he blossomed: He led the league in hitting (.392), at bats, hits, doubles, and runs batted in (174) in 130 games; and playing third, he also led the league in putouts, assists, and errors (55). That earned him an Oakland uniform for the last month of the season, where the level of competition was different. He hit .226 in the 15 games he got into, and maintained his fielding average: It had been .905 in Phoenix, and 5 errors made it .904 in Oakland.

Stengel, of course, was not one to be influenced by numbers, either .392 or .226. He knew what he had, and loved Martin for it from the start: a scrapper, pure and simple. Billy played the way he had lived on the Berkeley streets: Meet aggression with pre-emptive aggression, never back off, make up for lack of bulk by faster thinking. Best of all, he talked back and said what he thought. The Old Man (Stengel was already nearing sixty) had been that way himself.

So in 1948, with Martin playing all three infield positions in about three-quarters of the games, Stengel's Oaks won the Pacific Coast League pennant. And Casey went on to New York.

His replacement was Charlie Dressen, who was even shorter than Martin and just as fiesty, and just as perceptive as Stengel. He played Martin at second and short in 172 games on a team loaded with former major leaguers, which finished second. Billy hit .286, knocked in 92 runs, and led the league again in putouts—

and errors. The errors weren't a coincidence; they reflected his willingness to take chances, and in his subsequent major-league career he always posted high fielding averages.

Stengel had the Yankees buy his contract, and in 1950 he was a major leaguer: a utility player, spending part of the season back down at Kansas City, used in only 32 Yankee games with only 36 at bats, but a major league player. And befriended by Joe DiMaggio. At twenty-two.

In the spring of 1951, the Yankees switched training sites with the Giants, going to Phoenix instead of St. Petersburg. The sensation of the camp was a blond kid from Oklahoma with incredible speed and batting power from both sides of the plate. Mickey Mantle, naive, shy, and lionized, and Billy Martin, streetwise, tough, and unnoticed, took to each other quickly. A lifelong friendship began.

Mantle made the jump from the low minors to the champion Yankees that year, bogged down, had to return to Kansas City, came back, and wrecked his knee in the second game of the World Series. Martin was strictly a bench player. But in 1952, they were both regulars, and their parallel paths began. Mantle, the headliner, remained shy, what New Yorkers called "a hick"; Martin was talkative, brash, challenging, assertive. They began calling Martin "Billy the Kid," conjuring up the frontier outlaw glorified in so many movies and stories. Only older fans remembered that Southworth had once been called Billy the Kid, three decades back, at the Polo Grounds. But Billy the Kid II, himself, was unaware of the precedent as he was of his technical status as "junior." He liked the image and the implication, and fit it.

In the 1952 World Series, Martin had his first touch of fame. He made one of the great opportunistic plays of World Series history, racing in from second to catch a pop-up near the mound after the first baseman had lost sight of the ball, saving a seventh-game victory over the Dodgers. It was the fourth straight World Series victory for the Yankees and Stengel, equaling a record.

And in 1953, when the Yankees made it five straight by beating the Dodgers in 6 games, Martin established an individual record by getting 12 hits and batting .500. He was the regular second baseman on the most successful team ever; so much for the people in Berkeley who said he was too small.

But he spent almost all of the next two years in the army, going through a divorce, paying alimony. Precisely the two years that could have established his earning power were denied him.

Still, he got back in time to play all of the 1955 World Series (and hit .320), and was a regular again in 1956. But he played some third base now, and wasn't quite as quick as he had been. As the Yankees won another World Series, he played in all 7 games hitting .296 and making his career World Series batting average .333 for 27 games in four years.

But he never played in another one.

His twenty-ninth birthday came up in 1957 and it was a fateful one, altering the course of his life.

May 16 was an open date during a home stand, a Thursday. Yogi Berra's birthday had been on May 12. It was a natural time to have a birthday party. So Berra, Hank Bauer, Whitey Ford, Mantle, and a rookie pitcher named Johnny Kucks arranged the most innocent kind of outing imaginable for professional athletes: They went out to dinner with their wives. Martin, the guest of honor, had no wife at this time, having been divorced, and he didn't even bring a date.

After dinner, they decided to go to the most famous nightclub of the time, the Copacabana, to see the show.

Somehow, late in the evening, trouble developed between Bauer and a group of men at another table. It ended up with Bauer being accused of knocking out one of them. It became a police matter, and by dawn the whole "brawl" was all over the papers.

Weiss blamed Martin.

The Yankee general manager had disliked Martin from the start, and kept calling him a "bad influence" on Mantle. (If anything, Martin was Mantle's chief protector in the nightlife jungle, because the young Mickey, who didn't drink a lot, couldn't hold the liquor he did drink, and was a country-bumpkin innocent besides. And 1956, it would turn out, was Mantle's best season. Weiss used this incident, which became so heavily publicized, as the excuse for discarding Martin—who hadn't even been accused of any role in whatever fight took place.

The trading deadline of June 15 was four weeks away. When that day came, with the Yankees in Kansas City, Weiss traded Martin to the Athletics, the baseball equivalent of exile to Siberia in those days.

The shock embittered Martin for many years. He thought

Billy Martin

Stengel had failed to stick up for him. (Stengel had, but lost the argument; but Martin didn't know that.) As for Weiss, he was too shrewd to act merely on the basis of personal dislike. He certainly wasn't going to let go of Mantle, Berra, Ford, or Bauer (who were each fined $1,000, along with Martin), or of Kucks, who was only twenty-three, an 18-game winner as a sophomore in 1956, and pitcher of a shutout in the seventh game of the 1956 World Series. (Kucks, working for low wages, was fined only $500.) That left Martin—who had lost a step, and who was replaceable at second anyhow by a promising rookie named Bobby Richardson, Houk's protégé the two previous years at Denver.

Martin's years of wandering began. The deal with Kansas City involved six other players. At the end of the season, he was part of a thirteen-player trade that sent him to Detroit. After the 1958 season, a five-man transaction landed him in Cleveland. In mid-season, he got hit in the face by a pitch, suffering a broken jaw, and was through for the year. That winter, he was passed on with two other players to Cincinnati, in exchange for Cincinnati's second baseman, Johnny Temple. He played second base there in 1960, and got involved in his second case of exceptional notoriety.

On August 4, at Chicago, Martin was brushed back by Jim Brewer of the Cubs. He responded as countless players have before and since: He ran to the mound to throw a punch, and a brawl ensued. Brewer came out of it with a black eye and a fractured bone near his eye socket, although Martin denied being responsible for that particular blow. The league fined him $500, but that was routine.

What was not routine was that Brewer and the Cubs filed a million-dollar law suit against Martin personally.

Of all the thousands of major league baseball fights, this is the only one I know of—certainly the only widely publicized one—that brought about a suit for damages. Martin eventually had to pay tens of thousands of dollars in damages, and it took him years to pay off the debt; Brewer couldn't have been damaged too severely, since he went on to pitch in the majors for the next seventeen years with considerable success. Yet Martin was branded as an assailant for something that was accepted as absolutely routine in ballfield wars for one hundred years.

"And what no one ever mentions," Billy noted years later, "is the weeks I spent the year before recovering from a broken face. How can you not fight back if you see that happening to you again?"

But that winter he was traded again to the Milwaukee Braves, for whom he made only six pinch-hitting appearances even though Dressen was the manager. On June 1 he was traded back to the American League, to the Minnesota Twins, and played out the rest of the season there as a regular.

He was now thirty-three, and had been with seven different teams in five years. His performance had been remarkably consistent—.251, .255, .260, .246, .246—but he had slowed up and had no future. In midseason, the Twins had changed managers, from Cookie Lavagetto to Sam Mele, and the Griffith family, as frugal as ever in running its club's affairs, didn't need a $24,000 veteran at second base when it could have a $7,000 rookie (Bernie Allen). Yet all the Griffiths and in-laws, and Mele, liked Martin on a personal level and offered him a job as a scout. He needed the job, any job; he had remarried in 1957 and now had a young son, Billy Joe. He settled into a happy interval of three years as a Minneapolis suburbanite, growing tomatoes competitively with the Griffith clan, making his reports, and calming down.

He had never, until now, given much thought to managing. But if he were going to continue making a living in baseball, it would have to be in that direction. His philosophy had been broadened by experience.

At first, everything had centered on proving himself: that he could survive on the street, that he could play well enough to make a team, that he could be a pro, that he could reach the major leagues. His size, his poverty, his small-kid appearance added to the difficulty of winning acceptance and respect, and to be tougher, he had to be smarter, to figure more angles, to pay closer attention to everything. And, once abandoned by the Yankees, he had to prove himself again six times to new organizations every few months. He soaked up the mechanical and technical details of baseball as a composer might study music, to make it part of his instinctual self. But in behavior, Billy felt he had to be brash, fresh, pugnacious, assertive; otherwise, he might be taken for an easy mark or, worse still, considered of no consequence.

It was the last point that made his Yankee identity so much more important to him than to most other players. The Yankees symbolized the elite, and as one of them, he belonged. Being exiled not only tore apart his friendships with Mantle and Whitey Ford, and destroyed his trust in Stengel; it undermined his hard-won self-esteem.

Nevertheless, his spongelike mind swelled with input from so many different situations and contact with so many different people. He began to sort out what works and what doesn't, and why. As a scout, he sharpened his ability to evaluate the skills and shortcomings of every sort of player. No one might think of him as a manager yet, especially because of his pugnacious reputation. That Rickey edict "If you can't control yourself, how can you control others?" had become universal baseball law. So if he ever got the chance, he'd have to prove himself all over again. But he was preparing himself for that chance.

It came unexpectedly. Not quickly, and not according to plan.

In 1965, Mele asked Martin to become his third base coach. After some reluctance—he was feeling secure as a scout—Martin agreed. That year, the Twins won the pennant, their first since 1933, and Martin's input helped. He remained as coach through 1966 and 1967, as Cal Ermer replaced Mele as manager a third of the way into the 1967 season, and the team remained a contender. He started the 1968 season the same way.

In May, they asked him to go down to Denver, in the American Association, to be manager of their top farm club.

Martin had qualms. Would he ever get back to the majors? What if he failed? He had never tried to manage; when Mele had been fired, he wasn't even considered because he had no managerial experience, and he thought that was right. Now he had to face it. Could he?

He decided to try.

He was Billy the Kid no longer.

The Miracle Worker

The Denver team was 7–22 when he arrived. It played 58–28 under him, finished fourth, and made the playoffs. The Twins finished seventh that year, the last the American League would play as a ten-team circuit, and the Griffiths decided Ermer had to go and that Martin should be promoted. Within months of doubting he could manage at all, Billy was a major league manager.

The Twins were now in the six-team Western Division of the

twelve-team American League. They had a veteran lineup with lots of offense—Rod Carew, Harmon Killebrew, Tony Oliva—but shaky pitching, consisting mostly of men who had come from other organizations. Martin, of course, knew the roster and the farm system intimately: He had been studying it from the inside for nine years. But the general opinion was that this was an aging and deteriorating club in a weak division.

Martin finished first with it, winning 97 games for a 9-game margin over a young Oakland team. The only team with a better record was Baltimore, which won 109 and the Eastern Division title by 19 games. In the first American League Championship Series, the Orioles won three straight—4–3 in twelve innings to a two-out suicide squeeze bunt; 1–0 in eleven innings to a two-out line single just out of Carew's reach; and, back in Minnesota, 11–2.

That was disappointing but clearly a success. Jim Perry and Dave Boswell won 20 games each; in the preceding five years, neither had won more than 14. Ron Perranoski, age thirty-three, weighed in with 31 saves. Baseball managers don't get fired after a year like that.

But Martin did, almost immediately. One member of the Twins management was not a Griffith, and was an enemy. Howard Fox, the road secretary, had friction with Martin since his coaching days. In 1966, Billy actually punched Fox and knocked him out in an argument in Washington. When the playoffs ended, Martin wasn't even asked to attend the World Series with the rest of the Twin's management group, even though there would be an organizational meeting there. At that meeting, it was decided to fire him, but Calvin Griffith wasn't willing to say that when Martin called him. A week later, Billy heard on the radio that he was out.

Meanwhile, the Detroit Tigers also had an aging, power-hitting, pitching-problem club. It had won the World Series in 1968, when Denny McLain won 31 games in baseball's lightest-hitting year, but finished 19 games behind Baltimore in 1969 even though McLain won 24. Jim Campbell, an astute general manager, saw what Martin had done in Minnesota. Mayo Smith, the Detroit manager, was played out. In 1970 the Tigers dropped to fourth place and below .500, and McLain was suspended for half a season when it was learned that he had a side business as a bookie. It was time to change, and Martin was the man to change to.

Campbell hired Martin for the 1971 season.

Martin brought with him the pitching coach he had so much faith in, Art Fowler. A right-handed pitcher without much major league success, Fowler was forty-seven years old and still pitching at Triple-A level for Denver when Martin got there in 1968. When Billy went up to the Twins, he took along Fowler as his pitching coach, and the sudden success of Perry and Boswell was no coincidence. Martin had seen the special relationship Stengel had developed with Jim Turner and the special mother hen relationship that Turner (whom Martin used to make fun of) had developed with his pitchers. In Fowler, he had a man with whom he had great rapport—and who had the capacity to communicate to the pitchers as easily as Martin could communicate with him.

At Detroit, in 1971, without McLain, the Tigers bounced back to second place but still 10 games behind the Orioles, who were completing a three-year sequence of 318 victories and three straight World Series appearances. But in 1972, Martin brought the Tigers in first, ending Baltimore's reign, only to lose the playoffs again, this time in 5 tumultuous games to the new superteam, Oakland.

This time, the Detroit owner (John Fetzer) and Campbell were perfectly satisfied with the noble achievement. The friction that arose was of a different nature. Martin and Campbell disagreed thoroughly in their player evaluations. Martin insisted that the stars, who were all Campbell products from his days as farm system director, were too old, and that the present farmhands weren't good enough. He wanted trades. Campbell had two loyalties, to his old stars and to his present minor league organization. When Martin saw he was losing the argument, he sought security in another form: He asked for a three-year contract, figuring it would protect him against the losing record he thought would be inevitable. Campbell said no. On September 1, 1973, with the Tigers a distant third while Baltimore was running away with another division title, Martin was let go.

This would be a recurrent dispute for Martin for the rest of his life, the difference in how he and the front office evaluated talent. It goes to the heart of such conflict throughout baseball, and we'll return to it at the end of this chapter.

Seven days after being fired in Detroit, he was managing the Texas Rangers.

The Texas Rangers were, of course, the "new" Washington Senators, transplanted to the Dallas-Fort Worth area after the

The Moderns

1971 season. Their owner was Bob Short, a flamboyant sports figure and an old friend of Martin's from Minneapolis.

Short was a self-made success in the trucking business, a Notre Dame alumnus, a major figure in liberal Democratic politics, and a live wire in every respect. In the late 1950s, he had acquired a controlling interest—for $10,000—in the Minneapolis Lakers, a basketball team that had dominated the early years of the National Basketball Association as long as George Mikan was its center, but had fallen on hard times. However, Short did draft Elgin Baylor and Jerry West in successive years, and moved the team to Los Angeles in 1961—the first major basketball team to reach California. A year later he sold it (to Jack Kent Cooke) for $5 million.

A few years later, he bought the expansion Senators, who had never gotten off the ground after their creation in 1961. His master stroke was in persuading Ted Williams to come out of retirement and try his hand at managing (in 1969). This was a public relations coup, but the team remained terrible and Short's financial situation impossible. He got the league's permission to move to Texas because he got a seven-year guaranteed radio-television deal there with money up front. Williams, never cut out to be a manager anyhow, had enough after his fourth year (the first in Texas) and Short turned over the team to an untried young man named Dorrell (Whitey) Herzog. Since the team had no supply of talent, it did no better under Herzog than under Williams. So when Martin suddenly became available, Short begged him to take over.

Martin said, years later, that he didn't want to do it. He was bitter over being fired twice. But Short was someone he knew and trusted, and was asking for a favor, and knew how to press the right button: He offered Martin a contract that gave him absolute control over all personnel decisions.

That did it. Martin took over, and did no better that September than Williams and Herzog had with no material. The club that lost 100 games for Williams in 1972 wound up with 105 losses in 1973.

Then Short sold it.

The new ownership group was headed by Brad Corbett, who had not bought a major league baseball team to be a behind-the-scenes nonparticipant. The control clause in Martin's contract was valid, but certainly not welcome. The fights over players—

whom to bring up, whom to farm out, whom to trade, whom to seek, whom to play when and where and how much—started all over again.

Thanks to the contract, Martin's views prevailed—and the 1974 Rangers made a 27-game improvement, finishing second to the mighty A's and actually making a race of it in the Western Division. It didn't hurt that Martin had an ally in the front office in Bobby Brown, who had been finishing his Yankee career during Martin's early years there. Brown had gone on to become a cardiologist settled in Dallas, and had just retired from medicine. Corbett brought him in as an advisor and, thanks to this reentry to baseball, Bobby eventually became president of the American League.

The 1974 Texas Rangers were Martin's third straight miracle, but they were still a weak club with a weak organization. Corbett would certainly not renew the control clause in any new contract, and Martin wouldn't accept not having it, so they had to part company. When the team reverted to form and was 44–51 on July 25, 1975, Corbett fired him.

This time Martin was unemployed for eleven days.

The Yankees wanted him.

Through a series of machinations whose details must await the Dick Williams chapter, the Yankees were being managed by Bill Virdon with Gabe Paul as general manager and George Steinbrenner already highly visible as The Boss. Steinbrenner had taken Virdon for 1974 when his pursuit of Williams was stymied, and Virdon had exceeded expectations by bringing the team in second. But it was slipping out of the race behind Boston and Baltimore during July of 1975, and Martin was the answer on many levels.

The Yankees were completing their second season in Shea Stadium, waiting for the rebuilding of Yankee Stadium to be complete. The team had not won a pennant since 1964, under Yogi Berra, and the whole thrust of future promotion was going to be a return to former Yankee traditions and greatness. Martin had that association, and Mantle and Ford would be brought in as coaches. To Steinbrenner, that was the main thing.

To Paul, sharp baseball man that he was, Martin was a good choice for better reasons. Paul understood fully what Martin had accomplished, and how, in his three previous jobs. Gabe had been around long enough, and was self-confident enough, to feel that he could be the right buffer between Billy and George, whose personalities were bound to clash. (The one thing Martin demanded was authority; the one thing Steinbrenner couldn't stand to give to anyone else was authority.) The Yankees had, finally, collected considerable talent, including Catfish Hunter, the world's only free agent thanks to Charley Finley's mishandling of a contract. What they needed was a truly alert, experienced, fire-lighting manager-leader. Dark had thought, incorrectly, that he needed Paul out of the way to be in command at Cleveland. Paul knew that he'd have no trouble listening to, and trying to fill, Martin's needs.

So on August 1, 1975, Billy Martin was back in pinstripes, wearing the number 1 Pete Sheehy, the Yankee clubhouse factotum, had given him back in 1952. His exile had lasted eighteen years, one month, and sixteen days. And the chair he now occupied had once been filled by Stengel.

Yankee Yo-yo

Martin's managerial soap opera with the Yankees dominated baseball news for the next twelve years. The details don't need rehashing here. Only certain highlights need be cited:

1. Martin wanted more speed, defense, and left-handed power (for Yankee Stadium) than the Yankee roster had. Paul got it for him, with trades that brought Willie Randolph for second base, Mickey Rivers to play center and lead off, Dock Ellis to pitch, Oscar Gamble to hit homers. This transformed the character of the Yankee club. In 1976, it finished first for the first time in twelve years. It survived a dramatic 5-game League Championship Series with Kansas City, but was no match for the Cincinnati Reds in a 4-game World Series.

2. Free agency came into baseball during 1976, and Steinbrenner signed Reggie Jackson. This presented Martin with the classic challenge, in the tradition of Ruth and Huggins. A superstar who outshines the manager means trouble, and the manager's dominance must be established somehow for the sake of control of the rest of the team. Their conflicts received unprecedented coverage, thanks to advances in television, but the Yankees finished first again in 1977, beat Kansas City in 5 games again, and this

Billy Martin

time beat the Los Angeles Dodgers in the World Series in 6 games—with Reggie capping the sixth game at Yankee Stadium by hitting 3 home runs.

3. But Reggie was a minor problem for Martin compared to Steinbrenner, who was insatiable in flaunting his own authority. He injected himself into daily baseball decisions, the way Finley had in Oakland, without Finley's knowledge or consistency. He humiliated Martin in countless ways, publicly and privately, while interfering in personnel moves, practice schedules, and tactics. Paul, finding himself unable to deal with being in the middle, bowed out gracefully and went back to Cleveland as part of a new ownership package there. Steinbrenner brought in Al Rosen as general manager, with whom Martin had no previous relationship. Rumors (many planted by George) filled the air that Martin would be fired. By the middle of the 1978 season, tension was at breaking point. As the team was moving from Chicago to Kansas City the last week in July, Billy's emotions boiled over. He told newspapermen traveling with his club that he was fed up with Jackson (returning from an injury) and Steinbrenner (reportedly offering to trade him to Bill Veeck's White Sox for Bob Lemon, the Chicago manager who had just been dismissed).

"One's a born liar," said Martin, meaning Jackson, "and the other's convicted." That referred to Steinbrenner's conviction for perjury in connection with election law violations during the 1972 presidential election campaign.

And he insisted that they go ahead and print it.

The reaction can be imagined, but Billy didn't wait to be fired. He resigned. He issued a formal statement in Kansas City before Rosen even got there. He was through.

Rosen named Lemon, his former Cleveland teammate, manager of the Yankees.

The very next day Steinbrenner told Martin's agent he wanted to reinstate him as manager at the start of the 1979 season. What's more, he wanted to make the announcement at the Yankee Oldtimers' Day festivities that weekend.

They did it, and what a story *that* was.

Then the Yankees, under Lemon, once 14 games behind, caught the Red Sox, beat them in a 1-game pennant playoff at Fenway Park, polished off Kansas City in 4 games in the playoffs, and the Dodgers again in 6 of the World Series.

So Lemon had to stay, right? Right.

4. Lemon started the 1979 season with less success. His laid-back style had been the perfect antidote for the unbearable tension that had been generated by the middle of 1978; now Steinbrenner found his calm unbearable. Lem didn't even fight back. By June 18, with the Yankees at 34–31, George fired Lemon and reinstalled Martin. But 55–40 the rest of the way wasn't enough to catch Baltimore, Milwaukee, and Boston. The Yankees finished fourth.

Billy's nerves were frayed now too. He had started drinking more heavily and became nasty when drunk. Strangers would challenge him in a bar, there would be a scuffle (or a serious fist fight), and the "brawler" would be in headlines again. One such incident in the off-season after 1979 gave Steinbrenner an excuse to fire him.

And again, there was another job waiting.

5. Charlie Finley's empire had collapsed in Oakland. Free agency made it possible for his stars to leave, and they jumped at the chance. He had no money to spend in the open market. After seven straight years in contention, the A's finished last in 1977 (behind an expansion Seattle team), next to last in 1978, and last again in 1979, losing 108 games and drawing only 300,000 people. Finley didn't care. He was trying to sell the club to people in Denver.

When that deal fell through, however, he still had a club on his hands and the 1980 season was coming up. He offered the job to Martin.

Oakland, adjacent to Berkeley, was home. Martin was glad to return, and he stepped into a unique situation—a Finley team with Finley too disinterested to interfere.

It had a lot of young players, especially pitchers, and a flashy local kid named Rickey Henderson. Left completely alone by Finley (and with Fowler at his side as pitching coach), Martin produced a 29-game improvement and brought the A's in second behind Kansas City. With this material, he played what Stengel used to call "run sheep run" baseball, which was now tabbed "Billyball." Henderson stole 100 bases. The no-name pitchers were terrific, pitching complete games (since the bullpen was weak). Attendance nearly tripled, to 840,000.

And that attracted the interest of local ownership. The Walter Haas family, owners of Levi Strauss clothing, took the team off

Billy Martin

Finley's hands, for $12 million, for the express purpose of keeping it in Oakland (which was fighting to keep the football Raiders from moving to Los Angeles). The motivation was concern for the community; what made the deal viable was the presence in the package of Billy Martin.

6. The 1981 season was the one that was split in half by the two-month strike of the players. The A's won the first half, finished second in the second half, then polished off Kansas City in 3 straight in the special playoff to emerge as Western Division champions. But they were swept in the League Championship Series by the Yankees, now managed by Lemon again, as a late-season replacement for Gene Michael.

Billyball was the talk of the baseball world.

7. The Haas representative running the club was Roy Eisenhardt, a son-in-law, a law professor at the University of California. Bright, young, enthusiastic, he brought fresh pro-motional life to Oakland and to baseball in general—and he knew he didn't know enough baseball to try to give Martin advice. He gave Martin a fabulous contract with all sorts of perks and nomi-nal authority. But he was too vigorous a man to stay out of decision-making indefinitely. And he didn't like the image Mar-tin's off-field escapades, exaggerated or not, created. One word led to another and, in 1982, there was open antagonism. The team was a loser again, since all the pitchers collapsed (that is, re-turned to their pre-Martin ineffectiveness). Critics blamed Martin for "overusing" them in 1980 (a factually false accusation easily refuted by the record when one counted pitches thrown instead of innings). Martin blamed the pitchers for not staying in shape during the two-month strike. In any case, the 1982 A's finished fifth, losing 94 games, even though Henderson broke all records by stealing 130 bases.

Martin left, with both sides feeling betrayed.

But he had some place to go. George wanted him back.

8. Martin opened the 1983 season as manager of the Yankees. In a four-team race, they finished third, behind Baltimore and De-troit and ahead of Toronto, winning 91 games. Then there was another off-field explosion, and Steinbrenner took the manager-ship away again, giving it to Yogi while keeping Martin on the payroll. Yogi's Yankees finished third too, behind runaway Detroit and Toronto.

9. Less than three weeks into the 1985 season, Steinbrenner fired Berra and made Martin manager for the fourth time. The team was 6–10 when Billy took over, and played 91–54 the rest of the way. But in a September showdown with Toronto, it fell 2 games short.

10. Now Steinbrenner put Martin in the television booth and made Lou Piniella manager, according to a plan Martin was aware of during the 1985 season. Piniella's team finished a strong second in 1986 and a not so strong but respectable fourth in 1987, in what was then baseball's strongest division.

11. Even so, the 1988 season opened with Billy Martin as manager of the Yankees. That made it his fifth term, breaking the record of Franklin Delano Roosevelt. Piniella was now in the front office as general manager.

The Yankees won 9 of their first 10 games, finished April 16–7, and were 20–8 when they arrived in Texas on May 6. After that night's game (a loss) Martin was in a brawl in a nightclub. This time, he was the victim of a beating, not the instigator of the fight, but his reputation made cause and effect irrelevant: He was marked for another dismissal. It didn't come until June 23, when Steinbrenner also fired Fowler, and moved Piniella back to the dugout. Later, the pitching collapsed; the Yankees stayed in the race for a while, but they wound up fifth, even though they were only 3½ games out of first place.

So Steinbrenner fired Piniella and hired Dallas Green.

Let's summarize Martin's record:

At Minnesota, one season: to first place from seventh.

At Detroit, three seasons: to second from fourth, first, incomplete.

At Texas, one full season: to second from last.

At New York, three straight firsts after twelve years of nonwinning, if you include Lemon's finish of 1978.

At Oakland, three seasons: to second from last, first in a split season, fifth.

At New York, too complicated to sort out, but his five-term total as Yankee manager added up to 556–485 for .534.

In the ten seasons that he was allowed to operate from start to finish, he was first five times, second three times, third once, and fifth once.

When he had power, he used power. When he had speed, he used that. In every case, the pitching was better than it had been before he got there, and got worse again after he left. Any way the game could be played, he produced victories. No manager ever adapted better to the talent at hand.

Back in the late 1970s, he talked to me one day about his managing philosophy. Authority was always the key issue. He said,

> Players have to believe in the manager's authority or they can't do their best. The manager isn't always right; nobody is. But somebody has to make decisions, and the manager is the one—and if the players don't have conviction that your decisions are mostly right, they can't carry them out wholeheartedly. And a better idea done halfheartedly won't get as good a result as a lesser idea done wholeheartedly.
>
> But a lot of the time, you have to make a player do something he doesn't want to, for the good of the team, or to push him harder than he thinks he should be pushed. You can't do it if the player thinks, "Why listen to him? He's not the boss. He may be gone next year. I'll do it my way." When that attitude takes hold, teams don't win.

But that's not all. He went on:

> Managing is teaching, first of all. That's even more important than the winning itself. When you get a player whose potential you can see, and show him things that can make him better, and show him the things that can make him win, and then you can see him later realizing those things—it's like a graduation. It makes you feel satisfied even if he's no longer your player.
>
> For a team to win, a manager has to find ways to motivate different individuals. He has to judge correctly each man's abilities and weaknesses, and find the right ways and the right time to use them. He has to show them how something can be done better, and offer them loyalty and confidence. And he has to have authority, above all, because none of the other things can happen if the players don't have confidence in the manager's judgment, and in the fact that it is *his* judgment, not someone else's, that counts.
>
> So winning is the whole idea, sure; and that's what I'm trying to do. But the enjoyment comes from the things I put in it, the teaching, the problem solving, the answer to challenges. The victory at the end is only the proof that you've succeeded, and nobody can take that away from you once you've won. But the fun and the rewards are in what you do getting there.

Buried in the above speech is the phrase "judge correctly." This was the essense of all his conflicts with management, and it is the crux of managing problems in modern baseball. To see why this is so, we must recognize the fundamental difference in viewpoint of field manager and front office.

The Moderns

The manager thinks in specifics. He spends all his time conjuring up game situations, using past events as raw material, to figure out in advance what he wants to do in a given situation. In his mind, a ball game never has "a" hitter facing "a" pitcher; it's always specific people.

The front office thinks in generalities. One player is a "better" prospect than another according to his measured performance (speed to first, pitching velocity, weight, strength, accumulated statistics, emotional makeup). His quality is defined in career terms.

The manager, then, arrives at conclusions about what he wants. He thinks: "There will be games when I have men on in late innings with the score close and they'll bring in Eckersley (or Gossage or Johnny Murphy); who will I have on my bench to send up?" Or: "When my second baseman needs time off, who can fill in best and still help me in other ways when the second baseman does play?" Or: "These are the key opposing hitters I'm going to have to get out a dozen times each season in crucial situations if we're going to win; which pitchers have I got who can do that?

So when the manager tells the front office "I need a left-handed hitter" or "I'm not interested in that guy" or "Give me this kid from the minors" or "Don't take this reserve away from me," it's in the context of that huge imaginary jigsaw puzzle his mind has been creating and maneuvering all year long. He can't spell out all the hypotheticals, but he knows clearly what they are in his own mind.

The front office draws its conclusions from reading reports. Its skill consists of interpreting such reports correctly. But the reports are, by their nature, large-scale probabilities: "over a period of time, this player will hit so-and-so"; "he has power but only average speed"; "he has to work on holding the runner on." These may be 100 percent correct—but they don't tell the manager what he wants to know for *his* club, at *this* time for *current* needs. That kid may have power, and be headed for a 400-homer career someday, but can he do any good against the two dozen specific starting pitchers I know we're going to face?

The result is that the manager and the front office talk past each other unless they have exceptionally good rapport (which is what the Rickey system strove to achieve). However, the penalty for guessing wrong has different consequences. For the front office, the evaluation may prove out "sooner or later" and still be

Billy Martin

considered a success. For the manager, the games have to be won here and now, with little margin for error.

So when Martin said, "I want Elrod Hendricks here, not in Syracuse," he had a whole complex of reasons, interrelated and subtle. If he was correct, it would help win; if not, the cost would be immediate. But the front office (as in Detroit), which is urging him to stick longer with an older player because a terrific prospect is on the way, may indeed produce a fine prospect *eventually*—but only after the manager got fired and the club let a chance to win slip away.

This is a long way from where we started. McGraw, Mack, and Griffith faced no such differences: They *were* the front office. They could choose—this player to help me now, this one for the future—at their own discretion. McGraw could have conflict with an owner about allocation of money or clashes of personalities but not about evaluative judgment.

Rickey, recognizing the problem as a harassed manager, built unanimity of evaluation into his farm system idea. But in its heyday, that system had so many players at so many levels that the parent club's manager's needs could be taken off the shelf.

Since then, the systems have taken on a life of their own. The general manager, farm director, chief scouts, minor league managers, and coaches all have their own career concerns, and are judged by how convincing their paper work is. That's not to put them down; some are better than others at this, just as in any other job, and the paper work a vital function. But it's a different function, with different skills and different requirements, from the one the manager is asked to perform, which is to win games, now, in this league, with these players, under these conditions.

Billy Martin had the most finely honed sense of what it took to win, so his clashes with a front office were inevitable. He was not lucky enough to find a relationship like Huggins and McCarthy had with Barrow, or even Stengel with Weiss; few managers do. But he was too aggressive ever to give in—as most managers do—concerning his own judgment. In his approach to baseball and to life, he was the closest to a reincarnation of McGraw of any of them: small, combative, loved by some and hated by others, infallibly news-making, and smart.

In 1989, Steinbrenner dropped Green before the season was over and made Bucky Dent—the shortstop who had hit the decisive homer in the 1978 playoff game at Boston—Yankee manager. It was widely believed that he was going to give Martin a sixth shot in 1990 (when Martin would have been sixty-two).

But on Christmas night, 1989, Martin was killed in a car crash in upstate New York. He and a friend had been drinking. The reports were that the friend, who survived, was the one who was driving. Later, questions were raised about who was actually at the wheel. It couldn't matter now to Martin, either way; but if he was in the passenger seat, the symbolism of his ending would be complete. It would mean, again, that without being blameless, he paid the greater penalty for someone else's mistake.

18

Dick Williams

Utility Man

Dick Williams bounced around even more than Billy Martin. He spent longer in the minors, played more seasons in the majors, managed more in the minors, and more different big league teams. He even won more, getting to four World Series and winning two of them.

But there was one big difference. The recurrent dissatisfaction with Martin was always upstairs, in the front office. The dissatisfaction with Williams grew among his players. Plenty of players disliked, even hated, Martin, but many more swore by him and spoke of missing him when he was gone. Very few spoke well of Williams after playing under him for a few years.

No one questioned his knowledge and ability. Nor was there anything unique about the discipline and single-mindedness about winning that Williams demanded. What was missing was that vague but indispensable quality called "warmth." Martin made most players feel he was on their side, rooting for them to do well, mad at them at times but visibly forgiving. Williams projected contempt for all players who fell short of his standards of baseball behavior.

When he was fired from his last job, in Seattle in 1988, I had to write a piece about it for the *New York Times*. It summed up my view of him as well as anything I can say now, so here it is, as a starting point.

Dick Williams planned a graceful retirement, but he should have known it wouldn't work out that way. Nothing in his 42-year professional baseball career has ever come easily, and although he has tasted every level of success, he has usually moved on in an atmosphere of dissatisfaction.

The Moderns

When he started this season as manager of the Seattle Mariners, he said he intended to retire at the end of it, having set—presumably—baseball's least successful franchise on its feet at last. Instead, on Monday, just a month after his 59th birthday, he was dismissed. Most of his players were glad to see him go, condemning his "lack of communication."

As the manager of six different major league teams in 21 years, Williams never got the recognition his truly outstanding record merited. As a player for 13 big league seasons with five clubs, and part or all of nine years in the minors, he was never more than a journeyman, but he was able to play six positions and pinch-hit. As a person, he has always been unfailingly alert, smart and competitive, strong-minded to the point of stubbornness and abrasive in manner even though he could be charming when he wanted to be.

But charm was never his goal; winning was. And few baseball men have produced winners in as varied circumstances under unfavorable conditions as he did. Unfavorable circumstances, however, seemed to be his fate, and more often than not he couldn't overcome them.

He leaves the Mariners not noticeably different than they have been all along. In the 11 years since their formation as baseball's most recent expansion team (along with Toronto), they have never been in contention, never won even half their games and never reached the major league average in attendance.

Not even Williams could change that pattern, although he presided over historic turnarounds in Boston, Oakland and San Diego. In 1967, his first as a big league manager, he took a Red Sox team that had finished ninth the two previous seasons and won a pennant.

In 1971–73, in charge of the Athletics when they had already risen to second place but had not been a contender before that for 35 consecutive years in three cities, he won three straight division titles and two World Series.

And in 1984, he won a National League pennant with the Padres after they had failed to finish higher than fourth in a six-team division in all 15 previous seasons of their existence.

But there were no such miracles for him with the California Angels or Montreal Expos or the Mariners, and his hope of managing the New York Yankees in 1974, as Ralph Houk's successor, never materialized. And even his successful situations ended in bitterness and player dissatisfaction. One way or another, his abrasiveness outlasted his effectiveness.

Dick Williams

Yet his résumé is truly remarkable. Only one other man, Jimmy Dykes, managed six different clubs—and Dykes never won a pennant with any of them. Only one other man, Bill McKechnie, took three different clubs to a World Series (St. Louis, Pittsburgh and Cincinnati).

Only four others won pennants in both leagues—Joe McCarthy, Yogi Berra, Alvin Dark and Sparky Anderson—and they did it with only one team in each, teams that were habitual contenders.

More striking still is the breadth of William's experience in baseball, his interaction with so many notable people. He had the opportunity, as well as the ability, to absorb and internalize a vast amount of baseball thought.

He played for 10 different managers in the majors, including Charlie Dressen, Paul Richards and Walter Alston. He was a teammate, at one time or another, of six present managers—Anderson, Tommy Lasorda, Roger Craig, Whitey Herzog, Don Zimmer and Russ Nixon—and managed Tony La Russa briefly with the 1971 Athletics. He also played with former managers Gil Hodges, Bobby Bragan, Billy Gardner and Hank Bauer.

And he was, from the start, a Branch Rickey product. He entered the Brooklyn Dodgers system in 1947, at the age of 18, when Rickey's scouting-development mass production system was at its peak. He stayed in the Dodger system, bouncing back and forth to the minors, for 10 years before being traded to the American League, where he played for Baltimore, Cleveland, Kansas City and Boston. More thorough preparation for managing is hard to imagine.

Two years as manager in Toronto, then in the International League, preceded his Year of the Impossible Dream in Boston in 1967. But after two more seasons, he was gone, perceived as too demanding by his players. Taking over the Athletics, he had great young talent but an impossible boss in Charles Finley and endless turbulence.

After two straight seventh-game World Series victories, he resigned, planning to sign with George Steinbrenner's Yankees. But Finley held him to an unexpired contract, forcing Williams into the real estate business in Florida until, by midseason of 1974, Finley let him go to the Angels.

His Anaheim regime got nowhere, and he was out before the 1976 season ended. In the next four years, he turned Montreal into a contender, but was pushed out during September of 1981 even as the Expos were on their way to the playoffs.

In San Diego, starting in 1982, he had two .500 years leading to the glory of 1984. But by the end of the next season management wanted him out, and he left just before the 1986 season began amid a squabble over his staying on. A month into that season, he was hired by the Mariners, and, three days less than 25 months later, was fired by them.

He probably won't be around again, and won't be missed, in the fraternal sense, the way he might be if he were less crusty. But he has always been himself—no excuses, no compromises, no false heartiness—and he leaves the way he came in, strictly his own man, product of a sterner time, and proud of it.

When I wrote that last sentence, I was going on impressions formed at a distance over thirty years about a man I never knew well. Since then, I've read his autobiography, which spells out the background of that "sterner time."

He was born in St. Louis in 1928, and grew up rooting for those wild Cardinal teams and the hapless Browns of the 1930s. (He had an earlier connection with Branch Rickey than any of our other managers: He was one of the "knothole gang" kids let into the ballpark to build a future fan base, one of Rickey's innovations.) The family moved to the Los Angeles area, around Pasedena, when he was fourteen, and he went to high school and junior college there.

But the crux of the story is his father, and the boy's relationship with him.

The father was chronically unemployed or underemployed during the depth of the Depression, and a surly domestic tyrant of incredible proportions. He beat his children, had all but insane ideas about "discipline" and "never giving in," and conducted an unending emotional reign of terror that included the precept that "compromise" was unthinkable.

In St. Louis, the family lived in the maternal grandfather's house, largely supported by the grandfather. It moved to California when a relative got the father a job there. The father, overworked and a heavy drinker and smoker, developed heart trouble. When Dick was sixteen (as he tells it), he was playing in a high school football game when, at the end of a long run, he was tackled and suffered a broken ankle. His father came running down from the stands to see to his son, being carried off on a stretcher—and that night had a fatal heart attack. Williams says he blamed himself for his father's death, and never completely got rid of the guilt feelings. But he also internalized, more and more—even as a teenager—his father's mental framework, which I would describe as "Do it my way, and to hell with what anybody else thinks about it, and I'm going to tell you every chance I get why I think you're wrong."

Of course, I didn't know any of this in the years I came across Williams on the baseball beat. I had little occasion to deal with him extensively, but I didn't like him, for reasons of my own, which were superficial.

When he played with the Dodgers, I knew him enough to nod hello, but that's all. When he played elsewhere, the contact was even less. But when he became a celebrity with the Impossible Dream Red Sox of 1967, I got my first negative feedback. I was with the *New York Times* then, on one of the best of all baseball assignments, "front-running": that is, covering a non–New York team in the late stages of a close pennant race. By then, I was an experienced writer and identifiable in the baseball community, and had developed what I considered a good working relationship with managers of teams I wasn't covering regularly. I'd make clear I wasn't on their beat and not concerned about whatever ongoing controversies they had in their own town, and that anything I asked would be for the sake of information and my own understanding, not as a goad or a trap. It usually worked. But with Williams, I met automatic hostility and suspicion, the assumption that I (like the rest of the world) must be out to get him and that he didn't give a damn if I was, and an impatient annoyance at the simplest question or attempt at conversation.

Well, that was a relatively brief encounter under circumstances of great tension for him (greater than I knew at the time), so I didn't think much about it. But over the next twenty years, in Oakland, in Anaheim, and in San Diego, I found him acting the same way. He had every right, of course, to be that way; and I had every right not to like it. But when I heard players complain, as I've heard countless players complain about virtually every manager, I had a better understanding of what they meant in his case.

There was a notable exception to this pattern that I'll come to in a minute.

Shortly after he turned eighteen, in 1947, Williams signed with the Dodger organization. It was now Rickey's, and the scout who signed him had moved with Rickey from St. Louis to Brooklyn and remembered seeing Williams play as a kid on a semipro team sponsored first by the Cardinals, then by the Dodgers. After his graduation from Pasadena Junior College that June, Williams finished the season playing at Santa Barbara, up the coast a few miles, in Class C.

In the spring of 1948, he was one of the six hundred players who took part in the first session of the new Vero Beach complex, and returned to Santa Barbara. Late in the season, he was promoted to Fort Worth, Class AA, and played there in 1949 and 1950. The manager was Bobby Bragan, the first of the three central influences on Williams's baseball thinking. Bragan was (and is) a foremost Rickey disciple in the most passionate terms, and adept at the systematic teaching of basics. He also cut the cocky Williams down to size by forcing him to exert as least some self-discipline.

In 1951, the fateful year of the Bobby Thomson homer, Williams found himself on the Dodger bench in Brooklyn through unusual circumstances.

The Korean War was on. Williams was playing winter ball in Cuba with reasonable expectation of being promoted to the Dodger roster. Instead, he was drafted into the army. That was in February. He had a trick left knee, from football, but could be assigned to limited duty. In a camp baseball game, chasing a fly ball, he fell down a ravine and tore up the knee again. The doctors took a look at it, thought about liability, and gave him a discharge.

That was May. The natural move would have been to St. Paul, at Triple-A level, to resume baseball playing and prepare for the majors. The knee was all right. But baseball regulations weren't.

As a veteran of military service (three months), Williams had job protection: He could be carried on the Dodger roster for a full year without counting against the twenty-five-player limit. But he couldn't be taken *off* the Dodger roster, for minor league assignment, without going through waivers, and two other clubs were ready to claim him. The Dodgers didn't want to lose a good prospect, so they brought him to Brooklyn—to sit on the bench.

Dressen was the manager, and he related to Williams's feistiness right away. He made him the designated yeller, the bench jockey assigned to scream distracting insults at the opposition (and, if necessary, umpires). At this, Williams quickly became an all-time all-star, with Leo Durocher of the Giants his chief target. He became so proficient that before he was allowed to sit on the bench at the 1952 World Series (when he was injured), he was required by the league president to keep his mouth shut.

Jackie Robinson befriended him, but the other famous Dodgers did not. He found them cliquish and indifferent. For his part, he became notorious as a carouser. But he got little chance to play ball. He even sought permission from Commissioner Happy Chandler to be sent to the minors, but Chandler, though sympathetic, said, "Rules are rules." He was stuck in Brooklyn, unwanted and inactive, until May 29, 1952.

Nevertheless, Dressen liked him—and Dressen, he says, was the second great influence. When May 29 came around, the Dodgers not only kept Williams but started him in a few games. He might actually win the left field job.

Suddenly, on a hot August day in St. Louis, everything changed. He charged a sinking liner, didn't get it, fell, and suffered a triple dislocation of his right shoulder. He was never as good a ballplayer again. He couldn't throw from the outfield at all; he could get the ball from third to first on a bounce; and he couldn't hit as well as he once did.

Bad shoulder and all, he lasted twelve more years in the majors. The Dodgers sent him to Montreal for part of 1953, to St. Paul for part of 1954, and back to Fort Worth for all of 1955. That move was partly at his request: He had just married a girl from Fort Worth, and it gave them a chance to get settled. (His teammates included Sparky Anderson, Danny Ozark, and Maury Wills.) He started 1956 in Brooklyn, was sent to Montreal and, in June, was traded to the Baltimore Orioles.

The manager there was Paul Richards, his third great influence. (Maybe one of the things he got from Richards was the "You're too dumb to know what I'm talking about" attitude toward writers that put me off.) Williams played first, second, and third, and the outfield, and pinch-hit, and hit .286. Nevertheless, in June of 1957, he was traded to Cleveland (for Jim Busby), and in April of 1958 back to Baltimore. At the end of that season, he was traded to the Kansas City Athletics, not yet owned by Finley, for shortstop Chico Carrasquel. He played regularly there for two years—at three or four positions, mostly third—and had his two best seasons as a player (under managers Harry Craft and Bob Elliott). On the eve of the 1961 season, after Finley had bought the club, he was sent back to Baltimore, where he played as an all-purpose utility man for two more years.

At the end of the 1961 season, Richards left to take charge of the expansion Houston franchise, and he bought Williams's contract at the end of the 1962 season. But two months later, he traded it to the Boston Red Sox.

At Boston, the thirty-four-year-old Williams found himself in the famous "country club" atmosphere, and he didn't mind saying how much he despised it. They key word, to him, was "care": A player had to care, without limit, about winning; anything else was shameful, and anything that stemmed from total devotion to winning was justifiable. And an integral part of "caring" was "hating" any opponent. People could be—had to be—"driven" to do better, and whatever else Boston manager Johnny Pesky was doing, it wasn't that.

After two season of increasing uselessness at Boston, which finished seventh and eighth in the ten-team league, he was offered a deal by the farm director. Williams had been vociferous about how managers should operate. How about trying it in the minors? If he'd go to Seattle (Triple-A) as a player-coach, he'd get a chance to manage as soon as there was an opening. Williams said yes.

That winter, the Red Sox moved their team from Seattle to Toronto, and the Seattle manager didn't go with it. The job was open. Williams grabbed it. The salary was $10,000, a big cut from the $18,500 the Red Sox had paid him, but it was a chance to manage and worth it.

Williams felt prepared. The day he injured his shoulder, he started thinking about managing. He had spent every day and every game after that observing what managers did, how games and preparation worked out, channeling his competitive urge into someday winning as a manager. Bragan and Vero Beach had taught him the Rickey system, which he adopted completely. Dressen had taught him game alertness, daring, originality, and the little ways (including cheating) to win. Richards had taught him the importance and systematization of detail, especially concerning defense. And living poor was nothing new. All through his career, he had needed off-season jobs: unloading freight cars, stripping wallpaper, selling men's clothes, selling parimutuel tickets at a jai alai parlor in Florida, being a carpenter's assistant. And in 1956, he had converted to Catholicism, for the sake of his wife (who was from an Italian family) and children (three), so he had a better handle on his own emotions and behavior. He was ready.

He really was. His Toronto teams finished third and second, but won the International League playoffs each year. The Red Sox, meanwhile, fell to ninth for the same two years under Billy Herman. Herman was fired and Williams campaigned for the job at the top. And because of a front office shakeup that brought Dick O'Connell to the general manager's position, he got it. The salary was $35,000.

The Red Sox were considered a hopeless cause. Williams installed the Rickey teaching methods and his own ideas about discipline and the virtue of immediate criticism. Carl Yastrzemski responded with a triple-crown season, the pitchers got tough, and the Red Sox won the pennant on the final day of the 1967 season.

They lost the seventh game of the World Series to the Cardinals, but even in Boston there was no complaint about that. Williams was a hero who had performed a miracle. The trouble was, what could he do for an encore?

Not much, it turned out. The owner, Tom Yawkey, hadn't liked him from the start, and Williams showed his irritation at Yawkey's presence in the clubhouse (only after victories, Williams noted) and his pampering of stars like Yastrzemski. O'Connell got Williams a three-year contract, but Yawkey gave it reluctantly. A fourth-place finish in 1968 greased the skids. Running third in the new six-team Eastern Division in 1969 was enough excuse for Yawkey: Williams was fired.

It was just as well. He needed a year of peace. He had started drinking heavily after games. His home life was in turmoil, and he was on the edge of a separation. In 1970, he signed on as third base coach for Gene Mauch, managing the new Montreal Expos in the second season of their existence. Williams, like so many others, considered Mauch a baseball wizard. He had a happy and peaceful—one might say restorative—year in Montreal, despite his bitterness about Boston.

Then Charley Finley called.

The A's were on the verge of greatness. All those young players Dark had seen coming in Kansas City had grown up in Oakland under Bob Kennedy, Hank Bauer, and John McNamara in Finley's manager-a-year system. In 1968 they had crossed .500, and in 1969 and 1970 had finished second in the Western Division to Martin's and Bill Rigney's Minnesota Twins.

Now Finley wanted a live-wire manager, and knew all about Williams (as he did about everything going on in baseball). Williams didn't hesitate: Managing, once experienced, is addictive. He took over a ball club with far more talent than his Boston team of 1967, no great expectations among its fans, and no history of public turmoil in only its fourth year in a new location.

Library shelves are studded with books about the A's of 1971, 1972, and 1973, and most of them are fascinating. All that's relevant here, however, is how Williams managed them.

They finished first in 1971, but lost the League Championship Series to Baltimore. In 1972 and 1973, they went all the way to victory in 7-game World Series. Williams was no more immune to Charley's endless phone calls and specific instructions than his predecessors or successors, but he was a much sharper dugout general than Kennedy, Bauer, or McNamara, and the players could see that. Finley made him carry a designated pinch runner, a sprinter named Allan Lewis, "the Panamanian Express," so Williams used him productively (as Dark later used Herb Washington). Finley made him rotate three or four second basemen a game, using a pinch hitter each time one of them was to bat—even though everybody knew that Dick Green, the starter, was the best defensive second baseman in the game. Finley said grow mustaches, so they all grew mustaches (including Williams). He was as harassed as all other Finley managers.

But for that very reason, he had something going for him. The players were so busy hating Charley, they couldn't bother with hating him; in fact, the common enemy made them feel Williams was an ally—a feeling he never got from any other set of players. They appreciated his baseball acumen, and he knew how to help individual players get better. And because this free-spirited crew often engaged in intramural fights (some actually with fists), Williams's aloofness was a perfect fit. He didn't try to impose a strict curfew and other behavior codes as he had in Boston—he'd learned from that—so he didn't add to the turmoil but rode its crest.

And, as always, the fact of winning has charms to soothe a savage breast.

Dick Williams

Technically, his managing was first rate. Williams excelled at pitching changes (along with great starters, he had a great bullpen in which Rollie Fingers was first establishing his stardom). He juggled the lineup masterfully in the positions that weren't set, as Finley kept a steady stream of players coming and going, and his pinch-hitting choices came through a high proportion of the time. A year with Mauch had sharpened his game-situation skills, and the Dressen school of sign-stealing also paid off. He simply did a first-class job, and his players knew it, even if Finley didn't.

But friction was inevitable. After the World Series victory over Cincinnati in 1972, Finley became even more overbearing, and the players more sensitive. Every other day someone blew up at someone for something that was said or not said or misreported or whatever. The phone calls to Williams's house multiplied. By July, he was wondering how much more he could take.

As the pennant-winning manager in 1972, Williams was the American League manager for the All-Star Game, scheduled for Kansas City on Tuesday, July 24. The preceding Thursday, Williams had to undergo an emergency appendectomy, but he didn't let that stop him from taking part in an event that meant so much to his pride and competitiveness. Fresh from the hospital, he made it physically but suffered the emotional trauma of seeing a line drive break a finger on Catfish Hunter's pitching hand. (Catfish was out for a month, but came back and still wound up with 21 victories.) That afternoon, in the hotel lobby before the game, the uncharacteristic incident I referred to earlier occurred.

The *Times* had just moved me from New York to California, so I came east to cover that game with Joe Durso, who came from New York. We and Murray Chass were still, at that point, the paper's chief baseball writers. Joe and I ran into Williams in the lobby and for about half an hour enjoyed a most relaxed general conversation, the sort we were used to having with lots of others but not with Williams. Affable is the only word to describe him on this occasion. Actively friendly. Good humored.

It was so unusual that Durso and I joked about it afterwards. "What kind of medication must they have given him in the hospital? What's the opposite of ugly pills? Or is he having intimations of mortality?"

We thought no more about it then.

The A's did win the pennant again, but before they did Williams had made up his mind he couldn't stay. The A's won a nerve-wracking playoff series from Baltimore, and Williams had his future staked out: He would go to the New York Yankees, who had contacted him informally and secretly—and illegally, since he had another year to go on his contract with Finley.

The World Series with the Mets generated a particularly uncomfortable controversy. Mike Andrews, who had played for Williams in Toronto and Boston, was one of the second basemen Finley had acquired late in the season. In the twelfth inning of the second game, he booted a grounder and made a wide throw and the A's lost, 10–7. Finley, wanting to replace him with Manny Trillo—a roster substitution not allowable during the World Series—tried to get Andrews to sign (and Williams to certify) a false statement that Andrews was injured. The other players, of course, were as outraged as Williams, but Finley persisted and got Andrews to sign. The ploy didn't work, and the commissioner made Finley reinstate Andrews. The A's finally won in 7 games, but the emotional breaches were now irreparable.

Williams announced that he was quitting. Finley declared he would "not stand in his way." The move to the Yankees seemed set.

Why the Yankees? They had been purchased, in January of 1973, by a Cleveland syndicate headed by George Steinbrenner. Mike Burke, the president installed by CBS after it had completed its purchase of the team from Dan Topping in 1966, was to be part of the new group. Ralph Houk as manager and Lee MacPhail as head of baseball operations were a close-knit triumvirate that had not succeeded in restoring the franchise to former glory. By midseason, Houk made it clear that he could not tolerate Steinbrenner's mode of operation. He didn't resign formally until the day after the season ended, but insiders knew it was going to happen. Burke was eased out and MacPhail left a month later.

It was in that context that third parties—not Steinbrenner himself—sounded Williams out about coming to New York. Exactly when? In his book, Williams says it was "a couple of weeks before" the A's flew from Oakland to New York for the third game of the World Series with the Andrews case exploding in all directions. That would put it around October 3, the time the playoffs were just beginning.

But Durso and I wondered. Had there been such a possibility back in July? Was Williams suddenly so chatty with two representatives of the influential *New York Times* because he knew he might be going to New York? We had no evidence for such a suspicion; what's significant is that we thought of it, indicating how manipulative Williams seemed to us. "If that's true," I said to Joe, "we missed a big story by not following up our hunch that *something* was different."

To this day, I don't know (or much care) what the details and timing of the Yankee-Williams negotiations were. (I remembered that when the Yankees were interested in Alvin Dark in 1964, those explorations had been made in July.) But what mattered is what happened after the story became public, two days after the World Series.

Finley reneged. He wouldn't let Williams go without a fight. He demanded two hot prospects for the Yankees as compensation for letting Williams out of his contract. (The principle was not unprecedented: The Mets had traded a pitcher to Washington to get Gil Hodges as their manager, and later, when Finley himself wanted Chuck Tanner to move from Chicago to replace Dark in 1976, he would send catcher Manny Sanguillen to the White Sox as payment. The sticking point was the price.) The Yankees didn't want Williams that badly, and thought they could get a favorable ruling from American League president Joe Cronin. But if there is anything league presidents understand, it is the sanctity of contracts; all they really do is approve them, assign umpires, preside at meetings, and put their names on baseballs. Finley's rights were upheld—properly—and the Yankees dropped the subject.

They hired Bill Virdon, and Williams was left in limbo in Florida. Finley kept sending him paychecks, and Williams kept sending them back (so that he couldn't be assigned to some minor league scouting job, for instance), and went to work for the head of a conglomerate, giving motivational speeches to executives.

By midseason, the Angels were looking for a manager who could "take control." Gene Autry, an original owner of the expansion franchise since 1961, had nothing to show for thirteen years of operation. He was attracted to the reputation, success, and outlaw image Williams had acquired. He told Harry Dalton, his general manager, to hire him, and this time Finley (who owed his original move to Oakland to Autry's support) gave permission. On June 26, Williams became manager of the Angels.

Here Williams had the opposite of the situation in Boston: He was the owner's choice but not the general manager's, and that's even worse. And he had one similarity: The climate in the Boston clubhouse had been corroded by a superstar's presence, Yastrzemski; in Anaheim, Dalton had brought in Frank Robinson, whose prestige (and outspoken ideas) overwhelmed Bobby Winkles, the manager whose previous experience had been only as a college coach. The college had been Arizona State, where he turned out Rick Monday, Reggie Jackson, and Sal Bando, so his qualifications were fine; but the professional world is different, especially in the matter of internal politics, and Winkles wasn't equipped for that.

The star-manager relationship is classic: Huggins-Ruth, McCarthy-Ruth, Stengel-DiMaggio, Dark-Mays, Martin-Jackson, anybody-Hornsby, as we have seen. Williams solved the Robinson situation by appointing him team captain, giving sanction to his advising younger players.

The trouble was, most of the younger players couldn't play.

The Angels had Robinson, Nolan Ryan at his peak, a young pitcher named Frank Tanana, and just about nothing else.

Williams stayed for twenty-five months in three unrewarding seasons. The players detested him. He didn't think much of them either. Nor did he think much of the general manager. The farm system wasn't much. The rest of 1974 was 36–48; all of 1975 was 72–89; when it was 39–57 in July of 1976, after a shouting match with one of his players on the team bus, Williams was fired, while the nation was still celebrating its bicentennial.

The Anaheim experience did nothing to improve Williams's reputation or disposition. But he was still a very, very, very good baseball manager and these are always in short supply. Montreal needed one, because Mauch had finally packed it in after getting nowhere in six years with an expansion team, although he did leave behind a foundation. Mauch had a chance to go to a better club—the Minnesota Twins—and took it.

Williams applied for the job, and got it. He and his wife had enjoyed Montreal in 1970. They expected a peaceful time again.

Dick Williams

And this time, the general manager was someone Williams knew and could get along with. Charlie Fox, a street-tough New Yorker who had spent most of his life working for the Giants (whom he managed in San Francisco to a first-place finish in 1971), combined the old-fashioned virtues of Williams with a million-dollar personality that was the gregarious opposite of Williams's.

At Montreal, Dick's teaching (the Rickey system, through and through) took precedence over his whiplashing, and a young team improved. The young talent included Gary Carter and Andre Dawson. The move into Olympic Stadium buoyed everyone's enthusiasm. The 1977 team won 75 games, the 1978 team won 76, and the next two 95 and 90, finishing second to Pittsburgh in 1979 and to Philadelphia in 1980.

However, here a new problem arose, and neither Williams nor the front office knew how to handle it. This was the peak era of drug abuse in baseball, the late 1970s. Not just recreational drugs like cocaine and marijuana were widely used, but performance enhancers like "greenies" or "uppers" followed by "downers." This wasn't peculiar to baseball—it hit all sports, and a whole generation outside sports—but there was not, at this time, any institutional method or sophisticated guidance for dealing with it. For a man with Williams's rigid work ethic, and his habit of equating "inadequate" with "gutless," the drug scene was harder to ignore—or do anything about—than it was for most people.

Clubhouse confrontations continued, and in one of them Fox took a punch at one of the pitchers. That cost Charlie his front office job and John McHale, the president who had been a general manager before, stepped back down. Once again, Williams was working for an executive who didn't see things his way, and who listened to player complaints. In 1981, the team didn't start so well, and in June the two-month strike started. In due course, that meant it finished third in what was declared to be the first half of a split season. But whoever won the second half, after play was resumed in August, would qualify for a special playoff for the division title. On September 8, with 27 games to go, McHale fired Williams, giving the standard "failure to communicate" reason. Jim Fanning was pulled out of the front office to finish the season in the dugout—and the Expos won 17 of the games, finished first, and beat Philadelphia in the special playoff. Then they lost the

5-game regular playoff to the Dodgers, who went on to beat the Yankees in the World Series.

That was, by all rights, Williams's team, and it is still the most successful finish Montreal has ever had. But he was on the street again, bitter again, considered hard to get along with again, and again the best out-of-work manager available, since Martin was now with the A's.

During the off-season, there was another flirtation with the Yankees, but the real job offer came from San Diego. As an expansion team in 1969, the Padres were run by Buzzy Bavasi, who had left the Dodgers, for their first nine years. In 1974, about the time that Finley was preventing Williams from going to the Yankees, the franchise was almost moved to Washington, but Ray Kroc, the Chicagoan who had built the McDonald's hamburger business, stepped in and bought it to keep it in San Diego. After 1977, Bavasi left and Kroc took over the presidency himself. By the end of 1981, the franchise had finished above .500 just once in its thirteen seasons (in 1978 under Roger Craig), and had never placed higher than fourth. Kroc was ailing, so the active direction of the club was in the hands of his wife, Joan, his son-in-law Ballard Smith, and Jack McKeon, the general manager. That's the trio who signed Williams for three years at $190,000 a year—a long way from the $9,000 he had accepted to enter the managerial ranks at Toronto, seventeen years before.

McKeon, known as Trader Jack, did produce a lot of better players. Steve Garvey joined the team as a free agent. Ozzie Smith was traded to St. Louis for Gary Templeton. The pitching staff didn't have famous names but did have talent. Things improved quickly. In 1982, the Padres attained 81–81, and matched it in 1983, although still no higher than fourth. And in 1984, they put it all together and finished first with 92 victories. They lost the first 2 games of the playoffs at Chicago, but won the next 3 at home and reached the World Series, where the much stronger Detroit Tigers disposed of them in 5 games.

Williams was a miracle worker again.

And again, from his point of view, he was caught in a front office power struggle. Kroc had died, and his widow, Joan, controlled the money, with no pretense to knowing baseball or to showing much interest in it. Smith, who didn't know anything about baseball either, although he thought he did, protected his position by keeping her out of touch with day-to-day developments. McKeon,

Dick Williams

who did know baseball and had managed Kansas City once, wanted to manage again.

Things weren't so hot in the clubhouse either. Three starting pitchers caused a public relations storm by flaunting their membership in the John Birch society. A couple of players had hard-drug involvements. Williams himself had started to drink more during the pressures of the 1984 race, and the increasingly laid-back and selfish population of "today's ballplayers"—in his eyes—was harder and harder to take.

After a tie for third place at 83–79 in 1985, McKeon and Smith wanted Williams out while Joan Kroc wanted him to stay. McKeon fired Ossie Virgil, Dick's close friend and most trusted third base coach, and Mrs. Kroc had him reinstated. But two months later, a day before spring training was to start, she was won over to the other side and offered to buy out the remainder of Williams's contract—if he would go along with pretending to resign. There wasn't much choice. He had to swallow his pride and take the money.

Three months later he was in action again, taking over the Seattle Mariners, the only team with a worse history than the pre-Williams Padres.

This Seattle team had been created in 1977, with Danny Kaye as one of its original owners, and had failed financially as well as artistically. (The Seattle Pilots, an expansion team of 1969, had been transformed into the Milwaukee Brewers in 1970). The Mariners, starting their tenth season, had averaged 95½ losses a year when allowed to play a full schedule, and were 44–65 in strike-shortened 1981. That year, they had been purchased by George Argyros, a real estate developer based in Southern California, who had watched Williams's San Diego success. He also interviewed Billy Martin, who was in one of his nonmanaging cycles on the Yankee payroll, but settled on Williams.

Always convinced he could win if only people would do things his way, Williams took charge of a team that was already 9–20 in May. There were some talented players, but what Williams defined as an "uncaring" attitude and "gutlessness" under pressure was endemic. That season ended 67–95 in last place (seventh). But the 1987 team was the best in franchise history, flirting with .500 and finishing 78–84—a record good enough for fourth place, only 7 games out of first place, which Minnesota took with the worst first-place record in the history of the American League. (Don't laugh. The Twins went on to win the World Series.)

Argyros, in his own way, was no easier to get along with than Finley (but without, of course, Finley's total involvement and shrewdness). His delegate on the scene in Seattle was Chuck Armstrong, a Stanford Law School alumnus who was his business manager, also devoid of real baseball background. Their main concern became to sell or move the team, rather than to build a winner.

Williams was now fifty-nine years old, and accepting the idea that there was an unbridgeable generation gap between him and "the modern player." He announced that 1988 would be his last season. In May, after a 23–33 start, they asked him to leave now, and I wrote the piece that starts this chapter.

How do we sum him up as a manager?

Genealogically, pure Rickey.

Game management, talent evaluation, and strategic planning, right up there with the best.

Handling players, poor: too rigid, too frozen in his conviction that fear was the only motivator, that a whip was the necessary tool. What he wanted players to do was invariably right; how he tried to get them to do it proved self-defeating after a couple of years.

In his book, Williams described a showdown he had with a San Diego pitcher and made this comment:

"The conflict between Welsh and me became the talk of the clubhouse. That was good. It united the slouchers in their hate for me, which meant they'd probably play harder, if only out of spite. You know how I love that attitude. And the reasonable folks became united with me in my love for winning. . . . As I've said, the people who have the most trouble with me usually aren't the most productive."

That's a point of view from which he never strayed, and it is uncommon among the managers in this book. (Contrast it with Casey Stengel's maxim: "On every club there's ten guys who hate you, so make sure you room them together so they don't contaminate the rest.") He also believed, as most of the others did not, in immediate criticism of a player in front of others, instead of the "I'll chew him out later in private" school exemplified by Houk and subscribed to by Martin. (Well, McGraw did it, in a different age, but it hurt even him; remember Frank Frisch?)

To those who believe "hard-nosed" is the ultimate compliment and is the highest value to be sought above all others, Williams represented the perfect manager. To those who see the world in more complex terms, Williams was an outstanding manager who didn't do as well as he could have and should have because of that one-dimensional approach.

He called his book, *No More Mr. Nice Guy,* a reference to an old World War II joke about Hitler losing patience and threatening to do something *really* bad. It's an interesting choice, and I'm not sure Williams grasped all its implications. But he is, as I said, his own man and proud of it.

19

Earl Weaver

Mr. Nobody

Unlike Martin and Williams, Earl Weaver did not bounce around much, even though he was more ball-shaped than either. He worked for only three organizations, the Cardinals, the Pirates, and the Orioles, his whole baseball life.

Like Williams, he was born in St. Louis, on August 14, 1930, when Williams was a little more than a year old. But he grew up in entirely different circumstances. Williams and his family were outsiders; the Weavers were definitely insiders.

Earl's father handled the dry cleaning for both the Cardinals and the Browns, and from the time he was six, the son would tag along and visit the big league locker rooms for pickups and deliveries. His most affluent uncle was, among other things, a successful bookie who had season tickets for both clubs, and Earl himself was a regular customer of the Knothole Gang program for kids, so he used to see one hundred or so games a year at Sportsman's Park before he ever got to high school. When the whole 1944 World Series was played there, with the Cardinals beating the Browns in 6 games, the fourteen-year-old Weaver was able to walk up each day and buy a bleacher seat.

What's more, the father was a boyhood chum of Bill DeWitt, who had become Branch Rickey's office boy and, eventually, an owner of the Browns. And Earl senior's particular friend was Freddie Hofmann, a coach with the Browns in those days, who had been, in the course of a nine-year major league career, a roommate of Babe Ruth's.

So even before the Williams family moved to California, Weaver was a preteen-ager with finely honed skills in second-guessing Billy Southworth, Fred Haney, Luke Sewell, and dozens of visiting managers.

There was a key personality difference between Williams and

Weaver too. In his own way, Weaver was as combative, cocky, and competitive as Williams. (All these men are; it's an essential ingredient in their ability to become managers.) But Weaver had a sense of humor, about himself as well as the rest of the world, that Williams didn't. He had an internal personal security that neither Williams nor Martin grew up with (while Houk and Alston did). He had even more shouting matches with his players than Williams and Martin, on the bench and in the clubhouse, but these were open exchanges of emotion almost immediately forgotten by both parties (or at least put aside). Earl said what he thought, often in a profane vocabulary that could hold its own with Durocher's or Tommy Lasorda's, but it was more a matter of colorful rather than venomous self-expression. He retained a better sense of perspective, about himself and the world in general, than Williams and Martin were able to.

And, unlike them, he never realized his ambition to make the majors as a player. That failure probably made him a better manager than he might have been otherwise.

It wasn't something he found easy to accept. At the high school level, he was a fine player, a second baseman who could hit. He was small, about five feet six inches and 155 pounds, but so were McGraw and Huggins and McCarthy and, for that matter, Napoleon. Of course, McCarthy hadn't made it to the majors either, and Napoleon had never tried to hit a slider. But his high school team, which won two state championships, included Bobby Hofman, Roy Sievers, Bob Wiesler, and Jim Goodwin, who did wind up in the majors, and he held his own in that company. In fact, he caught the eye of no less distinguished a person than George Sisler, scouting for the Cardinals, who called his father about signing him.

"He won't be fourteen until August," said Earl senior, astounded and pleased. Sisler said he hadn't realized he was so young, and would keep an eye on him. Thereafter, both the Browns and the Cardinals invited him to all their tryouts, and another Cardinal scout—Walter Shannon, one of Rickey's most devout disciples— was particularly encouraging, while Freddie Hofmann took special pains with him at the Browns' workouts.

As Earl junior finished high school, Earl senior asked Hofmann for an honest evaluation of his son's chances. The honest answer was "Class A, no higher." The supportive father didn't speak to his good friend for more than a year after that.

Still, the father preferred the Browns and sought out DeWitt and the team's farm director, Jim McLaughlin. They offered him a Class B contract with a contingency bonus (to be paid if he were still with the team June 15). Earl junior was smart enough not to take it, went over to Walter Shannon, who gave him a Class B contract in the Cardinal chain for a smaller bonus, but up front. Earl junior had already figured out that when a club invested in a player beforehand, it would give him a longer look than a contingency player.

In the long run, Hofmann was dead right, and Shannon overoptimistic—but not really wrong either. Weaver played in the Cardinal chain for eight years. In the Illinois State League, the Western Association, and the Carolina League, he made all-star teams. At Omaha, in the Western League, he was a productive regular. But at Houston—Double A—he was a flop. In 1952 spring training, during Eddie Stanky's first year as manager of the Cardinal's, Stanky didn't see much in him and sent him to Houston, which bounced him back to Omaha. In 1953, they tried him at Columbus (Triple-A) but that manager—Johnny Keane—wasn't impressed either, and it was back to Omaha.

Now the Cardinals let him pass into the Pittsburgh organization—which had been taken over by Rickey after he left Brooklyn—and Weaver played at Denver and New Orleans, both Class A. A beaning in 1955 broke some bones under his left eye, and he never hit as well after that. But that winter he made good money playing winter ball in the Dominican Republic, and when he returned to New Orleans, he was shifted to Montgomery, which folded there and moved to Knoxville.

He was now about to be twenty-six, and ready to face the fact that he wasn't going to make it as a ballplayer. He had a wife and three kids to support. Like all ballplayers in those days, he had taken off-season jobs to make ends meet: as a warehouseman wrestling with galvanized steel, as a parking meter maintenance man, as a clerk in the tax collection office (his uncle's political connections accounting for the last two), as a unionized day laborer, as a hod carrier, as a stonemason's helper. As soon as the Knoxville season was over, he decided, he'd try to find a permanent job in civilian life. Meanwhile, with the team in last place in July, he was offered a $200 raise to take over as manager.

The first thing he did was bench his second baseman, the nonhitting Earl Weaver.

Earl Weaver

The next day, a fellow named Harry Dalton came through town. McLaughlin had moved with the Browns to Baltimore in 1954, and had hired Dalton as an assistant. The transferred and revitalized franchise, being run by Paul Richards, was thinking of acquiring Knoxville for its minor league system. Dalton was sent to scout the city, not the ball club, but he came back with a good report on Weaver, whose background he had looked up.

In September, Weaver became a management trainee with a loan company in St. Louis. It turned out that he had natural talents as a salesman and in dealing with people: He screened loan applicants, handled collections, tracked down delinquents. He was in line for promotion.

But in December, McLaughlin came through town. Would Weaver be interested in managing a minor league team for the Orioles? It would be for even less money than he got as a player ($3,500 for six months instead of $4,000), but the loan company said they'd be glad to have him back in the off-season. He took it.

And he stayed with that organization for the next thirty years.

Weaver managed at Fitzgerald and Dublin, in the Georgia portion of the Florida-Georgia League; Aberdeen, South Dakota, in the Northern League; Fox Cities, based in Appleton, Wisconsin, in the Three-I League; Elmira, in the Class A Eastern League for four years; and Rochester, at the top of the chain, in 1966 and 1967. Three of his teams finished first, five second, three third, but that wasn't the important part. In the organizational meetings to evaluate players, he emerged as an exceptionally accurate judge of talent. He was good with young players as a teacher and leader, but the main thing was his judgment. He was definite, outspoken, and rigorously hardheaded about what he thought, and he was proved right more often than most.

Somewhere back in the mid-1950s, he had been turned on to hypnotism, which he mastered as an amateur. He didn't try to use it in baseball, but it solidified his conviction that positive thinking and the power of suggestion could tap subconscious powers. While he was at Elmira, he was divorced from his first wife (whom he'd married at eighteen, and who was fed up with his work-related absences, since he also managed winter ball in Venezuela), and also met and married his second wife. He also spent an off-season as a used-car salesman, and was terrific at it.

The Moderns

The hypnotism and his gift for salesmanship are relevant to some of his later operations as a manager.

In 1966, the Orioles won their first pennant and swept the Dodgers in the World Series with Hank Bauer as their manager. Richards had moved on to Houston, Lee MacPhail was the club president, and Harry Dalton the general manager. In 1967, they fell all the way to sixth, losing 22 more games than they did in 1966. Dalton decided to fire all but one of Bauer's coaches and replace them with men Weaver had recommended in an organizational meeting. We've seen enough of managerial dynamics by now to understand how Bauer felt about *that.* But Dalton didn't take Weaver's recommendation for a first base coach; instead, he offered that job to Earl himself.

Aware of the internal political situation that this created, Weaver nevertheless accepted quickly. A key issue was pensions. He had never spent a day in the majors, so that was enough of an emotional motivation right there; but coaches, like players, qualified for pensions only by spending five years in the majors, while minor league managers got nothing. Weaver was thirty-seven, with no profession but baseball. He had to accept the opportunity.

By All-Star break, the Orioles were a respectable 43–37, in third place—but 12 games behind the Tigers (who would win the World Series that year). Dalton made the change he had wanted to all along, and fired Bauer. But instead of choosing Billy Hunter, the third base coach (the one who had remained, also on Weaver's recommendation), he promoted Weaver himself.

Earl who?

To the public at large, and even to many baseball people outside the Oriole organization, Weaver was totally unknown. Bauer had been a star with Stengel's perennial champion Yankee teams. Richards had been an elder statesman. Even Hunter had been a major league shortstop. Gene Mauch had just been let go in Philadelphia. Such recent World Series managers as Sam Mele, Yogi Berra, and Danny Murtaugh were floating around.

Earl Weaver?

The best way to show how right Dalton was is to simply list what happened next:

1968: 48–34 the rest of the way to finish second.

1969: 109 victories, 3–0 in playoff with Minnesota, lost World Series to the Miracle Mets 1–4.

1970: 108 victories, 3–0 in playoff with Minnesota, won World Series from Cincinnati 4–1.

1971: 101 victories, 3–0 in playoff with Oakland, lost World Series to Pittsburgh 3–4.

1972: 80–74 record, third behind Detroit and Boston.

1973: 97 victories, lost playoff to Oakland 2–3.

1974: 91 victories, lost playoff to Oakland 1–3.

1975: 90 victories, second to Boston.

1976: 88 victories, second to Yankees.

1977: 97 victories, tied for second with Boston behind Yankees.

1978: 90 victories, fourth behind Yankees, Boston, and Milwaukee.

1979: 102 victories, 3–1 in playoff with California, lost World Series to Pittsburgh 3–4.

1980: 100 victories, second to Yankees.

That's 12 consecutive full seasons with an *average* of 96 victories a year, plus a 26–20 record in postseason play.

He wasn't Mr. Nobody after *that.*

He had become, in fact, one of baseball's more recognizable personalities. That sports-page word, *colorful,* applied to him in spades.

He argued with umpires and got thrown out of games. He argued with his players in the dugout, in full view of the television cameras. He argued with writers, never running out of words and quotable observations. He promoted "rivalry" with Billy Martin, the colorful Yankee (as he appeared and disappeared). He made brilliant moves, some of them unorthodox, and moves that got second-guessed by everyone. He argued with his pitchers right out on the mound, while making a change. His running battle of words with Jim Palmer, his best pitcher, became part of American folklore.

And yet, there was something immensely good-natured in all of it. He was obviously free of malice—and all too often dead right. He didn't live by the "never hurt their feelings" code that was taking hold—but he never had a doghouse, either; yesterday's bawling out was always a thing of the past today.

I said he had a sense of humor that Williams didn't. More important, he was subtle where Williams was merely smart. To Williams (as to Houk and Alston), 2 and 2 meant 4, and that was that. Martin and Dark and Richards saw it might also mean 22 or 1 (that is, 2 over 2). But Weaver went beyond that and also considered that it could be 2.2 or, in the form of 22, the equivalent in base eight of 18 in base ten. (Stengel, aware of all that, might also wonder if it weren't two 5s or two 7s written upside down, depending on the penmanship.)

In the matter of style, Weaver acquired two primary reputations, which he fostered by commenting on them and encouraging the popular interpretation. One was that he was a "three-run homer manager" rather than a "move the runners along and get a run where you can" manager. The other was that he made early and extensive use of statistics, especially this-batter-against-this-pitcher records, in making decisions about lineups and substitutions.

I don't believe either one, and I don't believe he did.

He argued that it wasn't worth giving up a base for an out by using a sacrifice bunt, because you had a better chance of scoring from first with none out than from second with one out, or from second with none out than from third with one out. If you took your chances, you might get a big inning, and multirun innings win ball games.

Sure—in the abstract. He always had teams with players who *could* hit a three-run homer: Frank Robinson, Boog Powell, many others, interspersed in a well-balanced lineup in a basically symmetrical ballpark with short foul lines—plus outstanding pitching and defense. If he had Alston's personnel of the Dodgers of the mid-1960s, he would have bunted and squeezed and hit-and-run as much as anyone. Because he was such a good judge of talent, and because the Oriole organization was so effective and deep (thanks in part to his contributions), he saw to it that his clubs did have sufficient power to play the way they did. But he was too smart a manager not to adapt to whatever material he might have.

As for the statistics, I think his use of them was subtlety at its best. He understood how convincing they could be; remember, he was a natural salesman. He knew the character of the "modern player"—the character that bothered Williams so much—inside out, and understood that the new breed craved explanations for everything so that they wouldn't feel "bossed." The numbers were a beautiful device. Why is so and so playing instead of me today? Because you're 2-for-18 lifetime against this pitcher, and he's 6-for-12. What can you say to that?

In Earl's own mind, of course, he knew what he wanted to do

and why. Naturally, the numbers confirmed his opinion the vast majority of the time: He had formed his opinion by noticing and remembering—as all good managers do—what had happened to make the numbers what they were. But he didn't draw his conclusion *from* the numbers; he chose the numbers that suited his conclusion. When the statistics and his opinion didn't coincide, he followed his opinion, not the statistics.

Weaver tells a story on himself that illustrates the point. In an evaluation meeting just before the 1961 expansion, the Orioles had to choose one of two minor league pitchers to protect, Dean Chance or Arnie Thorslin. Both had pitched for him. The consensus was for Thorslin, whose statistics were much better: in winning percentage, hits allowed per inning, fast ball on the speed gun, and so forth. Weaver spoke up in favor of Chance. The organization decided on Thorslin, and the new Angels took Chance, who became an outstanding big league pitcher while Thorslin never made it.

Why had he argued against the figures? Because he knew more than they could tell, having watched both men. Chance was a terrible fielder, and many of the hits charged against him were grounders up the middle a pitcher should be able to field; subtracting those, his statistics would have been better than Thorslin's—and a pitcher can be taught to field his position better. Chance had better baseball instincts and already knew how to set up hitters. Besides, Thorslin had a throwing motion, across his body, that put too much strain on his arm; he couldn't last. (Within three years, Thorslin had a sore arm and was finished.)

No, statistics did not make Weaver outstanding. It was his judgment of abilities, enabling him to carry out the time-honored precept to not ask players to do what they couldn't and to find the one who could do what you needed. ("Why would you ask a man to execute if he can't execute?" Stengel used to say, explaining why someone hadn't bunted.)

The famous statistics were a marvelous teaching tool and a deflection of second-guessing: They impressed the hearer as "objective" facts. The writers and broadcasters loved them even more than the players, because they could pretend to think along—and especially second-guess—on the basis of numerical material available to them. But I don't think Earl took them nearly as seriously as he said he did, and he certainly wasn't their captive.

The Moderns

He was, then, a strange amalgam of our central themes.

As a talent scout, giving primary importance to his opinion of a player's ability and then letting him play, he was doing the Connie Mack routine. In playing for the big inning, he was carrying on what McGraw turned to late and McCarthy always practiced. And in being so integral a part of, and beneficiary of, the excellent system the Orioles built, he was living in the world Rickey created. The Oriole system had been modeled on Rickey's methods, although it differed in some of the details that were being taught about specific plays and ways to pitch (and Weaver instigated some of those adjustments). What made it so Rickeyesque was the systemwide uniformity, the attention to detail, the consistency of evaluation, and the demand for documentation: namely, all those statistics.

Finally, Weaver was exceptionally dedicated to staff operation. He trusted his coaches, and worked more closely with them and to a greater degree than most managers do. He believed in the consensus approach he had been part of in the minors, and saw the benefit of using it daily. He was clearly the boss, but he sought the opinion of those under him and gave them clearly defined duties, and he created a climate in which his players could speak out too. That led to the arguments—but it also told him what was on their minds and provided a cathartic release for them. Most managers have one intimate friend closer than other coaches: Martin had Fowler, Williams had Virgil, and so forth. Weaver built good relationships with almost all his coaches: Hunter, Jim Frey, George Bamberger, Ray Miller, Cal Ripken, Sr., Frank Robinson, all of whom subsequently managed in the majors. He was secure enough to welcome input without feeling threatened, shrewd enough to make use of it, and aware of how the visible unity of the coaching staff could stabilize the attitude of the players.

I got to know him better than most of the managers of teams I never traveled with and, as you can tell, I liked him. Williams welcomed a certain amount of turmoil on his club because, as he said, he thought it spurred players to greater effort; Weaver liked it because it was fun.

In the strike season of 1981, the Orioles didn't win either half, but their total record of 59–46 was third best in the fourteen-team league. By now, Weaver was thinking of retirement. He wasn't so old—just past fifty—but he'd been managing for twenty-five years. He had taken the Oriole job for $28,000, and had to fight for that much because the original offer was less than the $22,500 he was making—$15,000 as Bauer's coach, $7,500 from winter ball. Now he was making $200,000, and had investments. It was getting to be time.

The 1982 season started badly, and he announced that it would be his last. He hoped to go out a winner. In the second half, the Orioles put on a tremendous drive, won 33 out of 43, and tied Milwaukee for first place on the next-to-last day. But they lost that final game, and his regime was over.

He turned the team over to Joe Altobelli, who had played for him at Rochester and subsequently managed there. Joe had left the organization to manage the San Francisco Giants, had produced a fine second season there in 1978, but was summarily fired before the 1979 season ended. He took over the Yankee club in the International League at Columbus, won the pennant, and was named International League manager of the year for the third time. He spent the next two years as a coach with the Yankees, serving under three managers (none of them Martin) in Steinbrenner's Bronx Zoo, and was delighted to go back to the Oriole organization. All he did was win the 1983 World Series.

Weaver, meanwhile, remained connected with the club as a scout and consultant, in semiretirement. He did some broadcasting. The Orioles were under new ownership now, Edward Bennett Williams (the Washington lawyer) having bought it from Jerry Hoffberger (the Baltimore brewer and philanthropist), and it didn't have quite the same ideas about stability and patience. When Altobelli finished fifth in the East in 1984 despite an 85–77 record that was better than the Western Division's winner, the front office became disenchanted. When the 1985 team started out 29–26, they fired him and asked Weaver to come back to the dugout.

He couldn't say no, but you could see his heart wasn't in it, and in any case, the magic was gone. The organization as a whole was stagnating and headed for lean years. The team finished fourth, over .500 but 16 games behind Toronto, and in 1986 went all the way to the bottom at 73–89—Weaver's only losing record in the majors and his first since 1957 at Fitzgerald, Georgia, in his first full season as a manager.

This time he retired for good. The American League hasn't been quite as much fun since.

When he wrote his obligatory late-career book, in 1981, he chose as a title a phrase he had hanging on the wall in his office: *It's What You Learn after You Know It All That Counts.*

My sentiments exactly.

20

Sparky Anderson

Captain Hook

George Lee Anderson was born in Bridgewater, South Dakota, on February 22, 1934, on what was still automatically celebrated as George Washington's Birthday before such holidays were homogenized into pointless three-day weekends. Bridgewater is a town in the southeast corner of the state, population listed as 653, less than twenty miles due west of Pumpkin Center, which is just about that far west of the nearest metropolis, Sioux Falls (population 81,000).

The Andersons were poor by today's standards, but not by theirs. Nine of them lived in a two-story house: mother and father, two grandparents, an older sister, George, a younger brother, and two younger sisters. The grandfather painted houses, the father painted barns and silos and worked for the post office. The kids played ball in the summer, froze in the winter, and played hockey on ice without skates. The "rich family" in town had the only house with an indoor bathroom.

According to Sparky, he loved every moment of it.

When he was nine, the family moved to Los Angeles, to the ghetto later famous as Watts. There the house had a bathroom, but only two bedrooms. The boys and the grandparents shared one; the parents and the two younger daughters shared the other; the older sister slept on a couch in the living room. As the boys grew older, they moved their bed out to a porch for privacy, displacing a washing machine.

Shortly after moving there, while walking home from the first day of school, George was passing the field where the University of Southern California baseball team practiced. The campus was only a few blocks from his new home. A ball came flying over the fence. He retrieved it, and went inside the enclosure to return it.

That started a lifelong friendship with Rod Dedeaux, the USC baseball coach, who was nationally known for sending so many players to the major leagues and who knew everyone in baseball from Casey Stengel on down. Dedeaux made Georgie the team's batboy, a position he held for six years, and became a second father to him.

His own father, who had done some catching in semipro ball, was a tough man physically but gentle at heart. Dick Williams's father had told him, "Never give in". Anderson's father told him, "Be nice to people. That's the only thing in life that's free. It'll never cost you a dime to be nice. And you'll feel good."

Georgie felt good. To this, Dedeaux added an appetite for enthusiasm, kept after him about keeping up his grades in school, and taught him about the larger world.

While in high school, Anderson also played on an American Legion team that won the national championship in 1951 at Detroit's Briggs Stadium, as it was called then. By now, he had another influential guide. When he was fourteen, he had met Lefty Phillips, then a scout for Cincinnati, who drove him to games, taught him more baseball, and got him a summer job upstate. Phillips soon became affiliated with the Dodgers (still in Brooklyn), became a coach under Alston after the move to Los Angeles, and eventually managed the Angels. One of the kids he signed around this time was Don Drysdale.

And in February, 1953, Phillips signed the nineteen-year-old, small and slight, hustling and combative second baseman straight out of high school, to a Dodger system contract. Dedeaux had wanted Anderson to go to USC, but Georgie wasn't interested and knew he couldn't get admitted even with that kind of sponsorship. He took a $1,200 bonus, a $1,200 salary for the season, and went up to the Santa Barbara farm club in Class C.

He was a good-field, not-much-hit infielder. Both Dedeaux and Phillips were believers in the Rickey system. Now he was being schooled in it full bore. At Santa Barbara, he played shortstop and led the league in putouts. At Pueblo, Colorado, in 1954, he switched to second base and led that league in putouts. He moved up to Fort Worth in 1955 (where he was a teammate of Dick Williams's) and led that league in putouts and assists. He excelled at making the double play, which is the basic test of guts on a ball field. In 1956, he was up at Montreal, the top of the chain, hitting .298. In 1957, in a sort of lateral move, he was sent to Los Angeles in the Pacific Coast League, since the Dodgers had acquired that franchise prepatory to their move the next year. He played second and short and led the league in putouts, assists, fielding average (.985!), and games played, but hit only .260. In 1958, with the Dodgers in Los Angeles, Anderson was back at Montreal, leading the league in putouts and assists and fielding average.

He hadn't gone to college, but he now had the most thorough education in Rickey system baseball imaginable. His managers had been George Sherger, Gordie Holt, Tommy Holmes, Greg Mulleavy, and Clay Bryant, all insider legends of the Dodger system.

But the system was also firm in its evaluation process. A team that had Jim Gilliam playing second had no need for a Sparky Anderson. Instead of bringing him up, they traded him to Philadelphia.

The Phillies were in the process of finishing last for four straight years in the National League's last four seasons as an eight-team league. In 1958, Eddie Sawyer, who had won Philadelphia's last pennant with the 1950 Whiz Kids, had come back from retirement to replace Mayo Smith in midseason. He made Anderson his regular second baseman in 1959, and Sparky's contribution to last place was a .218 batting average.

In 1960, Sawyer quit after the first game of the season, and Gene Mauch began his managing career. But by then Anderson was back in the minors, at Toronto, where he played the next four years and never hit better than .257.

By now, however, he had his nickname: Sparky. At Fort Worth, he would argue vehemently with umpires. The radio announcer would describe such incidents as "sparks flying." Eventually, the announcer would say, "Here comes Sparky racing toward the umpire again."

People—except real friends—started to call him that all the time. As time went on, he accepted it and incorporated it into his public persona, but—he wrote in 1989—he considered Sparky and George to be two different people.

After his first pro season, he got married and started his own family. That meant he needed off-season jobs. He worked in a furniture factory making dinette tables, then in a factory making television antennae, then packing doughnuts, and—when he was already a minor league manager—selling used cars. In that job, he was the opposite of Weaver: He talked customers out of buying the lemons.

The Moderns

By 1964, it was clear Anderson wouldn't make it as a player. He was thirty-four. The Toronto club was being run jointly by the expansion Washington Senators and the Braves, who were preparing to move from Milwaukee to Atlanta. They made him the manager.

The next year, affiliations were shuffled and Toronto wound up as a Red Sox farm, with Dick Williams given the chance to manage it. Anderson signed on with the Cardinal system at Rock Hill, North Carolina, in the low minors. Then it was St. Petersburg, Florida, then Modesto, California. The Cardinal system, of course, was as thoroughly Rickey-based as the Dodger system, and many individuals had gone back and forth between them over the years. Sparky's indoctrination in Rickeyism was approaching the Ph.D. stage.

The general manager of the Cardinals in those years was Bob Howsam, who moved to Cincinnati in 1967. For 1968, he brought Anderson into the Reds' organization at Asheville, North Carolina, where he won the pennant. But in 1969, when Buzzie Bavasi left the Dodgers to take over the expansion San Diego team, Sparky took the opportunity to come to the majors as a coach for Preston Gomez, another dyed-in-the-wool Dodger system operative and the first Padre manager.

Howsam didn't forget him, however. The Reds were being rebuilt and collecting great talent, but the manager, Dave Bristol, was someone Howsam had inherited from the previous regime. We know how uncomfortable that makes a general manager. Bristol's teams were winning most of their games, but not really keeping pace in the pennant races being dominated by the Dodgers, Giants, and Cardinals. And Bristol couldn't match the teaching credentials Anderson had acquired in Howsam's eyes.

He made Anderson Cincinnati's manager for 1970.

It was another "Who's he?" situation, as with Weaver two years before. The baseball community knew Sparky; the public didn't. But this was becoming a real trend: Promote the men who did a good job for you within the system—Alston, Houk, Williams, Weaver. Anderson hadn't been long in the Cincinnati system, but he'd been in the systems Howsam knew and admired.

It worked. Sparky's first try out of the starting gate was a 102-victory regular season, and a 3–0 sweep of Pittsburgh in the playoffs. But the Orioles, still smarting from the previous year's World Series loss to the Mets, beat them in 5 games.

Sparky Anderson

Let's do what we did with Weaver. Here's Anderson's record:

1971: 79–83 for fourth place.

1972: 95 victories, 3–2 in playoffs with Pittsburgh, lost World Series to Oakland 3–4.

1973: 99 victories, lost playoffs to Mets 2–3.

1974: 98 victories, second to Dodgers.

1975: 108 victories, 3–0 in playoffs with Pittsburgh, 4–3 in World Series with Red Sox.

1976: 102 victories, 3–0 in playoffs with Philadelphia, 4–0 in World Series with Yankees.

1977: 88 victories, second to Dodgers.

1978: 92 victories, second to Dodgers.

That's a nine-year average of 96 victories and 26–16 in post-season.

So the Reds fired him.

Why?

The answer goes to the heart of the modern management question.

Sparky, like Weaver, was dedicated to the staff system and dependence on his coaches. It is one of the many football-organization concepts that has percolated into baseball and other sports. The modern game is too complex to be a one-man show at the directorship level. Too much information is available in a computer age, too many possibilities can be explored, too much interpersonal psychology is involved, and—above all—the competition is too stiff in an age when all rival clubs have access to the same resources, talent, and methods that only a few leaders used to have. So the manager—who is, nowadays, really the head coach—wants trusted, proficient assistants to whom he can delegate important tasks, from whom he can get valuable input and feedback, and with whom he can feel comfortable in an increasingly pressurized climate of modern media coverage.

The team Anderson put together in Cincinnati included Larry Shepard, Alex Grammas, George Scherger, and Ted Kluszewski. Shepard was the pitching coach, trained in the Dodger system back in the 1940s, with eighteen years of minor league managing experience before managing the Pirates in 1968 and 1969. Grammas, a Cardinal-product infielder who coached at third, had been at Pittsburgh when Shepard got there. Scherger had been Anderson's first manager at Santa Barbara, and had moved into the Cincinnati system later. Kluszewski had been a legendary home run hitter for the Reds in the 1950s, had gone into the restaurant business after completing his playing career in 1961, and had returned to the Reds as a minor league hitting instructor in 1969.

This group, with one change, was with Sparky all through the Cincinnati years. When Grammas left to manage the Milwaukee Brewers in 1976, he was replaced by Russ Nixon, who had spent twelve years catching in the American League and then managed for five years in the Cincinnati system.

And Joe Morgan, Pete Rose, and Tony Perez were like coaches on the field.

At the end of the 1978 season, the front office wanted to make changes in the coaching staff.

Sparky was flat-out against it.

Howsam was stepping out, possibly to take charge of a team in Denver, where a group expected to buy the A's from Finley. Dick Wagner, his assistant, was moving up to club president. The conglomerate ownership was taking a more active role, flushed with the success and attention brought to it by the Bid Red Machine. Just why it was decided to tamper with Anderson's staff isn't clear, but it obviously had something to do with front office politics.

Sparky kept saying no.

So they fired him along with the coaches.

It was a shock to all of baseball, but especially to Sparky. He knew he could get another job, with his credentials; in fact, six different clubs made him offers. But it made no sense. Nobody had been dissatisfied with him, and the only issue was loyalty (and his sense of what it took to keep winning). Still, he stuck by his father's teaching: In all the in-depth questioning that followed, he wouldn't blame anyone, wouldn't point fingers, wouldn't bad-mouth anything, wouldn't name the coaches involved. It was important to display class and, as he told his youngest son, to turn defeat into victory. And he did, by refusing to display any bitterness.

In June, Anderson accepted the job in Detroit, after turning down six others.

Jim Campbell, who had disagreed with Martin six years before, was the man who persuaded him. Houk had managed the Tigers from 1974 through 1978, and the talent flow had been restored. He told Anderson that Campbell was a good man to work for. Sparky,

Sparky Anderson

having learned his lesson, insisted on a five-year contract. Campbell, having learned his own lesson from Martin, had supplied Houk with one, and gave one to Sparky. And Sparky went about constructing the kind of staff he wanted. Dick Tracewski, a former Dodger infielder, was already there. Roger Craig came in as pitching coach. (He had already managed in San Diego.) Grammas, having been fired after two years of managing Milwaukee, had returned to Cincinnati and was at Atlanta in 1979. He came to Detroit in 1980.

It took them a while to put things together, but by 1983 they were in contention, losing out to Baltimore. Then, in 1984, they exploded: They won 35 of their first 40 games, the best start any major league team has ever had, wound up with 104, brushed aside Kansas City in 3 straight, and polished off the Padres in the World Series in 5 games.

Sparky was now the first manager in history to win a World Series in each league.

The Tigers ran third the next two years, then finished first again in 1987, after a titanic final week in which they won the last 4 games from Toronto to finish 2 games ahead of the Blue Jays. But they were knocked out in the playoffs by Minnesota (which went on to win the World Series 4–1).

In 1988, they led the league most of the time into August, then hit a bad slump and injuries, and still made enough of a comeback to finish second, only 1 game behind Boston.

But the talent was thinning out. The 1989 Tigers came apart completely and lost 103 games.

Sparky had what amounted to a nervous breakdown, and it prompted a reevaluation of himself, which he described in the book he wrote when the season was over, *Sparky!*.

He called himself a "winaholic." It's great to want to want to win, he said, but not to the point where it becomes "an obsession hazardous to your health or the well-being of your family." He couldn't face that the weak team he happened to have couldn't be "willed" into winning; it was trying, but it was losing. He had never experienced this before. So he put in more and more effort in dealing with the press, making his charity and public relations appearances, and worrying about how to fix things. By May, he was at the point of physical collapse, and had to leave the team. He spent three weeks home in California learning to unwind. "I was trying to cram 48 hours into a 24-hour day," he wrote. "I actually believed Sparky couldn't lose. That was for other guys. I got fooled. I can get beat."

He referred to Sparky in the third person because, he explained, it was an identity he manufactured over the years. It was a constantly upbeat, nonstop-talking, media-star personality quite different from the private George. It wasn't artificial, it was more like a split personality. He believed that part of his job was show business, that part of the enjoyment of the fans was display of enthusiasm. He considered Stengel the greatest showman baseball ever had, better even than Babe Ruth, and took any comparison as a compliment. Most of the comparisons arose when he tried his hand at radio broadcasting, in which he mangled grammar in the great tradition of Dizzy Dean and Casey while giving the listeners truly marvelous insights and witty observations. (He would do postseason games when his team wasn't in playoffs.) But the comparison was also made because of his winning record, and the obsession with winning finally made him sick.

He returned to the club, in early June, a calmer and saner man, and has been—by his own evaluation—a better manager since.

What does he think makes a good manager?

There are four elements to be handled, in his view: the dugout, his own conduct, understanding of his players, and dealing with the media. The dugout part is easy: Everybody knows what to do if you stay alert. The conduct is a given: Either you behave in a way that leads by example, or you don't. It's the understanding of players and the handling of the media that are hardest to achieve. Mastering all four won't guarantee success; but unless you do, your chances of success decrease dramatically.

I got to know him better than most nonhometown managers (as I did Weaver) for two reasons. The obvious one is that he was in so many playoffs, World Series, and All-Star games that I dealt with him a lot. The other was coincidental. In the 1950s, I happened to get particularly friendly with several of the St. Louis Cardinal players. (In those days, they came to New York eight times a year, for four series each with the Giants and Dodgers, and the Giants and Dodgers went there four times each; and when they were in a pennant race, I chased them elsewhere on front-running assignments.) In addition, I was getting to St. Louis a lot while covering the basketball Knicks. At any rate, one of those players was Grammas, so when he wound up in Cincinnati, I had an old acquaintanceship going there—just at the point in my own life when my age was giving me greater rapport with coaches and managers than with the suddenly too-young players.

One of Sparky's characteristics, in those years of the Big Red Machine, was that he had absolutely no hesitation in changing pitchers. He did not have a staff of star starters, nor one dominant game-end reliever (which he calls "the hammer"). He earned the nickname "Captain Hook"—not unique to him—for yanking pitchers. What it really showed, of course, was the firmness of his baseball judgments: I want *this* man to pitch to *this* hitter *this* way, *now*.

The overriding requirement for managing, Anderson felt, was to have no fear—no fear of what someone might say if the move didn't work, no fear of being fired, no fear of acting on your belief.

It's interesting, therefore, to note how he rated various managers when he wrote in 1990. Let's take just the ones that have chapters in this book.

McGraw is the greatest for numbers, and should be on a "pedestal." His 2,840 victories is the target all managers should aspire to reach.

Mack's 3,776 victories are not the same, because he owned his own club and managed to the age of eighty-eight. It's just not comparable.

Gene Mauch, Walter Alston, and Whitey Herzog were the best he managed against, Anderson said. Mauch was simply brilliant as a strategist and innovater. "If you had the best club, you had a chance to beat him; if he had the best club, you had no chance; if the clubs were even, he had the advantage. . . . I managed against him for a long time. . . . I always had the better teams." Mauch wasn't aloof (a common accusation), he was only intense.

Alston was calm. "He played chess on the field, but he was never fancy. . . . He rarely gambled. . . . If my team was better and I made all the right moves, I'd win; if his was, he'd win; but I knew I couldn't wait for a mistake from him. I knew I wouldn't get one. . . . He knew exactly what he had and what to do with it."

Dark was the best defensive manager, best able to protect a lead late in the game. "I attack a game in two stages, the first seven innings and then the last six outs. . . . Dark was the best when it came to the final six. . . . He was amazing, tough to manage against."

Herzog probably knows the game better than anyone in it now.

"Give Whitey 90 percent and the other guy 100 percent, and Whitey will win all the time. Give him 80 percent, and the other guy wins. But give him 90 and he's a lock."

Martin was tough to go against, because he had no fear. "How in hell can you bluff him into a move he shouldn't make? You can't. . . . He dared you to try something, dared you to challenge him. . . . He managed with the best of them."

Tommy Lasorda "has such a sensitive feeling for people. It might look like it's all for show, but the feeling is genuine. He really does love people. And a manager must love his players and show them that he cares. . . . He also has great showmanship. He's the closest thing we have to Stengel in that respect."

Do I like Sparky because his opinions agree with mine? Certainly not. I have the opinions I do because I've been smart enough to listen to Sparky and people like him. Our ideas coincide, when they do, because that's where I got them.

And I like something else about him, pertinent here. More than most, he has a sense of baseball history and baseball's place in the culture, in the emotional niche it fills for the people who follow it. He understands, even as a winaholic, that while winning is *his* business it's not *our* business—we the followers and enjoyers of it.

As I write this, Sparky is managing the Tigers, at the age of sixty-three. I hope he catches Connie Mack.

21

Tommy Lasorda

The Artful Dodger

That Tommy Lasorda represents the Dodger system, in its fullest form is hard to dispute, since he has been preaching that message coast to coast and worldwide for seventeen years with all media outlets turned up to maximum volume.

But underneath that lie rich veins of McGraw and Mack.

Like McGraw, Tommy grew up ready to fight—with his fists—at the slightest provocation, or no provocation. His autobiography (entitled *The Artful Dodger,* written in 1985) is a cheerful compilation of the brawls he engaged in until he became too old to hold his own—like McGraw.

And like Mack (and unlike McGraw) he understood early on the importance of encouragement, moral support, kindness, personal interest, and helpfulness in getting baseball players to do their best.

The word *love* has been sneaking into our discussions, and in Lasorda it becomes explicit. Martin, Weaver and Anderson talked about the need to love your players, even though you can't always show it, and that it has to be "tough" love. Houk didn't articulate that, but acted on it, and Stengel did it selectively. The ones like Dick Williams and Durocher, who didn't feel that way, are exceptions. And it shouldn't be surprising. Love, in this sense, is an ingredient of teaching in any activity: The teacher who doesn't love his or her pupils is rarely the best teacher. It does happen, but not often.

In Lasorda's case, love comes to the surface, explicitly expressed in word and gesture, without reserve or embarrassment. Those who dislike him—and plenty of people do—accuse him of insincerity in this respect and consider it part of his "act," calculated for effect. But they are wrong. He does have an act, and loves being on stage every moment, and much of it is calculated and practiced and perfected, purposefully directed at getting attention (like Stengel). And it is an act that turns some people off. But the love part is, in fact, a true part of his nature. It was instilled in him from childhood by a close family life, and being demonstrative about it was as much a part of his Italian ethnicity as grand opera and linguine.

We have here two topics of central importance to managing in the 1990s that are far removed from the baseball world of half a century ago: love and ethnicity.

From the beginning, as we have seen, command is the manager's central function. His orders must be followed—in the game, concerning training, in matters of discipline, and so forth. The nineteenth-century manager-coach had this authority automatically: He hired and fired with little restriction. His power was limited from time to time by the availability of alternative employers, but within the club it was absolute. After the turn of the century, when organized baseball systematized the monopoly, there were no real alternatives except for the brief Federal League episode in 1914–15, so holding a job—staying on the club—was the controlling consideration for players. The manager, more specialized but chosen by and backed by ownership, was as much an autocrat as an army general is to his troops. When ownership didn't back the manager, problems arose and teams paid the price in defeats. But by and large, most of the time, a player knew that the manager was boss, and the whole context of life, beyond baseball, included universal acceptance of a boss-employee relationship.

In such a climate, the manager's primary weapon was fear. A disobedient player could be, and would be, fired. (That is, sent back to the minors if not actually released.) If fear of imminent death by hanging "wonderfully concentrates the mind," fear of being fired has a similar effect, albeit to a lesser degree.

Now, when a player *knows* he has to do it the manager's way or not at all, he executes plays better, engages in disruptive grousing less often and less intensely, and even learns to improve whichever aspects of his game the manager wants him to improve. And the manager, living in the same social atmosphere, can convey his decisions directly. He has to make them clear, and he has to be proved right often enough to maintain confidence, but he doesn't have to worry about a player's feelings any more than he wants to, according to his own estimate of how that will help or hurt the player in question.

This was the situation in baseball pretty much into the 1960s, and the experience, at the playing level, of every one of the managers in this book. The most frequently used weapon, short of actual dismissal, was the fine: Cross me, and I'll take your money. And fear of losing $50 or $100 or (later) $500 was a real deterrent when the average salary was below $20,000.

But the world has changed a great deal in the last thirty years, beyond baseball as well as within it, and fear is no longer available as an instrument of control. The players make more money than the managers, have longer contracts, and have more leverage with the ownership, which signs those big checks. They have a strong union, which protects their rights in grievance procedures. Since expansion, only fringe players or newcomers have to worry about being sent out, and most experienced players know there are few replacements to challenge them, even when they don't do well. Besides, even if they do get fired, they've already made enough money not to feel economic pressure for many years. So the use of a threat has become pointless. A manager's declaration, "Do it my way, Or else . . ." is too easily answered by "or else what?" Fines big enough to mean anything, in proportion to pay, are simply not allowed, nor practical.

Yet exercising command is no less essential than ever, so the contemporary manager must find some other weapon to replace fear.

One alternative is love.

If the player is convinced that you, the manager, are for him, sincerely care that he does well in his career, he will be more disposed to accept your rule and try to carry out tasks wholeheartedly. Paradoxically, higher salaries often weaken confidence rather than strengthen it. (We'll discuss why in a moment). A manager who exudes love, in this sense, is best equipped to boost confidence when a boost is needed. When fear was paramount, it overrode despondency or uncertainty; the individual had to fight his own battle when confidence sagged. With financial security in hand, confidence about *performance* is more fragile, and a manager has to live with the consequences of its fluctuation.

By making visible his affection for his players, a manager can lower the tension they feel anyhow, and create a situation in which his orders are accepted because the player is convinced they are well-meaning orders, not arbitrary discomforts. Instead of second-guessing, resisting, or grudgingly carrying out some demand—to bunt, to be a role player, to miss a turn, to be platooned, to work on a weakness—a player who feels the manager cares about him *as a person* does what he's asked with less distraction.

Lasorda has been a wizard at projecting this feeling and establishing such a relationship. He not only pals around with his players, jokes with them, eats with them, plays games with them, but makes a point of knowing their wives and children and generating some degree of intimacy with them too, and of keeping up to date on what's happening in their personal lives.

This is difficult, and it has its own danger. Lasorda can do it because it is his true personality. He is being, as any good manager must be, himself. It can't be done as a ploy or scheme, because the phoniness comes through. And many of those who find phoniness in Lasorda do so because they honestly can't imagine themselves being like that. They're right. If they acted that way it *would* be phony. But Tommy is Tommy, and his effusiveness is real.

The danger is obvious. A manager is the one who must ask men to do things they don't want to do, and eventually fire them. He must strip them of their alibis, push them to extra effort, deny them comforts and rewards they feel they've earned, force them to make sacrifices for the sake of the whole, and (hardest of all) make hardheaded judgments about capability that may be painful to people you like best. "Falling in love with a player" used to be a managerial flaw, when love wasn't necessary. It meant sticking with someone who, objectively speaking, could no longer do what he used to (or it meant misevaluating him in the first place). That's still a flaw if it undermines managerial objectivity, so the manager who lets his love for his players show runs the risk of making the loved one feel betrayed when the inevitable uncomfortable situation arises. And having close relations with a few at the expense of the many sets up conflicts, so if you go the Lasorda path you have to get close to just about all of them—and that takes tremendous energy and effort, and a certain type of personality. That's what Lasorda has.

He is exceptional in how he shows it, but he's not the only one who feels it. Weaver, in his way, showed it by tolerating argument. Stengel, in his peculiar fashion and part of a harsher time, showed it in dollars: When a player gave him some extra effort of value (as Irv Noren did one year, playing on bad legs while Mantle was hurt, or a pitcher named Duke Maas who surpassed himself), Stengel would "give him another year" by keeping him on the payroll for an extra season when replacing him would have been justified.

So the formula is this: In the age of fear, a player could not afford to lose confidence; in the absence of fear, it takes being loved to restore confidence.

And why is confidence so crucial? Because, strangely enough, the more money you make, the more pressure you feel. Economically, you have more to lose when you finally fail, but that's not the big thing. Artistically and emotionally, you must live up to the excellence your price tag implies. You start to press, to try to do more than you can or did before, to justify in your eyes, and those of your peers, your incredible level of compensation. A slump becomes more devastating, and can result in only two possible states of mind: "I've got to try harder," which makes it worse, or "Don't panic, things will work out, at least I've got security," which makes it persist. A manager sensitive to his player's psyche can counteract either reaction better when the player knows he's "for" him.

An old anecdote from the opera world illustrates the confidence question. There was a great Russian basso, Feodor Chaliapin, who was as big a star in his time (the first quarter of this century) as any rock star is today. Late in his career, he was asked by Olin Downes, the music critic and an old friend, if he still got nervous before a performance. "More than ever," said Chaliapin. "But why?" said Downes. "What have you got to worry about? You're the great Chaliapin."

"That's just it," said Chaliapin. "I have to go out there and *be* Chaliapin."

That's the million-dollar player's problem too.

Love is not the only alternative to fear. Being consistently right is another. Durocher, Martin, Weaver—even McCarthy, back in the days when fear still rode high—convinced their players that they ought to be obeyed by showing that their decisions produced winning results.

But one way or another, today's manager must find something other than fear as a basis of authority, and one way or another, he must have authority. We saw, particularly in the cases of Martin and Dick Williams, what a problem that can be with the wrong front office relationship. In Lasorda's case, imbedded in the forty-year stability of the Dodger organization, that problem didn't arise, and his love-based solution worked well.

However, love wasn't the only string on Lasorda's bow. Another one, closely related to the first, was overt ethnicity.

Tommy is the first manager to flaunt his Italian identity. Martin was Italian, but neither his name nor his manner made a point of it. But there's no mistaking Lasorda, with his endless chatter about pasta, his relatives, his Catholic church anecdotes, and his stereotypical flair for talking with his hands and face simultaneously. He calls attention to his Italian heritage, with pride, humor, and no self-consciousness.

Why does this matter? Because a large fraction of the baseball population is black and Hispanic, to whom ethnicity is a serious business in a way most white Americans can't even imagine.

Self-identity for blacks and cultural foreigners (from the Caribbean mostly, in baseball) is something that has to be dealt with from childhood. Pride in one's distinct heritage has been an important issue, socially, culturally, and politically, for the last generation. Whatever progress various sports have made toward integration—and it's been fairly good on the playing field, terribly inadequate off—has been led by the self-awareness of the black players. Their sensitivity to unfairness and unthinking prejudice, honed by life experience, has raised the consciousness of the whites around them, making them recognize various forms of insult and injustice—totally unrelated to racial matters—they used to swallow without being aware of them.

So black ethnicity, asserting itself as something distinct and valuable, has become a facet of our society that didn't exist when baseball was a lily-white enterprise.

Now, Italian isn't black. But it's not traditional WASP, either. What Lasorda did was aver his ethnic distinctiveness, and that made it easier to communicate with every other specific ethnic distinctiveness. The underlying message is, "Hey, it's all right to be what you are. I'm proud of what I am, you be proud of what you are, I respect your difference, I expect you to respect my difference."

It's a powerful message. And his fluency in Spanish opens the door to that group of players in a way few managers can match (although more can than used to).

Tommy can use love because he's equipped to do so.

Tommy Lasorda

Finally, he understands that life must be fun and is uninhibited about making it fun. The celebrities in his dressing room, the mountains of food, the hobnobbing with glamorous show business figures from Frank Sinatra down—all of this helps make it fun to be around him. Not every player enjoys the carnival atmosphere, but enough do to create a joyful mood that spreads through the team's life-style.

Now, having said all that, we must face the amazing fact that Lasorda's reputation and career before he became a manager were based almost entirely on fights, conflict, dissatisfaction, and turmoil.

He was born September 22, 1927, in Norristown, Pennsylvania, the second of five sons of Sabatino Lasorda, an Italian immigrant in a town full of Italians. It is, actually, just outside of Philadelphia, but Tommy never left it until he was sixteen, and then when he had to go into Philadelphia for an All-Star amateur game, he didn't know how to get there and got lost.

The family was effusively loving, noisy, given to celebration, hard-working, poor, and happy. The father drove a truck in a nearby quarry. Tommy had two interests, baseball and fighting. He was absolutely certain he was going to be a major league pitcher and was a good enough fighter to get an offer to turn pro at fifteen. But he was committed to baseball. By that time he was playing some semipro ball, and confining his fisticuffs to regular bouts on the street. His idea of pitching was to throw knockdown pitches at anyone who got a hit off him. His idea of the right answer to any affront was getting in the first punch.

As a kid, he worked. He shoveled snow, shined shoes, sold fruits and vegetables door to door, laid track for the railroad, pressed pants in a military uniform factory, hauled ashes from peoples' homes to the dump, delivered hundred-pound sacks of potatoes. He was stocky of build, strong, left-handed. He was a good hitter as well as a pitcher, although he couldn't throw hard. His trademark was the curve.

In the summer of 1944, before he was seventeen, he signed with the Philadelphia Phillies to play at Utica. (His father didn't approve, but signed the contract for him because he didn't want his son to hold it against him some day that he wouldn't let him try a career he loved.) When he went to spring training in 1945, it was no farther away than Wilmington, Delaware, because World War II was still on and travel was restricted. He was actually sent

343

not to Utica but to Concord, North Carolina, in the Class D
Carolina League. He was not an instant success. He won 3 games,
lost 12, attacked his shortstop after he made an error that cost
him a game, and learned that you're not supposed to fight with
your teammates, only the other team.

When he was eighteen, Lasorda was drafted, and spent the next
two years in the army. With the war over, he spent most of that
time playing basketball and baseball on post teams and wound up
in charge of the athletic facilities at Fort Jackson, South Carolina.
While there, he found he could pitch for two nearby semipro
teams, and made more money that way than he would in professional leagues for many years afterwards.

He was out of the service in 1948, and was sent to Schenectady,
New York. He lost 12 again, but won 9. His best games, it turned
out, were against Three Rivers of Quebec, the Dodger farm team
in that Canadian-American League. So when the Phillies were
unimpressed enough to let him go into the minor league draft, the
Dodgers took him for the $4,000 fee.

Tommy was thrilled. As a kid, he had been a passionate fan of
the Yankees of the 1930s. The Phillies who signed him had been
baseball's laughingstock for years. But the Dodgers had won the
1947 pennant, in Jackie Robinson's first year. If they thought
enough of him to buy his contract, he was on his way to great
things.

The blood in his veins started to turn to Dodger blue.

In 1949, he was at the Vero Beach complex in its second year,
and was exposed to Mr. Rickey firsthand, along with six hundred
others. Tommy made good showings in camp games, and they
assigned him to Class A—a big jump—at Pueblo, Colorado. But
that seemed awfully far away for an Italian boy from the Philadelphia area. He asked if he could be moved, instead to the team in
Greenville, South Carolina, since he'd spent so much army time in
that general area. The Dodgers accommodated his wish.

He had a good year, only 7–7 in won-lost but a 2.93 earned run
average and almost as many strikeouts as innings—and almost as
many walks. He also, he reports, led the Sally League in fights. But
that's not what made it a good year. The important thing was that
he met a local girl, Joanne Miller, and married her within a year.
They had their fortieth wedding aniversary in 1990.

There was another significant experience in Greenville. The
manager was Clay Bryant, a tyrant who used the fear weapon to

the utmost, without trying to teach or encourage anyone. He would be a model for Lasorda's idea of how to manage: not that way.

That winter he was asked to play winter ball in Panama, and when he got to Vero Beach in the spring of 1950, they jumped him again, all the way to Montreal. He took off a week early to go Greenville to marry Jo, with a $500 loan from Rickey himself. (The club never let him repay it.) Then he reported to Montreal, where the manager was Walter Alston.

Alston, the opposite of Bryant, became Lasorda's model for how one *should* manage a ball club: Communicate, encourage, be tough but fair, motivate, win respect, give respect, but take no nonsense.

For the next four years, they were together in Montreal. Twice they finished first, twice second. Tommy was 9–4, 12–8, 14–5, and 17–8, and going crazy. He knew he belonged in the big leagues. In 1954, Alston went up to manage the Dodgers, after Dressen's unintended exit—and Lasorda was sent back to Montreal. He rebelled. He told Buzzie Bavasi (who had been the general manager in Montreal, but had also been promoted to Brooklyn) that he would quit baseball. Buzzie said fine, he'd help him get a job with a friend of his in a brewery, picked up the phone, and got him an offer for $125 a week. The Montreal salary was $9,000 for the season. Tommy went to Montreal.

By mid-July he was 14–5, and the Dodgers called him up. They were chasing the Giants in a tough race. But Alston didn't use him. It turned out that what Alston wanted from him was his yelling, to pep up a team that wasn't showing enough life. (Remember? These were the veterans who resented Alston's replacing Dressen.) Lasorda complained, and Alston told him off: "I'm the manager of this club and you'll do what I want you to do." Lasorda did.

Meanwhile, he was spending every winter in the Caribbean— Cuba, the Dominican Republic, Puerto Rico, Venezuela. It was a great experience, since so many other American players from other organizations were doing the same thing and they got to know each other. Tommy, unlike most, learned Spanish and, in his outgoing manner, got to know all the local people as well.

And yes, he was in one legendary fight after another.

In 1955, he was with the Dodgers as they got off to a 22–2 start and wound up, eventually, as Brooklyn's only World Series winner. But he didn't last that long. He didn't pitch at all until the Dodgers had a 10-game lead, and then got into only 4 games, pitching four innings and allowing 6 runs. Then the Dodgers ran into a roster problem. They had just signed a rookie left-hander for more than the bonus limit of $4,000, which meant they had to keep him on the major league roster for two years or lose him, and they thought he was a good prospect. His name was Sandy Koufax, and he did nothing useful in those two years; but his arrival pushed Lasorda back to Montreal. Tommy always uses the joke that it took the greatest pitcher in the world to knock him off the Dodgers, but it was no joke then. He went back, but he was despondent and less effective (9–8). He was ready to quit. It took a visit to Montreal by his father to talk him out of it, by putting his life into perspective.

In the spring of 1956, the Dodgers sold him to Kansas City.

Lou Boudreau was the manager, Spud Chandler the pitching coach. Tommy started 5 times, relieved 13, wound up 0–4.

That would be his major league career record: 0–4.

He did have one big fight, though, with the Yankees, triggered by an exchange of shouts with Martin. Shortly after that, the A's made a deal with the Yankees, and Stengel chose Lasorda's name off the list offered. He said he liked the way Tommy fought.

They didn't want him in New York, however, and sent him to Denver, where Houk was in charge of their fine farm club. Lasorda was only 3–4 as a pitcher, since his curves wouldn't break at that altitude. But when the team needed a boost during the playoffs, Houk encouraged him to start a fight. He did. It worked. Denver won.

In the spring of 1957, Lasorda was twenty-nine and facing the fact that he wasn't going to make it as a pitcher, although he still felt he'd never been given a fair chance. Wanting to stay in baseball, he asked Lee MacPhail to get him back to the Dodger organization, and Bavasi gave up a minor league infielder for him. The Dodgers assigned him to Los Angeles, just as they had Sparky Anderson, to the club that was holding their place for them until they could move themselves the next year. Tommy had a nondescript 7–10 year with the Pacific Coast League Angels, but he and Sparky engaged in some notable fights (with opponents, of course).

And who was the manager at Los Angeles? Clay Bryant.

In 1958, the Dodgers moved west, and made Spokane their West Coast farm club. But they still had Montreal, where they sent Bryant, and they needed a pitcher-coach for him. Lasorda made the tough choice. He could just pitch in Spokane for Gordie Holt, whom he liked, or work for Bryant and begin a coaching career. He chose future gain over present pleasure, and went to Montreal.

He really could pitch up there: 18–6, a 2.50 earned run average, 31 complete games, 5 shutouts, International League Pitcher of the Year. The next year, he was 12–8.

But he was now thirty-two and slowing down. In the middle of 1960, Bryant sent back a bunch of reports that Lasorda had a bad attitude, hated the Dodger organization, and was sabotaging him. Bavasi called him in and fired him, but Lasorda was able to prove that the reports were false, and that in fact Bryant had sabotaged *him.* The Montreal players also supported him. Bavasi, learning the truth, apologized, but couldn't send him back to Montreal. So Lasorda's new job was to be a scout, and his new immediate boss was Al Campanis.

The Lasordas settled in Norristown, and Tommy became a scout covering the northeastern region. It wasn't what he wanted, but as usual, he put his heart and soul into the job and got good at it. In 1963, they asked him to move to Los Angeles, to be closer to headquarters and to work the richer mines of talent in California. Again, it was a big decision, but Jo and the two kids said go for it, and they made the great American trek to the West Coast.

By now, each winter in the Caribbean, Tommy was managing instead of playing, making friends, having adventures, getting to know more and more baseball people.

In May of 1965, Bavasi and Campanis and Fresco Thompson called him in and gave him a new assignment. He could manage the rookie team in Pocatello, Idaho, which played a 60-game season after school let out in June. He had two mandates: Develop players without worrying about winning; and no more fights.

And he didn't have one until the fourth batter of the first game.

For all his experience, he didn't feel he knew that much about the strategic aspects of managing. He did know that you had to inspire and wring talent out of your players. The important thing was to pump them up and keep their confidence high, make them believe they could achieve. Tommy himself, from childhood, was absolutely sure he would win every time he played anything, and remained convinced in the face of evidence to the contrary all his life. He wanted to transmit that feeling to his players. It wouldn't guarantee victory, of course, but it couldn't hurt.

So for the next four years, he managed the best freshly signed

The Moderns

Dodger rookies and developed all his narrative and inspirational routines. His method was simple: He had the gift of spellbinding gab; he knew the best way to make a point was through some anecdotal story (a method his father had used at home with his five sons); and he found that the best way to find the appropriate facts for an illustrative anecdote was to make them up.

One of his most famous ones concerned his boyhood idols, the Yankees. His 1971 Spokane team lost 7 in a row. He told them that the 1927 Murderers Row Yankees, the greatest team of all time, with 110 victories and Babe Ruth hitting 60 homers, had lost 9 in a row. If a team like that could do it, they shouldn't get down about losing 7. His players responded by winning the next 6. "Did the Yankees really do that?" Jo asked him. "How would I know?" said Tommy. "But it sure sounded great to those kids."

But we're getting ahead of ourselves. After that first year, the Dodgers moved the team to Ogden, Utah, where it finished first in 1966, 1967, and 1968, overflowing with enthusiasm. Then Bavasi left to take over the expansion Padres, and Fresco Thompson, succeeding him as general manager, died within a few months. Now Campanis, who had spotted Lasorda as something special back in that first Vero Beach camp twenty years before and who had been his boss when Tommy began to scout, was general manager of the Dodgers.

He sent Tommy to the top of the system, Spokane in the Pacific Coast League. There he finished first in 1970 and third in 1971. In 1972 the Dodgers moved the franchise to Albuquerque, and Lasorda finished first there. By now, his clubhouse speech routines, and their revised versions for afterdinner speeches, were as perfected as the greatest vaudeville routines had been, and as slickly delivered as the shticks of his friends Sinatra and Don Rickles. (The public versions omitted the clubhouse adjectives.) He also continued to pitch batting practice with incredible stamina. The two things that never gave out were his left arm and his tongue.

In 1973, Danny Ozark, one of Alston's coaches at Los Angeles, left to become manager of the Phillies. The Dodgers brought Lasorda in to replace him. Tommy was ambivalent about it. He liked managing, not coaching. He knew he'd be in an awkward position answering the inevitable questions about being after Alston's job, or heir apparent. But the Dodgers roster now had seventeen players he had managed in the minors, and Alston made it clear he would be welcome. Anyhow, whatever the Dodgers said do, Tommy would do. He became, very quickly, the media star in that most media-crazed of all cities, Tinseltown.

Back in 1954, to Lasorda's chagrin, Alston had wanted him to pep up the Dodger bench in a sullen atmosphere in a close race. Here, Alston wanted him to give free reign to his flamboyant inclinations to maintain a lighter atmosphere on a club that had an aging manager and a flock of new-generation players. As an elder statesman and quiet by inclination, Alston had no clown in him. A constructive clown could help, as anyone who had ever seen Stengel in operation could tell.

So the Alston-Lasorda tandem worked beautifully. The 1974 Dodgers won the pennant, their first since 1966 and the retirement of Sandy Koufax. And they did their best to keep pace with Cincinnati's Big Red Machine in 1975 and 1976, but couldn't quite match the talent.

Lasorda was getting offers, of course, from other clubs, and at the end of the 1975 season faced a decision. Montreal offered him a three-year contract, now that Mauch was gone. Alston had just signed his twenty-third consecutive one-year contract with the Dodgers. The Montreal job would pay twice as much, and he'd be a manager again. But he wouldn't be a Dodger. He decided to stay. Then, just as the 1976 season was ending, Alston retired.

The baseball world considered Lasorda an automatic choice for the succession, but in reality he had no such guarantee. He went through an agonizing day of uncertainty. He was forty-nine years old. He was as ready as could be, steeped in every detail of Dodger methods, personally known to every Dodger, intimately aware of every Dodger problem, a public relations asset; and he had proved his organizational loyalty in unmistakable fashion by turning down the Montreal job. They *had* to give it to him.

Heck, Peter O'Malley, and Campanis knew all that. They called him in, told him, and announced it to the world on September 29, 1976.

The Dodgers, ever since moving to Los Angeles in 1958, had lived through fluctuating fortunes on the field, alternating dazzling success with fallow years. Walter O'Malley had once observed, long ago, that winning the pennant every year, the way the Yankees did, was not the best thing for business: Your fans got bored, taking victory for granted, and intolerant of occasional defeat. This best pattern was to win about every third year and be in contention most of the others. His formula was the equivalent of the famous football coach's remark about keeping the alumni "sullen but not mutinous."

So in 1959, only their second year in town, they had won the World Series, then flopped. Moving into their new stadium in 1962, they got to the World Series three times and lost a pennant playoff once in a five-year stretch, then went into deep decline for a couple of years after Koufax's departure. With a completely rebuilt roster and the beginning of divisional play, they just missed finishing first (by 1 game) in 1971, and became the chief pursuers of the great Cincinnati teams through the early 1970s. In 1974, they got to the World Series again, losing to Oakland.

Through all this, they were establishing 2.5 million as their normal attendance level.

It was Lasorda's job to keep that going, with another generation of players—his own minor leaguers.

So in 1977 and 1978, he won the pennant, losing the World Series to the Yankees both times in 6 games.

In 1979, he slipped to third, and in 1980 tied Houston for first, only to lose a 1-game playoff.

In the split season of 1981, he won the World Series. In 1982, he lost out to Atlanta on the last day, by 1 game.

In 1983, he won another division race, but lost the League Championship Series to Philadelphia.

Now the need for roster rebuilding was coming up at shorter intervals, and after a fourth-place finish in 1984, he finished first again in 1985 but lost the LCS to St. Louis.

1986 and 1987 were identical losing years, 73–89, but just when his detractors were starting to chortle that Mr. Big Mouth had run out of luck, he won the 1988 World Series, beating the New York Mets for the pennant and the Oakland A's in 5 games—both considered superteams.

And by now, the normal attendance level was over 3 million.

The 1989 team was distant fourth again, but in 1990 the Dodgers finished a strong second to Cincinnati and in 1991 were in first place most of the way, overtaken by Atlanta only on the final weekend. But in 1992 everything came apart and halfway to a last-place finish the Dodgers committed themselves to using the next generation of farm products.

As a personality, Lasorda had become baseball's best recognized figure, all over television in commercials and as a commentator as well as the most visible Dodger. Within the baseball community, there was a tendency to put him down in comparison to the "smart" managers, like Sparky and Williams and Tony LaRussa and Weaver and Martin. His exaggerated inspirational talks and his flamboyance tended to obscure the sound technical job he was doing in talent selection and game management. So the best way to put him into perspective is to make a table:

	Years (through 1992)	Finished		Won LCS	Won World Series
		1st	2d		
Lasorda	16	6	4	4	2
Martin	14	5	4	2	1
Herzog	18	6	2	3	1
Williams	21	5	2	3	2
Anderson	23	7	6	5	3
Weaver	17	6	6	4	1
LaRussa	14	5	0	3	1

I'd say he has held his own with the smartest.

My own experience is that he's much like Stengel in this respect: when you want to talk seriously to him, about baseball or life, away from a large audience, all the clowning drops away and you find yourself engaged with a very, very intelligent man.

My appraisal? I love 'im.

22

The Rest of the Story

By now, we should be familiar enough with the theme of managerial heritage to deal more consciously with a dozen other important figures of the postexpansion era. They are Whitey Herzog, Tony LaRussa, Roger Craig, Gene Mauch, Bill Rigney, Red Schoendienst, John McNamara, Chuck Tanner, Bill Virdon, Danny Murtaugh, Tom Kelly, and Bobby Cox. Most of the familiar names that have permeated our crisscrossing patterns so far will show up again in their lives. As we may have noted before, baseball is a small world.

Herzog (The White Rat)

In the table on the preceding page, Herzog's line shows six first-place finishes, three trips to the World Series, and one ultimate victory there. That he succeeded in both leagues—three of the division titles were in the American League, three in the National—qualifies him for the managerial elite, although all three of his league championships were in the National. But this competitive breadth was achieved on a very narrow geographical canvas—entirely within the state of Missouri. Although he got his first chance to manage with the Texas Rangers in 1973, his true career consisted of five years in Kansas City (three firsts, two seconds) and not quite eleven in St. Louis, where he had downs as well as ups and finally quit in frustration during the 1990 season.

He was a Stengel product through and through, and therefore in the McGraw line.

Dorrel Norman Elvert Herzog was born and brought up in the town of New Athens, Illinois. It's about forty miles southeast of St. Louis and might just as well be in north Germany, the way he describes it. Almost all of its population of farmers and miners came from a similar area around Hamburg, in the nineteenth and early twentieth centuries, and its way of life maintained their cultural tradition. The Herzogs, when Whitey was born on November 9, 1931, had been there for two generations. His mother's maiden name was Fanke and her mother's Maul. His paternal grandmother's maiden name was Kaiser. His father, Edgar, worked for the Mound City Brewing Company in town (pronounced New Ay-thens, by the way) and later for the Illinois Highway Department. His mother, Lietta, worked in a shoe factory. They, like their neighbors, believed in punctuality, cleanliness, and regular habits, and instilled those virtues in their children.

They also had their own ideas about names. They named their first son Therron Herman Herzog. The youngest was named Codell. Whitey came in between.

To the family, he was "Relly." The older brother was "Ronnie" until he so idolized Billy Herman, then with the Dodgers, that they started to use his middle name—Herman. Codell became Butzie.

Relly became Whitey when he first went into pro ball at McAlester, Oklahoma. A sportswriter there started calling him Whitey because his blond hair was so light. A few years later, when he was playing further up the Yankee chain in Denver, the "Whitey" was well established, but Johnny Pesky started calling him "the White Rat" because that's what they used to call Bob Kuzava, the left-handed pitcher who also had very light hair. So you might hear people call him Rat, or Whitey, or Relly (if they're from New Athens), but not Dorrel—which, through most of his early baseball career, came out in publications as Darrell or Dorrell.

This name business is interesting. George Anderson's "Sparky" made him feel like a different person. Alfred Martin became Billy, by transliteration from Italian, without even knowing he was Alfred. Even baseball fans might not identify Stanley Harris unless you said "Bucky." And Charley Stengel, of course, became Casey even to his own family.

And Anderson, you'll recall, said that Herzog "has a bit of the Old Man in him."

I say he had a lot more Stengel in him than that, and it showed more and more as he got older. His speech became more like Casey's over the years because, like Casey, his brain often went faster than his mouth. Herzog didn't take the same active pleasure in confusing listeners or exercise all the ulterior motives Casey used in perfecting his unique art form; but he was clearly an offshoot of the same school of word painting.

But that's not all. Whitey placed instinct, insight, remembered experience, and foresight ahead of documentation, rules, analytic gimmicks, and fancy theories. He grasped the way tiny details interplay with winning and losing and paid utmost attention to using them meticulously and with sophistication—but he didn't think the game is all that complicated. He knew that what really matters is how you can communicate the right thing at the right moment and get humans to do it properly; deciding what *is* the right thing is relatively simple. The game hangs not on solving mysteries, but on execution. And on character.

That's how Stengel looked at it too, and Whitey had extensive contact with the Old Man at key stages of his own career. So maybe it isn't all sheer coincidence that when Herzog chose a permanent home, where he built a house mostly with his own hands, it was outside of Kansas City—Stengel country—rather than St. Louis. Subliminal motivations do exist.

From New Athens, Whitey used to hitchhike and take buses into St. Louis to watch the Cardinals and the Browns. (He and Weaver and Williams must have attended many of the same games, without knowing one another.) But he never lived outside his home-town until he finished high school.

He was of normal height for an athlete, just under five feet eleven inches, but skinny. He was left-handed. The Browns were interested in him as a pitcher, but didn't offer a bonus (this was 1949) and he felt insulted. He said, "Now I know why you're in last place all the time, if you wanted to sign a wild-ass left-hander like me"—showing even at eighteen what would be the core talent of his eventually brilliant career: sound player evaluation.

The day after graduation, he and a teammate went to a Yankee tryout camp, and the Yankees saw him as a potential center fielder. They gave him a $1,500 signing bonus, bigger than they gave that same year to Mickey Mantle and Bill Virdon. This taught Whitey—upon reflection—the fallibility of scouting systems.

Herzog's playing career bears certain similarities to that of Dick Williams. He was a legitimately good prospect in a terrific system loaded with better prospects. He got in four seasons in the lower minors before spending two years in service, and became a pet of Stengel's in spring training in 1955. He seemed headed for the Yankees after a good year (.289 with 21 homers and 98 runs batted in) for Houk's first Denver team in 1955. Instead, he was traded off to Dressen's Washington Senators. He didn't hit there, went back to the minors for half a season, came back up, and was claimed on waivers by Kansas City, managed by Harry Craft, who knew the Yankee system—and suffered a bad leg injury. He spent five more years in the majors, with three teams, and hit respectably, but his speed was gone, and by 1964 he had moved into scouting and coaching for Finley's A's.

Williams had reacted to his evaporating dreams with bitterness and extra determination. Herzog had a different personality, and reacted by piling up friendships everywhere. In 1966, with Stengel and Weiss out of the Met picture and Bing Devine, the pure Cardinal product, in charge of the club, he joined the Mets as a coach and then moved into the minor league development system that had been set up by Eddie Stanky. (See what I mean about familiar names?) Stanky promptly moved on and Whitey ran it for the next five years, helping feed the 1969 Miracle.

In 1973 he went to Texas to succeed Ted Williams (on Ted's recommendation), only to be replaced by Billy Martin. He signed as a coach with the Angels under Bobby Winkles, and managed four games when Winkles was fired and Dick Williams was brought in. Whitey was content to continue coaching for Dick.

But in the middle of the 1975 season, the Royals, in their new jewel box stadium in Kansas City, fired Jack McKeon. The general manager now was Joe Burke, who had been Bob Short's right-hand man in Washington and Texas until Short sold out, and he knew Whitey. Remember rule number one? A general manager always wants his own man. Herzog suddenly had a first-rate squad at his disposal.

It finished that season second to the A's (under Dark), but then won three years in a row. Whitey's teams became marked by all-out base running (McGrawism in a nonhomer park), good pitching and defense, and good public relations with an outspoken, gregarious, Middle America native in the dugout. (In his four full seasons there, the Royals stole 811 bases.) But in each playoff, the Royals were nosed out by the Yankees, twice under Martin, once under Lemon.

Go back to the word *outspoken.* While Whitey was making friends by the carload, he wasn't being a hit with club owners who didn't like blunt-speaking truth sayers. He'd left the Mets after friction with M. Donald Grant, the club president. Now Ewing Kauffman, the Kansas City owner, didn't like him either—

especially because Whitey kept asking for multiyear contracts. As soon as he finished second (by 3 games to the Angels) in 1979, it was Good-bye, Whitey.

In June 1980, the call came from St. Louis, where the general manager, John Claiborne, had worked with Whitey in the Met system. But the man who counted was the owner, Gussie Busch. Whitey told him he needed a three-year contract because he saw what happened when players with long-term contracts (in the new free-agent era) complained: It was cheaper to fire the manager than them. Busch said, "He's right," and gave it to him.

By the end of the year, Herzog was also general manager. Busch was one owner who did like him: Whitey, raised on beer, would go out to the farm, drink beer with the boss, talk baseball, and pull no punches. Busch responded by giving him full control of the baseball operation.

Now he had what every manager needs: no front office friction and great farm system experience to make the most of the situation. His next nine years in St. Louis were beautiful: World Series winner in 1982, pennant winner in 1985 and 1987 in eventful playoffs, and World Series loser only in the seventh game.

Busch Stadium was like Kansas City's, artificial turf and distant fences. His teams ran, ran, ran. His pitching staff didn't depend on stars and he operated a bullpen by committee. He had as much fun as Stengel.

It all turned sour in 1990. The Cards had about eight players on the edge of free agency. Whitey couldn't get them aroused—and he didn't blame them so much as acknowledge his inability to get through to them. So he simply walked out.

His strongest point, all along, had been the ability to evaluate talent correctly. So Gene Autry, one of the owners who did like him and had always offered him a job when no one else did, made him general manager of the Angels in 1991, who had a bad year in 1992. But at sixty-two, his story may not be over.

Tony LaRussa (The Organized Man)

When I told Tony LaRussa that I was working on this book and wanted to talk to him about who had influenced him, he said, "Sure, and I think some of it may surprise you." In fact, it didn't, because the homework I had done made what he said fit perfectly with what I had learned.

The Rest of the Story

But before going any further, I must declare, in the interests of full disclosure, my strong prejudice in favor of LaRussa. Back in 1967, I had published my first book, *A Thinking Man's Guide to Baseball,* with a first chapter discussing hitting. (A total revision, *The New Thinking Fan's Guide to Baseball,* came out in 1991.) At the time, I was also writing a weekly column in *The Sporting News,* then the trade paper of the baseball community. One day I got a nice handwritten letter from a minor league player, saying he found the chapter on hitting interesting and sound, and discussing some aspects of it. The name meant nothing to me then: Tony LaRussa. I didn't hear from him again or meet him until he was a big league manager, more than a decade later, but I was convinced in 1967 that here was one of the finest baseball minds in captivity: If he thought well of what I had written, he had to be brilliant, right? Right. So if you want to discount what follows, go ahead. I can't pretend to total objectivity.

On the other hand, I don't have to, because once again the record speaks for itself.

A personality more different from Lasorda's is hard to imagine, but under the surface there are significant similarities in approach. LaRussa is a totally organized individual, almost compulsively so. Inside a ballpark, he exudes concentration about a serious business. He has a good education—he's a law school graduate and has passed the bar—and is at home with paper work and computer printouts. He doesn't make jokes, or even much small talk. In dealing with the media, he is just as controlled and within his game plan as in everything else, looking upon it as a solemn responsibility but never a lark. While Lasorda, in his pre-Ultraslim weight-loss phase, would eat anything within reach (and probably still does, but in sensibly smaller quantities), LaRussa pays great attention to healthful diet. He speaks out for animal rights. He knows and uses all the clubhouse words, but perhaps one-one-thousandth as often as Lasorda does, and with none of Tommy's gleeful vehemence.

But he's just as deeply involved with his ballplayers as people, not cogs in a machine, and just as dedicated to the psychological-inspirational aspects of the job. His manner and nature are different, so the character of the interaction is different, but it is no less a form of love. He's reticent and private and respects the privacy of others—but is totally aware of the emotional crosscurrents and undercurrents that form the fabric of his ball club's life. He, too, is following the basic rule: He's being himself.

The Moderns

And, like Lasorda, LaRussa has a violent temper that must be kept rigidly under control. Only he learned to do it at a much earlier age, and by conscious decision; Lasorda fully mastered it only when he turned forty and found himself too old to fight.

Tony was born on October 4, 1944—the day the All–St. Louis World Series opened with Earl Weaver sitting in the bleachers— in Tampa, Florida. His family had both Spanish and Italian roots, and he grew up in the postwar era when the Tampa area (like Florida generally) was experiencing explosive expansion. The baseball hero for kids like him and Lou Piniella (a contemporary Tampa resident) was, of course, Al Lopez. But all sorts of narrow social barriers were starting to break up in the 1950s, and optimism permeated American society.

A top-flight high school athlete, LaRussa signed a baseball contract as soon as he finished high school, at eighteen, in 1962. He signed with that newest eager beaver on the baseball scene, Charlie Finley, then in his second year of ownership of the Kansas City Athletics. Tony got a $50,000 bonus and played out the season at Daytona Beach, winding up for a few games in Bing-hampton, New York, for a taste of higher classification. He was tall, muscular, right-handed, and playing shortstop.

But playing baseball for money was not going to interfere with schooling, which was no less a priority. In the off-seasons he attended the University of Tampa, and eventually got a degree in industrial engineering at the University of Southern Florida in Tampa. Then he went to law school at Florida State, in Tallahasee, and got his law degree in 1978, the year he started managing in the minors. He passed his bar exam in December of 1979, a few months after he had become manager of the Chicago White Sox in midseason.

All the press guide biographies, and trivia buffs, note that he's only the fifth major league manager who was also a lawyer, and the other four are of interest to us here: Branch Rickey; Miller Huggins; Hughie Jennings, John McGraw's old sidekick; and, back in the nineteenth century, John Montgomery Ward, the man who led the Players' League revolt before turning into a staunch base-ball establishment supporter.

Whatever else you learn in engineering and law schools, you are indoctrinated into the importance of preparation, attention to detail, and the value of having things written down. These fit LaRussa's own inclinations and mental abilities like a glove. (I mean, a young minor league player perceptive enough to react to my book? An outstanding intellect, beyond dispute.)

However, intellect—as it says in my book—doesn't guarantee that you can make contact with major league pitches. In the course of sixteen years as a professional player, he spent parts (usually small parts) of six seasons in the majors, got into 132 games, and posted a career batting average of .199. So my book certainly didn't help him hit.

But his playing experience was managerial preparation of the highest quality. He played all four infield positions (second most of the time) and a bit in the outfield. He was exposed to the widest possible spectrum of teammates, opponents, managers, coaches, conditions, and circumstances. He played in 1,295 minor league games. That much exposure to baseball would teach a lot even to a dummy; LaRussa was not only no dummy, but an expert at studying. He learned plenty.

His chance to manage came in 1978. Bill Veeck had reacquired the White Sox and brought in Paul Richards. When LaRussa was with Atlanta and in its system, Richards and Lum Harris had liked him. The new Chicago regime made him manager at Knoxville and in midseason brought him up as a coach. He started 1979 managing Iowa, and was promoted to the top job when Don Kessinger quit with about a third of the season to go. Tony inherited a poor team, broke even with it the rest of the way, but had a terrible record in 1980. Meanwhile, the Veeck operation went broke and the new owners of the White Sox were a syndicate headed by Jerry Reinsdorf, which kept Rollie Hemond as general manager—and Rollie kept LaRussa.

What LaRussa thought would surprise me was the influence he ascribed to Richards. But watching him operate in Oakland, and having already researched much of this book, I found that quite natural. His managing style is McGrawism filtered through the meticulous orderliness and record-keeping of the Richards approach.

His in-game style is aggressive—a running offense and frequent pitching changes, with a demand for total concentration. That's McGraw. But his emphasis on pregame preparation is Richards-tainted Rickeyism. No detail, of technique or attitude, is too small to pay attention to. And he took to greater lengths two concepts less fully developed by others: a coaching staff carefully chosen for teaching ability, specialist knowledge, cohesion, and stability;

and explicit roles for every pitcher, not just for starters and finishers.

In Chicago, when all is said and done, he had mediocre talent. But his 1982 team (after the strike year of 1981) climbed to third (87–75) and in 1983 it ran away with the division by 20 games, only to lose the playoffs to Baltimore. It was back to losing in 1984, but back to third and 85–77 in 1985. In 1986, however, the owners changed general managers, bringing Ken Harrelson in from the radio booth—and guess what? By midseason LaRussa was out.

Within three weeks he was managing the A's, the best move the Haas family could make. After dropping Martin, they had tried to run an "intelligent" organization on a committee system, with little success. To LaRussa, they made it clear that the vital baseball judgments would be his: Whatever the table of organization might say, his evaluations and ideas would be given prime consideration.

It all worked like a charm. By 1987, the A's were at 81–81 (after five losing years) and then came three straight pennants—the first such feat since the Yankees of 1976–78. The talent was tremendous, out of a fine farm system aided by astute trades and free-agent signings. But it was LaRussa who knew what to do with it—and, unlike all other winning teams in the 1980s, kept it going.

It all broke down in 1991, and the A's finished fourth, albeit with a winning record. But in 1992, he brought his team back to a divisional championship, the fourth in five years, in what was the best managing job of his career and one of the best ever. An unprecedented run of injuries to front-line players required him to juggle line-ups, get the most out of bench players and maintain intensity through "adversity." Rarely has a manager succeeded while being forced to stray so far from his original plans.

He is the McGraw line in a particularly interesting and relevant way. He has adapted those time-honored principles to completely contemporary high-tech methods in a very different world. The comparison in my mind goes like this: Tom Edison, Henry Ford, the Wright brothers, and Alexander Graham Bell were inventor-promoters who had to figure out systems from scratch, with few existing tools. They built what they needed and broke new ground in terms of organization as well as mechanical development. They were supertinkerers, inspired, original, and eventually rich. McGraw and Mack and Rickey were like that.

But those who presided over space flights to the moon, the

refinements of IBM's operations, the development of jet planes, and the expansion of telephone communication were not such solo operatives. They had enormous tool complexes at their disposal and had to deal simultaneously with external factors like politics and publicity on a level that didn't exist in earlier times. They didn't work with their hands, but directed people who did. They had to function at more complex levels of sophistication, more with computer screens and written reports than with screwdrivers and pencils. Yet, at bottom, they were doing the same thing as their predecessors: making decisions, setting goals, solving problems, envisioning a result, turning out a product, or achieving a result.

The modern manager is like that, and LaRussa is further along than most in pursuing eternal goals (victory) by modern methods (available technology).

No less than McGraw, he wants complete control of everything that happens in the ball game. But in an age when being a dictator is impossible and counterproductive, his means of control are maximum information and preparation. His troops obey because he has proven to them that his orders are based on reality and lead to results. McGraw saw insubordination as a threat, and a cause of defeat; LaRussa sees insufficient information, insufficiently grasped, as the threat.

No less than McGraw, LaRussa responds to hunch and feel and a daring move to catch the opponent off guard, and revels in the mental combat of outguessing the other manager. But he bases the hunch and the intuition on what he has studied so much, not merely on what he sees at the moment.

No less than McGraw, he believes in aggressive offense, the primacy of pitching, the need for outstanding and consistent defense to make the pitching pay off.

No less than McGraw, he believes in practice, practice, practice, and good physical conditioning. But he has more devices and expert advice at his disposal about how to practice what, and—it goes without saying—more advanced medical knowledge available.

McGraw, no less than LaRussa or Lasorda, wanted to grasp the psyche of each of his players. But he lived in a world that had much more primitive ideas about how psychology worked. (He was good at it, make no mistake; but it was rudimentary manipulation rooted in generating omnipresent fear and the ability to punish.) Lasorda's expressive love and LaRussa's restrained and private interactions reflect, in a way, different schools of modern psychology, but they have the same aim: to make players as functional as possible by dealing with the personal problems that decrease, by distraction, potential performance.

And like McGraw, LaRussa has an iron will. For all the difference in his chosen techniques, he is as convinced as McGraw ever was that the methods and opinions he has worked out for himself are the only right ones—maybe not the only right ones for someone else, but the only right ones for him.

When I rewrote my baseball book, in 1990, I asked him to critique the chapter on managing; not edit it, but just make a general comment. He picked on one thing. He thought I minimized how much a manager can do in controlling and achieving constructive change in troublesome personalities, and how many new wrinkles can be thought up, and are being thought up, by today's managers.

He's probably right. But he's certainly himself. In my personal scouting system, I rate him an OSC: one smart cookie.

Roger Craig (Humm Baby)

Dodger system through and through, with a Casey Stengel leavening: That's Roger Craig, the manager. He has won only one pennant (1989) and one other divisional title (1987) with the San Francisco Giants, but his influence has been greater than his record because of his distinction as a pitching coach and because of the modern managerial qualities he represents. It's the last part that's of special interest to us in this book, because his amalgam of Dodger training and special relationship to Stengel as an Original Met tie together so neatly the Rickey-McGraw joint heritage.

Won-lost records, we should know by now, are made by teams, not managers. Craig became an outstanding manager, and is worth studying, because his personality and methods encompass so many of the strands we've been tracing.

In 1962, as an Original Met, Craig won 10 games—one-fourth of the 40 the team won—and lost 24. In 1963, he got national attention in the course of an 18-game losing streak that lasted three months, and finished 5–22. As Stengel took pains to point out, you have to be a very good pitcher indeed to lose 20 games, or you wouldn't be used often enough to have the chance. Roger did it two years in a row.

The Rest of the Story

And he kept his sanity, which is the main point. That's the experience that put the finishing touch to his managerial potential. The Dodger system had schooled Craig in the techniques of the game and the value of being organized. Watching Stengel, and interacting with him, he learned about the emotional and psychological side of dealing with adversity—and a lot of additional technical items too.

He learned how to take losing without letting it sap one's desire for, and dedication to, winning. He learned how an atmosphere could be kept light without getting out of control. He learned how to avoid pointless blame of players who were doing their best but simply didn't have it, how one could use every ounce of what a player did have to offer, and how encouragement and enthusiasm could help the receptive player. (Many Mets weren't receptive, but he saw how Stengel helped the ones that were.)

Those early Met years were hilarious for everyone except the players. Craig had the maturity and perception to see all sides of the situation, and to internalize the central message: Never give up. The spirit must be willing no matter how weak the flesh gets. That became the core of Craig's philosophy. The core itself is not unusual; most outstanding competitors have it. What Craig learned from Stengel was that it was possible to convey, enhance, instill, stimulate, sustain, and, if necessary, renew that feeling.

So when he turned to managing, he used the same love motif that Lasorda used, but in tune with his own low-key personality instead of Lasorda's explosive one; he expressed incurable optimism and stressed positive thinking as assiduously as Houk; and with every player, he drove home the central point that has become indispensable today: I'm on your side.

Meanwhile, in his approach to game management, he adopted the free-thinking, chance-taking, intuitive approach to offense that stemmed from McGraw through Stengel. His decisions to squeeze-bunt, hit-and-run, steal bases—when personnel permitted it—were remarkably like Martin's, and not at all like Alston's.

But he was, above all, a thinking man's pitcher, and his special skill became handling a pitching staff. Much of this he got from Alston in principle, although he never shared Alton's conservativism. Much of it rested on the fact that he himself knew so much about pitching mechanics and the remedy for flaws. And since he was so strong on personal relationships—the supportive father figure as he grew older, an admirer of the strong, silent Western hero in good novels and movies, exuding individual confidence and competence without making a fuss—he became the ideal pitching coach in a time when managers were giving that job a high degree of autonomy (as Stengel did with Turner, Houk and others with Johnny Sain, LaRussa with Dave Duncan, and so forth). The pitchers were "his chickens" and could rely on him to be their mother hen.

Craig's career can be reviewed briefly. A native of Durham, North Carolina, he signed at twenty with the Dodger system during the last year that Rickey was in charge of it. After two seasons in the low minors and two in the army, he was still in Class B in 1954. But they jumped him to Montreal (AAA) for 1955, and when he was 10–2 in July, brought him to Brooklyn because the pitching staff had a series of injuries. He won 5 games before the season ended and 1 in the World Series that gave Brooklyn its greatest glory.

He moved with the Dodgers to Los Angeles, developed arm trouble, recovered, and was considered expendable when the list had to be made for stocking expansion teams. After his two years with the Mets, he was traded to St. Louis and helped the Cards win the World Series in 1964. He moved on to Cincinnati and Philadelphia and, through as a pitcher, back to the Dodger system as manager at Albuquerque in 1968.

When Bavasi left the Dodgers to take over the expansion San Diego team in 1969, he brought Craig in as pitching coach for Preston Gomez. When Gomez wound up managing Houston (after Durocher) in 1974–75, Craig went with him. He was back in San Diego, under John McNamara, when Dark came in—the only manager who never appreciated him—and then wound up as manager (as we've seen in Dark's story). He lasted two years, then spent four as Sparky Anderson's pitching coach in Detroit, including the glory year of 1984. He spent 1985 scouting until the call to San Francisco came in September.

Bob Lurie, owner of the Giants, had decided to turn direction of the club over to Al Rosen after years of disappointment. Rosen chose Craig, as a matter of scouting judgment, since there had been no prior close relationship between them. But mentally, they were on the same baseball wavelength, and that necessary condition for success—front office rapport with the dugout—was in place. From 100 losses the Giants went to 84–78 in 1986, then finished first, then slipped back in an injury-plagued year, and then won the pennant in 1989. They faded again late in 1990, and hit bottom in 1991 and 1992, when Craig's own health also suffered.

The Rest of the Story

Why should Craig be considered special? Because he proved to be a wizard at squeezing victories out of pitching staffs that didn't have that much inherent talent. I have mountains of statistics that demonstrate this point, which I won't cite here. Take my word for it in this case. But the fact is that despite a truly abnormal sequence of physical accidents, dependence on aging arms in some cases and not-quite-ready rookies in others, and the absence of even one really outstanding staff leader, the Giants were able to get enough good innings, day after day, out of the available material to stay in contention and even win. In the face of one disruptive event after another, Roger somehow got things back on an even keel sooner than anyone could expect.

How? Primarily through his positive thinking, individual approach to every player's problems, and ability to instill and restore confidence. He is most identified with the split-fingered fast ball technique about which he has preached so much and taught so widely. (It's a variation of what others call a fork ball—a ball gripped with fingers wide apart so that the arm motion of a fast ball produces an off-speed delivery that rotates less and dips sharply at home plate.) But that's really a distortion. It's only one of a dozen technical and mechanical aids Craig has been able to teach. His ability to identify with a pitcher's psyche and to think fast during the game are more important. Like Lasorda, LaRussa, and Sparky Anderson in his later phase, he can relate to today's ballplayers and their needs on the right level, even though he himself knows how different a world he came from.

Of all the managers I have covered, starting with Stengel, none ever handled pitching staffs any better than Craig. Since I've been able to follow the Giants closely in recent years because of where I live, I believe he has performed miracles repeatedly. But in the 1991 season, which started so badly for the Giants, he was sixty-one years old and, as we used to say in a time when older metaphors were common, even a train stops.

When he came to San Francisco, he introduced the phrase "Humm Baby," whose history he could not identify. It was common in his part of North Carolina, he said. It can mean "Way to go!" or "Let's go" or "Go get 'em" or "Nice goin' " or "How about that?" or "We win" or perhaps a dozen other things. It's another case where something is easier to recognize and use than to define and explain. Humm Baby became a catchword used in promotion, repeated by all the media people in contact with Craig, a rallying cry in the clubhouse. And for me, it sums up one of his most endearing and valuable qualities: You know what he means even when you don't know what he means.

When I made a checklist of managerial duties, and ran it past LaRussa, he didn't exactly endorse it but he didn't find much wrong with it, either. It goes like this:

1. Run the game.
2. Handle the pitching staff.
3. Make out lineups and choose personnel.
4. Evaluate abilities (your own and the opposition's).
5. Motivate and discipline players.
6. Deal with the rest of the organization.
7. Deal with the media and the public.
8. Teach.
9. Delegate authority to coaches.
10. Integrate the demands of the job with your personal life.

I give Roger Craig no less than a B-plus on every one.

Gene Mauch (Mastermind)

If being respected by one's peers were the sole criterion for managerial greatness, Gene Mauch would be a Hall of Famer. No one of his time, roughly the 1960s through the 1980s, has been more often praised by fellow professionals for his baseball acumen. Those who disliked him—and these were never in short supply—and most baseball fans dismiss him with the ultimate shrug, "never won." He did, in fact, win two divisional titles, both with the California Angels, but since he got no further, the record worshipers can brush him aside as a failure by their definition.

For our purposes, we can't ignore him because he represents a main theme. We started out saying we'd examine those who not only won but were influential. Mauch didn't win as much as the others did, but he was certainly influential. And his managerial lineage is a blend of Rickey training and McGraw outlook in a manner distinct from the others we've seen. He is unquestionably an important figure in our story.

More than any other baseball man of his era, Mauch is singled out by players and rival managers alike as a brilliant student of the game. "He knew more about the details of every position, and all the little technical things, than anyone I came across," one player with twenty years of experience told me. We've already seen how other managers cited his ability to plan ahead and

The Rest of the Story

foresee events within a ball game as a formative influence on them. He was, no one would deny, an intellect of the game of the highest order.

And yet, won-lost records aside, many considered him lacking something as a manager. The significance here is that many who liked him and admired his knowledge felt that way, not just his detractors. Piecing together what various players have told me, I get the following picture: Mauch knew so much and was so intense about putting it to use that he intimidated his own players in a counterproductive fashion.

What we're talking about now would be impossible to deal with in a newspaper column, but at the end of this book we've covered enough ground to see it in perspective.

Mauch knew more baseball, in the technical sense, with deeper insight, than almost anyone around him or in the opposing dugout. He tried, tirelessly, to impart the appropriate gems of information to his players. But he did it so tirelessly, in such detail, with such intensity, that he aroused the wrong reaction. Players would begin to worry more about doing what Mauch wanted than about winning itself. The difference is subtle, but not uncommon in the performing arts. It often arises between a soloist and a high-powered teacher in classical music, or between an actor and a certain director: The effort to please—or, to put it more accurately, to do it "correctly" according to the teacher's precepts—transcends the fundamental artistic communication that must come from the performer in a "natural" way. Technique obscures content.

At the same time, Mauch believed—not incorrectly, as we have seen—that a manager must keep a certain distance from his players. (Lasorda is one of the few exceptions to this rule.) As a personality, he was unable to bridge the gap this creates with the modern player. He had all of McGraw's dictatorial tendencies in principle, without McGraw's streak of meanness, but he had no way of softening the harsh relationship this implied. If Mauch had been dealing with the players of McGraw's time, it wouldn't have mattered; the rule of fear was accepted then. In the later world, when managerial authority could not be based simply on fear, mollification was needed. We've seen how others, notably Lasorda, LaRussa, and Craig, found ways to do that consistent with their own personalities. Mauch was unable to do it.

And his intimidation was not the McGraw type of intimidation.

The Moderns

The fear he generated did not focus on insecurity: "Do it my way, or I'll fire you, or fine you, or at least chew you out in front of everyone." It was an intellectual intimidation. It made the player think, "What am I doing wrong now? What is it he wants me to do that I'm not doing? How did I just screw up in his eyes?" And then, fatally, "I'd better make sure I do the right thing," or, at a certain point, "To hell with it, I can't satisfy him anyhow."

I believe Mauch never understood he was having this effect, or at least the extent to which he was having it, and an anecdote illustrates why I think so.

Ron Fairly played for Mauch for five years at Montreal, a veteran on an expansion club full of less experienced (and often less talented) players. Fairly would be taking ground balls at first base during batting practice, and would suddenly find Mauch standing there and staring at him. Fairly would wonder, "What's he looking at? I'm catching all of them. What does he see that I'm doing wrong? Why is he studying me?" Later, he'd be in the outfield, and he'd see Mauch watching him there. Then he'd see Mauch at the second base position, staring at the batting cage.

Finally, Fairly asked him about the second base incident. Mauch explained. The day before, the second baseman had looked uncomfortable on a couple of plays. Mauch wanted to understand why—not to blame the player, but to understand better and perhaps offer an idea to help. But to understand, he wanted to go out to the position and watch the ball coming off the bat, as the second baseman would see it. Maybe there was something in the background of the stands that was in the line of vision. Maybe it was something else. Maybe it was the way the first bounce came up on that particular field. He just wanted to see for himself.

So in reality, he wasn't really staring at the players who thought his attention was on them, but only figuring out some baseball problem in his own mind. They, of course, couldn't know that. All they knew was that there was the boss, frowning, and that when he ever did speak to them it was about how to do this or that better, or avoid this or that mistake.

Mauch was robbing the players of an essential condition: relaxation.

He was being too sophisticated for too many of his players.

It's a phenomenon that turns up in brilliant professors in some scientific fields. A large portion of the class simply can't keep up. The best students can, and the best players did with Mauch—and that's why so many who became managers respected him, because they had comparable dedication to understanding as much as possible and the kind of minds that could absorb the subtleties; that's what made them managers themselves. To a significant portion of the twenty-five-man squad, however, Mauch was simply making them so uncomfortable in trying to make them play better that they wound up playing not as well as they could. The tension would take its toll over time, even while certain mechanical movements did improve.

Even so, he had the misfortune of being dealt weak hands, in terms of material, most of his career. He could and did improve it, dramatically, but only up to a certain level. Then the tension would make the squad freeze at that level, and eventually slip back.

The result was that he managed for twenty-seven years, a career length exceeded only by Mack, McGraw, and Bucky Harris, and managed more games than Stengel, Durocher, Alston, McKechnie, and McCarthy, who follow the top four on that particular list, but lost more games than he won.

Well, so did Mack and Harris.

Gene was born in Salina, Kansas, November 18, 1925. He went into Rickey's Dodger system at seventeen, in 1943, as an infielder. He never could hit much, and after actually playing a few games at Brooklyn in 1944, put in his time in the military draft, and came back to baseball at St. Paul in 1946.

As a middle fielder, he had nowhere to go with Pee Wee Reese and Jackie Robinson on the parent club. In the next few years, he kicked around in five organizations until the Braves made him a player-manager at Atlanta at the age of twenty-seven in 1953, the year the Braves moved from Boston to Milwaukee. But he felt he wasn't ready, so he returned to playing, in the Coast League. He came up to the Red Sox, and when they offered him their top farm club in Minneapolis in 1958, he took it.

Now he was ready. He had two good years and was suddenly called to Philadelphia when Eddie Sawyer, the manager, quit after Opening Day. The Phils finished eighth (and last) for the third straight year and in 1961 got national attention with a 23-game losing streak in a 107-loss season. But Mauch was gaining widespread respect, got over .500 in 1962, and finished fourth in a ten-team league in 1963. The less said now about 1964 the better: It was considered amazing that they were leading the league so soon after 107 defeats, but when they led by 6½ games with 12 to play, they were considered a cinch. Then they lost 10 straight and were beaten out by the Cardinals. Mauch tried to use two ace pitchers on two days' rest, three times each; it didn't work, and Mauch was never allowed to forget it.

In 1968, he was finally fired, but was promptly hired to manage the expansion Montreal franchise. He struggled for seven years, with less talent than his original Phillies, but never reached .500. That was enough. Then he spent five seasons at Minnesota, improving but not winning. Then the Angels (by this time run by Bavasi) brought him in just before the 1981 strike started, and he finished first in 1982—only to lose the playoff to Milwaukee.

Mauch went to the front office the next two years, with McNamara managing, but was back in the dugout in 1985 because a new general manager, Mike Port, wanted it that way. He lost out to Dick Howser's Kansas City team by 1 game, then finished first in 1986—only to lose the playoff to the Red Sox after coming within one pitch of victory in the fifth game after winning 3 of the first 4. He was now past sixty, and during spring training of 1988, after a brief illness, he retired.

What's significant here is his talent and his flaw. He was uncanny at anticipating, planning, and even arranging what would happen in a ball game. He'd tell players that such and such would develop, and a few innings later it would, partly because he manipulated the game into that situation. So he was accused of "overmanaging," and maybe he was; but if all the things he thought of and noticed could have been executed, he would have won all the time.

And that's the other side. How do you get players to execute? In the old days, apart from the fear factor, you simply discarded and replaced those who couldn't respond with those who could: There were plenty of capable players for only sixteen teams with well-stocked minors. But after expansion, thinned-out minors rushed every slight sign of promise upward too quickly, replacements were hard to find, and long-term contracts with no-trade clauses precluded replacing many players anyhow. Mauch could not adjust to that world, any more than Dick Williams could, and that negated his conceptual brilliance.

In the managerial scheme, however, Mauch increased the vocabulary of the managers around him not only by showing them new twists and ways to anticipate but by stimulating them to follow their own thoughts in the directions he pointed.

And, perhaps, as much as he understood about techniques and

tactics, he didn't understand pitchers well enough—not pitch*ing,* the craft, but pitch*ers,* the people. He could have used an intimate friend as chief lieutenant to be a coach who could bridge the communication gap with that special breed, but he seldom found (and possibly didn't want) such a partner (like Martin's Fowler). It might have helped.

So the bottom line is that others got more benefit out of Mauch's ideas than he did himself.

Bill Rigney (Underrated)

Of all the managers I have ever met, I have had the longest running conversation with Rig. It started as no more than a few hellos when he was playing for the Giants in 1951, but got serious one day in 1955 when he was managing in Minneapolis and the parent Giants came through for an exhibition game. In 1956, he succeeded Durocher as manager of the Giants when I was traveling with them more than with the other two New York teams. He moved west with the Giants two years later, but we never lost touch, and when I moved to the coast fifteen years after that, there he was in his native Oakland. He managed the Giants again in 1976, when Bob Lurie bought them, and became an advisor to Walter Haas when that family bought the A's from Finley. I never fail to seek him out whenever I go to the Oakland Coliseum, and he never fails to have something illuminating to say about the current scene when we get past our reminiscing rituals.

Now, Rigney is easy to classify: he modeled himself, consciously, on Durocher, to the point of picking up mannerisms and voice inflections. He was, however, an entirely different kind of person than Leo—warm, kind, well-behaved, steeped in traditional values, and entirely free of Leo's less endearing qualities. But in baseball terms, Durocher was his guru, not only because of Leo's own quick-thinking approach to the game, but because of the McGraw and Rickey elements he was passing along. Rigney tried to manage like Leo and talk like Leo (but with less than one-tenth the profanity), yet he radiated congeniality. Leo could be charming when he wanted to be, but only when he wanted to be. Rigney was just plain naturally charming.

Born in Alameda, which is adjacent to Oakland, he was nineteen in 1938, when he entered pro baseball. He went to Spokane, a farm club of the Oakland Oaks of the Pacific Coast League at a time when only the Cardinals and the Yankees had fully developed farm systems. He bounced back and forth between Oakland and lower teams for a couple of years, then became the regular shortstop of the Oaks in 1941 and 1942, until World War II pulled him into service for three years. When he came back, in 1946, his contract belonged to the New York Giants and he went straight to the Polo Grounds, where Mel Ott was coming off a fifth-place wartime-season finish en route to a last-place finish with veterans back in action. Rig played third and short on the team that prompted Leo's remark, from the Dodger dugout, about nice guys finishing last.

His manager at Oakland had been Johnny Vergez, who had played third base for the Giants for the last two years of McGraw's regime and the first two years of Terry's, so he came with some feel for Giant traditions. In 1947, playing 130 games at three different infield positions, but mostly second, he contributed 17 home runs to the team's record-breaking total of 221, and in the middle of the 1948 season Durocher came over from Brooklyn to replace Ott. Leo used him regularly, at all three positions, in 1949, but then acquired Stanky and Dark, and Rigney became strictly a reserve for the next four years.

There was no question about his desire to manage, or his ability to put to use the studying he was doing so avidly. In 1954, the Giants gave him their Minneapolis club. Stoneham, already disillusioned with Durocher but persuaded by the players to keep him on, was thinking beyond the present; and his nephew, Chub Feeney, acting as Horace's general manager, also saw Rigney as a possible successor. Both liked him personally.

In Minneapolis, Rig placed third in 1954 and first in 1955. (The general manager at Minneapolis was Rosy Ryan. Remember him? Relieving in the 1923 World Series and having McGraw send word to the mound on how to strike out Babe Ruth with the bases full? These baseball interconnections are endless.) Durocher was definitely out as the 1955 season ended. Rigney had shown he deserved promotion.

So in 1956, he began his big league managing career in the Polo Grounds. World champions as recently as 1954, the Giants had dissolved quickly. They had Willie Mays at his most brilliant, not much else at other positions, and a truly weak pitching staff. In their last two years in New York, the Giants finished sixth on

The Rest of the Story

merit, and enthusiasm died completely when, in August of 1957, Stoneham made the formal announcement that they'd be leaving for California.

In those circumstances, Rigney decided to let Mays run. Willie had won the batting championship in 1954 and had hit 51 home runs in 1955. Now, for the next four years, he led the league in stolen bases. And with all that, what he was *really* good at was fielding. We used to joke that some of those road trips might never have ended if Willie hadn't hauled down so many shots to every part of every outfield: The home teams would still be at bat.

And that, ironically, became a problem when the move to San Francisco took place in 1958.

As a native of the East Bay, Rigney was welcomed as a returning hometown hero. The Giant farm system, which was a good one, had held back some of its best prospects from San Francisco delivery, and here they came: Orlando Cepeda, Bob Schmidt, Jimmy Davenport. The one thing San Franciscans were sensitive about was comparisons to New York: They considered themselves highly cultured and sophisticated, and were afraid that New York, then clearly the entertainment and communications capital of the world, didn't appreciate their merit. All that talk about Mays being better than anybody must be typical New York hype; they knew good ballplayers when they saw them, and these new Giant kids were *good.* Taking nothing away from Willie, of course, he was certainly a star; but he wasn't as good as those New Yorkers claimed—nobody could be—and he wasn't their own; the newcomers were.

This presented Rigney with the classic managerial problem in reverse form: He had a superstar on his hands, with whom he had excellent rapport—but the fans and media didn't share that feeling. (One reason was that Seals Stadium, where the Giants played the first two years, didn't have the kind of center field acreage the Polo Grounds did, so Willie's prodigious feats afield were not so visible because there was not that much room to roam. He caught everything, but he didn't have to go as far as he could.) Rigney had to walk a fine line in praising Mays without shortchanging the others, or overpraising the others at Willie's expense. It was a kind of difficulty that could not have arisen in the old days.

He handled it well and, in fact, handled the whole ball club well. But he then ran into a phenomenon that would haunt the rest of his career: winning too much too soon.

The Moderns

His 1958 and 1959 Giants were pennant contenders, winding up only 3 games out in 1959 behind the Braves and Dodgers, who tied for first. That pushed expectations way out of shape, so when the 1960 season began in the newly built Candlestick Park—which was totally unsuited to the power hitters he had—a June losing streak was enough to get him fired, even though the team was still in good shape with a 33–25 record.

The American League, however, was preparing to expand to ten teams in 1961, and Rigney became the first manager of the Los Angeles Angels (who didn't change their name to California until they moved to Anaheim five years later). He was an ideal manager for an expansion team. He talked while he managed, so there was a lot to be learned, and he loved to teach. His enthusiasm was infectious. His ability to make personal contact was an asset even though, at this time, the old boss-employee relationship still held. His Durocher style—hunch, gamble—was grounded on the soundest fundamentals, and he also liked the game to be fun.

So the 1961 Angels, purposely dealt a rotten hand the way all the expansion teams were, finished eighth in the ten-team league, only ½ game behind Minnesota (the transplanted Washington Senators) and 9 ahead of the other expansion team (the new Senators) and Finley's first Kansas City team, which tied for last.

And the 1962 Angels actually finished third, chasing the dominant Yankees well into August and finishing only 10 games out (behind Minnesota). It was a terrible mistake, we told him; he should have gone up one notch at a time—seventh, sixth, fourth, then maybe third; this way he was doomed. We were joking—but we were right. The next year the Angels were back in ninth. Then they were fifth (above .500), seventh, sixth, fifth. If not for 1962, this might have been considered orderly progress (since no other expansion team ever finished in the first division its second year). As it was, instead of getting credit for doing something remarkable early, he was blamed for not living up to that unreasonable level.

When the 1969 Angels got off to an 11–28 start in the new two-division twelve-team setup, Rig was fired. But when the Twins dropped Billy Martin after finishing first in 1969, they hired Rigney and finished first again in 1970.

And that, again, was too much too soon. Dropping to fifth in 1971, he was dropped himself with the team at 36–34 in the first week in July in 1972. He stayed out of uniform until 1975, when he acted as a coach (and scout) for John McNamara with San Diego, and was named manager of the Giants again when Bob Lurie bought the team in 1976. But that attempt to revive associations of early San Francisco glory went nowhere because the team wasn't much (as it hadn't been for Wes Westrum in 1975 and wouldn't be for Joe Altobelli in 1977). Rig's managing career was over.

But his influence and presence were not over. Among his former Angels who went on to manage were Jim Fregosi (whose endless questions had Rig referring to him as "my assistant manager" even in his earliest years), Bob (Buck) Rodgers, Joe Adcock, and Del Rice. Among the Giants who had played for him were Dark, Westrum, Jim Davenport, Whitey Lockman, and Joe Amalfitano, and, albeit briefly, Red Schoendienst. His successor at Minnesota was Frank Quilici, his utility infielder. Rigney turned to broadcasting and special scouting assignments, and when the Haas family bought the A's from Finley, he became a part of their official family as an advisor, which he still is as this book is being written.

He was a good judge of talent and good with people. He preached the fundamental "counterclockwise" game, earning runs the old-fashioned way, one base at a time.

"Just get everything you're supposed to get, in the scoring opportunities that come up, and you'll win," he'd say. "And don't give the other side more chances than they earn." Pitching and defense were certainly most important, but, unfortunately, most of the time the teams he had were deficient in exactly that. To sum Rig up in one word, use *underrated.*

John McNamara (Professional)

Underrated also applies to John McNamara. It is fashionable for sportswriters and radio-television commentators to sneer at baseball's "buddy system," and to depict experienced managers as "retreads," being chosen again and again by the tight in-group of owners because the owners are (1) stupid, (2) bigoted, (3) afraid to "try" someone new, (4) prisoners of inertia. Ballplayers, even more than media observers, express this view. The implication, of course, is that the critic (especially if it's a ballplayer) is wiser, more honest, more noble, better informed, and all-around smarter than the dumbbells who actually hired someone who failed to win last year's World Series.

I don't buy any of that, of course, and this book so far demonstrates why. Like any popularly held theory, it has elements of fact, but in this case facts don't add up to truth.

There is an excellent reason for hiring "recycled" managers. It is a profession that has no formal educational program that can produce a "qualified" graduate. You can't get a college degree in it, or pass the equivalent of a bar exam, or be subjected to peer review like a doctor or scientist, or learn anything from a book. You can learn it only by doing it—and the only available "credential" a prospective employer can look at is the fact that you did it before. And, as I've said so often, the *evaluation* of how well you did it in a previous job does *not* rest on that team's won-lost record. Fans and writers are free to label people as "winners" or "losers" any way they like; but someone running a multimillion-dollar business does not choose an important executive on such trivial criteria. The fact is that most managers who have been fired one place are hired in another because the new employers— owners and general managers—think they have demonstrated their ability in knowing the game, accumulating experience, handling people, judging talent, living with the media, and the rest.

In addition, the congeniality factor, between a manager and his bosses, is crucial. We have seen, time and again, how badly things work when there isn't enough trust, similarity of outlook, and honest friendship between front office and dugout. So it is not only natural but sensible for the front office to seek out someone already familiar, someone who is a known quantity from former contact in other contexts. In this sense, what looks like mere buddy-ism from the outside is simply prudence. The relationship with your manager is going to be an intimate one. Wouldn't you hire someone you already like, know, and respect? Why would you seek out a stranger?

So even in theory, the so-called buddy system is not only understandable but universally practiced in almost every other human field of endeavor.

But factually, the charge is simply untrue. The number of "recycled" managers is actually quite small in proportion to the total. We notice the ones who are rehired, but ignore the many more who get one shot and never another—not because they lost games, but because they didn't convince any alternate employer that they were desirable. And every manager, without exception, got a first job somewhere, sometime, somehow: That employer "took a chance" on a new face, didn't he?

And, in fact, the managers in this book—representing the cream of the crop, even if you disagree with some choices and feel others should have been made—got their opportunities at a remarkably early age, after all. Most displayed their abilities in minor league managing jobs, but they had to be given those, untried. Some served as major league coaches, some didn't. Some managed, then coached, then managed again. Durocher, Dark, Frisch, Huggins, Cronin, Harris, and Yogi Berra all reached the World Series as managers without managing a minor league club for even one day (although Harris did much later in his career). It's simply false to say newcomers don't get a chance.

So if a manager who has been fired by one club is hired by another, it doesn't show that the second club is run by dummies, but that the manager has something to offer. The nature of the job, and of sports promotion, is that dismissing a manager is the standard reaction to failing to win—not because the manager is the one who's at fault, but because no comparably easy public relations step is available. So all the experienced managers on the open market are there to be hired because they left a team that recently lost; if it had kept winning, they wouldn't have been fired (although Yogi was in 1964).

McNamara is an excellent case in point. He had neither the personality nor the self-promotion skills to be considered a genius by the media (or his players), nor the good fortune to have consistently strong rosters. Yet he did so many good jobs, in so many places, that there was always another employer ready to use him—and they weren't his drinking buddies, either.

John Francis McNamara was born in Sacramento on June 4, 1932. (Does the date ring a bell? It's the day after McGraw turned the Giants over to Terry.) A catcher, John attended Sacramento State, then turned pro with Fresno in 1951 at the age of nineteen. That was in the Cardinal system. He kicked around the minors for years until he got a chance to manage at Lewiston, in the Northwest League, in 1959. This was a farm club of Kansas City (before Finley bought the A's), and Mac gradually went up the ladder in Finley's system, helping develop all those future stars at Birmingham in the middle 1960s. When the A's moved to Oakland in 1968, he went along as a coach under Bob Kennedy and, the next year,

The Moderns

Hank Bauer. Finley made him the manager late in the 1969 season and for all of 1970. The A's were second both those years (to Minnesota) and the stage was set for Dick Williams and the championship years.

McNamara spent 1971–73 as a coach with the Giants (who finished first in 1971), and in 1974 Bavasi made him manager of the Padres, just bought by Ray Kroc. Early in his fourth season there he was replaced by Dark, and in 1978 he served as a coach for the Angels (who changed managers in midseason from Dave Garcia to Jim Fregosi). That's when the Reds, startling everyone by dropping Anderson, brought McNamara in, and he promptly won the division in 1979, losing the playoff to Chuck Tanner's Pirates. He was third in 1980, with only one less victory, and won more games than anyone else in the strike-split season of 1981 but didn't finish first in either half and got shut out of the playoffs. When the Reds were in last place in July of 1982, he was gone.

In 1983, however, Mauch moved into the Angel's front office and McNamara became the manager there. He finished only 3 games behind Kansas City in 1984, but then Mauch went back to the dugout and McNamara was hired by the Red Sox. (Their most active owner, Haywood Sullivan, had known him since the days in Kansas City.) In 1986, he finished first, outlasted Mauch in that eventful 7-game playoff, and was 1 out away from winning the World Series in the tenth inning of the sixth game when a wild pitch and the grounder through Bill Buckner's legs reversed everything and gave the Mets a chance to win the seventh game. So instead of being Boston's biggest hero since Paul Revere, he was just a fifth-place manager in 1987 and was axed on July 14 (Bastille Day) of 1988 with the team at 43–42.

In 1990, he took over the Cleveland Indians, a long-term hopeless cause, where his fourth-place finish was the team's highest in fourteen years, and he was fired halfway through the 1991 season.

McNamara is hard to classify in our scheme, although he started in the Rickey-created Cardinal system. The best term for him is *eclectic:* sound, self-controlled, a low-key encyclopedic baseball man without frills and therefore easy to overlook; affable, but not "good copy"; able to deal with the full spectrum of player personalities, but not inspirational. With good players, he won; without them, he lost. He was an excellent teacher, good evaluator, conservative in-game tactician. If there were a Ph.D. in baseballistics, he'd have one. But a man who could finish first or

The Rest of the Story

second with four different teams, in widely different circumstances, and manage about 2,300 games in eighteen years during a forty-year career is not somebody's buddy, or a retread, or a member of some private in-group. He's simply someone who has proved he's darn good at a uniquely difficult job.

Bill Virdon (Second Choice)

Also underrated, in my opinion, was Bill Virdon. More self-effacing than McNamara, less colorful a personality than any of the other winners of the 1980s, he achieved more than people realize. Since he had not been fully appreciated as an outstanding center fielder during his playing career, this was consistent with his inherent lack of glamor. But, in a space of nine years, he won a division title in Pittsburgh as a rookie manager, finished a close second with the Yankees after that mighty franchise had been in the doldrums for a decade, and finished first with a Houston team for the first time in its history. And when allowed to manage a full season, he finished lower than third only once.

All his life he seemed to be a second choice. He was signed by the Yankee system in 1950, at the age of nineteen, when the search for a successor to Joe DiMaggio was in full swing—a year behind Mickey Mantle. It took Virdon four years, the normal progression then, to reach Triple-A level at Kansas City—by which time Mantle was a star, so the Yankees traded him to St. Louis to squeeze out another pennant from the aging Enos Slaughter (which they did). This didn't make Virdon a hit with the sentimental Cardinal fans, even though he spent all of 1954 at Rochester and didn't reach St. Louis until 1955. He promptly won Rookie of the Year honors, hitting .281 with 17 homers and playing outstanding defense—but the Cardinals were being run by Frank Lane, the mad wheeler-dealer, who traded even managers. Early in 1956, Lane shipped him off to Pittsburgh for a less proficient outfielder (Bobby Del Greco) and a pitcher (Dick Littlefield) who stayed only a couple of months before being passed on to the Giants on the way to his greatest distinction: playing for ten different major league teams in a nine-year career.

Trader Lane rarely made a worse deal. Virdon settled into center field with the Pirates and became one of the mainstays of an improving team that won the 1960 World Series.

The Moderns

Virdon held down center field for the Pirates for nine years of consistent, high-quality—and often unnoticed—play. In 1966, turning thirty-five, he knew it was time to think about the future and he went down to Williamsport, in the Eastern League, to manage. The next year he was up at Triple-A, managing Jacksonville in the International League, and in 1968 came back to Pittsburgh as a coach, first under Larry Shepard and then under Danny Murtaugh, for whom he had played. When Murtaugh retired again after winning the 1971 World Series, Virdon was promoted and brought the team home in first place again, but lost the League Championship Series to Anderson's Cincinnati Reds in the last half of the ninth inning of the fifth and deciding game on a wild pitch.

In September of the following year, the National League East was having the craziest of all pennant races: the one in which five teams were alive on the final weekend and Berra's Mets finally won with an 82–79 record, just 3 games over .500. On September 7, with the Pirates at 67–69 and no worse off than anybody else, Murtaugh came back and the team wound up third.

That's when the Yankees tried to get Dick Williams from the A's, and Finley stopped them, and as the impasse dragged on, the Yankees had to do something. So they signed Virdon (second choice again) in January of 1974.

The Yankees were not in good shape. Steinbrenner and his group had bought the team from CBS only the year before. Ralph Houk had quit in disgust. Gabe Paul had been brought in to act as general manager because Lee MacPhail had become president of the American League. They didn't even have their own ballpark: Yankee Stadium was being torn up for a complete reconstruction, and the Yankees would have to play the 1974 and 1975 seasons in Shea Stadium, as temporary guests of the Mets.

Taking a team everyone expected to finish near the bottom, Virdon showed (according to Phil Pepe, who was covering the club for the *Daily News*) "organization, patience, perseverance, courage, and optimism." From 60–61 on August 20, a stretch drive pushed the Orioles, eventual winners, to the limit. The Yankees weren't eliminated until they lost a ten-inning night game at Milwaukee on October 1, the next-to-last day of the season, and made Earl Weaver and his coaches extremely nervous even though the Orioles were winning 13 of their last 14 games to hang on to the lead. (I know how nervous they were because I spent that Saturday night in their Detroit hotel suite listening to the Milwaukee game on the radio; they had beaten the Tigers 7–6 that afternoon, and the Yankee loss gave them a 2-game lead with 1 to play.)

Wouldn't this make Virdon a hero in New York? Nope. The next season, the Yankees were 53–51 on August 1, but as soon as Billy Martin became available (by being fired in Texas), Virdon was out. He had managed the Yankees a year and a half without ever getting to occupy the home dugout in Yankee Stadium—his original goal—because the Yankees didn't go back there until 1976.

But Virdon had a new job even before that. Less than three weeks after being let go by the Yankees, he replaced Preston Gomez as manager of the Houston Astros.

He stayed seven years, and went about his business of building a good ball club methodically. The Astros had climbed painfully above the .500 level in the early 1970s after their first decade as an overmatched expansion franchise, but in 1975 had tumbled back to last place (and finished 45 games behind the division-leading Reds). Virdon got a 17–17 split in the games he managed, and in 1976 had the club back to third place and at the .500 level the next two years. In 1978, the Astros tumbled to fifth again, but bounced back sharply in 1979 and finished second to McNamara's Reds by only 1½ games. And in 1980, they finally finished first in melodramatic style. They came to Dodger Stadium for the last 3 games of the season with a 3-game lead over the Dodgers, and lost three one-run decisions to create a first-place tie. Then they won the single-game playoff, 7–1.

That put them in the League Championship Series against Philadelphia, and they lost the fifth and deciding game only in the tenth inning, 8–7. The Phillies went on to win the World Series.

Next came the strike year, and by winning the second half, the Astros qualified for the special playoff round against the Dodgers. The Astros won the first 2 at Houston, lost the next 2 at Los Angeles, and were down to a deciding game again. This time, Jerry Reuss outpitched Nolan Ryan, 4–0, and the Dodgers went on to win the LCS from Montreal and the World Series from the Yankees.

There is a school of thought that says, at this point, "Aha! That's it. He can't win the *big one!*"

I think that's nonsense (as should be clear by now). First of all, managers don't win or lose individual ball games, players do. What a manager is supposed to do is *get* you to the "big one," and Virdon had been doing that regularly.

But that was to be the last time. In 1982, the Astros were back to fifth place, and before the season was over Virdon was replaced by Bob Lillis.

But another team was in trouble. Dick Williams had left Montreal late in 1981, and Jim Fanning had come out of the front office just to finish that season. That ended successfully enough (in the LCS loss to the Dodgers) that he managed the whole 1982 season, in which the Expos finished a close third behind St. Louis and Philadelphia. But he was not a permanent answer, and Virdon's credentials were impressive. Over the past five years, the Expos had compiled as good a won-lost record as anyone in the division. An experienced pilot was just what the situation called for.

Alas, there was disappointment again. In first place as late as mid-September, the Expos lost 12 of their last 20 and wound up third, 10 games behind Philadelphia. And 1984 was worse. Nothing went right. There were injuries. The offense died. Attendance at Olympic Stadium dwindled. By the end of August, the Expos were settled in fifth place, and Virdon let his boss, John McHale, know that he didn't intend to return in 1985. McHale said, Okay, leave now, and Fanning finished the season again—this time in fifth.

Virdon's managing had one aspect we haven't stressed enough so far. All managers try to create, to some degree, an "us against the world" mentality within the ball club. It's the most obvious and time-tested way of creating unity, extra effort, and mutual support. Different managers do it in different ways, and at different times, with more or less emphasis. Many channel the always plentiful hostility toward the media to this end, since complaining about fan support is pointless (although often done) and hating the opposition is a given. But this sort of unity-under-siege is a common—and effective—device in all sports.

Virdon stimulated this feeling in his players not by overt action, but by his nature. He did nothing to produce or increase xenophobic impulses—but he was so clearly not a darling of the media that his players automatically felt he was more "one of them" than many managers who were media stars. I don't know if this ever even occurred to Virdon, but his simple, honest, blue-collar, no-baloney approach to his job came across to his players as a positive. His personal views were quite conservative, even old-fashioned, and he certainly had none of the psychological manipulation tricks used so well by Lasorda and Martin; but his very absence of flamboyance made it easier to get along, constructively, with the emerging generation of players.

Up to a point. By the middle 1980s, the big stars were so big themselves that they had no idea what blue collar might mean.

Categorizing him is simple enough. Although he started in the Yankee system, he was a Rickey-heritage product through the Pittsburgh branch of Rickey's creations.

Chuck Tanner (The Smiling Irishman)

A smiling Irishman with the gift of charming gab that movie stereotypes have made us associate with such a person, Charles William Tanner, Jr., was born on July 4, 1929, in New Castle, Pennsylvania, part of the same Pittsburgh hinterland that later gave the football world Joe Namath and Joe Montana. A three-sport star in high school, he entered the Boston Braves system at seventeen in 1946, as a left-handed outfielder. It took him nine years to work his way up the system being built by John Quinn, a Rickey disciple, through Owensboro, Eau Claire, Pawtucket, Denver, and Atlanta, with brief side trips to Milwaukee (still in the minors) and Toledo, to the parent Braves—by then in Milwaukee and starting the 1955 season. On April 12, he was sent up to bat for the first time, in the eighth inning, and hit a home run.

His playing career went downhill from there. He hit .247 in 97 games that year and .238 as a pinch hitter in 60 games the next. Midway through the second season, 1956, Fred Haney replaced Charlie Grimm as manager. The Braves went into 1957 with an outfield of Hank Aaron, Bill Bruton, and Wes Covington, with no less than Bobby Thomson and Andy Pafko in reserve. (Pafko, you'll recall, was the Dodger left fielder over whose head Thomson's 1951 playoff homer had sailed. Baseball is not only a small world, it keeps turning up strange bedfellows.) That Milwaukee team was good enough to win the World Series, and it didn't need any help from Tanner. In June, he was sold to the Cubs on waivers.

At the end of the 1958 season, he was traded to the Red Sox, who sent him to Minneapolis, where he played for Mauch. He hit

.319 there in 1959, and in September the Indians bought him and brought him to Cleveland. He didn't make it there either, and wound up at Toronto in 1960. He split 1961 between Toronto and Fort Worth. The Indians sold him that September to the Los Angeles Angels, completing their first year, and he was there just long enough to say hello to manager Bill Rigney before winding up back in Triple-A at Dallas–Fort Worth, where he hit .315. It was only big league pitching that he couldn't hit.

So it was time to turn to managing. He was thirty-three, and had certainly received a well-rounded baseball and geographic education. The general manager of the Angels was Haney, Tanner's last manager at Milwaukee, and he gave Chuck a job at Quad Cities in the Midwest League, baseball's lowest classification, now called Class A. Quad Cities represented Davenport and Bettendorf, Iowa, and Moline and Rock Island, Illinois. (When I was covering basketball, this had been the home of the Tri-Cities Blackhawks—excluding Bettendorf—who became the Milwaukee Hawks and then the St. Louis Hawks and are now the Atlanta Hawks). He produced the third-best record in the ten-team league, but had the highest attendance.

Everywhere he went, Tanner made friends. He was evangelical in his promotion of the great national game, the way Stengel was and Lasorda would be, and unshakably upbeat and optimistic in whatever he said to his players and to the media.

He stayed in mid-America for two years, moved up to El Paso in 1965 and 1966, and to Seattle in 1967. In 1968 he was back in El Paso and then, for the next two years, in Hawaii at the top of the Angel's system. In 1970, after finishing first in the Southern Division, he lost the playoff to Lasorda's Spokane team, and left immediately to take up his new position as manager of the Chicago White Sox.

The Sox were in trouble, on their way to 106 losses, the worst record in their long history as charter members of the American League. On September 2, Arthur Allyn, the owner, fired his general manager, Ed Short, and brought in Rollie Hemond, who had been farm director for the Angels. The next day, on Hemond's recommendation, he hired Tanner to replace Don Gutteridge as field manager. Since Tanner was still involved in the Pacific Coast League playoffs, he didn't actually take over until September 14, but got there in time to lose 13 of the last 16 games.

But Chuck was full of ideas. Of all the men he had played for, he told me once, the most influential was Andy Cohen, back in

The Rest of the Story

Denver. "I was just a kid, and not the best kid at that," he said. "Andy not only taught me baseball, but took me under his wing and made me grow up as a person." And who was Andy Cohen? Well, back in the late 1920s, just before Tanner was born, Andy had been one of McGraw's pet projects at the Polo Grounds. He was a little second baseman and identifiably Jewish. McGraw was convinced that a Jewish player in New York could attract a big new following—as Tony Lazzeri was doing among Italians in Yankee Stadium across the way (before DiMaggio), and as Rickey realized the black players would later on. The concept may have had merit, but neither Cohen nor the Giants were good enough to make it work. Andy hit .274 and .291 in 1928 and 1929, but in those two seasons that was below the league average—and Babe Ruth was in his heyday across the river. Cohen spent most of the rest of his life managing and teaching in the minors, but did get to manage one major league game: for the Phillies, the day after Eddie Sawyer quit in 1960 and the day before Mauch arrived.

Tanner, therefore, came to managing with a thorough grounding in McGrawism, and the two main points he adopted were run-run-run and don't be afraid of original thoughts. (The dictatorial part was foreign to his nature, and he never tried that. At the same time, the Braves and Angels systems were Rickeyesque. He had two pet theories. One was that base stealing and hit-and-run disrupt the defense. The other was that pitchers can be used in unorthodox ways. "Why couldn't you have a staff of nine guys and have three of them pitch three innings each every third day?" he'd ask. "They'd stay fresh and hitters couldn't get a third and fourth crack at them late in a game." In all the years he managed, he never actually tried it, but he never stopped talking about it.

What he did do when he got to Chicago, however, was remarkable enough. He and Hemond cleaned out most of the veterans and brought in younger players, whom Tanner platooned like crazy. The team won 23 more games, finished a respectable third behind Oakland and Kansas City, and tripled its home attendance. But the eye-opener was Wilbur Wood.

Tanner found this knuckle-ball pitcher working in the bullpen, where he had led the league for three straight years in appearances: 88, 76, and 77. And he'd been effective: 32 victories and 52 saves. Tanner and his pitching coach, Johnny Sain, decided he should be a starter, and could often work with short rest (since a knuckle ball is supposed to be no strain on the arm). So for the next five years he led the league in starts—42, 49, 48, 42, and

43—and posted won-lost records of 22–13, 24–17, 24–20, 20–19, and 16–20.

Still, the White Sox couldn't contend in a division dominated by the A's. But Chicago was the home of Finley, the insurance man, even though his team was in Oakland. A garrulous Irishman certainly seemed more congenial than a Bible-quoting Southerner, so when he dropped Dark at the end of 1975, he hired Tanner. (Maybe Tanner's availability encouraged him to get rid of Dark, since it was known that the White Sox, bought by Veeck, were bringing back Richards and didn't want Tanner.) So in 1976, Tanner moved in at Oakland.

Catfish Hunter and Reggie Jackson were already gone, but the rest of the stars were still there—impatient to become free agents at the end of the season now that the new system had been agreed to by midyear. They played well for Tanner and might have won for a sixth straight year, but a Finley caper derailed them. He tried to sell Vida Blue, Rollie Fingers, and Joe Rudi for $3 million at the June 15 trading deadline, only to have the deals nullified by Commissioner Bowie Kuhn; then he refused to let the three play for two weeks while he pursued his battle (which ended in a law suit) with the commissioner, and let them return only when the rest of the team threatened to strike. The A's lost momentum and wound up 2½ games behind Herzog's first Kansas City champion.

Meanwhile, Tanner found foot speed at his disposal, and let it rip. His A's stole 341 bases, averaging 2.12 a game, a figure exceeded only by McGraw's 1911 Giants (who stole 347 in 153 games). How's that for heritage?

Tanner, of course, couldn't take Finley any more than anyone else could, and an opportunity to go home arose. The Pittsburgh Pirates had an opening, and were willing to give Finley their fine catcher, Manny Sanguillen, in exchange. Tanner became manager of the Pirates for the 1977 season, and stayed nine years.

His 1977 and 1978 teams chased the Phillies down to the wire. In 1979, the Pirates won everything, including a 7-game World Series from Baltimore after trailing 1–3. Their theme song was "We Are Family." Good feeling peaked. Tanner kept talking and playing a daring game from the dugout.

But good times don't last. The 1980 and 1981 seasons, punctuated by talk of strike and the actual strike, saw the Pirates fade. In 1982 and 1983 they had identical 84–78 records, good only for fourth place the first time but for second behind the Phillies in

The Rest of the Story

1983. But the next two years they fell to last, losing 104 in 1985.

The drug culture that had become so prominent in all sports in the early 1980s had hit the Pirate clubhouse hard. In the most publicized case, seven players testified against a pusher operating inside Three Rivers Stadium. Tanner, personally, was not involved, but his authority was shot and his reputation tarnished. If he didn't know what was going on, he should have; if he suspected, he hadn't acted. There was a trial, the pusher was found guilty, and seven players (from various clubs) who testified against him were slapped on the wrist by Commissioner Peter Ueberroth.

But Pittsburgh had bigger problems than that. The Galbreath family, which had owned the team for almost forty years, sold out, and a cooperative including the city government was formed to keep the franchise from moving elsewhere. There was no room for Tanner in the new setup.

But there was in Atlanta, where Ted Turner, the TV mogul, had his once powerful team in shambles. Bobby Cox was made general manager for 1986, and he brought in Tanner. It didn't help. At that point, the talent simply wasn't there. The Braves finished sixth in 1986 and fifth in 1987, and early in the 1988 season he was fired.

Tanner had the right temperament, viewpoint, and enthusiasm to deal with the modern ballplayer, but not enough of a knack for maintaining discipline. His game concepts were thoroughly McGrawian. He was one of the most entertaining and instructive men I ever met in baseball, and a prominent figure on the stage of the 1970s and 1980s. But in terms of accomplishment and influence, he didn't match the main figures of this book.

Still, he managed more than 2,700 big league games, and won more than 1,300, and as Sparky Anderson would say, that's not chopped liver.

Danny Murtaugh (The Toast of Pittsburgh)

This story, like the one that follows, can be told very briefly. Murtaugh was a small, tough, talkative Irish infielder in the McGraw, McCarthy, Weaver, Anderson mold. (Well, McCarthy wasn't so garrulous, and Weaver and Anderson weren't Irish, but you get the idea.) By training, however, he was Rickey system in its later phase. He was born in Chester, Pennsylvania, near Philadelphia, October 8, 1917. He entered Rickey's Cardinal system in 1937, at nineteen, and couldn't stick at Triple-A in Columbus in 1939, so he spent the next two years in Houston and was sold off, as surplus, to the Phillies, then the epitome of futility. He played there as a regular, usually second base, for three years, then spent two years in service in World War II. When he came back in 1946, he was bounced back down to Rochester, and the Boston Braves drafted him from that roster. But they sent him to play at Milwaukee (where Alvin Dark met him) in 1947 and traded him to Pittsburgh in a five-player deal at the end of the season. He played as a regular in 1948, and as a reserve the next three years. But he stayed in the Pittsburgh organization the rest of his life.

In 1951, when Rickey came over from Brooklyn, Murtaugh was made a manager at New Orleans, charged with training what Rickey intended to be his new triumphant chain. It took longer than Rickey expected because, among other things, conscription had remained in force and young men kept having two-year interruptions of all careers by military service, but in the long run it paid off. Danny spent three years in New Orleans and was managing Charleston, West Virginia, in the American Association in 1955 when he was brought up to the parent club as a coach under Bobby Bragan (the Rickeyiest of Rickey disciples). On August 3, 1958, Bragan was fired, and Murtaugh became manager.

He was, of course, familiar with most of the players, and the team was ready to mature. It was still seventh that year, but second to Milwaukee in 1958. The three-way race to the wire in 1959 among Los Angeles, Milwaukee, and San Francisco left Pittsburgh in fourth place, but in 1960 the Pirates were ready to assert themselves. They not only won the pennant, they upset the lordly Yankees of Stengel's final year in a 7-game World Series ended by Bill Mazeroski's ninth-inning home run at Forbes Field.

Danny was the toast of Pittsburgh and underdog lovers everywhere. But in the next four seasons, the Pirates were sixth, fourth, eighth, and sixth, and his halo was tarnished. He was replaced by Harry Walker for 1965, and turned to scouting duties for the organization. Harry's teams finished third behind the Dodgers and Giants in the close races of 1965 and 1966, with a strong finish each year. But when the team was 42–42 just past the middle of the 1967 season, Walker was canned and Murtaugh was brought back. It made a tremendous difference: The Pirates were 39–39 the rest of the way, and finished sixth in the ten-team league.

Now Danny became director of player development, while Lar-

The Rest of the Story

ry Shepard became manager. Shepard finished sixth again in 1968 and, when the six-team Eastern Division was created in 1969, third behind the Miracle Mets and Durocher's Cubs.

Back into the dugout went Danny, for his third try, and this time he hit the jackpot: first place in 1970, followed by an LCS loss to Cincinnati; and a World Series triumph in 7 games again in 1971, this time against Baltimore. Mr. Underdog had done it again.

Now wanting to try for an encore, Murtaugh went back to the front office for special scouting duties and turned the team over to Virdon. But late in 1973, he took it back, and in 1974 finished first again. This time he lost the LCS to Alston's Dodgers, but he brought the Pirates home first again in 1975, only to be eliminated by Anderson's Cincinnati team approaching its peak. He won the same number of games, 92, in 1976, but that left him 9 games behind the Phillies, and he announced his retirement.

He was fifty-nine. Two months later he suffered a stroke and died. By managing the same team on four different tours of duty, he had set a major league record, which Martin would soon break. But Martin's in-again, out-again routine was all turmoil; Murtaugh's was all sweetness and light. The general manager of the Pirates through all his years was Joe L. Brown, a close friend and a Rickey product. (Joe was the nephew of Joe E. Brown, the movie comedian, and as a teenager had lived for a while with Mr. and Mrs. Dizzy Dean, and had come up the Pittsburgh organizational ladder when Rickey joined it through Hollywood.) In fact, it was right after Brown announced his resignation that Murtaugh announced his own.

Danny was just a flat-out good manager. He knew the game, he made decisions with guts, he was a fine evaluator of talent, and a good teacher. He had rapport with players, old and young alike, and just about anybody else he came across. His death took some sunshine out of the baseball scene, because he would have been a pressroom star among the scouts for twenty more years if he had lived.

Red Schoendienst (The Toast of St. Louis)

Murtaugh turned out to be a one-organization man once he got to Pittsburgh. Schoendienst was a St. Louis organization man at the beginning and, after an eventful detour, forever.

Of all the modern managers in this book, Albert Fred Schoendienst was the best player, making the Hall of Fame. As a freckle-faced redheaded teenager of nineteen, he entered the Cardinal system in 1942, made it to Rochester in one year, and became the regular second baseman of the Cardinals in 1945. He was a switch-hitter who could be relied upon for an average around .300, and an outstanding fielder. He and Stan Musial became close friends, and his looks, his cheerful disposition, and the proximity of the Mississippi River led some of us refer to him as Huckleberry Finn, although his personality wasn't really anything like that. The best words for him were *solid, reliable,* "no trouble to anybody," and "a pleasure to be around."

In his first twelve years with the Cardinals, he made the All-Star team eight times. But just before the trading deadline in 1956, Trader Frank Lane sent him to the Giants in a four-for-four swap that brought Al Dark and Whitey Lockman to St. Louis (and Dick Littlefield, the traveling man, to the Giants). Bill Rigney's first Giant team was going nowhere, and exactly a year later, the Giants traded Red to Milwaukee for three players, one of whom was Bobby Thomson himself, returning to the Polo Grounds.

Red was the final piece in the championship puzzle the Braves were putting together. He helped them win two pennants in a row and beat the Yankees in the 1957 World Series. (The Yankees got even in 1958.)

In 1959, he came down with tuberculosis—and was cured in time to come back and play the second half of the 1960 season. But the Braves gave him his release at that point, and he went back to St. Louis, where his heart had always been. He played as a reserve in 1961 and 1962, and in 1963 became a coach for Johnny Keane. When Keane went to the Yankees after the 1964 World Series, Red was a natural choice for the Cardinals not only because his credentials were in order but because Cardinal fandom needed the emotional repair of having an old favorite in place after all the 1964 turmoil.

By the baseball world in general, Red wasn't seen as terrific managerial potential. Among other things, he seemed too nice a guy. And a seventh-place finish in 1965 didn't dazzle anyone. Those St. Louis people, we felt, had chosen sentiment over efficiency once again.

In 1966, the Cardinals moved into the new Busch Stadium, with its artificial turf and a spacious outfield, from the cozier old Busch Stadium (with its short right field). This required a different style of play, with more emphasis on pitching and defense and baseline speed. Good managers adapt. Red turned out to be a good manager.

The 83–79 record in 1966 was only good for sixth place. But the next two years, the Cardinals won pennants by healthy margins. They beat the Red Sox in a 7-game World Series in 1967, and lost to the Tigers in 7 games in 1968, after leading 3–1.

The Redhead had everyone's respect.

The next year, divisional play began, and Red managed the Cardinals for eight more years. He never finished first again, but came in second three times and third once. But after a fifth-place finish in 1976, it was time for a change. The Cards (with Bing Devine back in office, briefly) dipped down into their system and promoted Vern Rapp. Schoendienst went to Oakland and spent two years as a coach for the dismantled A's, an island of sense and stability where Finley was juggling Jack McKeon and Bobby Winkles back and forth in the managerial chair.

In 1979, Red returned to St. Louis as a coach for Ken Boyer, and finished out the 1980 season as manager when Boyer was fired. For the next ten years, he served Whitey Herzog as a coach, and when Herzog walked out in 1990, he stepped in and managed until Joe Torre arrived a month later. Then he resumed his coaching duties, and was still in uniform in 1991, at the age of sixty-eight, while the Cardinals under Torre were doing better than the experts had expected.

As a manager, Schoendienst was an orthodox Rickeyite, nothing fancy, sound in standard tactics. He was good at keeping the clubhouse attitude relaxed and positive, a good evaluator, a calming influence. An inspirational motivator? No. A tough competitor? Yes. Description? A good baseball man, in the best sense of the phrase.

Tom Kelly (Another Mr. Nobody)

Certainly the least known and least lionized of the current managers, Tom Kelly won the World Series with his Minnesota teams of 1987 and 1991, each time winning the seventh game at home in the Metrodome. He had no distinction as a player (an outfielder), no flamboyant personality, and no impact on the baseball public even after his first World Series exposure. But his very self-effacing qualities fit well with the demands of the free-agent, milliondollar-player, organization-oriented world baseball has become.

The Moderns

He was born in 1950, in Minnesota, but grew up in New Jersey. His father pitched in the minors, in the Cardinal and Giant organizations, and Jay Thomas Kelly became an outstanding athlete at high school and junior college levels. In 1968 he had the distinction of being drafted (fifth round) by the Seattle Pilots in the only draft they ever conducted. (After their one season of 1969, the Pilots were moved and reorganized into the Milwaukee Brewers.) He entered the Twin chain in 1971 at Charlotte, played three and a half years at Tacoma, got up for half the 1975 season in Minneapolis (hitting .181) and was back in Tacoma as manager in 1977, at the age of twenty-six.

He spent 1979–82 at lower levels, in Visalia and Orlando, with great success, and came to the Twins in 1983 as a coach under Billy Gardner and then Ray Miller. He replaced Miller in September of 1986, with the team in last place, and wound up sixth. The next year, 85–77 was good enough to finish first—one of the lowest first-place percentages ever—and he disposed of Anderson's Tigers 4–1 and Herzog's Cardinals 4–3. In 1988, he had a better record, 91–71, but wound up far behind the revived LaRussa Athletics. In 1989, the Twins fell to fifth and in 1990 to last place, and it was taken for granted that Mr. Nobody would be canned. Instead, they became the first team to go from worst to first in 1991 (although they hadn't really been "worst" in 1990, since the Yankees had a worse record in the Eastern Division cellar). In 1992, his Twins led the first half of the season but were overtaken by LaRussa's revived A's.

Kelly, then, is a Twins system product, which is an amalgam of Griffith and later Yankee influences. The Griffiths sold the team in 1984 and the new owners installed Andy MacPhail as general manager—son of Lee MacPhail and grandson of Larry. Andy grew up when his father was deeply involved with the Yankees (as well as Baltimore) and for a while used Ralph Houk as an advisor after Houk left the Red Sox. But even before that, under the Griffiths, Frank Crosetti as a coach and Martin as coach and manager had crossbred some Stengelism into the organization. Of all the managers in this book, Kelly is at the earliest stage of his career.

Bobby Cox (The Developer)

Kelly's opposing manager in the 1991 World Series was Bobby Cox, whose background is Dodger and Yankee and a fitting mixture of Rickey-McGraw for our final citation.

The Rest of the Story

He was good enough to get a $40,000 signing bonus from the Dodgers when he came out of a California high school in 1959 (before there was a draft), and spent seven years in the minors getting a thorough indoctrination into Rickeyism while being cut off from the parent club by more talented infielders. Eventually, he was traded to the Atlanta Braves (at the end of their first season in Atlanta) and played 1967 on their farm club in Richmond. He was traded to the Yankees and played a couple of years for Houk, but by now his knees were shot because of injuries and he was ready to stop playing at the age of thirty. Houk and Lee MacPhail, however, recognized his qualities from the start: keen baseball intelligence, exceptional conscientiousness and work ethic, solid personal values. (The first story I wrote about him was when he showed up for spring training in Fort Lauderdale in 1968. He had driven across the country with his wife and three small kids and arrived too late in the day to find the Yankee road secretary and his hotel room assignment—so they parked the car on the beach and slept in it, to make sure he wouldn't be late reporting for work the next morning.)

The Yankees sent him to manage at Fort Lauderdale in 1971, West Haven (Connecticut) in 1972 and Syracuse (their top club then) for the next four years. In 1977 he joined Martin's staff in Yankee Stadium as a coach, and in 1978 was hired by Ted Turner to manage the Atlanta Braves, who had finished last two years in a row. They finished last again in the first two years under Cox, but he knew how to build. They reached .500 in 1980, and after the split season of 1981, finished first for Joe Torre in 1982. But by that year, Bobby had moved to Toronto to work on an even bigger development job with a five-year-old expansion team that had never been out of last place.

In four years there, he turned the franchise completely around into the contender it has been ever since. He got a club record 78 victories in 1982, won 89 in each of the next two years (for fourth and second), and 99 in 1985 for the Eastern Division title. The Blue Jays lost the playoff in 7 games to Kansas City, and Turner wooed him back to Atlanta by giving him the general managership.

Cox had Tanner as his field manager, but the system had been stripped of talent and Cox concentrated on rebuilding that. He replaced Tanner with Russ Nixon early in 1988, but the team stayed in the cellar anyhow, and took over the dugout from Nixon midway through 1990—and finished last again.

The Moderns

But the groundwork effort was paying off. The system was producing quality players, especially pitchers, and the structure now had that priceless ingredient, unity of field manager–general manager thinking. After the 1990 season, Cox showed the true benefit, and the proper approach, to the free-agent system: He signed three players who were not top-level (or top-dollar) stars, but who could give his club what it needed. Terry Pendleton, third baseman from St. Louis, became the league's MVP. Sid Bream, from Pittsburgh, supplied offense and played first base; and Rafael Belliard, from Pittsburgh, anchored shortstop. These blended with the system talent (Dave Justice, Ron Gant, Tom Glavine) and previous acquisitions (John Smoltz, Lonnie Smith) for another "worst to first" achievement (and their 1990 record really was the worst among the twelve National League teams).

Then he took essentially the same group and won the 1992 race much more decisively, sooner, by a bigger margin—and got it back into the World Series, the first manager to repeat since Lasorda in 1977 and 1978. And there he faced the Toronto franchise he had first put on its feet eight years before, managing against Cito Gaston, whom he had brought to Toronto as a coach in 1982.

Cox projects even-keel stability, not "brilliance," but sharp-eyed determination not to overlook anything, and all the virtues of patience. His concepts of training and evaluating are classic Dodger system; his way of playing the game and running the ball club have deep McGraw roots through Houk's inheritance from Stengel. For managing a major league baseball team in the 1990s, no better combination can be imagined.

A Final Word

There has been no attempt, throughout, to make this a comprehensive treatment of the subject, historically or analytically. We've been tracing the evolution of baseball-manager thinking through certain practitioners and their descendants. What emerges most clearly is how interconnected baseball activities and experiences are: It's a small world. We've been trying to get some feel for what it's like, not a definitive description of all that can be learned about it.

To sum up, then, let's go back to the list of tasks at the end of the Craig section and see how these fit with our four originators. (We'll include Griffith here.) We'll use "N.A." for "not applicable."

I can't vouch for the unassailable accuracy of such a report card, and wouldn't want to try. What's valid is the process. I think managers can be looked upon in this way, or some similar way, and a better understanding can be gained of what it is they do and how they do it.

But if we don't do anything else, we can enhance our comprehension of the baseball manager's life and function by keeping in mind one inescapable three-point formula.

1. The manager, and only the manager, gets the first guess.
2. Everyone else has the luxury of the second guess.
3. It takes guts to make the first guess.

	McGraw	Rickey	Mack	Griffith
1. Run the game	Outstanding	So-so	Relaxed but sharp	Aggressive
2. Handle pitching	Outstanding	Good	Outstanding	Outstanding
3. Choose line-ups, roster	Outstanding	Outstanding	Outstanding	Very good
4. Evaluate abilities	Outstanding	Outstanding	Outstanding	Very good
5. Motivate and discipline	By fear	By education	By kindness	By example
6. Deal with bosses	Good early, bad late	So-so	NA	NA
7. Deal with media and public	Very good	Very good	Very good	So-so
8. Teach	Very good	Outstanding	Very good	Good
9. Delegate authority	Poor	Excellent	Very good	Good
10. Integrate personal life	Poor	Excellent	Excellent	Excellent

Appendix

The Genealogy

The derivation of modern managers in the following table uses the following, somewhat arbitrary, criteria.

An asterisk (*) indicates World Series winner.

The team name under "Heritage" indicates the system within which that manager got the bulk of his training. The name in parentheses following the team name indicates the main architect of that team's system. It's Rickey for Cardinals from 1930 on, Dodgers from 1943 on, Pittsburgh from 1952 on, and Orioles, by derivation of disciples, from 1955 on.

A manager's name under "Heritage" indicates someone the modern manager actually played for, with the name in parentheses indicating that mentor's original line.

A hyphenated entry (Rickey-McGraw) indicates a joint influence, such as the line derived through Durocher.

In three cases, the derivation is not unambiguous.

LaRussa is marked *mixed*. His minor league experience was so broad that he was exposed to various systems. But the emphasis he himself gives to the Richards influence, as well as his in-game approach, puts him in the McGraw line.

McNamara is marked *unclassified* because he had broader exposure than anyone else to all the systems of his time.

Fanning is marked *unclassified* also. He played in the Chicago Cubs organization when it had no clear direction, and by the time he came down from the Montreal front office to manage, in the 1980s, he had his own administrative background.

Appendix

* won pennant   First-Place Finishers 1961–91

Manager	Team and Year	Heritage
Anderson	Reds 1970*, 1972*, 1973, 1975*, 1976*; Tigers 1984*, 1987	Dodgers (Rickey)
Lasorda	Dodgers 1977, 1978, 1981*, 1983, 1985, 1987, 1988*	Dodgers (Rickey)
Weaver	Orioles 1969,* 1970*, 1971*, 1973, 1974, 1979*	Cardinals (Rickey)
Herzog	Royals 1976, 1977, 1978; Cardinals 1982*, 1985*, 1987*	Stengel (McGraw)
Martin	Twins 1969; Tigers 1972; Yankees 1976*, 1977*; A's 1981	Stengel (McGraw)
Williams	Red Sox 1967*; A's 1971, 1972*, 1973*; Padres 1984*	Dodgers (Rickey)
Alston	Dodgers 1963*, 1965*, 1966*, 1974*	Dodgers (Rickey)
Murtaugh	Pirates 1970, 1971*, 1974, 1975	Pirates (Rickey)
LaRussa	White Sox 1983; A's 1988*, 1989*, 1990*, 1992	Mixed (McGraw)
Houk	Yankees 1961*, 1962*, 1963*	Stengel (McGraw)
Dark	Giants 1962*; A's 1974*, 1975	Durocher (Rickey-McGraw)
Howser	Yankees 1980; Royals 1984, 1985*	Houk (Stengel, McGraw)
Ozark	Phillies 1976, 1977, 1978	Dodgers (Rickey)
Berra	Yankees 1964*; Mets 1973*	Stengel (McGraw)
Lemon	Yankees 1978*, 1981*	Lopez (Stengel, McGraw)
Frey	Royals 1980*; Cubs 1984	Orioles (Rickey)
Mauch	Angels 1982, 1986	Dodgers (Rickey)
Cox	Blue Jays 1985; Braves 1991*, 1992	Dodgers-Yankees (Rickey-McGraw)
McNamara	Reds 1979; Red Sox 1986*	Unclassified
Morgan	Red Sox 1988, 1990	Pirates (Rickey)
Schoendienst	Cardinals 1967*, 1968*	Cardinals (Rickey)
Virdon	Pirates 1972; Astros 1980	Yankees-Pirates (McGraw-Rickey)
Dave Johnson	Mets 1986*, 1988	Weaver (Rickey)

Appendix

Manager	Team and Year	Heritage
Leyland	Pirates 1990, 1991, 1992	Tigers (Mack-McGraw)
Mele	Twins 1965*	Red Sox (Griffith)
Bauer	Orioles 1966*	Stengel (McGraw)
Smith	Tigers 1968*	Yankees (McGraw)
Darrell Johnson	Red Sox 1975*	Stengel (McGraw)
Rigney	Twins 1970	Durocher (Rickey-McGraw)
Fregosi	Angels 1979	Rigney (Rickey-McGraw)
Kuenn	Brewers 1982*	Tigers (Mack-McGraw)
Altobelli	Orioles 1983*	Orioles (Rickey)
Kelly	Twins 1987*, 1991*	Twins (Griffith)
Gaston	Blue Jays 1989, 1992*	Padres (Rickey)
Hutchinson	Reds 1961*	Tigers-Cardinals (Mack-McGraw-Rickey)
Keane	Cardinals 1964*	Cardinals (Rickey)
Harris	Braves 1969	Richards (McGraw)
Hodges	Mets 1969*	Dodgers (Rickey)
Fox	Giants 1971	Giants (McGraw)
Tanner	Pirates 1979*	Braves (McGraw-Rickey)
Green	Phillies 1980*	Phillies (Rickey)
Owens	Phillies 1983*	Phillies (Rickey)
Fanning	Expos 1981	Unclassified
Torre	Braves 1982	Braves (McGraw-Rickey)
Lanier	Astros 1986	Giants (McGraw)
Craig	Giants 1987, 1989*	Dodgers-Stengel (Rickey-McGraw)
Zimmer	Cubs 1989	Dodgers (Rickey)
Piniella	Reds 1990*	Martin (Stengel, McGraw)

Index

Index

Index

Index

Index

San Francisco Giants, 15, 101, 158, 194, 202, 258–267, 311, 325, 362, 364–365, 373, 375
   see also New York Giants
Sawyer, Eddie, 329, 369
Scheffling, Bob, 220, 260
Schoendienst, Red (Albert Fred), 194, 375, 389–391
Season of '49, 153
Seattle Mariners, 298, 313–314
Seattle Pilots, 392
   see also Milwaukee Brewers
Selee, Frank, 23, 29, 59, 61
Senators *see* Washington Senators
Sewell, Luke, 218, 316
Shannon, Walter, 318
Shawkey, Bob, 119, 121
Shea, Bill, 158
Shepard, Larry, 380, 388–389
Sherger, George, 329
Shibe, Ben, 23, 70, 81
Short, Bob, 286, 355
Short, Ed, 384
Shotton, Burt, 92, 170, 216, 217, 226
Slattery, Jack, 119
Smith, Ballard, 312–313
Smith, Mayo, 329
Southworth, Billy, 96, 133, 142, 257, 316
   Boston Braves, 212
   St. Louis Cardinals, 212–214
Spalding, Al, 8–10, 12, 22, 24, 29, 41
   Chicago White Stockings, 8–9, 11
Sparrow, Harry, 110
Stankey, Eddie, 173, 176–177, 183, 214, 224, 257, 318, 355
Steinbrenner, George, 25, 210, 251, 271, 287–292, 295, 299, 308, 325
Stengel, Casey, 105, 138–160, 165, 168, 176, 181, 183, 191–192, 230, 241–248, 252, 254, 266, 274, 276, 278–279, 281, 285, 288, 295, 314, 320, 322, 334, 336–337, 340, 346, 348, 352, 354, 356, 362–363, 365, 369, 384, 388, 394
   Boston Bees, 146–147
   Brooklyn Dodgers, 144–146
   Milwaukee Brewers, 151
   New York Mets, 158–160, 204
   New York Yankees, 153–158, 227
Stoneham, Charles, 64, 67, 95, 110, 170
Stoneham, Horace, 119, 170–171, 173, 175, 258–259, 264, 266, 372–373
Stouffer, Vern, 269–270
Stovall, George, 89
Street, Gabby, 96, 166, 187, 217
Sullivan, Haywood, 267, 378

Tanner, Chuck (Charles William), 309, 378, 383–387, 393
Temple, William C., 23, 36
Temple Cup Series, 23, 35, 37, 40
Terry, Bill, 67, 144–145, 166, 170, 190, 198, 213, 217, 377
Texas Rangers, 285–287, 352

Thinking Man's Guide to Baseball, A, 357
Thompson, Fresco, 226–227, 347–348
Tigers *see* Detroit Tigers
Topping, Dan, 127, 152, 157, 241–242, 248–249, 308
Toronto Blue Jay's, 291–292, 333, 393–394
Torre, Joe, 207, 391
Turner, Ted, 387
Twins *see* Minnesota Twins

Ueberroth, Peter, 387

Veeck, Bill, Jr., 136, 151, 181–182, 211, 215, 219, 359
Veeck, William, Sr., 118
Vergez, Johnny, 372
Virdon, Bill, 287, 309, 379–383, 389
Von der Horst, Harry, 24, 39

Wagner, Dick, 332
Walker, Harry, 176, 214, 388
Wallace, Bobby, 89
Ward, John Montgomery (Monte), 17, 18, 19, 21, 23, 35, 40, 358
Washington Senators, 65, 70, 76, 113, 122, 132, 209–211, 285, 330
Weaver, Earl, 135, 236, 316–326, 329, 331, 337, 340–341, 350, 358, 380, 387
   Baltimore Orioles, 320–326
Webb, Del, 127, 152, 157, 241
Weiss, George, 122, 127, 151–152, 154, 157–159, 165, 204, 219, 240–243, 248–249, 280, 295
Westrum, Wes, 159, 171, 176–177, 194, 234, 261, 375
White Sox *see* Chicago White Sox
Williams, Dick, 207, 271, 287, 297–315, 316, 322, 324, 328, 337, 341, 350, 355, 380, 382
   Boston Red Sox, 305
   California Angels, 309–310
   Montreal Expos, 310–313
   Oakland Athletics, 305–308
   San Diego Padres, 312–313
   Seattle Mariners, 313–314
Williams, Edward Bennett, 325
Wilson, Jimmie, 151
Woodward, Woody, 207
Wright, Harry (William Henry), 5–8, 9, 10–11, 13, 22, 23, 27, 29, 34
   Cincinnati Red Stockings, 6–8, 11, 13
Wrigley, William, 118

Yankees *see* New York Yankees
Yawkey, Tom, 80, 305
Young, Dick, 231

Zimmer, Don, 299

404